Compleat   C

Compleat C

J. F. Peters III
SAINT JOHN'S UNIVERSITY
COLLEGEVILLE, MINNESOTA

H. M. Sallam
MANKATO STATE UNIVERSITY
MANKATO, MINNESOTA

A RESTON BOOK
Prentice-Hall
Englewood Cliffs, New Jersey

To our families and students.

Library of Congress Cataloging-in-Publication Data

Peters, James F.
    Compleat C.

    Includes bibliographies and indexes.
    1. C (Computer program language)   I. Sallam, Hamed M.
    II. Title.
QA76.73.C15P47   1986   005.13′3   85-14502
ISBN 0-8359-0977-8

TRADEMARKS:

Bell Laboratories: UNIX   *Heath Company:* H8
Digital Equipment Corporation: *IBM:* System 360 / 370, IBM-PC
   DEC, PDP, VAX, RAINBOW   *Apple Corporation:* Apple IIe

A Reston Book published by Prentice-Hall
A Division of Simon & Schuster, Inc.
Englewood Cliffs, N.J. 07632

© 1986 by Prentice-Hall, Englewood Cliffs, N.J. 07632

All rights reserved. No part of this book may be reproduced in any way, or by any means, without permission in writing from the publisher.

10 9 8 7 6 5 4 3 2 1

PRINTED IN THE UNITED STATES OF AMERICA

Contents

Preface xi

1 Overview 1

AIMS 1

1.1 Introduction 1
1.2 Machine Organization 3
1.3 Keyboard Symbols and Machine Codes 3
1.4 The C Programming Language 5
1.5 The C Preprocessor 7
1.6 C Syntax 8
1.7 The Source Books: K & R and J & W 9
1.8 Debugging a C Program 10
1.9 Summary 11

REVIEW TERMS AND SYMBOLS 12

EXERCISES 13

RELATED READINGS 13

2 Beginning C Programming 14

AIMS 14

2.1 Introduction 14
2.2 Program Development Cycle 17

v

vi Contents

2.3 The C Vocabulary 20

2.4 Tokens, Syntax Diagrams, and Identifiers 20

2.5 Statements 22

2.6 Comments 22

2.7 Indexed Repetition: For-Loops 24

2.8 Expressions, Operators, and Operands 27

2.9 Bug Clinic: Prefix and Postfix Operators 29

2.10 Type Int 32

2.11 #include and #define 34

2.12 Formatted Output with Printf() 38

2.13 Formatted Input with Scanf() 41

2.14 Summary 47

REVIEW TERMS AND SYMBOLS 49

EXERCISES 50

LAB PROJECTS 53

SELECTED SOLUTIONS 54

RELATED READINGS 56

3 Primer on Functions 57

AIMS 57

3.1 Introduction 57

3.2 Function Syntax 59

3.3 Local and Global Variables 62

3.4 Refinement: More on the Use of Type Char 64

3.5 Refinement: Selection of a Figure to Draw 69

3.6 Calls by Value and by Reference 70

3.7 Observations and a New Function: Strcpy() 74

3.8 Functions That Return a Value 77

3.9 Using a Return Statement to Define a Power Function 80

3.10 Refinement: Using Type Unsigned Instead of Type Int 83

3.11 Further Refinement: Using Type Double Instead of Type Int 84

3.12 Another Refinement: Improving the Format of a Table 84

3.13 Scope 84

3.14 Local Variables in Blocks on the Same Level 87

3.15 Storage Classes 87

3.16 Summary 95

REVIEW TERMS AND SYMBOLS 97

EXERCISES 98

LAB PROJECTS 101

SELECTED SOLUTIONS 103

RELATED READINGS 114

Contents **vii**

4 Types and Operators 115

Aims 115

4.1 Introduction 116
4.2 Type Char 116
4.3 String Constants 121
4.4 Type Int Qualifiers: Short, Long, Unsigned 128
4.5 Type Float and Double 136
4.6 Boolean Operators 138
4.7 Bitwise Operators 139
4.8 Compression of Assignment Statements 148
4.9 Summary 151

Review Terms and Symbols 153
Exercises 154
Lab Projects 156
Selected Solutions 156
Related Readings 168

5 Control Structures 169

Aims 169

5.1 Introduction 170
5.2 Sequential Control 171
5.3 Selection Control Structures 172
5.4 Iteration Control Structures 178
5.5 Application: Random Numbers 191
5.6 Summary 201

Review Terms and Symbols 202
Exercises 202
Lab Projects 204
Selected Solutions 206
Related Readings 221

6 Arrays 222

Aims 222

6.1 Introduction 223
6.2 Constructing Arrays 227
6.3 Library of Functions 231
6.4 Arrays of Random Numbers 232
6.5 Pointer Constants and Pointer Variables 240
6.6 Arrays of Pointers 243

viii Contents

6.7 Arrays of Strings: Jagged Arrays   246

6.8 Application: Finding the Smallest and Second Smallest Number   249

6.9 Extended Precision Products with Arrays   256

6.10 Multidimensional Arrays   258

6.11 Summary   264

REVIEW TERMS AND SYMBOLS   266

EXERCISES   266

LAB PROJECTS   269

SELECTED SOLUTIONS   272

RELATED READINGS   296

7   Structures   297

AIMS   297

7.1 Introduction   298

7.2 Pointers to Structures   299

7.3 Initializing Structures   301

7.4 Functions and Pointers to Structures   301

7.5 Operations with Pointers to Structures   304

7.6 Array of Structures   307

7.7 Arrays of Pointers to Structures   307

7.8 Refinement: Counting Bytes Used by Structures   309

7.9 Swapping Pointers to Structures   312

7.10 Refinement: Selection Sort of Structures   312

7.11 Refinement: Varying the Sort Key   316

7.12 Refinement: Introducing a Select( )Function   316

7.13 Editing a Structure   316

7.14 Refinement: Selecting a Member to Edit   320

7.15 A Hash Search for a Structure   321

7.16 Refinement: Keeping Track of the Cell Used   334

7.17 Refinement: Keeping Track of the Comparisons Used   334

7.18 Refinement: Deletions and Insertions   335

7.19 Refinement: Editing a Hash Table Entry   335

7.20 Nested Structures   335

7.21 Creating New Type Names with Typedef   336

7.22 Unions   338

7.23 Summary   338

REVIEW TERMS AND SYMBOLS   340

EXERCISES   340

LAB PROJECTS   342

SELECTED SOLUTIONS   343

RELATED READINGS   388

Contents   ix

8   Linked Lists   389

AIMS   389

8.1   Introduction   390

8.2   Recursion   390

8.3   Appending Nodes to a Linked List   394

8.4   Inserting a Node into a Linked List: Insertion Sort   396

8.5   Deleting a Node from a Linked List   399

8.6   List Processing   401

8.7   Refinement: A Complete List Processing Program   402

8.8   Multilinked Lists   411

8.9   Binary Trees   412

8.10 Building a Binary Tree   412

8.11 In-order Tree Traversal   414

8.12 Refinement: Visiting a Tree Node   414

8.13 Deleting a Node from a Binary Tree   417

8.14 Analysis of a Tree Sort   417

8.15 Summary   420

REVIEW TERMS AND SYMBOLS   421

EXERCISES   422

LAB PROJECTS   425

SELECTED SOLUTIONS   426

RELATED READINGS   436

9   Files   437

AIMS   437

9.1   Introduction   437

9.2   Building a File of Random Numbers   439

9.3   Inspecting the Contents of an External File   440

9.4   File of Structures   440

9.5   Refinement: Using a Sentinel   448

9.6   Refinement: Directory of Available Files   448

9.7   Using an External File to Build a Binary Tree   449

9.8   Refinement: Using a Sentinel   449

9.9   Treesort of an External File of Names   453

9.10 Refinement: Choosing Files to Sort   454

9.11 Refinement: External Sort   459

9.12 Direct Access Files   459

9.13 Refinement: Another Use for a File Directory   461

9.14 Refinement: Specifying the Output File   463

9.15 Summary   464

x Contents

REVIEW TERMS AND SYMBOLS   465
EXERCISES   465
LAB PROJECTS   467
SELECTED SOLUTIONS   467
RELATED READINGS   470

Appendixes   471

A Character Representations in ASCII and EBCDIC   473
B Common Syntax Errors in C Programs   475
C The C Language   480

Glossary   488

Index of Programs   491

Index of Functions   493

Index of Syntax Diagrams   494

Index of Symbols and Terms   495

Preface

The term *art* has to do with skill in doing something as a result of knowledge and practice. Also associated with the idea of art is the use of techniques, where one applies the principles of a subject. Art also has to do with both *imitation* of artful objects and the design of new objects. The skill it takes to produce works of art carries with it a sense of design, a sense of structure, and a perception of form. Instead of bits and pieces scattered about in a work, there is a molding of the bits and pieces into forms that both please and tend to explain themselves.

One of the aims of this book has been to provide complete, structured programs that will be helpful to a beginning C programmer. A deliberate effort has been made to avoid fragments as much as possible. Instead, complete programs and functions have been presented, which will be helpful in the design of new C programs.

Functions are the building blocks of good C programs. It is helpful to think of a function as a tool, something that can be used over and over in more than one program. The effort it takes to develop a new C function pays off. A function used to build a file of integers, or to draw a line, or to build an array will usually carry over into more than one program.

Finally, C is a gentle art. According to the *Oxford English Dictionary,* the term *gentle* has to do with noble or excellent things, belonging to a good family. The C language is part of a good family of languages (C , Pascal, PL/I, Ada, Modula-2) that encourages the development of structured programs. A structured

xii Preface

program will typically rely on canonical control structures (if, while, do, for, but, not, goto), the use of modules (functions or procedures), and stepwise refinement as a means of perfecting a beginning program.

Note for the Student

You will probably find the chapter summary and review terms a helpful overview of what is covered in each chapter. Selected solutions to chapter exercises and lab projects are given in the back of the book.

Before you start, you may find it helpful to look at Appendix B (the Bugbook), showing examples of common sources of errors in C programs. You might find it helpful to start a bugbook of your own, a record of the mistakes you find yourself making. You should also determine the debugging tools that are available for your system. See if there is a *lint* program, for example.

You will also find Appendix C helpful, since it gives some of the typical methods used to compile and run a C program. It also gives a cross reference of all standard and new C functions used in this book.

Finally, see newlib.h in Appendix C, which is a minimal library you might want to consider using with your beginning C programs. The use of a personal library in a C program is discussed in Chapter 2 and again in Chapter 4.

Note to the Instructor

You will find that this book has the following features:

1. Syntax diagrams for principal C constructs (BNF diagrams are given in Appendix C), which are helpful in organizing a discussion of portions of the C language.
2. A fairly broad spectrum of problems is used to illustrate features of C :
   Gries's coffee can problem
   Extended precision arithmetic
   Extensive work with strings
   Cryptography problems
   Random numbers for simulations and simple games
   Sorts
   Searches
3. Stepwise refinements of most programs presented.
4. Short as well as major programs in later chapters.
5. Detailed examples of the low-level features of C , as well as its higher-level features.

6. Running comparison of constructs in C with similar constructs in Pascal.
7. Treatment of the efficiency (the expected running time) of the sorts and the hash search.
8. A comprehensive treatment of the C language.
9. A distinction between exercises (for individuals) and lab projects (for groups) in Chapters 2 through 9.
10. Chapter aims, introductions, and summaries, that run parallel with chapter contents, and review terms and symbols, and related readings for each chapter.

We will be happy to share with you copies of the programs used in any of the figures or for any of the solutions. These are available on RX50, quad density, 5 ¼-inch diskettes for the Rainbow-100 or DECMATE™ or on magnetic tape. They can be obtained by writing to the publisher.

Finally, feel free to write to us if you have any questions or suggestions or improved programs and/or solutions.

*　　　　　*　　　　　*

Acknowledgments

We wish to acknowledge the help and suggestions given by Ken Hortsch, Karl Glander, Tracy Gauthier, Mark Tristani, Thomas Plum, Patrick Holmay, and Lori Kaufenberg at St. John's University, as well as Patricia Rayner at Reston.

J. F. Peters III
H. M. Sallam

Overview

[C] is not tied to any one operating system or machine; and although it has been called a "system programming language" because it is useful for writing operating systems, it has been used equally well to write major numerical, text-processing and database programs.

B. W. Kernighan and D. M. Ritchie*

AIMS

- Introduce Generic Concepts Concerning Machine Organization of a Typical Host Machine for a C Compiler.
- Give Historical Background of C and Indicate How It Differs from Its Predecessors.
- Discuss the Functions of a C Compiler.
- Discuss Two Features of the C Preprocessor Program.
- Suggest Some Debugging Tools.
- Introduce the Initials K & R and J & W.

1.1 INTRODUCTION

C is a small, powerful, and portable programming language. C allows a programmer to take full advantage of the machine on which it is to be used. It does this by supplying a model of the computer that is close to the target machine being used. C supplies dozens of operators that make it possible to get close to the target

---

*The C Programming Language, Prentice-Hall, Inc., Englewood Cliffs, N.J., 1978.

2 Overview   CHAPTER I

hardware, if we wish. For example, it supplies bitwise operators, which allow us
to work on the bit level of the machine. It also allows a C programmer to be free
of the constraints of a particular machine in developing solutions to problems that
demand the use of a high-level language on an ideal machine rather than a particular target machine.

Although C began as the systems language for the UNIX™ operating system
on a PDP-11™ in 1972 at the Bell Laboratories, C is now available on a variety
of machines and under a variety of different operating systems. Evidence of the
portability of C is given in Table 1.1.

TABLE 1.1   Sample C Compilers

Compiler	Operating System	Machine
Aztec C/1.5G	CP/m 80	Rainbow-100/Apple IIe
Aztec C/65	Apple	Apple IIe
BDS C	CP/m 80/2.0	Heath H8
C/80 C/2.0	CP/m 80	Heath H8
Telecon C	CP/m 80	Heath H8
Whitesmith C	CP/m 80	Heath H8
Whitesmith C	RSTS/E	PDP-11
Whitesmith C	RSX-11	PDP-11
Whitesmith C	RT-11	PDP-11
c-systems C	PC-DOS	IBM PC
Caprock small C	PC-DOS	IBM PC
Xenix-286 C	XENIX	IBM PC AT
MS C 3.0	MS-DOS	IBM PC
Lattice C	PC-DOS	IBM PC
Supersoft C	PC-DOS	IBM PC
C	UNIX	VAX-11
C	UNIX	PDP-11

Johnson and Kernighan (1983) mention that C offers a compromise between
a very high-level language like BASIC and an assembly programming language.
That is, the model computer made available by C is close to the target machine.
C does this with a generous provision of storage classes, including a register storage class that is used by a C compiler in an advisory fashion. C also lets a programmer get close to the target machine with a generous selection of operators,
including bitwise operators that allow a C programmer to work on the bit level of
a target machine. C does this without the restrictions and system dependency
found in an assembly language.

C also lets a programmer work with an idealized machine and be removed
from the constraints found in a typical assembly language. C allows us to work

CHAPTER I   1.3 Keyboard symbols and machine codes   3

with high-level language constructs: functions with parameter lists, powerful and diverse control structures, and the use of pointers to handle dynamic allocation of storage.

This chapter introduces some basic concepts about machine organization and the C language. The emphasis in this chapter and in this text is not on the constraints of a particular machine or operating system. The emphasis is rather on the features of C considered standard by its author, Dennis M. Ritchie. This is possible, thanks to the recommendations by Ritchie concerning the standard features of C described in the June 1983 Bell Laboratories publication entitled *The C Programming Language—Reference Manual*. It is the standardized C recommended by Ritchie that forms the basis for the presentation in this book. This reference manual is a helpful supplement to that provided by Kernighan and Ritchie (1978).

1.2 MACHINE ORGANIZATION

A sketch of the organization of a typical computer is shown in Figure 1.1. The *central processing unit* (CPU) of a computer is made up of a control unit and arithmetic and logic unit. A program entered by a user from a keyboard or retrieved from a secondary storage device like a disk is kept in a processor's main memory unit. The instructions and data from a program must be transferred bit by bit from main memory to registers inside the processor. The arithmetic and logic operations of a processor are carried out with the contents of processor registers.

A *register* is a small, high-speed storage area inside a processor. Various kinds of registers are indicated in Figure 1.1. A general-purpose register, for example, can be used as an accumulator or as a scratch pad used by the processor in making calculations. These registers are also useful in identifying the location of program data in main memory. A general-purpose register is of interest to a C programmer, since C has a register storage class that can be used to speed up calculations with a small number of commonly used variables.

Memory on a computer can be explained in terms of bits. The term *bit* is a contraction of the words *binary* and *digit*. A *memory location* in a computer is a set of connected (contiguous) bits. A *memory address* is a set of bits used to tag (identify) a memory location. The C language makes it possible to determine and change, if necessary, the memory address used by variables in a C program.

1.3 KEYBOARD SYMBOLS AND MACHINE CODES

Each keyboard symbol is associated with a unique bit string, the encoded form of a symbol we type. A processor works with bit strings; humans work with symbols. The two come together through code tables that convert a typed symbol to a bit

4 Overview

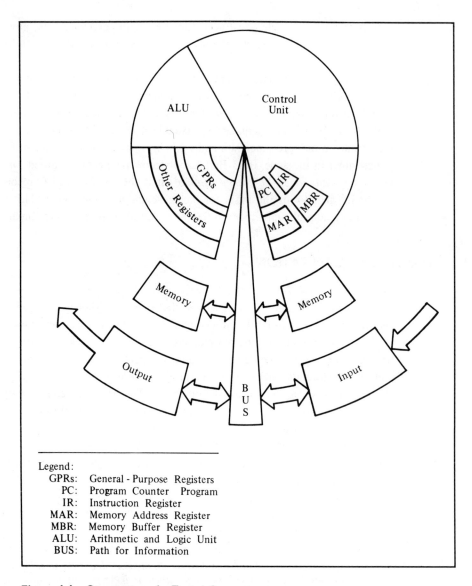

Figure 1.1 Organization of a Typical Computer

string and return to a user a symbol corresponding to a bit string. Two systems of encoding keyboard symbols are used with C compilers:

1. The 7-bit ASCII code (ASCII stands for American Standard Code for Information Interchange). There is also an 8-bit version of the same table.

CHAPTER I   **1.4 The C programming language 5**

2. The 8-bit EBCDIC code developed by IBM™ for its System/360 and used on its System/370 (EBCDIC stands for Extended Binary Coded Decimal Interchange Code).

These two tables are given in Appendix A. Some sample symbols and their corresponding binary and hex codes in both systems are given in Table 1.2.

The ASCII table is the more commonly used table, especially on non-IBM systems. C makes it easy to determine which coding system is being used by a computer. Included in the standard C function library is a printf() function, which makes it possible to format output to a screen. In Chapter 4 we show how this function can be used to print out the corresponding machine code being used for a keyboard symbol. Using a printf() control string, these codes can be printed in octal (base 8), hexadecimal (base 16), and decimal (base 10). The discussions in this text will be limited to ASCII codes.

TABLE 1.2 Sample Keyboard Symbols and Codes

	Binary Bit String				
	ASCII Code			*EBCDIC Code*	
Symbol	*Binary*	*Hex*		*Binary*	*Hex*
0	0011 0000	30		1111 0000	F0
1	0011 0001	31		1111 0001	F1
2	0011 0010	32		1111 0010	F2
3	0011 0011	33		1111 0011	F3
Y	0101 1001	59		1110 1000	E8
c	0110 0011	63		1000 0011	83
=	0011 1101	3D		0111 1110	7E

1.4 THE C PROGRAMMING LANGUAGE

C began as a systems language for the UNIX operating system on a PDP-11 at the Bell Laboratories in 1972. Dennis M. Ritchie designed C as an alternative to the B language, which had been developed at the Bell Laboratories. The B language was a short-lived offspring of the BCPL language, which was another systems language developed in 1969 by Martin Richards at Cambridge University. BCPL stands for Basic Combined Programming Language.

C gets its name from being the successor of the B language. The BCPL and B languages are "typeless" languages, whereas C is a weakly typed language. In B and BCPL, the only type was the machine word; special operators and function

6 Overview CHAPTER I

calls were used to access other kinds of objects. By contrast, C has three fundamental data types: integers, floating-point numbers, and characters.

The main distinction between C and its predecessors is the provision of data
types by C. Even so, C is not a strongly typed language because it permits type
conversions within a program. C shares with Band BCPL a selection of control
structures:

1. Blocks: sequential control
2. If: selection control
3. While, for, do: iteration control
4. Switch: case statement

C also provides pointers, a powerful programming tool that permits dynamic
allocation of memory during the execution of a program and address arithmetic.
C also permits internal functions (also called procedures in Pascal) and external
functions.

C relies on the use of four separate programs to process a source text written
in C. For example, when we type

cc yes.c

to compile the yes.c source text, the following four programs are used to obtain
an executable task module:

1. A preprocessor program (ccp), which is mainly concerned with file inclusion and text replacement. (We explain this in the next section.) The ccp
   program also strips away comments from the source text when it builds
   the expanded source text.
2. A translator program (cc, itself), which translates the expanded source
   text from the preprocessor program down to the assembly language level.
   The cc program will produce error messages for syntax errors in the expanded source text (these can usually be found in a log file).
3. A second translator program (as), which translates the assembler text
   from the cc program down to the bit string level. This assembly language
   program (as) produces what is known as an object module, with provi-
   sional (temporary, relocatable) memory addresses for the lines of
   machine code in the object module.
4. A linking loader program (ld), which brings the object module from the
   assembly language program (as) together with other object modules that
   might be needed. The result is an executable load module, which is des-
   ignated by a.out or, in some compilers, by yes.tsk.

The relationship between the four C compiler programs and a source text is shown in Figure 1.2.

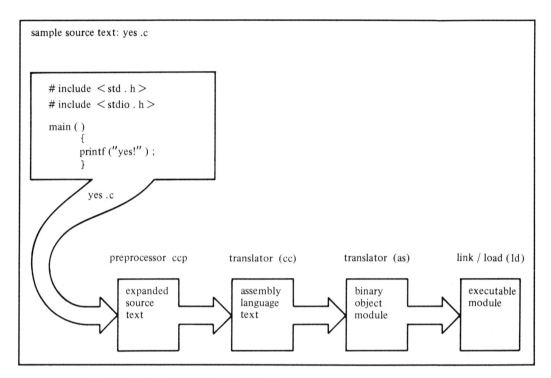

Figure 1.2 Processing a C Source Text

1.5 THE C PREPROCESSOR

The C preprocessor program (ccp) has four functions:

1. File inclusion (#include directs ccp to do this).
2. Token replacement (*define directs ccp to do this).
3. Conditional compilation.
4. Building an expanded source text without any of the comments that might be present in an original source text.

The pound sign (#) sets up a control line between the preprocessor program and the original source text. For example, the line

#include <stdio.h>

8 Overview   CHAPTER I

in Figure 1.2 tells the preprocessor to replace the given line with the complete contents of the standard input/output library file. When pointed brackets are used with the *include* directive, the preprocessor looks only in standard places for the named file. It does not look in the directory containing the reference to the source text, such as yes.c. If we use

#include "newlib.h"

this tells the preprocessor to look in the directory for the source text to find the newlib.h file. The double quotes (") are used to tell the C preprocessor about another file it should include with the source text. If the preprocessor does not find a file referenced with double quotes in the source text directory, it will also look in standard places for the same file.

The word *include* is an example of a preprocessor directive. A directive tells the preprocessor to do something. The word *define* is another commonly used preprocessor directive. For example, the control line

#define MAX 50

tells the preprocessor to replace any occurrences of the identifier MAX in the source text by the token 50. The identifier MAX is an example of what is sometimes called a *macro,* and the #define sets up what is called *macro substitution.* There are two forms of the #define:

#define identifier token string
#define identifier (identifier, . . . , identifier) token string

The #define control line can be broken or undone by using, for example,

#undef MAX

anywhere inside an original source text.

The #include and #define directives are used throughout this text. They are very useful programming tools. They are explained in more detail in the next chapter.

I.6 C SYNTAX

C is terse. For an untrained eye, the terseness of a C source text can be a problem. One of the commonest sources of syntax errors in beginning C programs is the use of braces { }, instead of the words *begin* and *end* found in Pascal, to mark the boundaries of a program block. This problem can be solved in beginning C programs by using the following *define* directives:

CHAPTER I   **1.7 The source books: K & R and J & W   9**

```
#define begin {
#define end   }
```

So, for example, the source text in Figure 1.2 can be rewritten as shown in Figure 1.3. We use this technique in the first few chapters of this text.

A *noise* word is used to improve the readability of a statement but contributes nothing to the use of the statement by a compiler. For example, an if statement in **C** is written as follows:

```
if condition statement;
```

We use, for example,

```
if x > o
    printf("Yes!");
```

We introduce the noise word *then* into this statement using the following technique:

```
#define then

        .

        .

        .

main()
    {

        .

        .

        .

    if x > o
        then printf("Yes!");

        .

        .

        .

    }
```

I.7 THE SOURCE BOOKS: K & R AND J & W

In this text we will often compare a construct in **C** with its counterpart in Pascal. What might be called the Pascal book was written by Kathleen Jensen and Niklaus Wirth in 1974. This book contains a Pascal reference manual written by Wirth,

10 Overview   CHAPTER I

```
#include <std.h>

#include <stdio.h>

#define begin {

#define end   }


main()

    begin

        printf("Yes!");

    end
```

Figure 1.3 Sample C Source Text

who created Pascal about the same time Ritchie was creating **C**. It has become
commonplace to refer to this book using J & W.

Similarly, what is usually called the **C** book was written by Brian Kernighan
and Dennis Ritchie in 1978. The **C** book (or K & R) contains a complete **C** reference manual in Appendix A.

1.8 DEBUGGING A C PROGRAM

A *bug* in a program is an error (a problem or glitch). Basically, there are two types
of program bugs:

1. *Syntax errors.* An improper form is used in a source text. *Example:* using
   a left brace, {, instead of a right brace, }, or vice versa, to mark the
   boundaries of a program block. Missing semicolons, commas, or braces
   are other sources of bugs. A misspelled word will produce an error message.
2. *Logic errors.* An improper formula or condition used to control execution, for example, will result in a logic error.

Syntax errors are the easiest to find and correct. With **C** under UNIX, use,
for example

lint yes.c

to help isolate syntax errors. For **C** compilers without the lint program, a log file
is usually set up automatically whenever the cc compile command is used. The

CHAPTER I   1.9 Summary   11

Whitesmith C compiler for PDP-11 systems, for example, always sets up a log file each time a source is compiled. The log file will indicate which lines of a source text are troublesome to the C compiler. Errors tend to multiply like rabbits. A simple missing left brace can lead to a misinterpretation of the lines of text following the missing brace. Instead of one error, it is possible to have 15 syntax errors.

In Appendix B (no pun intended), we give some sample debugging tools useful in checking for both syntax and logic errors. A logic error is usually more difficult to fix, at first. Misuses of data types or data structures like arrays or strings can often lead to logic errors. A logic error can be either of the following two types:

1. A can't-do request. *Example:* dividing by zero, or trying to use an array that is too small.
2. A shouldn't-do request. *Example:* a poorly defined condition used to control execution of a program block, or performing an operation when another operation should be performed instead.

A tried-and-true method of debugging programs is to *keep a record of all programming errors made* (a bugbook). The errors you make will probably be *partly* those commonly made by others (see Appendix B) and partly those you alone tend to make. Your own bugbook will help you in future programs. Get used to identifying those errors you yourself are prone to make; this is Knuth's recommendation (1973, p. 189).

Another helpful debugging tool is the use of *test data.* Program correctness can be measured in terms of results that can be checked by another program, a calculator or table, or by hand.

1.9 SUMMARY

C is a programming language that was developed by Dennis M. Ritchie during the early 1970s at the Bell Laboratories. It is part of a trio of compilers that was started in 1969 by Martin Richards: BCPL, B, and C. The C language is the lexicographic and logical successor of the middle member of this trio, the B language also developed at the Bell Laboratories. The main distinction between C and its predecessors is its provision of three fundamental data types: integers, floating-point numbers, and characters.

C is terse. C programs tend to be very concise, intricately and admirably crafted.

C is a language that demands considerable skill and the awakening of a perception of the organization of the host machine for a C compiler. C allows a pro-

12 Overview

CHAPTER I

grammer to work on the bit level of a host machine, to do address arithmetic. **C** also allows a programmer to use high-level, structured programming constructs. In other words, **C** lets a programmer work on what would normally be the assembly language level, as well as the higher-order language level, depending on the application.

C is subtle. **C** permits type conversions within a program. Statements (but not functions) can be nested and compressed. **C** has more than the usual number of operators, far outstripping Pascal, for example, in its provision of operators.

C encourages an art of programming. Its preprocessor makes it possible to set up stand-alone functions that can be *included* in more than one source text. The result is the construction of libraries of functions that can be used across a spectrum of programs. Thanks to the *include* directive, **C** programs (what we see in a *new* source text) can be terse and elegant. And thanks to the *define* directive, **C** programs can be fashioned using personalized (and stylized) constructs. The preprocessor program encourages a creative approach to programming.

REVIEW TERMS AND SYMBOLS

Term	*Meaning*
accumulator	register used by a CPU to do arithmetic and hold operands (or addresses of operands) used in calculations by the processor
ASCII	American Standard Code for Information Interchange
B	derived from BCPL
BCPL	Basic Combined Programming Language (1969)
bit	binary digit, unit of information in a machine
C:	derived from B by D. M. Ritchie (1972)
1. ccp	preprocessor
2. cc	translator to assembly language
3. as	translator to machine language
4. ld	linker/loader to produce executable module
control line	connection between source text line and preprocessor
CPU	central processing unit, which handles the control, arithmetic, and logic operations of a processor
debugging tools:	ways to identify program problems
1. lint	syntax checker for **C** under UNIX
2. bugbook	list of errors made
3. test data	sample input to check program results
define	preprocessor directive used for token replacement
EBCDIC	Extended Binary Coded Decimal Interchange Code
Errors:	
1. syntax error	improper form used in source text
2. logic error	misuse of a data structure, a poor interpretation of an algorithm
include	preprocessor directive to include a file with a source text

CHAPTER I   **Related readings   13**

Term	*Meaning*
J & W	Jensen and Wirth, the Pascal book, 1974
K & R	Kernighan and Ritchie, the C book, 1978
memory address	set of bits used to identify a memory location
memory location	set of contiguous bits in main memory
noise word	word used to improve readability of an expression
preprocessor	text substitution program used by C
register	small, high-speed storage inside a processor

EXERCISES

1. Does your system have a lint program for syntax-checking a C source text? If not, what debugging tools are available with your C compiler?
2. What is the difference between a memory location and a memory address?
3. Give the ASCII and EBCDIC codes in binary and hex for the lowercase letters. See Appendix A for the ASCII and EBCDIC tables.
4. How many registers can be used as accumulators on the host system for your C compiler?
5. Which C compiler does your system use?
6. Fill in Figure 1.1 with information about the host computer for your C compiler in terms of the following things:
   a. Number of bytes in main memory.
   b. Number of accumulators available.
   c. Types of input/output devices available.
   d. Disk space available.

RELATED READINGS

Feuer, A. R., and **N. Gehani,** editors, *Comparing and Assessing Programming Languages: Ada, C and Pascal.* Englewood Cliffs, N.J.: Prentice-Hall, Inc., 1984.

Jensen, K., and **N. Wirth,** *Pascal User Manual and Report.* New York: Springer-Verlag, New York, Inc., 1974; also, 1985 (for second edition).

Johnson, S. C., and **B. W. Kernighan,** "The C Language and Models for Systems Programming," *Byte,* Vol. 8, No. 8 (August 1983), 48–63.

Kernighan, B. W., and **D. M. Ritchie,** *The C Programming Language.* Englewood Cliffs, N.J.: Prentice-Hall, Inc., 1978.

Knuth, D. E., *The Art of Computer Programming,* Vol. 1 (Fundamental Algorithms). Reading, Mass.: Addison-Wesley Publishing Co., 1973.

Ritchie, D. M., *The C Programming Language,* Reference Manual in UNIX Time-Sharing System. UNIX Programmer's Manual, Vol. 2. New York: Holt, Rinehart and Winston, 1983, pp. 247–278.

Thomas, R., "C Tutorial: Getting Started," *UNIX/World,* Vol. 1, No. 2 (March/April 1984), 46–53. Los Altos, Calif.: Tech Valley Publishing, Inc., 1984.

2

Beginning C Programming

C is a general-purpose programming language featuring economy of expression, modern control flow and data structure capabilities, and a rich set of operators and data types.

D. M. Ritchie and others*

AIMS

- Introduce C Syntax.
- Introduce Features of the Program Development Cycle.
- Begin Using Formatted Input and Output.
- Begin Setting up a Local Macro Library.
- Begin Discussion of C Data Types.
- Examine the Tokens of a C Program.
- Distinguish Types of Expressions and C Statements.
- Introduce Use of the For Statement.

2.1 INTRODUCTION

Creating a new program often means creating new instructions. The aim of the new instructions is to tell a computer to do something. Suppose, for example, that we want to tell a computer to draw the sideview of a robot on a ramp shown in Figure 2.1. Before we worry about how to tell a computer to draw this picture in

---

*"The C Programming Language," *Bell System Technical Journal,* Vol. 57, No. 6, July–August, 1978.

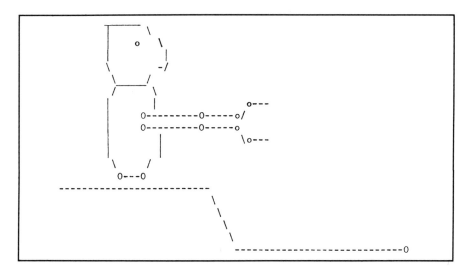

Figure 2.1 Sketch of CP34

a *particular* programming language, we can try using our own words to write down the new instructions:

> begin
>   drawcp34;
>   drawramp;
> end

The next trick is to *define* these instructions in terms of the vocabulary of a particular programming language. We do this using C in Figure 2.2. The *drawcp34* and *drawramp* instructions have been defined using parameterless functions in C. Each "definition" is in terms of another function, puts(). This function is part of the standard C library of functions. In general, its format is

> puts(string)

where *string* is any of the keyboard characters put inside double quotes. The entire collection of keyboard characters is given in the ASCII table shown in Chapter 1. The puts() function reads "put string." It contributes a <return> after its target string is printed.

    Notice that the new instructions are placed inside the function *main*(). Every C program has this function. We use main() as a command center, directing a computer to draw a sideview of a robot called cp34, and then to draw a ramp below cp34.

```c
#include <stdio.h>

drawcp34()
      {
      puts("                                ");
      puts("       _____\\\\             ");
      puts("      |        o    \\\\           ");
      puts("      |             |           ");
      puts("      \\\\      -/             ");
      puts("       \\\_____/             ");
      puts("       /        \\\\             ");
      puts("      |          |        o--- ");
      puts("      |    0--------0-----o/    ");
      puts("      |    0--------0-----o     ");
      puts("      |              \\\\o---                    ");
      puts("      |                     ");
      puts("       \\\\      /             ");
      puts("        0---0                 ");
      }

drawramp()
      {
      puts("------------------------");
      puts("                        \\\\");
      puts("                        \\\\");
      puts("                        \\\\");
      puts("                        \\\\");
      puts("                         ---------------------------0");
      }

main()
      {

            drawcp34();
            drawramp();

RUN C22
```

RUN C22

```
      _____\
     |        o    \
     |             |
     \       -/
      _____/
      /        \
     |          |        o---
     |    0--------0-----o/
     |    0--------0-----o
     |              \o---
     |
      \      /
       0---0
------------------------
                        \
                         \
                          \
                           ---------------------------0
```

Figure 2.2   C Program to Draw CP34

CHAPTER 2   **2.2 Program development cycle**   17

The braces { } mark the beginning and end of a **C** function block. They serve the same purpose as the begin/end in Pascal procedures. Later, we show how these braces can be replaced by begin/end to make a **C** program more readable, especially to those who are familiar with Pascal or ALGOL.

Finally, notice that each instruction is terminated with a semicolon (;).

You might put your imagination to work in terms of defining the following instructions using puts():

```
main()
begin
        drawcp34();
        drawramp();
        drawbeeper();
        drawoutlet();
end
```

That is, add to the cp34 picture a sketch of a beeper for cp34 to pick up and an outlet cp34 can use to charge its batteries. We leave the creation of these new **C** functions as an exercise.

In this chapter we begin a discussion of the program development cycle. These are stages usually followed in developing new programs. Some of these stages are implicit in the preceding discussion. We also introduce the **C** vocabulary, along with syntax diagrams for some of the elementary **C** statements and functions. Finally, we give a running comparison of familiar Pascal statements and their **C** equivalents.

2.2 PROGRAM DEVELOPMENT CYCLE

There are recognizable stages in the development of a program in any language. For example, in developing a program to draw a sideview of cp34 on a ramp, we can extract some of these stages. We did the following things:

1. Start with a problem (a picture of cp34 we want to *tell* a computer to duplicate).
2. Draw up a preliminary list of instructions to solve the problem.

```
drawcp34;
drawramp;
```

3. Define these instructions in terms of separate modules (we used functions in **C**) in terms of the vocabulary of a computer language.
4. Test the program (get a sample run).

18 Beginning C programming

5. Begin writing a cp34 robot manual (explain the program, suggest extensions, make refinements of the original program).

We can get *very* busy in step 2 of the preceding cycle (solving the problem). It depends on a clearly stated description of the problem. Programs are always being changed, refined, tuned, and made more useful. After the preliminary design modules have been built in step 2, it is usually necessary to refine them, step by step. This leads to more testing and more documenting (manual writing).

These stages in the program development cycle are shown in more detail in Table 2.1. One of the more subtle features of this cycle is the use of assertions about a program. It is usually a good idea to pinpoint relations in a program that should remain invariant when a program is run.

For example, suppose we have the following lines of code in **C**:

```
while (1)
    {
    scanf ("%f %f", &a, &b);
    if (a >= 0.0)
        if (b > 0.0)
            c = b / a;
    }
```

This is equivalent to the following Pascal fragment:

```
while 1 > 0 do
    begin
    readln (a,b);
    if (a >= 0.0) and (b > 0.0)
        then
            c = b / a
    end;
```

In either case, values for a and b are taken from a keyboard. Then, in each case, the input is evaluated. If the two conditions are satisfied, a ratio c is computed. This allows us to make the following assertion about these lines of code:

$$c >= 0 \quad and \quad b = c * a$$

As long as these lines of code continue to be executed, this relation remains invariant. If c is computed, it will always satisfy this invariant assertion.

It is helpful to put invariant assertions in the comments of a program. Why? These assertions will give you something to fall back on if it becomes necessary to debug a program. Debugging is made easier by checking if invariant assertions hold true.

CHAPTER 2   **2.2 Program development cycle   19**

TABLE 2.1   Program Development Cycle

. *Cycle Stages*	. *Illustrated Stages*

1. Specification
  1.1 Problem definition
  1.2 Functions to perform
	1. Specification
	  1.1 Duplicate picture
	  1.2 Draw picture of cp34 on a ramp

2. Design
  2.1 Modularization (separate the
  tasks to perform) *Note:* avoid
  lumping tasks together
  2.2 Stepwise refinement (think of
  possible ways to improve the
  modules)
	2. Design
	  2.1 drawcp34;
	  drawramp;
	
	  2.2 drawsideview; refine
	  drawtopview; drawcp34
	  drawfrontview; function
	  drawramp;

3. Coding
  Use vocabulary of a computer
  language to define instructions
	3. Coding
	  Use puts() and main() in **C**

4. Program Correctness
  4.1 Test the program (does it work?)
  4.2 Verify (is the output correct?)
  Test assertions made in program
  comments
	4. Program Correctness
	  4.1 Print duplicate of picture
	  4.2 Has a duplicate of robot picture
	  been printed? Test assertion: a
	  duplicate will be printed

5. Documentation
  Write a manual about program
	5. Documentation
	  Begin cp34 robot manual

Both of the preceding while-loops are infinite loops. They run forever. This is a coincidence, not the basis for the invariant relation, which depends solely on the values of a and b. In either a finite or infinite loop, the preceding relation remains invariant.

The scanf() function is a standard **C** formatted input function, which we explain later. It takes its formatted input from an input stream coming from a keyboard. The &-prefix in &a, for example, is used to specify the address (memory location) of the variable a, which will receive a value typed at a keyboard. The %f indicates that the value in the input stream will be a floating-point number like 1.618.

What is an *invariant assertion*? It is a claim about the values of variables in a program. It is a claim that is checked when it is necessary to debug a program, to check its *production* of values of program variables. A good discussion of invariant assertion is given by Dijkstra (1976).

20   Beginning C programming CHAPTER 2

Finally, **C** programming encourages the development of program modules instead of lumping program instructions inside main (). Why? In **C**, it is easy to develop separate functions that can be used by more than one program. These functions are put into libraries. It makes sense to separate as much as possible the tasks performed by functions. This will increase the usefulness of a particular function in various programs. In this chapter, we show how these libraries can be set up using the #include **C** preprocessor command.

2.3 THE C VOCABULARY

Every programming language has its own vocabulary. The vocabulary for **C** is shown in Table 2.2. The **C** vocabulary is expressed in terms of the Backus–Naur form (BNF). The BNF equal symbol (=) reads "is defined by." The BNF vertical line symbol (|) reads "alternatively." The BNF period symbol (.) terminates a BNF production. For example,

$$\text{binary digit } = 0 \mid 1.$$

reads

"binary digit" is defined by '' 0 or 1''

BNF productions can be used to exhibit the syntax of statements in a programming language. We show how this is done in terms of **C** statements in Appendix A.

The 29 word symbols in Table 2.2 are the reserved words in **C**. This is a shorter list of reserved words than the 35 reserved words given for Pascal by J & W (1974).

2.4 TOKENS, SYNTAX DIAGRAMS, AND IDENTIFIERS

Tokens are the smallest units in a computer program. For example, in **C** the tokens are in three groups:

1. Special symbols like = = or = .
2. Word symbols like *if* or *while*.
3. Identifiers like *result* or *drawcp34*.

The statements of a programming language are built in terms of these tokens. Each statement will have its own syntax or *acceptable* use of tokens.

Since BNF productions are sometimes not easy to read, syntax diagrams are used as an alternative representation of language syntax. *Syntax diagrams* are also called railroad charts, since they can be read in terms of an imaginary locomotive traversing a syntax diagram from left to right.

2.4 Tokens, syntax diagrams, and identifiers 21

TABLE 2.2   C Vocabulary

Special symbols	= | == | != | & | && | + | ++ | / | - | -- | | | ^ | << | >> | ˜ | * | &= | += | -= | |= | ^= | <<= | /= | >>= | *= | % | . | _ | %= | (|) | [|] | { | } | ' | " | ? | : | | | → | /* | */ | , | ; | .
Word symbols	auto | break | case | char | continue | default | do | double | else | enum | extern | float | for | goto | if | int | long | register | return | short | sizeof | static | struct | switch | typedef | union | unsigned | void | while.
Letters	a | b | c | d | e | f | g | h | i | j | k | l | m | n | o | p | q | r | s | t | u | v | w | x | y | z | A | B | C | D | E | F | G | H | I | J | K | L | M | N | O | P | Q | R | S | T | U | V | W | X | Y | Z.
Digits	0 | 1 | 2 | 3 | 4 | 5 | 6 | 7 | 8 | 9.

For example, identifiers for variables, constants, and functions in C have the syntax shown in Figure 2.3. This syntax diagram for a C identifier reads "letter followed by zero or more letters, underscores, or digits." The following is a list of C identifiers:

x	draw_line	result_05
x1	sea_lane	catch22
x_1	result	C_index
drawcp34	result_01	C_symbol

The maximum number of characters in a C identifier will vary, depending on the compiler. As a rule, only the first eight characters are taken as significant. This means that

until_123
until_124

will probably be indistinguishable to a C compiler, since the ninth character is not used by the compiler. Also, reserved words in C cannot be used to introduce variables, constants, or functions.

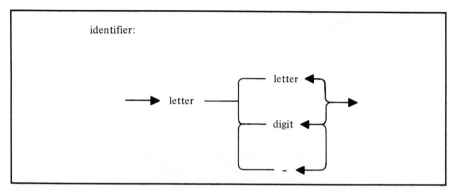

Figure 2.3 Syntax for a C Identifier

2.5 STATEMENTS

Statements in C tell a computer to do something. A *statement* specifies an action for the computer to perform. Statements in C are either atomic or compound. An *atomic* statement is executed separately. The statements in the *drawcp34()* function, for example, are atomic.

Compound statements represent a sequence of actions within a block. For example, the statements inside the braces in the following infinite while statement represent a compound statement:

```
while (1)
{
puts("* * * * * *");
puts("*         *");
puts("*C is terse.*");
puts("*         *");
puts("* * * * * *");
}
```

The statements inside this block are executed, as long as the condition tested by C in the while loop is satisfied. In this case, they will always be executed.

2.6 COMMENTS

Comments in C are put between left, /*, and right, */, symbols. For example, in terms of the invariant assertion we mentioned earlier, we can make the following comment:

CHAPTER 2   **2.6 Comments** **23**

```
/*assertion:                              */
/*     result >= 0 and x = result * y     */
/*                                        */
    while (1)
       {
       scanf("%f %f", x, y);
       if (x >= 0.0)
         if ( y > 0.0 )
           result = x / y;
       }
```

Comments should be used sparingly. The following is a helpful "comment" that can be used to separate the chief parts of a longer C program:

```
/* - - - - - - - - - - - - - - - - - - - - - */
```

For example, in the program in Figure 2.2, we could have used the following framework:

```
#include <stdio h>
drawcp34()
   {
   .
   .
   .
   }
/* - - - - - - - - - - - - - - - - - - - - - */
drawramp()
   {
   .
   .
   .
   }
/* - - - - - - - - - - - - - - - - - - - - - */
main()
   {
   .
   .
   .
   }
```

That is, the rows of hyphens help separate the parts of a program. In a longer program, this is helpful.

2.7 INDEXED REPETITION: FOR-LOOPS

In C, indexed repetition is obtained by using a for-loop. By *indexed repetition,* we mean controlling how many times one or more actions are iterated by using an index. For example, consider the following parallel repetitions:

Repetition without a for-loop	*Repetition with a for-loop*

{
 drawcp34;
 drawcp34;
 drawcp34;
 drawcp34;
 }
	for (i = 1; i <= 4; i = i + 1)
	 drawcp34;

In this example, the integer variable *i* is used as the index variable to control the iteration of drawcp34.

A syntax diagram for a C for-loop is given in Figure 2.4. We illustrate the three expressions in the for-loop diagram in terms of the preceding example, which has the following structure:

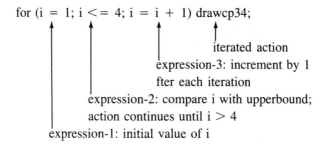

The expression $i = i + 1$ reads "*i* is assigned the value of *i* plus 1." This expression has the following simplified form:

$$i = i + 1 \quad \text{is the same as} \quad ++i$$

So we can write the preceding for-loop as follows:

for (i = 1; i <= 4; ++i)
   drawcp34;

It is important to notice that the action that is iterated by a for-loop is specified by a statement. In C, a statement can be either *atomic* or *compound*. In the preceding example, the for-loop is written in terms of an atomic statement. Only a single action is specified in an atomic statement. We can just as easily iterate

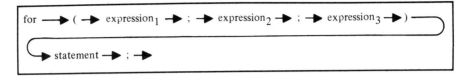

Figure 2.4 For-Statement Syntax

the actions specified by a compound statement. For example, we can use a for-loop to print a picture of a cp34 beeper (a robot toy!) and print the value of the index variable with each iteration. This is done as follows:

```
for (i = 0; i <= max; ++i)
{
drawbeeper();
printf("\n\n index equals %5d \n", i);
}
```

This for-loop includes the use of a printf() statement, which is a standard C function to handle formatted output to a terminal. We explain how a printf() works in detail later. In general, a printf() has the following structure:

$$\text{printf (format, output)}$$

In the preceding example, the *format* of the output specified by a printf() is given inside the double quotes. This output format specifies the following things:

1. Two <return>s with "\n\n" ["\n" reads "newline" and calls for a CR (carriage return) and LF (line feed)].
2. Print the following string:

$$\text{index equals}$$

3. Print a decimal value with

$$\text{"\%5d"}$$

(this allows five places for the printed number, which is right justified).
4. Print a final <return> with

$$\text{"\n"}$$

We show a C program to carry out this idea in Figure 2.5. The final printf() in Figure 2.5 has an added format specification with

26 Beginning C programming   CHAPTER 2

```
#include <stdio.h>
                        /*define drawbeeper instruction*/
drawbeeper()
        {
        printf("    o    \n");
        printf("    |    \n");
        printf("  << >>   \n");
        }

main()
        {
        int i,max = 5;
        for (i = 0;i <= max;++i)
                {
                drawbeeper();
                printf("\n\t\t\index equals %5d\n",i);
                }
        }

RUN C25
     o
     |
   << >>

                    index equals     0

     o
     |
   << >>

                    index equals     1

     o
     |
   << >>

                    index equals     2

     o
     |
   << >>

                    index equals     3

     o
     |
   << >>

                    index equals     4

     o
     |
   << >>

                    index equals     5
```

Figure 2.5 C For-Loop

CHAPTER 2   **2.8 Expressions, operators, and operands   27**

$$''\backslash t\backslash t''$$

This calls for two horizontal tabs before the string is printed.

Notice, in addition, that *max* is declared to be of type *int* (or integer), which is discussed in detail in the next section. For now, notice that, at the same time the data type of max is declared, it is also given a value. That is,

$$\text{int max} = 5;$$

says max is type int *and* equal to 5.

We can force a for-loop to iterate indefinitely by using the following structure:

$$\text{for (1)}$$
$$\text{statement;}$$

For example, the palindrome

$$\text{Aha! Aha! Aha!}$$

will be printed forever on *separate* lines by using the following loop:

```
main()
{
for (1)
     printf("Aha! Aha! Aha! \n");
}
```

2.8 EXPRESSIONS, OPERATORS, AND OPERANDS

An *expression* is a representation of a value. An expression can be simply a number (a discrete value), an identifier for a variable or a constant, an identifier for a function, or an expression with either a unary or binary operator. The following is a sampler of possible expressions:

233	(discrete value)
-5	(unary operator -, with discrete value 5)
x	(identifier)
i + 1	(the + operator with operands i and 1)
+ +i	(the same as i = i + 1)
sqrt(2)	(square root of 2)
p && q	(p and q)
21 - 2 * 3	(= ?)

28 Beginning C programming CHAPTER 2

```
x - 2 * y
x % y               (x mod y)
drawcp34()
box[2]              (array element identified by box[ ])
55 / 6              (55 div 6 = 9)
55.0 / 6.0          (=9.16667)
21 - (2 * 3)        (= ?)
(21 - 2) * 3        (= ?)
```

The evaluation of an expression containing one or more operators depends on the precedence and associativity of the C operators used. An *operator* specifies an operation to be performed. *Operator precedence* determines which operator gets evaluated first, if an expression without parentheses has more than one operator. Parentheses can be used to control the order in which the parts of an expression are evaluated. *Operator associativity* specifies whether evaluation of an expression is from left to right (with + and *, for example) or from right to left (with + + or the unary operator -, the minus sign).

For example,

$$21 - 5 * 3 + 2 = 21 - (5 * 3) + 2$$
$$= 21 - 15 + 2$$
$$= (21 - 15) + 2$$
$$= 6 + 2$$
$$= 8$$

The parentheses in this statement have the highest precedence. Their associativity is from left to right. Evaluation begins with the expression inside the parentheses. The times operation (*) has higher precedence than either subtraction (-) or addition (+). All three operations are left associative, so this expression is evaluated from left to right, starting with the operator with highest precedence. This expression can be written with parentheses as follows:

$$(21 - (5 * 3)) + 2 = 21 - 5 * 3 + 2$$

We can change the order in which the operations are performed by changing the parentheses. For example, we can *construct* the following expression:

$$((21 - 5) * 3) + 2 = (16 * 3) + 2$$
$$= 48 + 2$$
$$= 50$$

A summary of C operators used with integers (type *int* in C) is given in Table 2.3.

CHAPTER 2   **2.9 Bug clinic: prefix and postfix operators   29**

TABLE 2.3   C Operators

Operator(s)	Precedence	Associativity
+ + -- (unary) -	1	Right to left
* / % (mod)	2	Left to right
+ -	3	Left to right
= (assigned)	4	Right to left

1 = highest precedence

The following is a list of short examples to illustrate the use of the operators in Table 2.3 not mentioned so far.

Operator	*Sample C expression*	*Equivalent Pascal expression*
--	--x (same as x = x - 1 in C)	x := x - 1
/	55 / 6 (= 9)	55 div 6 (= 9)
% (used *only* with type int)	55 % 6 (= 1)	55 mod 6 (= 1)
=	x = x + 25	x := x + 25

In Figure 2.6, we show a program with a sampler of uses of these operators in terms of type *int*.

2.9 BUG CLINIC: PREFIX AND POSTFIX OPERATORS

The program in Figure 2.6 exhibits the use of + + and -- as *prefix* operators in

$$+ +x \text{ and } --x$$

Notice that x, for example, is given an initial value of 100. Then

$$\text{printf} (+ +x) \text{ prints } 101 \text{ (or } x = x + 1)$$
$$\text{printf} (--x) \text{ prints } 100 \text{ (or } x = x - 1)$$

When + + is used as a *prefix* operator, C will increment the + + operand by 1, first. Then printf() exhibits the incremented value of x.

Similarly, when -- is used as a *prefix* operator, C will decrement the -- operand by 1, *first*. Then printf() exhibits the decremented value of x.

The program in Figure 2.6 also exhibits the use of + + and -- as *postfix* operators in

$$x + + \text{ and } x--$$

30 Beginning C programming   CHAPTER 2

```c
#include <stdio.h>

compute()
       {
       int x = 100;

       printf("Sampler of uses of C arithmetic operators\n\n");
       printf("-----------------------------------------------\n\n\n");
       printf("\t\t 2 - 5 * 3 + 2 = %4d\n\n", 2 - 5 * 3 + 2);
       printf("\t\t (2 - (5 * 3)) + 2 = %4d\n\n", (2 - (5 * 3)) + 2);
       printf("\t\t (2 - 5) * 3 + 2 = %4d\n\n", (2 - 5) * 3 + 2);
       printf("\t\t 55 / 6 = %4d\n\n", 55 / 6);
       printf("\t\t 55.0 / 6.0 = %4.2f\n\n", 55.0 / 6.0);
       printf("\t\t 55 mod 6 = %4d\n\n", 55 % 6);
       printf("\t\t ++5 = %4d\n\n", ++5);
       printf("\t\t --100 = %4d\n\n", --100);
       printf("\t\t ++x = %4d\n\n", ++x);
       printf("\t\t --x = %4d\n\n", --x);
       printf("\t\t x now equals %4d\n\n", x);
       printf("\t\t --x produces %4d\n\n", --x);
       printf("\t\t now x equals %4d\n\n", x);
       printf("\t\t x++ produces %4d\n\n", x++);
       printf("\t\t now x equals %4d\n\n", x);
       printf("\t\t x-- = %4d\n\n", x--);
       printf("\t\t Aha!--now x equals %4d\n\n", x);
       printf("-----------------------------------------------------\n\n\n");
       }

main()
       {

       compute();

       }


RUN C26

Sampler of uses of C arithmetic operators

-----------------------------------------------

                    2 - 5 * 3 + 2 =   -11

                    (2 - (5 * 3)) + 2 =   -11

                    (2 - 5) * 3 + 2 =    -7

                    55 / 6 =    9

                    55.0 / 6.0 = 9.17

                    55 mod 6 =    1
```

Figure 2.6 Calculations with C Arithmetic Operators

CHAPTER 2   2.9 Bug clinic: prefix and postfix operators   31

```
++5  =      5

--100  =    100

++x  =    101

--x  =    100

x now equals   100

--x produces    99

now x equals    99

x++ produces    99

now x equals   100

x-- =   100

Aha!--now x equals     99

-------------------------------------------------------
```

Figure 2.6   *continued*

The postfix operator $++$ is applied to x when x has a value of 99. Notice that

$$\text{printf}(x++)$$

has no apparent change in x. That is,

$$\text{printf}(x++) \text{ prints } 99$$

What about the $x++$ operation? This takes place *after* the printf() is executed by C. If we had used

$$\text{printf}(x++, x++)$$

on x with an initial value of 99, you can verify that the first $x++$ occurs prior to printing, and the second $x++$ occurs *after* the printf() is executed. This is left for an exercise.

Similarly, notice that

$$\text{printf } (x\text{--})$$

produces no apparent change in x. For example, when x begins with a value of 100, then

$$\text{printf } (x\text{--}) \text{ prints } 100$$

32 Beginning C programming

The action of -- as a *postfix* operator is carried out by C after the printf() is executed. You might wonder what happens if x is given an initial value of 100 and the following printf() is executed:

$$printf \ (x--, \ x--)$$

2.10 TYPE INT

In C, type *int* will range over a subset of the integers. The limits of this subset will depend on the computer used. Some sample type *int* ranges are shown in Table 2.4.

TABLE 2.4 Type Int Ranges

Computer System	Range					
Apple IIe	-2^{15},	. . . ,	0,	. . . ,	$2^{15} - 1$
PDP 11/70	-2^{15},	. . . ,	0,	. . . ,	$2^{15} - 1$
VAX-11/780	-2^{31},	. . . ,	0,	. . . ,	$2^{31} - 1$

$2^{15} = 32{,}767$ (for a 16-bit machine)
$2^{31} = 2{,}147{,}483{,}647$ (for a 32-bit machine)

In C, the range of integers

$$0, \ . \ . \ . \ , \ max$$

can be extended to $2^{word \ size} - 1$, using type *unsigned*. For example, the PDP 11/70 is a 16-bit machine; this is the word size of the PDP 11/70. It has 16-bit words. So an *unsigned* integer will be in the range

$$0, \ . \ . \ . \ , \ 2^{16} - 1 \ (= \ 65535)$$

On a VAX-11 system, the long words are each 32 bits. A C unsigned integer on a VAX-11 will be in the range

$$0, \ . \ . \ . \ , \ 2^{32} - 1 \ (=4, \ 294, \ 967, \ 295)$$

The maximum *unsigned* value of an integer available to C is implementation dependent. To determine the maximum signed and unsigned integers usable by C on your system, you can use the program given in Figure 2.7. This program was run on a PDP 11/70, which is a 16-bit machine. To use this program on a VAX-11 system, change *max* and *limit* as follows:

double max = 31;
double limit = 32;

CHAPTER 2   **2.10 Type int   33**

```
#include <math.h>
#include <stdio.h>

compute()
        {
        double max = 15.0;          /*for PDP 11/70 signed maxint*/
        double limit = 16.0;        /*for PDP 11/70 unsigned maxint*/
        double log(),exp();         /*specify double precision floating*/
                                    /*output for these functions*/

        max = exp(max * log(2.0)) - 1.0;
        limit = 2.0 * max + 1.0;
        printf("signed maxint =   %10f", max);
        printf("\n\n-------------------------------------\n\n");
        printf("unsigned maxint = %10f", limit);
        }

main()
        {
        compute();
        }


RUN C27

signed maxint =        32767


-------------------------------------

unsigned maxint =      65535
```

Figure 2.7 Signed and Unsigned Maxint Values

VAX-11s are 32-bit machines. Type *double* is a C floating-point data type, which we explain in detail later. On a PDP 11/70, type double floating-point numbers use 32 bits.

The C math functions log(x) and exp(x) used in Figure 2.7 require the use of type *double* arguments. These two functions have the following features:

Function	*Result*
exp(x)	Returns a double floating-point value for e^x
log(x)	Returns log e x as a double floating-point value

The log(x) function is a natural logarithm. It returns the exponent necessary to compute the power of the Euler number e, which equals x. That is,

$$\text{if } y = log(x) \quad \text{then } x = e^y$$

The Euler number e is approximately equal to 2.71828 and can be computed by

34   Beginning C programming

using

$$e = \lim (1 + \frac{1}{n})^n$$

$$n \to \infty \qquad \text{(where } n \text{ approaches infinity)}$$

$$= 1 + \frac{1}{1!} + \frac{1}{2!} + \frac{1}{3!} + \frac{1}{4!} + \cdots$$

Log(x) in **C** is the same as ln(x) in Pascal. The combination of the exponential and logarithmic functions can be used to compute powers of numbers. For example, suppose we want to compute b^n. This can be done as follows: Let

$$y = b^n$$

Then take the ln of both sides of this equation,

$$ln\ y = ln\ b^n$$

and rewrite using the law of logarithms in terms of the logarithm of a power:

$$ln\ y = n\ ln\ b$$

Then exponentiate both sides of this equation:

$$e^{ln\ y} = e^{n\ ln\ b}$$

where

$$y = e^{ln\ y}$$

which gives

$$b^n = e^{n\ ln\ b}$$

or, using **C** functions, we compute b^n using

$$exp(n * log(b))$$

It is also possible to compute powers of numbers using an iteration instead of the exp() and ln() functions. We show how to do this later.

2.11 #INCLUDE AND #DEFINE

The #include command tells the **C** preprocessor to include a specified library in the processing of a **C** program. It has two forms:

#include form	Explanation
#include <name.h>	This specifies a standard **C** library like stdio.h
*include "name.h"	This specifies a user-constructed local source library

CHAPTER 2   2.11 #include and #define   35

For example,

#include <stdio.h>

tells the C preprocessor that functions in the standard I/O library will be used. To create a personal C library called lib.h, for example, use an editor to prepare the source text. For example, suppose we want to set up a personal library with the #include commands we usually use. The source text for this library would have the following form:

/*lib.h: a user-defined library*/
#include <stdio.h>
#include <math.h>

To use this library in a program, write

#include ''lib.h''
main()
    {
    puts (''Hello, world!'')
    }

The C preprocessor also makes it possible to create macros using the #define command. For example,

#define bell ''\007''

can be used in

printf(bell)

in place of

printf(''\007'')

The preprocessor will replace all occurrences of *bell* by ''\007'' wherever *bell* is used in the source text, *except* where bell appears inside quotes. For example,

1. printf(bell, bell, bell)   will ring the keyboard
                                     bell three times;
2. printf(''bell, bell, bell'')   will print

                                     bell, bell, bell

It happens that 007 is the ASCII code in octal for the keyboard bell.

The same technique can be used to define constants and *convenient* noise words. For example, we can set up the following constants and noise words in our local (personal) library:

36   Beginning C programming

```
#define e 2.7182818284        /*constant*/
#define pi 3.1415926535       /*constant*/
#define begin   {             /*noise word*/
#define end      }            /*noise word*/
#define then                  /*noise word*/
#define var                   /*Pascal turf*/
#define const                 /*Pascal turf*/
```

The **C** preprocessor will replace occurrences of the constant *e*, for example, with 2.7182818284 wherever it appears in a source text, except when *e* appears inside quotes. The #define command can be used on any program line as well as in a personal library. The #define must always begin in column 1 of a source text.

The #define command can also be used to define functions. For example, we can use

#define writeln printf(''\n'') /*<ret>*/

which can be used like a Pascal *writeln* to move the cursor to the next line. We illustrate the use of these definitions with the personal library lib.h in terms of a modified version of Figure 2.5. We show source text for lib.h in Figure 2.8. The

```
#include <stdio.h>
#include <math.h>

/*constants: */

#define e 2.7182818284                      /*Euler´s number*/
#define PI 3.1415926535


/*printf() controls*/

#define beep "\007"                         /*ASCII code for kb bell*/

/*noise words: */

#define begin {
#define end }
#define then
#define var /*var*/
#define const /*const*/

/*functions: */

#define writeln printf("\n")                /*produces cr + lf*/
```

Figure 2.8   User-Defined C Library

CHAPTER 2   2.11 #include and #define 37

modified version of the program in Figure 2.5 is given in Figure 2.9. Notice that
the original

$$\text{printf(''\textbackslash n\textbackslash t\textbackslash t index equals \%5d \textbackslash n'', i)}$$

has been replaced by

> writeln;
> printf(''\t\t index equals %5d'', i);
> writeln;

which is less terse but perhaps more readable. The use of begin/end in place of
the braces {} does make early C programming easier. Why? One of the most common sources of errors in beginning C programming is in the use of these braces
to set up compound statement blocks or to mark the boundaries of a function. It
is easy to overlook one of these braces in the early stages of C programming. It
is also safe to argue that the use of begin/end contributes to the readability of a
source text. Statement blocks are easier to pick out. If nothing else, the use of
begin/end instead of braces makes Pascal programmers more at home.

So, in the early stages of C programming, we will use begin/end. Later we
will return to the use of braces.

```
#include "lib.h"                    /*Tell C preprocessor about lib.h*/


drawbeeper()
        begin
        printf("    o    \n");
        printf("    |    \n");
        printf("  << >>   \n");
        printf(beep,beep,beep);
        end

main()
begin
        var
                int i,max = 5;

        for (i=0;i <= max;++i)
                begin
                drawbeeper();
                writeln;
                printf("\t\t index equals %5d",i);
                writeln;
                end
end
```

Figure 2.9 Use of Personal C Library

38 Beginning C programming

2.12 FORMATTED OUTPUT WITH PRINTF()

The syntax diagram for a printf() is given in Figure 2.10. The *control string* of a printf() can minimally specify a *string constant,* which are characters surrounded by double quotes such as

"A way a long a last a loved a long the"

from the last page of James Joyce's *Finnegan's Wake* or a *null string,* which is written as

" "

which puts the null character '\0' into memory. The printing of a string constant can be *controlled* using standard C symbols for ASCII control characters. These are shown in Table 2.5. These printing controls can be used more than once inside the same control string. For example, we used multiple tabs in the last printf() in Figure 2.9.

It is also possible to print a single quote or a backslash using the following printf() conventions:

"\\"   to print a backslash
"\'"   to print a single quote

Finally, in Table 2.6 we show the conversion characters that can be used in a printf() to format an optional argument list following the control string inside the double quotes. For example,

printf("%c for %3s", 'e', "Euler");

will print

e for Euler

We can surround the argument 'e' with single printed quotes by using

printf("\' %c \' for %s", 'e', "Euler");

It is also possible to specify a field width of a string. The *field width* for a string is the number of columns to be used in printing a string that is right justified inside the field. For example,

printf("%10s %20s", "search", "running time");

will print the 'h' in *search* in column 10 and the 'e' in *time* in column 30. A single character surrounded by single quotes like 'e' is a character constant. We use a "%c" format to print character constants.

2.12 Formatted output with printf()

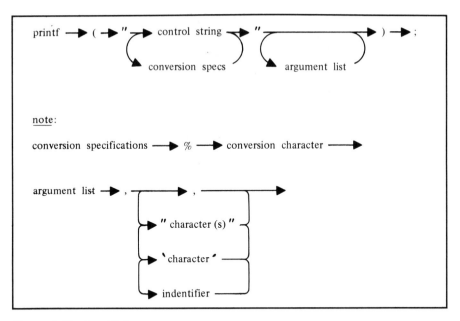

Figure 2.10 Printf() Syntax

TABLE 2.5 C Symbols for ASCII Control Characters

Symbol	Format	Result
n	"\n"	cr + lf (newline)
t	"\t"	Tab
b	"\b"	Backspace
r	"\r"	Carriage return
f	"\f"	Form feed
ddd	"\ddd"	Octal code for user-defined ASCII code

[a]Examples of "\ddd":

007	"\007"	Ring kb bell
012	"\012"	Line feed
013	"\013"	Vertical tab
014	"\014"	Form feed

40   Beginning C programming

TABLE 2.6   Printf Output Format Specifiers

Output Specifier	Format Specified
%c	Print character like 'e'
%s	Print string like 'Oh: C!'
%d	Print decimal integer
%e	Print floating-point number in exponential format
%f	Print floating-point number
%g	Print floating-point number in e-format or f-format (**C** will choose the shorter format of the two)
%o	Print integer in octal
%x	Print integer in hex
%u	Print unsigned integer

For the most part, we will use

''\d''   for integers
''\f''   for floating-point numbers

with printf() to handle numeric output. **C** data types themselves are considered in detail later. For now it is important to know the flexibility of these numeric format specifications. The syntax diagrams for these two formats is given in Figure 2.11. It is necessary to use ''%d'' to format the printing of expressions of type *int*. There is an optional field width, which can be specified with conversion characters like d or f. For example,

printf(''%10d'', 2)

will set up a field width with 10 columns and print the 2 in the tenth column. This is helpful in setting up a table with integer entries with varying numbers of digits. The printf() will right justify each entry.

The ''%f'' format is used with floating-point expressions used in a printf(). An optional field width can be specified for either the integer part, or the fraction part, or both parts of a floating-point number. For example, we can use the following field width specifications:

Format	*Sample*
''%.4f''	29.0000 (fraction field is given a width of 4)
''%10.2f''	3.75 (specifies both parts will have a total width of 10, with a width of 2 for the fraction)
''%10.0f''	7 (fraction part ignored, with number given a total width of 10)

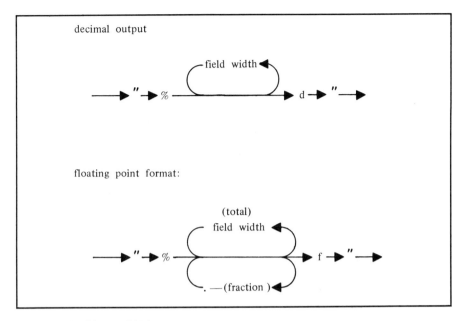

Figure 2.11   %d and %f Syntax

We illustrate the use of the d- and f-formats in Figure 2.12, and we also illustrate the use of ''%s'' to format a string output. That is, we use

printf(''%10s %20s'', ''format'', ''output'')

which puts the 't' in *format* in column 10 (it is right justified in terms of the specified field width). The same is true of ''output'', which is right justified in the next 20 columns of the table printed. In this program, we also introduce a drawline() function. This gets incorporated into the local library lib.h after this, since it is useful in dressing up output and in building the sections of printed tables in later programs.

2.13 FORMATTED INPUT WITH SCANF()

The syntax diagram for a scanf() is given in Figure 2.13. Each member of the scanf() argument list has an ampersand (&) prefix. Why? Each scanf() argument represents a memory *address* of a variable. This is a place in computer memory where the corresponding content in the input stream specified by the control string is deposited. The *input stream* is the sequence of characters that has been typed from a keyboard.

```
#include "lib.h"

drawline()
        begin
        int i;

        for (i = 1;i <= 80;++i)
                printf("-");

        end

sampler()
        begin

        printf("%40s", "golden ratio (almost)");
        writeln;
        drawline();
        writeln;
        printf("%10s %10s %20s\n\n", "format", " ", "output");
        drawline();
        writeln;
        printf("%10s %10s %20.4f\n\n", "%20.4f", " ", 377.0 / 233.0);
        printf("%10s %10s %.18f\n\n", "%.18f", " ", 377.0 / 233.0);
        printf("%10s %10s %20.0f\n\n", "%20.0f", " ", 377.0 / 233.0);
        printf("%10s %10s %20f\n\n", "%20f", " ", 377.0 / 233.0);
        printf("%10s %28s %f\n\n", "%f", " ", 377.0 / 233.0);
        drawline();

        end

main()
        begin

        sampler();

        end

RUN C212

                    golden ratio (almost)
--------------------------------------------------------------------------------
    format                          output

--------------------------------------------------------------------------------
    %20.4f                          1.6180

    %.18f               1.618025751072961400

    %20.0f                               2

    %20f                                 2

    %f                                   2


--------------------------------------------------------------------------------
```

Figure 2.12 Floating-Point Output Sampler

2.13 Formatted input with scanf()

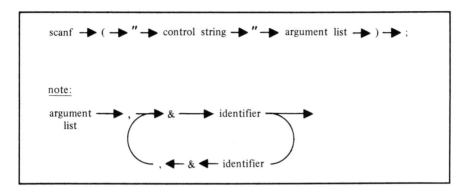

Figure 2.13 Scanf() Syntax

For example, suppose "%d %d" is used with the arguments &x and &y in

scanf("%d %d", &x, &y);

and the following characters are typed at a keyboard:

6765   10946

The space separates the two sets of characters. The first %d in the scanf() control string specifies that 6765 is an integer to be stored in location x. Then the remaining characters following the space in the input stream are "put together" in terms of the %d specification. The integer 10946 is deposited into a memory location with the symbolic address y. Now, for example, if the identifier x is referenced immediately after the execution of this scanf(), it will reference (identify) a value 6765.

The preceding input stream contains the ASCII codes for the corresponding ASCII characters typed at a keyboard. In terms of this input stream, we have the following ASCII codes:

ASCII character	*ASCII code (in octal)*	*ASCII Bias = 60 removed*
6	66	66 - 60 = 6
7	67	67 - 60 = 7
6	66	66 - 60 = 6
5	65	65 - 60 = 5
Space	40	Continue!
1	61	61 - 60 = 1
0	60	60 - 60 = 0
9	71	71 - 60 = 11 (octal)
4	64	64 - 60 = 4
6	66	66 - 60 = 6

44 Beginning C programming

To "put together" the first argument in the input stream, the procedure in Figure 2.14 mimics what C does in telling a processor how to handle the input stream. This procedure is not given in terms of a programming language. It is Pascallike because it uses Pascal noise words and the Pascal assignment operator ($:=$). It is a form of pseudocode, which is easily adapted to a programming language like C, which gives access to the keyboard input stream.

Try this procedure out on one of the arguments in the preceding input stream. For example, we can do this in terms of "putting together" 6765 as follows:

1. Take ASCII 66 (octal) from the input stream.
   digit $:=$ 66; (note: digit does not equal space
         code = 40);
   digit $:=$ digit - 60 = 66 - 60 = 6; (drop bias);
   no $:=$ no * 10 = 0 * 10 = 0;
   no $:=$ no + digit = 0 + 6 = 6;
2. Take ASCII 67 (octal) from the input stream.
   digit $:=$ 67; (digit <> 40 (octal));
   digit $:=$ digit - 60 = 67 - 60 = 7; (drop bias);
   no $:=$ no * 10 = 6 * 10 = 60;
   no $:=$ no + digit = 60 + 7 = 67;
3. Take ASCII 66 (octal) from the input stream.
   digit $:=$ 66; (digit <> 40 (octal));
   digit $:=$ digit - 60 = 66 - 60 = 6; (drop bias);
   no $:=$ no * 10 = 67 * 10 = 670;
   no L= no + digit = 670 + 6;
4. Take ASCII 65 (octal) from the input stream.
   digit $:=$ 65; (digit <> 40 (octal));
   digit $:=$ digit - 60 = 65 - 60 = 5; (drop bias);
   no $:=$ no * 10 = 676 * 10 = 6760;
   no $:=$ no + digit = 6760 + 5 = 6765;
5. Take ASCII 40 (octal) from the input stream.
   digit $:=$ 40;
   (Aha! This is the flag, so store
   6765 in location x or &x);

C was developed on PDP-11 computer systems. However, now C has spread to many other systems. Many of these other systems use hex (base 16) instead of octal for ASCII codes. So the preceding procedure needs to be adapted to a non-PDP-11 environment. This is easy.

CHAPTER 2   **2.13 Formatted input with scanf()**   45

```
procedure read number;

var   base, no, digit, flag : integer;

begin

Initialize variables:

    no := 0;

    base := desired base (use 10, here);

    flag := 40 (ASCII code for a space in octal);

repeat

get ASCII code from input stream:

    digit :=  ASCII code;

    if digit <> flag

        then

            begin

                digit := digit - 60;  (*drop ASCII bias*)

                no := no * base;  (*append zero to no*)

                no := no + digit;

            end

    until digit = flag

    end;  (*read number*)
```

Figure 2.14   Numeric Input Procedure

You will need to check the ASCII codes in hex given in Appendix A to see this. Notice that the ASCII bias is 30 (hex) instead of 60 (octal) for the numerals 0 through 9. Our example can be rewritten using these hex codes and the hex codes for the digits in the input stream on a VAX-11 system, for example. This revision is left as an exercise.

The various conversion characters that can be used in the control string of a scanf() are given in Table 2.7. We summarize these ideas about printf() and scanf() in terms of a von Neumann time machine in the program in Figure 2.15. This program

char name [30]

46 Beginning C programming

TABLE 2.7 Conversion Characters Used by Scanf()

Conversion Character	What Happens to Characters in the Input Stream as a Result
c	ASCII code taken as character
s	ASCII codes taken as string
d	ASCII code(s) used to *produce* single integer
f	ASCII codes used to *produce* single floating-point number
lf	ASCII codes used to *produce* double-precision floating-point number

sets aside 30 bytes for a string with the *name* identifier. A *string* is an array of bytes or a row of contiguous bytes in computer memory. The ''%s'' specifies that the input stream contains characters that will be loaded into an array of bytes identified by the *name* identifier. Notice, in this case, that the ampersand (&) prefix is not given to *name* in

$$\text{scanf (''\%s'', name)}$$

Why? The *name* identifier already *points* to the memory location of the leading byte of the name-string. The *name* identifier specifies an address.

```
#include "lib.h"

jvntimer()
      begin
      char name[30];
      int year;

      for (1)
              begin
              printf("\n\n Your name: ");
              scanf("%s", name);
              printf("\n\n Your birth yr:  ");
              scanf("%d", &year);
              writeln;
              drawline();
              printf("\n\n\n %s , \n", name);
              printf(" you were born %4d", year - 1946);
              printf(" yrs after(before) the birth of the JVN machine.");
              writeln;
              drawline();
              writeln;
              end

      end
```

Figure 2.15 Von Neumann Time Machine

CHAPTER 2   2.14 Summary   47

```
main()
      begin

             jvntimer();

      end


RUN C215


  Your name: Susu


  Your birth yr:  1967

  ------------------------------------------------------------------------


  Susu ,
  you were born   21 yrs after(before) the birth of the JVN machine.
  ------------------------------------------------------------------------


  Your name: Ken


  Your birth yr:  1902

  ------------------------------------------------------------------------


  Ken ,
  you were born  -44 yrs after(before) the birth of the JVN machine.
  ------------------------------------------------------------------------


  Your name: ^C
```

Figure 2.15   *concluded*

2.14 SUMMARY

A C program can be characterized in terms of its tokens. A *token* is the smallest individual unit of a program. There are three types of tokens to consider in a C program:

1. Word symbols like 'for' or 'int'.
2. Special symbols like '&' or '='.
3. Identifiers like 'printf' or 'drawcp34' or 'max'.

48 Beginning C programming   CHAPTER 2

A program is built in terms of these tokens. The word-symbol tokens of C are the *reserved words* of C. These reserved words cannot be used as identifiers for user-defined instructions or variables. Their use is restricted and well defined by the creator of C, Dennis Ritchie of Bell Laboratories. The complete set of the first two types of tokens is given in Table 2.2.

There are two types of statements in C. An *atomic* statement in C specifies a single action and it is always terminated by a semicolon (;). A *compound* statement in C specifies one or more actions to be performed by the computer. A compound statement is always bracketed by braces { }. A compound statement always begins with a left brace ({) and always terminates with a right brace (}). A compound statement is also called a block by K & R (1978).

This means a C function is also a block, since a C function identifier specifies zero or more actions bracketed by braces. A favorite function block among Clophiles is the following:

```
main()
{
puts("Hello, world!");
}
```

The program development cycle begins with a person dreaming up new (and old) instructions. These instructions are used to characterize the solution to a problem, a method with definite steps that can be used in obtaining a problem solution. The new instructions are defined in C using functions. Eventually, these functions (*explained* instructions) can be put into external files that can be used in other programs and by other users. We saw an example of this happening in this chapter. The *drawline()* function was first used in Figure 2.12. It was then incorporated into the local library lib.h and used as a library function in Figure 2.15. The revised copy of lib.h can be found in Appendix C.

The standard C functions printf() and scanf() are used to handle formatted output and input. The formatting used in the control strings of these functions governs the use of an input stream. An *input stream* is a stream of characters coming from a keyboard. Actually, it is a stream of ASCII character codes rather than the typed characters that are formatted by these C functions. These are powerful functions.

The argument list in a printf() is optional. The control string of a print(f) can be used by itself to print a string of characters. Character, string, and numeric output can be formatted and controlled by a printf(). You probably recognized the following equivalences between the printf() and a Pascal write statement:

CHAPTER 2   **Review terms and symbols   49**

printf() in C	*write in Pascal*
printf("%6d", 2);	write(2:6);
printf("%20s", "Eureka!");	write('Eureka!':20);
printf("%10.2f", 3.14);	write(3.14:10:2);

The arguments for a scanf() function are *addresses*. Except for array identifiers like *name* in Figure 2.15, each scanf() argument has an ampersand (&) prefix.

Finally, #include and #define are commands for the C preprocessor. A #include tells the preprocessor about a library that will be used by a C program. Each of the programs in this chapter used

$$\#include\ <stdio.h>$$

to make functions like printf() available to a program. A #define is used to set up personal, local macro libraries. These will contain texts that the C preprocessor will insert into a source text wherever a library identifier occurs. For example, we used this preprocessor facility to introduce begin/end noise words in place of the somewhat elusive braces {/}.

REVIEW TERMS AND SYMBOLS

Term	*Meaning*
&	ampersand prefix in scanf() arguments
atomic statement	specifies single action
block	compound statement
{ }	braces used to bracket a compound statement (used to bracket boundaries of function block)
BNF	Backus–Naur form
BNF production	representation of language syntax
character constant	single character surrounded by single quotes
comment	characters between /* and */
compound statement	specifies one or more actions
control string	used by printf() and scanf() to specify I/O and its format
conversion character	used to printf() and scanf() to format I/O stream (*examples:* c, s, d, f)
#define	specifies macro for C preprocessor
double	double-precision floating-point data type in C
exp()	power of *e*
expression	representation of a value
for	indexed repetition (for-loop)

50 Beginning C programming   CHAPTER 2

Term	*Meaning*
#include	specifies library for **C** preprocessor
input stream	string of ASCII codes
invariant assertion	claim about a relation that does not vary
int	signed integer data type in **C**
J & W	K. Jensen and N. Wirth
K & R	B. Kernighan and D. Ritchie
log()	natural log
macro	specifies text to be inserted by preprocessor
newline	\n
operand	a quantity or symbols(s) that is (are) operated on
operator	specifies operation
operator associativity	evaluation of an expression from left to right or right to left (direction of evaluation within a statement)
program development cycle	specify/solve/code/test/document
postfix operator	*Example:* x + + or x-- for x of type int
prefix operator	*Example:* + +x or --x for x of type int
printf()	formatted output
scanf()	formatted input
signed integer	type int {. . . ,-2,-1,0,1,2, . . }
statement	specify action
string constant	characters surrounded by double quotes
syntax	arrangement of tokens used by a part of a language (especially a statement)
syntax diagram	graphical representation of language syntax
tokens	smallest parts of a computer program
unsigned	subset of natural numbers and {0}

EXERCISES

1. Give examples of three types of tokens.
2. Give a syntax diagram for an English surname.
3. How does a syntax diagram differ from an actual railroad chart? (Give an example of each in your example.)
4. Using your imagination in terms of the needs and surroundings of a typical robot, write a **C** program that contains functional definitions for each of the following main() functions:

    a. main()
    ```
        begin
            drawcp34();
            drawramp();
            drawbeeper();
            drawoutlet();
        end
    ```

CHAPTER 2   **Exercises 51**

    b. main()
        begin
            drawbeeper();
            ringbeeper();
        end
        Note: make beeper ring 10 times

    c. main()
        begin
            drawsideview();
            drawfrontview();
            drawtopview();
        end

    d. main()
        begin
            drawantenna();
            drawcp35arm();
            drawcp35();
        end
        Note: show cp35 with attached
        arm and antenna and show
        these items detached from cp35

  5. Write a **C** program to draw the photon beam shown in Figure 2.16. Imagine that this photon beam is being projected by a cp35 clone, which is off the edge of the page. (The cp35 clone is ''out of sight''!) *Hint:* Use nested for loops-and use ''/b'' for a backspace and the index of the outside loop to control the production of the photon beam within the inside loop.

Figure 2.16 CP35 Clone Photon Beam

  6. The photons projected by the cp35 clone in Figure 2.16 appear in columns 1, 3, 6, 10, 15, 21, 28, 36, ... Develop a formula that can be used to determine which columns will contain photons. Use your formula to determine where the ninth and tenth photons will be printed.

  7. Add to the program in Exercise 5 the following feature: each time a photon is ''printed,'' ring the keyboard bell.

  8. Make an invariant assertion about the program in Exercise 5 in terms of the relation between the index variable of the inner loop relative to the index variable in the outer loop.

  9. Which of the following represent an error? Why? (Assume *x, y* are type int.)
    a. for (1)   **b.** printf(+ 8);
        printf(+ +7);

52 Beginning C programming   CHAPTER 2

    c. printf("%10S", 'ok');   **d.** printf("%c = %4d", '7', 7);
    e. printf("\n\n\n\n\n %d\"", 2);   **f.** scanf("%d %d", x, y);
    g. scanf("%d %s", &x, y);   **h.** scanf("%s %s", x, y);

10. Which of the following are not legal user-defined identifiers?
    a. x9   **b.** x_9   **c.** x-9
    d. x.9   **e.** int   **f.** begin
    g. 8th   **h.** e   **i.** real
    j. &   **k.** a_b_c   **l.** block

11. Give an example of an expression that is not an identifier.

12. Evaluate the following expressions, assuming that x has an initial value of 500 before an expression using x is evaluated:
    a. + +x   **b.** 21 % 5 % 2 * 7 + 1
    c. 21 * 5 % 2 % 7 + 1   **d.** 21 + 5 % 2 * 7 + 1
    e. 21 - 5 - 3 * 7 % 2   **f.** 21 - 21 - 21 * 21 + 21 % 21
    g. 2 * 2 * 2 % 10   **h.** 2 * 21 * 2 * 2 % 10
    i. 2 * 2 * 2 * 2 * 2 % 10   **j.** 2 + (+ +x) + (x--)

13. Write a **C** program to verify the claims (assertions!) you have made about each of the expressions in Exercise 12.

14. Write a **C** program to approximate the value of e using

$$e = 1 + \frac{1}{1!} + \frac{1}{2!} + \frac{1}{3!} + \frac{1}{4!} + \cdots$$

Note: The denominators of these fractions are factorials, with

$$
\begin{aligned}
1! &= 1 &&= 1 \\
2! &= 1 \times 2 &= 1! \times 2 &= 2 \\
3! &= 1 \times 2 \times 3 &= 2! \times 3 &= 6 \\
4! &= 1 \times 2 \times 3 \times 4 &= 3! \times 4 &= 24 \\
&\quad\;\cdot \\
&\quad\;\cdot \\
&\quad\;\cdot \\
n! &= 1 \times 2 \times \cdots \times (n-1) x n &= (n-1)! x n
\end{aligned}
$$

Hint: use data type double for e and "\f" to format the output.

15. Use "%0" and "%x" to print the octal and hex codes used by your system for the digits 0 through 9.

16. Rewrite the procedure in Figure 2.14 for an implementation of **C** that uses hex codes for the ASCII table.

17. Use the procedure in Exercise 15 to construct the number 10946 taken from the input stream by scanf() with a %d format.

CHAPTER 2   **Lab projects   53**

LAB PROJECTS

1. Write a C program that does the following:
   a. Prompts the user for the ages of 5 robots.
   b. Keeps a running total of the ages.
   c. Prints the average age of the robots.
   Give a sample run.
2. Write a C program that does the following:
   a. Prompts the user for the number of copies each of the front view, side view, and top view of cp34 to be printed.
   b. Uses the value given by the user to control the repetition of printing cp34 views, with each set of three views on a separate line.
3. Write a C program that does the following:
   a. Prints the following heading:

x	exp(x)	log(x)

   b. Prints 20 rows of this table for integer values of from 1 to 20.

54 Beginning C programming

CHAPTER 2

SELECTED SOLUTIONS

Exercise 15

```
#include "lib.h"

table()
    begin
      int i;
      printf(" %12s %10s %8s","decimal","octal","hex");
    writeln
      for (i = 1; i<= 75;++i)
         printf("\-");
    writeln

      for (i = 0; i < 17; ++i)
         printf(" %9d %11o %10x \n",i,i,i);

      for (i = 1; i < 76; ++i)
         printf("\-");

    end


main()

    begin

        table();

    end


RUN CE215
```

decimal	octal	hex
0	0	0
1	1	1
2	2	2
3	3	3
4	4	4
5	5	5
6	6	6
7	7	7
8	10	8
9	11	9
10	12	a
11	13	b
12	14	c
13	15	d
14	16	e
15	17	f
16	20	10

CHAPTER 2   **Selected solutions   55**

Lab Project 3

```
#include "lib.h"


table()
   begin
     int i;
     double j = 0.0;
     double exp(),log();
     double eu = 0.0;
     double count = 1.0;
     double   l = 0.0;

     printf(" %7s %15s %15s \n","x","exp(x)","log(x)" );
     for (i = 1; i<= 75;++i)
        printf("\-");
        writeln;

     for (j = 1.0; j <= 20.0; ++j)
     begin
          eu = exp(j);
          l = log(j);
          printf(" %7.0f %15.4f %15.4f \n",j,eu,l);
        end;

     for (i = 1; i < 76; ++i)
        printf("\-");
        writeln;

     end



main()

   begin

       table();

   end


RUN CL23

        x          exp(x)         log(x)
-------------------------------------------------------------------------
        1          2.7183         0.0000
        2          7.3891         0.6931
        3         20.0855         1.0986
        4         54.5982         1.3863
        5        148.4132         1.6094
        6        403.4288         1.7918
        7       1096.6332         1.9459
        8       2980.9580         2.0794
        9       8103.0839         2.1972
       10      22026.4658         2.3026
```

56 Beginning C programming

CHAPTER 2

Lab Project 3 *concluded*

11	59874.1417	2.3979
12	162754.7914	2.4849
13	442413.3920	2.5649
14	1202604.2842	2.6391
15	3269017.3725	2.7081
16	8886110.5205	2.7726
17	24154952.7536	2.8332
18	65659969.1373	2.8904
19	178482300.9632	2.9444
20	485165195.4098	2.9957

RELATED READINGS

Dijkstra, E. W., *A Discipline of Programming.* Englewood Cliffs, N.J.: Prentice-Hall, Inc., 1976, Chapter 8 ("The Formal Treatment of Small Examples") on invariant assertions.

Feuer, A. R., and **G. Narian,** editors, *Comparing and Assessing Programming Languages: Ada, C, and Pascal.* Englewood Cliffs, N.J.: Prentice-Hall, Inc., 1984, pp. 110–116, "UNIX Time-Sharing Systems: The C Programming Language," by D. M. Ritchie and others.

Jensen, K., and **N. Wirth** (J & W), *Pascal User Manual and Report.* New York: Springer-Verlag, New York, Inc., 1974.

Kernighan, B., and **D. M. Ritchie** (K & R), *The C Programming Language.* Englewood Cliffs, N.J.: Prentice-Hall, Inc., 1978, especially the C Reference Manual in Appendix A.

Thomas, R., "The C Tutorial: Getting Started," *UNIX/World,* Vol. 1, No. 2 (March/April 1984), pp. 46–51. Los Altos, Calif.: Tech Valley Publishing, Inc., 1984.

3

Primer on Functions

The procedure serves as a device to abbreviate the text and, more significantly, as a means to partition and to structure a program into logically coherent, closed components.

*Niklaus Wirth**

AIMS
- Introduce Functions with Parameters.
- Distinguish between a Call by Value and a Call by Reference.
- Distinguish between Actual and Formal Parameters.
- Distinguish between Global and Local Variables.
- Discuss the Scope of a Variable.
- Introduce Storage Classes Used in C Programs.
- Introduce the Use of Strcpy() and the Switch Statement.

3.1 INTRODUCTION

Creating a program is comparable to putting together a string of pearls. Dijkstra (1972, p. 60) suggested this. A pearl is a procedure name that references lines of code that explain (define) the procedure name. For example,

```
begin
    enquiry();
    printheading();
    drawdottriangle(size, copies);
end
```

Systematic Programming: An Introduction, Prentice-Hall, Inc., Englewood Cliffs, N.J., 1973, p. 93.

58   Primer on functions   CHAPTER 3

can be characterized as a string of pearls. There is an art in the selection of the procedure names to put into a text. They should, as much as possible, tell you what the string (text) is about. In this example, the text makes it possible to carry out the give and take, with resulting dot triangle shown in Figure 3.1.

```
Object:  draw an equilateral dot triangle like the following :

                                 .
                               . .
                             . . .

Height of triangle : 1
No. of copies : 1

-------------------------------------------------------------------------

                      Dot triangle(s)

     height                              No. of copies

        1                                     1

-------------------------------------------------------------------------
```

478   **Figure 3.1** Sample Give and Take

A function in C is comparable to a procedure in Pascal or PL/1. This chapter introduces the elementary features of functions in C programming. It introduces enough of these features to make it possible to write C programs that are strings of pearls, to use functions to encapsulate separate program tasks.

In this chapter we present both parameterless functions like enquiry() and printheading() as well as functions with parameters like

drawdottriangle(size, copies)

In doing so, we will, among other things, flesh out the procedure names in the preceding block.

Functions in C have an optional return statement, which makes it possible to return the value of an expression to a calling procedure. This is a powerful programming tool, which is also discussed in this chapter.

A key concern in C programming is the scope of the variables used in a C program. We deal with this issue in this chapter. Finally, we discuss storage classes used in C programming.

3.2 FUNCTION SYNTAX

A syntax diagram for a C function is given in Figure 3.2. Notice that only the function identifier, parentheses ( ), and braces { } are necessary. Everything else is optional. That is, it is possible to define a function that does nothing. The following is an example of an "empty" C function:

riverrun()
{
}

A function without a parameter list is a *parameterless function*. The jvntimer() used in Chapter 2 is an example of a parameterless function. The heading

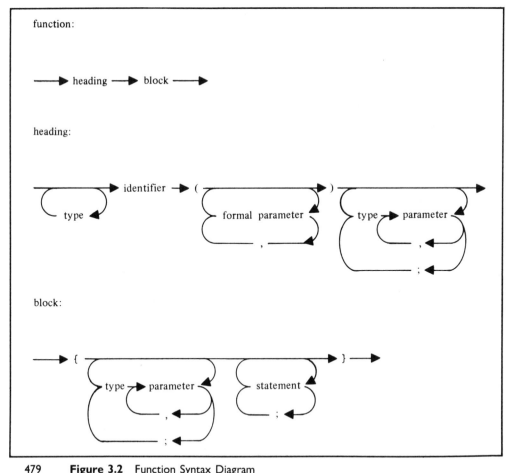

Figure 3.2 Function Syntax Diagram

60   **Primer on functions**

CHAPTER 3

for this function does not contain formal parameters and it does not return a value to the calling function. Since jvntimer() does not return a value to the calling function main() in Figure 2.15, the function heading does not begin with a type declaration. Finally, since the function heading contains no formal parameters, it also does not have corresponding type declarations.

The exp() and log() functions used in Figure 2.7 are examples of functions with formal parameters. A *formal parameter* in a function heading is a place-marker. A formal parameter does not represent a value. Only its position in a function heading is significant. Formal parameters are initialized during the execution of a function call.

The function

drawdottriangle(size, copies)

in the suggested text in Section 3.1 also has a formal parameter list. The formal parameters are *size* and *copies*. Whenever there is a formal parameter in a function heading, its data type is declared. This is done immediately after the right parenthesis of the function heading. Formal parameters in a function heading are separated by a comma (,), not a semicolon (;). A type declaration for a formal parameter can contain a list of parameters separated by commas. Type declarations themselves are separated by semicolons. A heading for the *drawdottriangle()* function is given next:

```
drawdottriangle(size, copies);
int size;            /*specify no. of rows*/
int copies;          /*specify no. of copies*/
```

This function will not return a value to a calling function. So its heading will not begin with a type declaration, which is used to specify the data type of a returned value.

Before we attempt to write out the complete drawdottriangle() function, we start with a simplified version of this function. We will use

drawdottriangle(size);

instead, specifying only the height of the triangle to be printed. The heading and block for this simplified function are given in Figure 3.3. The block for this function has the following local variables:

```
int rows, cols;
char dot = '.';
```

The function parameter *size* is used as an upper bound on the *row* variable, which is used as an index variable in the outer for-loop. Notice the value of the *row*

CHAPTER 3   **3.2 Function syntax 61**

```
drawdottriangle(size)
int size;                               /*equilateral triangle height*/

        {
        /*local variables: */

        int rows,cols;                  /*index variables*/
        char dot = '.';                 /*fabric of triangle*/

        for (rows = 1;rows <= size;++rows)
                {
                printf("\n\t\t");
                for (cols = 1;cols <= rows;++cols)
                        printf("%2c", dot);
                }
        }
```

Figure 3.3 Function with One Formal Parameter

variable is used as the upper bound on the *cols* variable used in the inner loop.
Finally, notice that

$$printf(''\%2c'', dot);$$

prints a space and a dot ('.') each time the printf() is executed.

   A program illustrating the use of this simplified version of drawdottriangle()
is given in Figure 3.4.

```
#include "lib.h"

drawdottriangle(size)
int size;                               /*equilateral triangle height*/

        begin
        /*local variables: */

        int rows,cols;                  /*index variables*/
        char dot = '.';                 /*fabric of triangle*/

        for (rows = 1;rows <= size;++rows)
                begin
                printf("\n\t\t");
                for (cols = 1;cols <= rows;++cols)
                        printf("%2c", dot);
                end
        end
```

Figure 3.4 Calling a Function with One Parameter

62 Primer on functions

CHAPTER 3

```
main()
        begin

        drawdottriangle(3);
        writeln;
        drawdottriangle(5);
        writeln;
        drawdottriangle(10);

        end

RUN  C34
                    .
                    . .
                    . . .

                    .
                    . .
                    . . .
                    . . . .
                    . . . . .

                    .
                    . .
                    . . .
                    . . . .
                    . . . . .
                    . . . . . .
                    . . . . . . .
                    . . . . . . . .
                    . . . . . . . . .
                    . . . . . . . . . .
```

Figure 3.4 *concluded*

3.3 LOCAL AND GLOBAL VARIABLES

A more elaborate version of the drawdottriangle() function is given in Figure 3.5. The variables defined *inside* a function block are local to that block. We will see in a bit that the same local variable used in one function will not retain values obtained as a local variable in another block. The safest way to pass values of variables between functions is through the use of function parameter lists.

We can also set up variables that are global within a program. That is, these variables are available equally across function boundaries. For example, we can do this as follows in terms of two global variables: *peak* and *image*. The positioning of these globals relative to three functions is given as follows:

CHAPTER 3   3.3 Local and global variables   63

```
drawdottriangle(size, copies)
int size;                               /*equilateral triangle height*/
int copies;                             /*no. of copies of image*/


      {
      /*local variables: */

      int rows,cols;                    /*index variables*/
      char dot = ´.´;                   /*fabric of triangle*/
      int xerox;                        /*another index variable*/

      for (xerox = 1;xerox <= copies;++xerox)
         for (rows = 1;rows <= size;++rows)
               {
               printf("\n\t\t");
               for (cols = 1:cols <= rows;++cols)
                       printf("%2c", dot);
               }
```

Figure 3.5   Function with More Than One Formal Parameter


```
int peak = 0, image = 0;  /* 2 globals */
enquiry()

      .

      .          /*get values for peak and image*/

      .

   end
printheading()

      .

      .          /*use peak and image*/

      .

   end
drawdottriangle(size, copies)

      .

      .

      .

   end
main()
      begin
      enquiry()          /*call enquiry fn*/
      printheading()     /*call printheading fn*/
      drawdottriangle(peak, image)
      end
```

64   Primer on functions   CHAPTER 3

Notice that the actual parameters *peak* and *image* are passed to the drawdottrian-
gle() function from main(). An *actual parameter* is a parameter used in a function
call. It is an argument in a function call. The variables *peak* and *image* are used
as actual parameters inside main(). They are used as arguments in drawdottriangle-
(peak, image). These variables are given default values when they are declared as
globals. It is good practice to provide default values for global variables.

In distinguishing between *local* and *global* variables, we are really starting
to talk about the *scope* of a variable. In general, if a variable is declared outside
a function, it is available to those functions defined below it. A global variable is
declared (and, usually, initialized) before any functions are defined.

A program to illustrate the use of global variables in connection with the
preceding three procedures is given in Figure 3.6. Notice that the identifiers for
the formal parameters *size* and *copies* in

drawdottriangle(size, copies)

are not the same as the actual parameters *peak* and *image*. Formal parameters have
no significance, except as place-markers. As a rule, the identifiers for formal parameters will not be the same as the identifiers used for actual parameters.

The program of Figure 3.6 has no provision for allowing the user to select
a symbol besides a dot (.) to print copies of various triangles. We show how to
add this feature to the program next.

3.4 REFINEMENT: MORE ON THE USE OF TYPE CHAR

Type char in **C** declares a variable to be an ASCII character. For example, if we
use

char ch[0];

the identifier *ch* points to a character array (also called a *string*) with *one* element.
The identifier *ch* is the symbolic address of this array element. The address of the
first element of this array can also be written as ch[0] or ch + 0. We can use this
idea to set up a global variable ch to be used by enquiry() and printheading(). This
variable can also be introduced as an actual parameter in the drawdottriangle()
call. To do this, we expand the triangle function as follows:

drawtriangle(size, copies, symbol)
int size;
int copies;
char symbol[0]; /*new formal parameter!*/

We have also made the function identifier more general by dropping the *dot*. If

CHAPTER 3   **3.4 Refinement: more on the use of type char   65**

```
#include "lib.h"

int peak = 0, image = 0;                        /*2 global variables*/

enquiry()

        begin

        printf("\n\n Height of triangle:  ");
        scanf("%d", &peak);
        printf("\n\n No. of copies:  ");
        scanf("%d", &image);
        printf("\n\n");

        end


printheading()

        begin

        drawline();
        printf("\n\n %30s \n\n", "Dot Triangles");
        printf("%16s %32s \n\n", "Height", "No. of copies");
        printf("%12d %28d \n\n", peak, image);
        drawline();

        end

drawdottriangle(size, copies)
int size;                                       /*equilateral triangle height*/
int copies;                                     /*no. of copies of image*/

        begin
        /*local variables: */

        int rows,cols;                          /*index variables*/
        char dot = '.';                         /*fabric of triangle*/
        int xerox;                              /*another index variable*/

        for (xerox = 1;xerox <= copies;++xerox)
           for (rows = 1;rows <= size;++rows)
                begin
                printf("\n\t\t");
                for (cols = 1;cols <= rows;++cols)
                        printf("%2c", dot);
                end

        end

main()
```

Figure 3.6 Program with Global Variables of Type Int

66 Primer on functions   CHAPTER 3

```
       begin

       enquiry();
       printheading();
       drawdottriangle(peak, image);


       end


RUN C36

 Height of triangle:   3


 No. of copies:  2


 ------------------------------------------------------------------------

                   Dot Triangles

          Height                    No. of copies

            3                            2

 ------------------------------------------------------------------------
                      .
                      . .
                      . . .
                      .
                      . .
                      . . .
```

485   **Figure 3.6** *concluded*

we use scanf() in terms of ch, it is necessary to use ''%s,'' not ''%c.'' Why? We set up ch as a string with

<mark>char ch[0];</mark>

However, if we printf() in terms of the ch-string, <mark>we can</mark> be selective about which <mark>part</mark> of the string is printed. For example, we can use

printf(''%c'', ch[0])

We show a program to carry out this idea in Figure 3.7.

CHAPTER 3   **3.4 Refinement: more on the use of type char   67**

```
#include "lib.h"


int peak = 0, image = 0;                /*2 global variables*/
char ch[0] = ´a´;                       /*another global*/

enquiry()

        begin

        printf("\n\n Height of triangle:  ");
        scanf("%d", &peak);
        printf("\n\n No. of copies:  ");
        scanf("%d", &image);
        printf("\n\n Symbol to use:  ");
        scanf("%s", ch);

        end


printheading()

        begin

        printf("\n\n\n");
        drawline();
        printf("\n\n %30s \n\n", "Symbol Triangles");
        printf("%16s %32s %16s \n\n", "Height", "No. of copies", "Symbol");
        printf("%12d %28d %20s", peak, image, " ");
        printf("%c \n\n", ch[0]);
        printf("\n\n");
        drawline();

        end

drawtriangle(size, copies, symbol)
int size;                               /*equilateral triangle height*/
int copies;                             /*no. of copies of image*/
char symbol[0];                         /*symbol to use in drawing
triangle*/

        begin
        /*local variables: */

        int rows,cols;                  /*index variables*/
        int xerox;                      /*another index variable*/

        for (xerox = 1;xerox <= copies;++xerox)
           for (rows = 1;rows <= size;++rows)
                begin
                printf("\n\t\t");
                for (cols = 1;cols <= rows;++cols)
```

Figure 3.7 Program with a Global String Variable

68 Primer on functions   CHAPTER 3

```
                              printf("%2c", symbol[0]);
                    end
        end
main()
        begin

                enquiry();
                printheading();
                drawtriangle(peak, image, ch);

        end
```

RUN C37

Height of triangle: 8

No. of copies: 2

Symbol to use: !

            Symbol Triangles

         Height   No. of copies   Symbol

           8   2   !

             !
             ! !
             ! ! !
             ! ! ! !
             ! ! ! ! !
             ! ! ! ! ! !
             ! ! ! ! ! ! !
             ! ! ! ! ! ! ! !
             !
             ! !
             ! ! !
             ! ! ! !
             ! ! ! ! !
             ! ! ! ! ! !
             ! ! ! ! ! ! !
             ! ! ! ! ! ! ! !

Figure 3.7   *concluded*

CHAPTER 3   **3.5 Refinement: selection of a figure to draw   69**

3.5 REFINEMENT: SELECTION OF A FIGURE TO DRAW

The drawtriangle() function can be refined into a drawfigure() function, which allows the user to choose a figure to draw. This can be done by using the **C** switch statement, which has the following form:

```
switch (expression)
    {
    case value:
        statement;
        break;

        .

        .

        .

    case value:
        statement;
        break;
    default:
        statement;
        break;
    }
```

For example, we can introduce a choice parameter in the drawfigure() function as follows:

```
drawfigure(size, copies, symbol, choice)
int size, copies, choice;
char symbol [0];
    begin
    int rows, cols, xerox;
    switch (choice)
        begin
        case 1:
            /*draw triangle*/
            break;
        case 2:
            /*draw square*/
            break;
        case 3:
            /*draw line*/
            break;
```

70 Primer on functions CHAPTER 3

```
            default:
                printf("error: not a valid choice!");
                break;
        end
    end
```

In place of the indicated comments for each case, it will be necessary to insert **C** code needed to print the indicated figure. For case 1, the **C** code that replaces the comment will be identical to the code used to print a triangle in Figure 3.7. This refinement is left as an exercise. The *default* label of the *switch* statement is reached, if a valid choice is not made. The *break* statement causes the processor control to jump to the closing end (brace) of the switch statement.

3.6 CALLS BY VALUE AND BY REFERENCE

If a function is called with the value of an actual parameter, then a *call by value* is used. A call by value transmits a value to a function relative to one of its formal parameters. A formal parameter that receives a value is called a *value parameter*. Except for one example, all the function calls used in this chapter have been calls by value. For example,

drawdottriangle(peak, image)

used in Figure 3.6 is a call by value. First, we determined values for the actual parameters peak and image using the enquiry() function. Then the values of these actual parameters were passed to the drawdottriangle() function in the main() block.

If a function is called with the address of a memory location, then a *call by reference* is used. A call by reference transmits an address to a formal parameter of a function. A formal parameter that receives an address is called a *variable parameter* (it is also called a *name parameter*). A call by reference does not transmit a value to a function. For example,

drawtriangle(size, copies, ch)

used in Figure 3.7 contains a call by reference. That is, ch is the symbolic address of a string. This identifies the address of the first character of this string. It is not the value ch[0] that is passed to the drawtriangle() function, but rather the address where ch[0] can be found. It is this address that is used by drawtriangle() to pinpoint the location of the character it will use.

The program in Figure 3.7 illustrates the use of the combination of call by value and call by reference. What is the difference between the results of these calls? In a *call by value,* the value of an actual parameter is used as the value of a local function variable. Changes in a value parameter (a formal parameter that *receives* a value in a call by value) do not change the value of the actual parameter in the calling function. In other words, a call by value is a *one-way street*.

By contrast, a *call by reference* is a *two-way street*. Changes in a memory location identified by a variable parameter are not local changes. The results of the use of a variable parameter inside a function are accessible to the calling func-

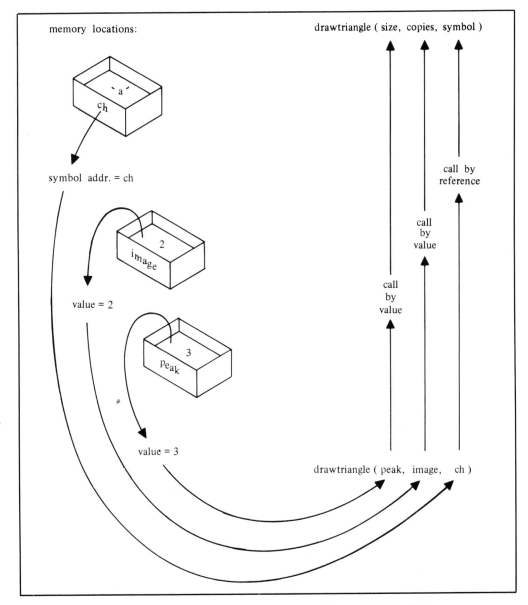

Figure 3.8 Graphical Interpretation of a Call by Value and Call by Reference

72 Primer on functions   CHAPTER 3

tion. The difference between a call by value and a call by reference is illustrated graphically in Figure 3.8. Here *size* and *copies* are value parameters. Size receives a value of 2; copies, a value of 3. Size and copies are used as local variables in the drawtriangle() function. *Symbol* is used as a variable parameter. It receives the address of 'a', not 'a' itself. Changes to location ch are made by drawtriangle() through *symbol*, which is a *local alias* for ch.

   We also illustrate the difference between a call by value and a call by reference in the following program. What we do is introduce a function called echo(), which operates on each of its formal parameters. The echo() function is given in Figure 3.9. The parameters *x* and *y* are value parameters; ref is a variable parameter. Each time this function is called, the local variables *x* and *y* produce a *local* change. The actual parameters used to call this function are not affected by echo(). The *ref* parameter in the echo() function produces a change in the content of the memory location referenced by the symbolic address transmitted to echo(). A program to illustrate the use of echo() is given in Figure 3.10.

```
echo(x, y, ref)

int  x, y;              /*local variables receiving values*/

char ref[10];           /*local alias for ch in main()*/

        {

        x = x + 10;    /*change x-value*/

        ++y;           /*change y-value*/

        printf("%10s", "Enter name: ");

        scanf("%s", ref);

        }
```

Figure 3.9 Function with a Local Alias

CHAPTER 3   **3.6 Calls by value and by reference   73**

```
#include "lib.h"

echo(x, y, ref)
int x, y;                                /*local variables receiving
values*/
char ref[10];                            /*local alias for ch in main()*/
        begin

        x = x + 10;                      /*change x-value*/
        ++y;                             /*change y-value*/
        printf("\n\n %10s", "Enter name :  ");
        scanf("%s", ref);
        printf("\n\n %20s", "local values");
        printf("\n\n %10c %10c %20s", ´x´, ´y´, "ref"):
        writeln;
        drawline();
        printf("\n\n\n %10d %10d %20s", x, y, ref);
        writeln;
        drawline();

        end

main()
        begin
        int this = 5,that = 8;
        char ch[10]

        strcpy(ch, "Goldberry");
        printf("%25s %20s", "Initial ch-string:". ch);
        printf("\n\n\n");
        drawline();
        for (1)
                begin
                strcpy(ch, "Goldberry");   /*copy string into ch*/
                echo(this, that, ch);
                printf("%10s %10s %20s", "this", "that", "ch");
                printf("\n\n %10d %10d %20s", this, that, ch);
                end

        end


RUN C310

    Initial ch-string:          Goldberry


------------------------------------------------------------------------

 Enter name :  Susu
```

Figure 3.10   Program with Calls by Value and Reference

74 Primer on functions   CHAPTER 3

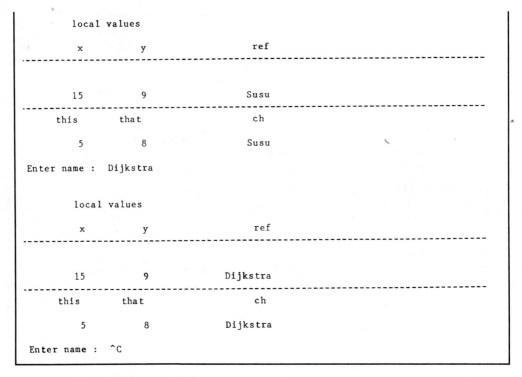

Figure 3.10 *concluded*

3.7 OBSERVATIONS AND A NEW FUNCTION: STRCPY()

The program in Figure 3.10 behaves predictably. How? The initial values for *this*, *that*, and *ch* are as follows:

this	that	ch
5	8	Goldberry

The identifiers *this* and *that* represent actual parameters. The values of these actual parameters are passed to the *x* and *y* formal parameters in echo(). The echo() function produces a local change in *x* and *y*.

The echo() function also produces a change in the *ref* string. The *ref* identifier is a local alias for the array of characters with the beginning address symbolically represented by the *ch* identifier. A *local alias* is another name for a memory location. Cooper (1983) suggests the use of the term *local alias* to identify a formal parameter used in a call by reference. This is an apt description of the ref parameter in the echo() function. Why?

CHAPTER 3   **3.7 Observations and a new function: strcpy() 75**

The change in the ref string produces a corresponding change in the ch-string. That is, after we return from the echo() function, the ch-string has the *same* string assigned to the ref string. They are, in fact, the same string.

Inside the echo() function the following results are obtained:

x	y	ref
15	9	Susu

When the processor transfers control back to main() after the first visit to echo(), the following things are printed:

this	that	ch
5	8	Susu

In other words, the actual parameters *this* and *that* have not been changed by echo(). The values of *this* and *that* are still the same. However, the ch-string no longer contains "Goldberry." Instead, the ch-string contains "Susu." A call by value does not produce a change in the actual parameters used. The changes to the corresponding value parameters x and y do not change *this* and *that*. A call by reference does produce a change in the memory locations referenced in such a call. The changes to the corresponding parameter (with a local alias) ref do produce a change in the ch-array.

The main() function in Figure 3.10 introduces the use of another standard C library function: strcpy(). The identifier *strcpy* stands for "string copy." The strcpy() function has the following form:

strcpy (pointer to string$_1$, pointer to string$_2$)

The first argument of strcpy() is a pointer to an array of characters in memory. A *pointer* is a symbolic address for a memory location. A pointer *points* to the beginning address for the first cell of an array. Each pointer in the strcpy() function must point to an array of type char.

The second argument in the strcpy() function can be a string constant. A string constant like

"A way a lone a last a loved. . ."

also serves as a pointer. It points to the first element in the string constant, that is, the letter A. So, for example,

strcpy(ch, "Goldberry");

in Figure 3.10, puts the characters of "Goldberry" into the ch-array. This idea is illustrated graphically in Figure 3.11. After the strcpy() function is executed in

76 Primer on functions   CHAPTER 3

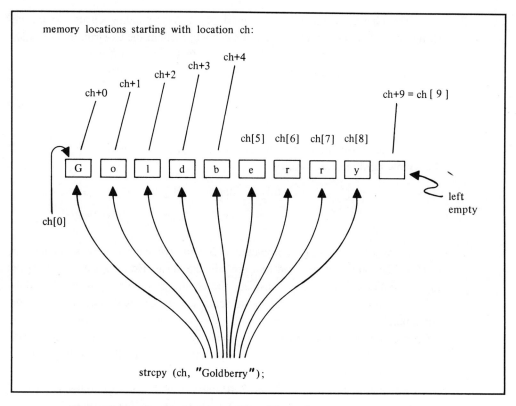

Figure 3.11 Graphical Interpretation of Strcpy()

Figure 3.10, the letter G in "Goldberry" is in ch[0], the letter o in ch[1] or location ch + 1, and so on. It is easy to verify this. This is left as an exercise.

Finally, notice that the use of the scanf() function in echo() *apparently* empties out the trailing (unused) cells of the ch-array. Notice that

$$printf("\%20s", ch)$$

prints

Susu

and not

Susuberry

It is also easy to verify if ch[4] through ch[8] still have the characters of "berry." How? Print the ch-array character by character, starting with ch[0]. This can be done using a for-loop. This is also left as an exercise.

CHAPTER 3   **3.8 Functions that return a value 77**

3.8 FUNCTIONS THAT RETURN A VALUE

The *return* statement can be used inside a function block to return a value. The syntax for a return statement is given in Figure 3.12. For example, the following function called *bump* returns an increment of the actual parameter in the function call:

```
int  bump(x)
int  x;
    {
    return  ( + +x);
    }
```

```
return ──▶ ( ──▶ expression ──▶ ) ──▶ ; ──▶
```

Figure 3.12 Syntax for Return Statement

The bump() heading includes a type declaration *int*. This specifies the data type of the returned value. Data type *int* is the *default* type for a returned value. There-fore, it is not necessary to declare type int in the function heading, if we are return-ing an integer to the calling function. That is, the following structure for bump() will also work:

```
bump(x)
int  x;
    {
    return  ( + +x);
    }
```

More than one return statement can be used in the same function block. For example, the following function returns a selected value:

```
change (choice, x)
int choice, x;
    {
    switch(choice)
        {
        case  1:
        return  ( + +x);
        break;
```

78 Primer on functions   CHAPTER 3

```
case 2:
return (--x);
break;
case 3:
return (x*x);
break;
default:
printf("\n\n %40s", "Error: not a valid choice");
return (233);
break;
}
}
```

This function illustrates possible uses of the *return* statement. We use return (233) after printing an error message. It is also possible to use a plain

return;

which returns no value to the calling function. The 233 returned when the default label is reached is an arbitrary value. It was put there merely to illustrate another form of the return statement. A program to carry out this idea is given in Figure 3.13.

```
#include "lib.h"

change(choice, x)

int choice, x;

        begin
        switch (choice)
                begin
                case 1:
                return( ++x );
                break;
                case 2:
                return( --x );
                break;
                case 3:
                return( x * x );
                break;
                default :
                printf("\n\n %40s", "Error: not a valid choice!");
                return(233);
                break;
                end

        end
```

Figure 3.13 Program with Several Return Statements

CHAPTER 3   3.8 Functions that return a value   79

```
main()
        begin
        int oldx = 5;
        int y = 3;

        printf("%20s %4d", "sample = ", change(y, oldx));
        for (1)
                begin

                printf("\n\n");
                drawline();
                printf("\n\n Enter integer: ");
                scanf("%d", &oldx);
                printf("\n\n Menu: ");
                printf("\n\n %10c %40s", ´1´, "See increment of your entry");
                printf("\n\n %10c %40s", ´2´, "See decrement of your entry");
                printf("\n\n %10c %40s", ´3´, "See square of your entry");
                printf("\n\n Enter choice: ");
                scanf("%d", &y);
                printf("\n\n");
                printf("%20s %4d", "result = ", change(y, oldx));
                end

        end
```

RUN C313

            sample =   25

 Enter integer: 89

 Menu:

            1   See increment of your entry

            2   See decrement of your entry

            3   See square of your entry

 Enter choice: 1

            result =   90

 Enter integer: 233

Figure 3.13 *continued*

80 Primer on functions   CHAPTER 3

```
Menu:

        1                    See increment of your entry

        2                    See decrement of your entry

        3                   See square of your entry

Enter choice: 2


        result =    232

-----------------------------------------------------------------------

Enter integer: 89

Menu:

        1                    See increment of your entry

        2                    See decrement of your entry

        3                   See square of your entry

Enter choice: 3


        result =   7921

-----------------------------------------------------------------------

Enter integer: ^C
```

Figure 3.13   *concluded*

3.9 USING A RETURN STATEMENT TO DEFINE A POWER FUNCTION

In Figure 3.14, we show a power function that uses a return statement to return a
number raised to a power. The power() function is almost identical to that suggested by K & R (1978). This function is written with the assumption that an integer value will be returned to the calling function. We illustrate the use of this function in a program to build a powers table. In this program, we allow the user to
select the base and the range of exponents specified. We show a program to do
this in Figure 3.15. This program introduces the use of the *if* statement in **C**. We
examine this statement in detail later. For now, notice that it has the following
form:

CHAPTER 3   **3.9 Using a return statement to define a power function   81**

```
power(b, n)

int b;                      /*b = base*/

int n;                      /*n = exponent*/

    {

    int i;                  /*index variable*/

    int p = 1;              /*initial value for product*/

    for (i = 1; i <= n; ++i)

            p = p * b;

    return (p);

    }
```

Figure 3.14   K & R Power Function

> if (expression)
>   statement;

By introducing the noise word *then* from the local library lib.h, it is also possible to write

> if (expression) then
>   statement;

which will make Pascalers more comfortable. The *if-expression* in the buildtable() function in the program of Figure 3.15 is as follows:

> count % 4 = = 0

This is used as a Boolean condition in the if-statement. One number is divisible by another, if the division does not produce a remainder. If count is divisible by 4, then

> count % 4

will equal zero. If this happens, then the processor will execute

> printf(''\n\n'')

which follows the if-expression. That is, the machine checks the truth value of

82   Primer on functions   CHAPTER 3

the if-expression. If it finds that count is not divisible by 4, it skips to the next statement,

$$++count$$

This gives us a way to print the powers table in four columns.

```
#include "lib.h"

int x = 1,low = 1, high = 1;                      /*globals*/

enquiry()
        begin
        printf("\n\n Enter base low high:   ");
        scanf("%d %d %d", &x, &low, &high);
        printf("\n\n");
        end

printheading()
        begin
        printf("%30s %4d %10s", "powers of", x, "table");
        printf("\n\n");
        printf("%10s %4d %1c %2d", "range: ", x, ^^, low);
        printf("%5s %4d %1c %2d", "to", x, ^^, high);
        printf("\n\n");
        drawline();
        printf("\n\n");
        end

power(b, n)
int b;                                            /*base*/
int n;                                            /*exponent*/
        begin
        int i;                                    /*index*/
        int p = 1;                                /*power with init. value*/

        for (i = 1;i <= n; ++i)
                p = p * b;
        return( p );

        end

buildtable()
        begin
        int count = 0;                            /*column counter*/
        int j;                                    /*index*/

        for (j = low;j <= high; ++j)
                begin
                printf("%10d",power(x, j));
                ++count;
                if (count % 4 == 0)
                        printf("\n\n");
                end
```

Figure 3.15 Program to Build Powers Tables

CHAPTER 3   **3.10 Refinement: using type unsigned instead of type int**   **83**

```
        end

main()
        begin
        enquiry();
        printheading();
        buildtable();
        end


RUN C315

 Enter base low high:  2 0 14


                    powers of    2       table

    range:      2 ^  0    to     2 ^ 14


-----------------------------------------------------------------------

        1           2           4           8

       16          32          64         128

      256         512        1024        2048

     4096        8192       16384


RUN C315

 Enter base low high:  3 0 9


                    powers of    3       table

    range:      3 ^  0    to     3 ^  9


-----------------------------------------------------------------------

        1           3           9          27

       81         243         729        2187

     6561       19683
```

      Figure 3.15 *concluded*

3.10 REFINEMENT: USING TYPE UNSIGNED INSTEAD OF TYPE INT

The program in Figure 3.15 can be improved by using type *unsigned* instead of type *int*. How? Use

84 **Primer on functions** CHAPTER 3

$$\text{printf("%10u", power(x, j));}$$

and declare *p* to be

$$\text{unsigned int p;}$$

This will enlarge the range of powers that can be printed in the table printed by the program in Figure 3.15. This refinement is left as an exercise.

3.11 FURTHER REFINEMENT: USING TYPE DOUBLE INSTEAD OF TYPE INT

The table printed by the program in Figure 3.15 can be improved further by using type *double* instead of type *int*. How? This time, use

$$\text{double power (b, n)}$$

and use

$$\text{double p} = 1.0;$$

Then use

$$\text{printf("%18.of", power(x, j));}$$

to print the floating-point numbers returned by power. The printed numbers will be printed as whole numbers. This refinement is left as an exercise.

3.12 ANOTHER REFINEMENT: IMPROVING THE FORMAT OF A TABLE

A column should be added next to each column of powers printed by the program in Figure 3.15. This column should contain the exponents used to obtain each of the corresponding powers. The table can have the following form:

n	b^n	n	b^n	n	b^n

The b^n heading should be in terms of the actual value of *b* selected by the user. For example, if the user selected $b = 2$, then you should print the following headings:

n	2^n	n	2^n	n	2^n

This refinement is also left as an exercise.

3.13 SCOPE

The scope of a variable in a **C** program depends on the position of the type declaration that introduces a variable. If a variable is introduced before any function, it

CHAPTER 3   3.13 Scope   85

has global scope. it can be used across function boundaries. If a variable is introduced inside a function block, it has local scope.

In C it is not possible to nest one function inside another. This distinguishes
functions in C from procedures in Pascal or PL/1, which can be nested. However,
it is possible to nest blocks inside a C function. And it is also possible to declare
variables inside more than one function block. For example, we show nested
blocks inside the cruncher() function given in the program in Figure 3.16.

```
#include "lib.h"

cruncher()
        begin                                /*outer block*/
        char letter = ´k´;
        char name[10];
        int bump = 21;

        strcpy(name, "Goldberry");
        printf("%40s \n\n", "initial values in outer block:");
        printf("%10c %20s %20d", letter, name, bump);
        printf("\n\n");
        drawline();
        printf("\n\n");
                begin                        /*inner block*/
                char letter = ´A´;
                char name[10];
                int bump = 34;

                strcpy(name, "Ishmael");
                printf("\n\n %40s", "inner block values:");
                printf("\n\n %10c %20s %20d", letter, name, bump);
                printf("\n\n");
                drawline();
                printf("\n\n");
                end                          /* end of inner block*/

        printf("%40s", "check on outer block values:");
        printf("\n\n");
        printf("%10c %20s %20d", letter, name, bump);

        end                                  /*end of outer block*/

main()
        begin

        cruncher();

        end
```

Figure 3.16 Nested Blocks

86 Primer on functions   CHAPTER 3

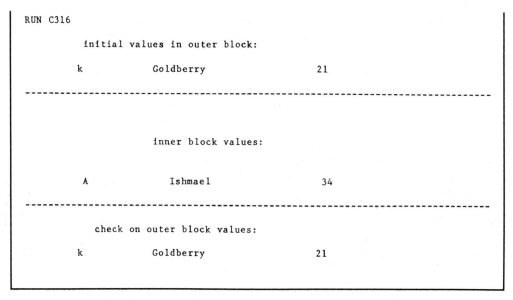

Figure 3.16 *concluded*

The program first prints

letter	name	bump
k	Goldberry	21

which are the initial values for the local variables in the outer block of cruncher(). The inner block of cruncher() begins with declaration of its own local variables. Even though the same identifiers from the outer block are used in the type declarations in the inner block, the local variables use entirely *different* memory locations. The program of Figure 3.16 prints

Inner block values

letter	name	bump
A	Ishmael	34

from the inner block. The local variables in the *outer* block of Figure 3.16 are not affected by the local variable changes in the *inner* block. Evidence of this fact comes from the final lines printed by the program in Figure 3.16.

Check on outer block values

letter	name	bump
k	Goldberry	21

CHAPTER 3   **3.15 Storage classes   87**

In general, what happens to local variables of an inner block is "unknown" to outer blocks. On the other hand, if a variable in a **C** program is global, then what happens to a global variable is "known" to all blocks within a function. Nesting function blocks will not hide what happens to a global variable within an inner block. The term *known* is used in the sense that an outer block can make use of changes made to a global variable within an inner block.

There is still the question of what happens to a global variable that is declared as local to a function block. That is, what happens to a global variable, if a global identifier is used as the identifier for a local variable? This question is left as an exercise.

3.14 LOCAL VARIABLES IN BLOCKS ON THE SAME LEVEL

Blocks in a **C** function can also be set up on the same level. Local variables declared in blocks on the same level cannot be shared between blocks on the same level. The initial block of a **C** function is on level 1. Local variables on level 1 can be used by blocks inside the level 1 block. A block set up immediately inside a level 1 block is on level 2. There can be more than one block on level 2, for example. Each block on level 2 can have its own local variables.

For example, the program in Figure 3.17 has a function called watermusic(). This function has two blocks on level 2, each with its own local variables. The local variables from the level 1 block of watermusic() are available to both level 2 blocks. Notice that *raindrop* and *echo* are both used in the level 2 blocks. The identifier *plip* is used as a local variable in both level 2 blocks. The H_wt and O_wt variables in the first level 2 block are not available to the second level 2 block. Notice that the changes made to *plip* within the level 2 blocks do not change the *plip* string set up in the level 1 block.

It is easy to verify that, if *plip* is not used as the identifier of a local variable in the second level 2 block, a

printf("%s", plip)

in the second level 2 block will print the level 1 *plip* string. The use of *plip* as a local variable in the first level 2 block will not be known in the second level 2 block.

3.15 STORAGE CLASSES

C storage classes are given in Table 3.1. Every **C**-type declaration specifies three things:

1. Identifier for a memory location.

88   Primer on functions   CHAPTER 3

```
#include "lib.h"

#define pinggg "\007"                          /*source of sound*/

watermusic()
        begin                            /*level 1*/
        char plip[20];
        char raindrop = ´!´;
        char echo[20];

        strcpy(plip, "plip! plip! plipp!"); /*init. plip-string*/
        strcpy(echo, "plippp! plippp!");
        printf(pinggg,pinggg,pinggg);
        printf("%40s \n\n", "initial music on level 1");
        printf("%10c %20s %5c %20s", raindrop, plip, raindrop, echo);
        printf("\n\n");
        drawline();
        printf("\n\n");
                begin                        /*level 2*/
                double H_wt = 1.0079;        /*hydrogen wt*/
                double O_wt = 15.9994;       /*oxygen wt*/
                char plip[20];

                strcpy(plip, "plop! plop! plopp!");
                printf("%40s \n\n", "music from 1st block on level 2");
                printf(pinggg,pinggg,pinggg);
                printf("%8.4f %20s", H_wt, "for hydrogen wt");
                printf("%8.4f %20s", O_wt, "for oxygen wt");
                printf("\n\n");
                printf("%10c %20s %5c %20s", raindrop, plip, raindrop, echo);
                printf("\n\n");
                drawline();
                end

                begin                        /*2nd level 2 block*/
                char plip[20];

                strcpy(plip, "pippp! pippp! pip!");
                printf("%40s \n\n", "music from 2nd block on level 2");
                printf(pinggg,pinggg,pinggg);
                printf("\n\n");
                printf("%10c %20s %5c %20s", raindrop, plip, raindrop, echo);
                printf("\n\n");
                drawline();

                end

        /*return to level 1*/

        printf("\n\n %40s", "final music from level 1");
        printf("\n\n");
        printf("%10c %20s %5c %20s", raindrop, plip, raindrop, echo);
```

Figure 3.17 Parallel Blocks

CHAPTER 3   3.15 Storage classes   89

```
        end
main()
        begin
                watermusic();
        end


RUN  C317
                initial music on level 1
        !    plip! plip! plipp!      !      plippp! plippp!
----------------------------------------------------------------------------

        music from 1st block on level 2
    1.0079       for hydrogen wt 15.9994          for oxygen wt
        !    plop! plop! plopp!      !      plippp! plippp!
----------------------------------------------------------------------------
        music from 2nd block on level 2


        !    pippp! pippp! pip!      !      plippp! plippp!
----------------------------------------------------------------------------

                final music from level 1
        !    plip! plip! plipp!      !      plippp! plippp!
```

Figure 3.17 *concluded*

2. Data type of a variable.
3. Storage class used.

For example, the declaration

$$\text{int bump;}$$

inside a function block indicates that *bump* identifies an integer variable. That is, the computer memory reserved by C for the bump variable will be used to hold integers. Implicit in this declaration is an indication of *how* this computer memory

90   Primer on functions

TABLE 3.1   Storage Classes

Specifier	Objects	Explanation
Auto	Variables *within* function blocks	Temporary storage set up for a variable in a function, persists as long as execution continues inside a block. This is the default class for internal variables.
Static	Variables and functions	Reserves storage that persists during the execution of a program, not just while a block or function is being executed.
Extern	Variables and (by default) functions	Globally accessible variables and functions. Storage for an external variable is permanent within the execution lifetime of a variable, making its content accessible across function boundaries. All functions are in the extern storage class by default.
Register	Variables only	Limited to variables of type int or char or to memory addresses (pointers); advises C to use a register for a variable, if possible, to speed up execution.

for bump will be used in a C program. Also implicit in this declaration is an indication of how much memory to reserve for a variable of type *int*. The storage class implicit in this declaration is *auto*.

3.15.1 Storage Class Auto

The *auto* storage class is the default storage class for C-type declarations within a function block. We could have also used

auto int bump;

A local variable inside a function block with auto storage class can be thought of as a variable with *temporary* storage. The processor will reserve storage for a local variable of class auto as long as that variable is being used within a block. This is temporary storage. Why? Once processing within a function block is finished, the processor no longer reserves the memory used for a local variable with class auto. The values of local variables with class auto are lost. If processing moves to a block with local variables with class auto, the processor opens up new storage for the auto class variables. This will happen no matter how many times a block with auto class variables is revisited during the execution of a program.

Storage class auto is the most commonly used storage class. We have used this storage class almost exclusively until now.

It is possible for the local variables of a function block to retain previously obtained values. This is made possible by using the *static* storage class.

CHAPTER 3   3.15 Storage classes   91

3.15.2 Storage Class Static

The static storage class makes it possible for the local variables of a block to retain old values. For example, in Figure 3.17 we could have used the following type of declarations:

static double H_wt;
static double O_wt;

Then, if we revisit a block containing these variables, they will retain the values obtained during the preceding visit. We illustrate this with a modified version of the program in Figure 3.18.

```
#include "lib.h"

cruncher()
        begin
        static double. x = 1.61803, y = 5.0;
        auto char ch[40];
        auto int i;

        strcpy(ch, "Tumty ti tumty ti tum toes!");
        printf("\n\n %40s", "Initial values for level 1 variables: ");
        printf("\n\n %10c %10c %20s", ´x´, ´y´, "ch");
        printf("\n\n %10.5f %10.5f %30s", x, y, ch);
        printf("\n\n");
        drawline();

            for (i = 1;i <= 3; ++i)
              begin
                  begin                          /*level 2 block*/
                  static double H_wt = 1.0079;
                  static double O_wt = 15.9994;
                  static char atom[20];

                  printf("\n\n %40s", "Values from 1st level 2 block: ");
                  printf("\n\n %10s %10s %30s", "H_wt", "O_wt", "atom");
                  printf("\n\n %10.5f %10.5f %30s", H_wt, O_wt, atom);
                  printf("\n\n Enter name of atom: ");
                  scanf("%s", atom);
                  ++H_wt;
                  ++O_wt;
                  end

                  begin                          /*level 2 block*/
                  double u = 233.0;
                  int v = 5;
                  static symbol = ´@´;
```

Figure 3.18 Use of Static Storage

```
            printf("\n\n %40s", "Values from 2nd level 2 block: ");
            printf("\n\n %10c %10c %20s", ´u´, ´v´, "symbol");
            printf("\n\n %10.5f %10d %20c", u, v, symbol);
            symbol = ´!´;                /*assign new symbol*/
            ++u;
            ++v;
            end
    end

/*return to level 1 block*/

printf("\n\n %40s", "Final values for level 1 variables: ");
printf("\n\n %10c %10c %20s", ´x´, ´y´, "ch");
printf("\n\n %10.5f %10.5f %30s", x, y, ch);
printf("\n\n");
drawline();
        end

main()
        begin

                cruncher();

        end


RUN C318

    Initial values for level 1 variables:

            x          y                ch

        1.61803    5.00000    Tumty ti tumty ti tum toes!

--------------------------------------------------------------------------------

            Values from 1st level 2 block:

            H_wt       O_wt                          atom

        1.00790    15.99940

    Enter name of atom: oxygen


            Values from 2nd level 2 block:

            u          v                symbol

    233.00000          5                      @

            Values from 1st level 2 block:

            H_wt       O_wt                          atom

        2.00790    16.99940                            oxygen
```

Figure 3.18 *continued*

CHAPTER 3   3.15 Storage classes   93

```
    Enter name of atom: carbon


            Values from 2nd level 2 block:

         u              v              symbol

     233.00000          5                 !

            Values from 1st level 2 block:

        H_wt        O_wt                        atom

     3.00790    17.99940                        carbon
    Enter name of atom: hydrogen


            Values from 2nd level 2 block:

         u              v              symbol

     233.00000          5                 !

        Final values for level 1 variables:

         x              y                  ch

     1.61803     5.00000    Tumty ti tumty ti tum toes!

    ------------------------------------------------------------------
```

Figure 3.18   *concluded*

3.15.3 Observations on Static and Auto Class Variables

The program in Figure 3.18 proves nothing about the static variables x and y in the level 1 block. Why? All processing is done inside the level 1 block of the cruncher() function. It is not revisited when processing the level 2 blocks of this function is complete. The processing done in the level 2 blocks of the cruncher() function is a continuation of the processing started at the top of the level 1 block.

The results of using static variables do show up in the processing of the level 2 blocks in the cruncher() function of Figure 3.18. How? The initial values of the static variables of the first level 2 block are printed as follows:

H_wt	O_wt	atom
1.00790	15.99940	

94 Primer on functions CHAPTER 3

Before the processor exits from the beginning level 2 block, each of its local variables is changed. The values of H_wt and O_wt are incremented by 1. The string variable *atom* is also assigned a string with

$$\text{scanf("\%s", atom);}$$

Then the processor exits from the first level 2 block and begins execution of the next level 2 block. This time the local variables of the second level 2 block are printed:

u	v	symbol
233.00000	5	@

Notice the local variables u and v of the second level 2 block are given the storage class *auto* by default. The results of these declarations in the second level 2 block show up when this block is revisited during the second pass of the for-loop. Notice that the local variables u and v are incremented by the processor before it exits from the second level 2 block. Finally, notice that the variable symbol of type *char* is in the extern class. Before exiting from this block, the following statement assigns a character to *symbol:*

$$\text{symbol = '!';}$$

The processor revisits the first level 2 block during its second pass through the for-loop. This block has local variables that are in the static storage class. The old values of *these* local variables have not been lost. This fact shows up in the second printing of the values of these variables:

Values from first level 2 block		
H_wt	O_wt	atom
2.00790	16.9994	oxygen

In other words, the first level 2 block has its own private storage, which stays intact when the processor exits from this block. This is not the case with the variables u and v in the auto storage class in the second level 2 block. Evidence of this can be found by checking what gets printed when the processor revisits the second level 2 block. Its old values of u and v are lost. It starts over with the initial values of u and v. However, the old value of symbol has been retained. That is, the old value of symbol is '!'.

It is possible to verify the retention of the values of the static variables x and y in the level 1 block of the cruncher() function. This can be done by producing a change in x and y inside the cruncher() function. For example, use

$$++x;$$
$$++y;$$

CHAPTER 3   3.16 Summary   95

Then call the cruncher() function more than once from main(). This change in Figure 3.18 is left as an exercise.

3.15.4 Storage Class Extern

All functions are in the extern storage class. Variables in the extern class can be declared either inside a function block or outside any function. Variables declared outside a function are in the class *extern*. The explicit use of the *extern* specifier in the type declaration of a variable indicates to the processor that a variable will be declared in the current file or another file that has been linked with the current file. Variables in this class give us a means of passing variables between functions. However, the preferred way to pass variables between functions is through the use of parameter lists.

Why? Variables in the extern class can be changed within any function block having access to one of these globals. This makes the use of external variables error prone.

3.15.5 Storage Class Register

Storage class register is limited to variables of type int and char and to addresses (pointers) to memory locations. The processor will use a register for the storage of a variable or address in this register class, if one of its registers is available. Since the number of general-purpose registers in a processor is small, it may not be possible for the processor to use a register for a variable or an address in this class. If a register is not available, the auto storage class is used.

Why use the register storage class? A general-purpose register is storage within the central processor, rather than primary memory. This means speedier execution relative to register contents. Why? The contents of a register are immediately available to a central processor. Before a processor can use the content of a memory location, it must first transfer the contents of a memory location to one of its registers. These transfers between a CPU register and main memory slow execution of a program.

The register storage class should only be used for heavily used variables. K & R (1978) mention that future versions of the C compiler will probably eliminate the need for register declarations.

3.16 SUMMARY

A function in C consists of a heading and a block bracketed by braces { }. A function specifies zero or more actions to be carried out by a processor relative to the function heading. A function specifies a task for a processor to perform. A func-

96 Primer on functions

CHAPTER 3

tion is a pearl. A program is a string of pearls. This analogy by Dijkstra suggests that a program be put together so that it has symmetry. Actually, Dijkstra suggests thinking of a function identifier as a pearl. Taking Dijkstra's idea, a string of pearls in a program can be "woven" initially without regard to the lines needed to flesh out a function.

We can start putting together a program as a string of pearls in terms of function identifiers that suggest tasks to be performed by a processor. In other words, start with names of tasks that need to be performed. The art of computer programming reduces to judicious selection of the names of functions that need to be created after the initial fitting of the pearls. We tried this in terms of

```
begin
    enquiry();
    printheading();
    drawdottriangle();
end
```

Then a function like enquiry() gets fleshed out to meet the needs of a program, or, possibly, an old pearl gets used in a new string of pearls. The printf() or scanf() function is an example of an old pearl.

In effect, a function becomes a tool that is potentially useful in many programs. A function tends to be a little universe. It can be used to encapsulate the parts of an algorithm needed by a program. This is a notion suggested by Aho, Hopcroft, and Ullman (1983).

A *function heading* has two optional features: (1) a type declaration for a value returned by a function and (2) a formal parameter list. The default data type returned by a C function is *int*. A function returns a value to a calling function using the *return* statement.

There are two types of formal parameters: (1) *value parameters,* which receive values from arguments in a function call, and (2) *variable parameters,* which receive *addresses* of memory locations (not values) from arguments in a function call. Value parameters are used as local variables in a function. The changes to a local variable do *not* change the original argument used in a function call. Changes made to a memory location identified by a variable parameter are not local. These changes are permanent and "known" by the calling function.

One C function cannot be put inside another C function block. That is, C functions cannot be nested. This distinguishes C functions from Pascal and PL/1 procedures, which can be nested.

Blocks can be nested in a C function. Figure 3.16 illustrates the use of nested blocks. Each block can have its own set of private variables. There can also be more than one block on the same level below the level 1 or initial block of a C function.

CHAPTER 3   **Review terms and symbols** **97**

The scope of a variable in a **C** program is dependent on the position where it is declared in a source text. A variable declared at the beginning of a source text is *global* to all functions in the source text.

A variable declared inside a function block is a *local variable*. It is available to all blocks nested *below* the block in which it is declared. Local variables are not available to other blocks on the same level or in parallel with a block containing a local variable. Figures 3.17 and 3.18 illustrate the uses of local variables in blocks on the same level.

By default, all local variables are in the auto storage class. This is the most commonly used storage class for local variables. It is temporary storage set up for a variable as long as execution continues inside a block. Changes made to auto class local variables are lost each time a processor exits from a block containing variables in this class.

Local variables in a block can be made to retain their values by declaring them to be in the static storage class. This is especially useful in later programming in **C**. Global variables are in the extern class. They also retain their values throughout the lifetime of a program in execution.

By default, all **C** functions are in the extern storage class. One **C** function made known to a program can be called by any function within that program. There are several methods for making a function known to a program. Functions in separate object modules can be linked together. The preprocessor can be told to include a source text containing a needed function. Finally, a function declared within a source text is known to all functions within the same source text.

The notion of a storage class is one of the subtler features of **C**.

REVIEW TERMS AND SYMBOLS

Term	*Meaning*
actual parameter	argument in a function call
block	compound statement, one or more lines of code bracketed by { }
call by value	use an argument in a function call to pass a value to a function
call by reference	use an argument in a function call to pass an address to a function
formal parameter	place-marker
formal parameter list	parameter list in a function heading
function	heading + block (cf. procedure in Pascal)
global variable	variable declared outside a function, available across function boundaries
local alias	formal parameter that is another name for a memory address identified in a call by reference

98 Primer on functions CHAPTER 3

Term	Meaning
local variable	variable declared in a function block
parameterless function	function without a parameter list
scope of a variable	availability of a variable to functions and function blocks
storage class	specifies (1) how much memory to use and (2) lifetime of storage used during program execution
1. auto:	default storage for variables declared *inside* function blocks. *Lifetime:* temporary, while a block containing an auto class variable is being processed
2. static:	private, permanent storage for variables or functions. *Lifetime:* during entire execution of program
3. extern:	permanent storage for variables declared outside function blocks and for functions. *Lifetime:* during entire execution of program
4. register:	auto class variables of type int or char or addresses (pointers) that are kept in registers, if available. *Lifetime:* same as auto class
strcpy(x, y)	copies string pointed to by y to string pointed to by x
switch (choice)	selection of block to execute based on value of choice variable
value parameter	a formal parameter that receives a value from a function argument
variable parameter	a formal parameter that receives an address from a function argument; a local alias for a memory location identified by an argument in a function call (cf. var parameter used in Pascal procedures)

EXERCISES

1. What are the differences between local and global variables in a **C** program?
2. Give two methods used to pass values of variables between functions.
3. What is the default storage class for the following items?
   a. Local variables
   b. Global variables
   c. Functions
4. Explain the term *scope of a variable*.
5. What is the scope of each of the following?
   a. Global variable
   b. Local variable
   c. x in Figure 3.15
   d. Raindrop in Figure 3.17
   e. H_wt and O_wt in Figure 3.17
   f. x and y in Figure 3.18
   g. Atom in Figure 3.18

CHAPTER 3   Exercises   99

6. Give the storage class and type of each of the following functions:
   a. Choice() in Figure 3.13
   b. Power() in Figure 3.15
   c. exp() in math.h
   d. log() in math.h

7. What is the difference between a call by value and a call by reference?
8. What is a formal parameter?
9. What are the two types of formal parameters?
10. What is an actual parameter?
11. What is meant by the term *local alias*?
12. Indicate the storage class corresponding to the following descriptions of storage specified for a variable x:
   a. x retains its value within a block.
   b. x retains its value within a program.
   c. x has storage allocated to it only during execution of the statements in the block containing x.
   d. A register is used for x.
   e. For x declared as follows in a block:

$$int\ x;$$

   f. For x declared as follows in a block:

$$char\ x;$$

13. Modify the program in Figure 3.10 as follows: in main(), print out the characters of the ch-array individually after each call of the echo() function. This can be done by using

```
for (i = 0; i <= 9; ++i)
    printf("%c", ch[i]);
```

Run the program for "Susu" as input to the echo function and determine if "berry" is still left in the ch-string after the assignment of the new string.

14. Use

```
main()
{
enquiry();
}
enquiry()
{
char line[80];
strcpy(line, "Eureka!");
forward(line);
backward(line);
}
```

to print the line string forward and backward. In other words, introduce a function

100 Primer on functions   CHAPTER 3

forward() that can be called by main to print a string forward. Similarly, introduce a
function backward() that will print a string backward.

15. Enhance the program in Exercise 14 so that the user can enter the string that is to be
    printed forward and backward. Run your program for
    a. "Hello, world!"
    b. "C is terse."
    c. "Programming is designing, creating new programs (Wirth)."

16. Carry out the refinement in Section 3.10 for the program in Figure 3.15. Run the new
    program for the following sets of values:
    a. Base = 2, low = 0, high = 15;
    b. Base = 4, low = 0, high = 7;
    c. Base = 8, low = 0, high = 5;

17. Carry out the refinement in Section 3.11 for the program in Figure 3.15. Run the new
    program for the following sets of values:
    a. Base = 2, low = 0, high = 20;
    b. Base = 3, low = 0, high = 20;
    c. Base = 16, low = 0, high = 20;

18. Carry out the refinement in Section 3.12 for the program in Exercise 17. Run the new
    program for parts (a), (b), and (c) of Exercise 17.

19. What happens to a global variable if its identifier is used for a local variable? Use

```
/*modified version of Figure 3.16*/
int bump = 5;       /*addition to Figure 3.16*/
cruncher()
    {
    .
    .
    .
    }
main()
    {
    cruncher();
    printf("bump = %2d", bump);
    }
```

in Figure 3.16 to illustrate your answer.

20. What happens to the contents of memory locations identified by static variables after
    a processor exits from a function containing such variables? Use the following modifi-
    cation of main() in Figure 3.18 to illustrate your answer:

```
main()
    {
    cruncher();
    cruncher();
    }
```

Note: Remove the for-loop in the cruncher() function to cut down the length of the
run.

21. Write a C program picture() that uses a *switch* statement to determine which of the
    following the user wants printed:

CHAPTER 3   **Lab projects 101**

a. Symbol triangle
b. Symbol square
c. Coordinate axes
In terms of each choice, allow the user to specify dimensions and the symbol to be
used to print each picture.

LAB PROJECTS

1. A Fibonacci sequence typically begins with 0 and 1 and each succeeding term is defined
   in terms of the preceding two terms. This gives the following sequence:

$$0, 1, 1, 2, 3, 5, 8, 13, 21, 34, 55, \ldots$$

   where $F(0) = 0$, $F(1) = 1$, and $F(n) = F(n - 1) + F(n - 2)$. Write a function in
   Fibonacci() that allows the user to pass a pair of adjacent Fibonacci numbers and that
   returns the next Fibonacci number of the adjacent pair. Then
   a. Write a C program that uses Fibonacci() to allow the user to print out the next Fibonacci number after an adjacent pair supplied by the user.
   Run the program for
   b. $F(10) = 55$, $F(11) = 89$
   c. $F(21) = 10,946$, $F(22) = 17,711$
2. Improve the program in Lab Project 1 so that it does the following things:
   a. Prompts for a beginning pair of adjacent Fibonacci numbers.
   b. Prompts for the number of Fibonacci numbers inside a for-loop.
   c. Prints the indicated sequence
   Run your program for
   d. $F(0) = 0$, $F(1) = 1$, $n = 22$, and print

$$F(0), F(1), \ldots, F(22)$$

   e. $F(10) = 55$, $F(11) = 89$, $n = 14$ and print

$$F(10), F(11), \ldots, F(14)$$

3. Write a C function drawnotriangle() to print a triangle of Fibonacci numbers like the
   following:

```
0
1   1
2   3   5
8  13  21   34
```

   This time
   a. Prompt for the number of rows in the printed triangle, which always starts with zero.
   Run your program for
   b. Rows $= 3$
   c. Rows $= 6$
4. Improve the program in Lab Project 3 so that the user can choose the beginning two
   numbers of the printed Fibonacci triangle; run your program for
   a. Beginning pair $= (2, 3)$, $n = 5$
   b. Beginning pair $= (0, 1)$, $n = 5$

102   Primer on functions   CHAPTER 3

5. Write a C function printletter() that uses the following formal parameters,

symbol	/*supplies address of a character*/
height	/*specifies height of a letter*/
letter	/*specifies a letter of the alphabet*/

and prints a letter with the height specified using the specified symbol. For example, using

$$symbol = '*'$$
$$height = '5'$$
$$letter = 'c'$$

this function will print

```
* * *
*
*
*
* * *
```

The width is left fixed. Write a program that uses the letter() function. Run your program for

a. Symbol = '.'
   Height = '5'
   Letter = 'A'

b. Symbol = '!'
   Height = 5
   Letter = 'L'

c. Symbol = '*'
   Height = '5'
   Letter = 'T'

d. Symbol = '@'
   Height = 10
   Letter = 'J'

CHAPTER 3   **Selected solutions   103**

SELECTED SOLUTIONS

Exercise 15

```
#include "lib.h"

char line[80]=´´;

forward(string)
        char string[80];

        begin
        int i;

        for (i = 0;i <= 80;++i)
          printf("%1c",string[i]);
        writeln;
        end

backward(string)
        char string[80];

        begin
        int i;

        for (i = 80;i >=0; --i)
          printf("%1c",string[i]);
        writeln;
        end

enquiry()
        begin
        printf("Enter a string-:> ");
        scanf(" %s ",line);
        writeln;
        end

main()
        begin
        enquiry();
        forward(line);
        backward(line);
        end


RUN CE315

Enter a string-:> Hello,_World!

Hello,_World!


!dlroW_,olleH
```

Exercise 15 *concluded*

```
RUN CE315

Enter a string-:> C_is_terse.

C_is_terse.


.esret_si_C


RUN CE315

Enter a string-:> Programming_is_designing,_creating_new_programs_(Wirth).

Programming_is_designing,_creating_new_programs_(Wirth).


.)htriW(_smargorp_wen_gnitaerc_,gningised_si_gnimmargorP
```

Exercise 16

```
#include "lib.h"

int x = 1,low = 1, high = 1;                    /*globals*/

enquiry()
        begin
        printf("\n\n Enter base low high:  ");
        scanf("%d %d %d", &x, &low, &high);
        printf("\n\n");
        end

printheading()
        begin
        printf("%30s %4d %10s", "powers of", x, "table");
        printf("\n\n");
        printf("%10s %4d %1c %2d", "range: ", x, ‾^‾, low);
        printf("%5s %4d %1c %2d", "to", x, ‾^‾, high);
        printf("\n\n");
        drawline();
        printf("\n\n");
        end

power(b, n)
int b;                                          /*base*/
int n;                                          /*exponent*/
        begin
        int i;                                  /*index*/
        unsigned int p = 1;                     /*power with init. value*/

        for (i = 1;i <= n; ++i)
                p = p * b;
        return( p );

        end
```

104

```
buildtable()
        begin
        int count = 0;                          /*column counter*/
        int j;                                  /*index*/

        for (j = low;j <= high; ++j)
                begin
                printf("%10u",power(x, j));
                ++count;
                if. (count % 4 == 0)
                        printf("\n\n");
                end

        end

main()
        begin

enquiry();
printheading();
buildtable();
end
```

RUN CE316

 Enter base low high: 2 0 15

                    powers of   2   table

    range: 2 ^ 0   to   2 ^ 15

----

           1   2   4   8

          16   32   64   128

         256   512   1024   2048

        4096   8192   16384   32768

RUN CE316

 Enter base low high: 4 0 7

                    powers of   4   table

    range: 4 ^ 0   to   4 ^ 7

----

           1   4   16   64

         256   1024   4096   16384

106 Primer on functions CHAPTER 3

Exercise 16 *concluded*

```
RUN CE316

 Enter base low high:  8 0 5


                     powers of     8        table

    range:      8 ^  0    to     8 ^  5


-----------------------------------------------------------------------------


          1        8       64       512

     4096     32768
```

Exercise 17

```
#include "lib.h"

int x = 1,low = 1, high = 1;                    /*globals*/

enquiry()
        begin
        printf("\n\n Enter base low high:  ");
        scanf("%d %d %d", &x, &low, &high);
        printf("\n\n");
        end

printheading()
        begin
        printf("%30s %4d %10s", "powers of", x, "table");
        printf("\n\n");
        printf("%10s %4d %1c %2d", "range: ", x, '^', low);
        printf("%5s %4d %1c %2d", "to", x, '^', high);
        printf("\n\n");
        drawline();
        printf("\n\n");
        end

double power(b, n)
int b;                                   /*base*/
int n;                                   /*exponent*/
        begin
        int i;                           /*index*/
        double p = 1;                    /*power with init. value*/
```

CHAPTER 3   Selected solutions   107

Exercise 17   *continued*

```
        for (i = 1;i <= n; ++i)
                p = p * b;
        return( p );

        end

buildtable()
        begin
        int count = 0;                          /*column counter*/
        int j;                                  /*index*/

        for (j = low;j <= high; ++j)
                begin
                printf("%18.0f",power(x, j));
                ++count;
                if (count % 4 == 0)
                        printf("\n\n");
                end

        end

main()
        begin

enquiry();
        printheading();
        buildtable();
        end


RUN CE317

 Enter base low high:  2 0 20


                powers of    2       table

   range:    2 ^  0   to   2 ^ 20


-------------------------------------------------------------------------------


                1                 2                 4                 8

               16                32                64               128

              256               512              1024              2048

             4096              8192             16384             32768

            65536            131072            262144            524288

          1048576
```

108   Primer on functions

CHAPTER 3

Exercise 17   *concluded*

```
RUN CE317

 Enter base low high:  3 0 20


                  powers of   3      table

   range:    3 ^  0   to    3 ^ 20

 ------------------------------------------------------------------------


                 1                3                9               27

               81              243              729             2187

             6561            19683            59049           177147

           531441          1594323          4782969         14348907

         43046721        129140163        387420489       1162261467

       3486784401

RUN CE317

 Enter base low high:  16 0 14


                  powers of   16      table

   range:    16 ^  0   to    16 ^ 14

 ------------------------------------------------------------------------


                 1               16              256             4096

            65536          1048576         16777216        268435456

       4294967296      68719476736    1099511627776   17592186044416

  281474976710656  4503599627370496 72057594037927936
```

CHAPTER 3   Selected solutions   109

Exercise 21

```
#include "lib.h"

drawtriangle(size,dot)
int size;                               /*equilateral triangle height*/
char dot[0]; /*symbol to print*/

        begin
        int rows,cols;                  /*index variables*/

        for (rows = 1;rows <= size;++rows)
                begin
                printf("\n\t\t");
                for (cols = 1;cols <= rows;++cols)
                        printf("%2s", dot[0]);
                end
        end

drawsquare(size,dot)
int size; /*width and height*/
char dot[0]; /*symbol to print*/

        begin
        int rows,cols;

        for (rows = 1;rows <= size;++rows)
          begin
          printf("\n\t\t");
          for (cols = 1;cols <= size;++cols)
            printf("%2s", dot[0]);
          end
        end

drawaxis(size,dot)
int size; /*x and y axis length*/
char dot[0]; /*symbol to print*/

        begin
        int x,y;

        for (y = 1;y <= size+size;++y)
          begin
          for (x = 1;x <= size;++x)
            printf("  ");
          printf("%s", dot[0]);
          writeln;
          if (y == size) /*if 1/2 way then print x axis*/
            begin
            for (x = 1;x <= size+size;++x)
              printf(" %s", dot[0]);
            writeln;
            end
          end
```

110 Primer on functions   CHAPTER 3

Exercise 21   *continued*

```
        end

picture()

        begin
int choice,size;
char symbol[0];

        printf("menu:\n");
        printf("\t1) draw a triangle\n");
        printf("\t2) draw a square\n");
        printf("\t3) draw coordinate axis\n\n");
        printf("choice-:> ");
        scanf("%d", &choice);
        writeln;
        printf("size-:> ");
        scanf("%d",&size);
        writeln;
        printf("symbol-:> ");
        scanf("%s", symbol[0]);
        writeln;
        switch (choice)
          begin
          case 1:
            drawtriangle(size,symbol);
            break;
          case 2:
            drawsquare(size,symbol);
            break;
          case 3:
            drawaxis(size,symbol);
            break;
          end

        end

main()
        begin
        picture();
        end


RUN CE321

menu:
        1) draw a triangle
        2) draw a square
        3) draw coordinate axis

choice-:> 1

size-:> 3
```

CHAPTER 3   **Selected solutions**   111

Exercise 21   *concluded*

```
symbol-:> !


                    !
                    ! !
                    ! ! !


RUN CE321

menu:
        1) draw a triangle
        2) draw a square
        3) draw coordinate axis

choice-:> 2

size-:> 4

symbol-:> *


                  * * * *
                  * * * *
                  * * * *
                  * * * *


RUN CE321

menu:
        1) draw a triangle
        2) draw a square
        3) draw coordinate axis

choice-:> 3

size-:> 4

symbol-:> $

            $
            $
            $
            $
  $ $ $ $ $ $ $ $
            $
            $
            $
            $
```

Lab Project 5

```
#include "lib.h"

printletter(symbol,letter,height)
char symbol,letter;
int height;

        begin
        int i;

        switch (letter)
          begin
          case 'A':
            printf("    %c\n", symbol);
            printf("  %c  %c\n", symbol, symbol);
            printf(" %c    %c\n", symbol, symbol);
            printf("%c      %c\n", symbol, symbol);
            for (i = 1;i <= 8;++i)
              printf("%c", symbol);
            writeln;
            for (i = 1;i <= height;++i)
              printf("%c      %c\n", symbol, symbol);
          break;
          case 'L':
            for (i = 1;i <= height;++i)
              printf("%c\n", symbol);
            for (i = 1;i <=7;++i)
              printf("%c", symbol);
            writeln;
          break;
          case 'T':
            for (i = 1;i <= 7;++i)
              printf("%c", symbol);
            writeln;
            for (i = 1;i <= height;++i)
              printf("   %c\n", symbol);
          break;
          case 'J':
            for (i = 1;i <= 7;++i)
              printf("%c", symbol);
            writeln;
            for (i = 1;i <= height;++i)
              printf("   %c\n", symbol);
            printf("%c  %c\n", symbol, symbol);
            printf(" %c%c\n", symbol, symbol);
          break;
          end
        end


main()
        begin
        char symbol,letter;

int height;

    printf("Enter your letter (A,L,T,J), symbol, & height.  (?,?,#) ");
    scanf("%c,%c,%d", &letter, &symbol, &height);
    writeln;
    printletter(symbol,letter,height);
    end
```

Lab Project 5   *concluded*

```
RUN CL35

Enter your letter (A,L,T,J), symbol, & height.  (?,?,#) A,.,5

        .
      .   .
    .       .
  .           .
  ..........
  .           .
  .           .
  .           .
  .           .
  .           .


RUN CL35

Enter your letter (A,L,T,J), symbol, & height.  (?,?,#) L,!,5

!
!
!
!
!!!!!!!


RUN CL35

Enter your letter (A,L,T,J), symbol, & height.  (?,?,#) T,*,5

*******
   *
   *
   *
   *
   *


RUN CL35

Enter your letter (A,L,T,J), symbol, & height.  (?,?,#) J,@,10

@@@@@@@
     @
     @
     @
     @
     @
     @
     @
     @
@    @
  @@
```

RELATED READINGS

Aho, A. V., J. E. Hopcroft, and **J. D. Ullman,** *Data Structures and Alogrithms.* Reading, Mass.: Addison-Wesley Publishing Co., 1983, Section 1.6.

Cooper, D., *Standard Pascal User Reference Manual.* New York: W. W. Norton & Company, 1983.

Dahl, O.–J., E. W. Dijkstra, and **C. A. R. Hoare,** *Structured Programming.* New York: Academic Press, Inc., 1972, pp. 1–83.

Kernighan, E. W., and **D. M. Ritchie,** *The C Programming Language.* Englewood Cliffs, N.J.: Prentice-Hall, Inc., 1978, Section 1.7 and Chapter 4.

4

Types and Operators

On the one hand, the mathematical basis of programming is very simple. Only a finite number of zeroes and ones are to be subjected to a finite number of simple operations, and in a certain sense programming should be trivial. On the other hand, stores with a capacity of many millions of bits are so unimaginably huge and processing these bits can now occur at so unimaginably high speeds that the computational processes...we are invited to invent...have outgrown the level of triviality by several orders of magnitude.

E. W. Dijkstra*

AIMS
- Show Uses of Fundamental Data Types in C.
- Introduce Type Int Qualifiers: Short, Long, and Unsigned.
- Show How Casts Are Used, and Type Conversions C Volunteers.
- Introduce the Use of Pointers.
- Distinguish between String Constants and Character Constants.
- Introduce Boolean and Bitwise Operators.
- Show How Assignments Can Be Compressed and Nested.
- Discuss the Role of Operator Precedence and Associativity in the Evaluation of an Expression.
- Distinguish between IBM 360/370 and PDP-11/VAX-11 Bit Strings.
- Show How to Use Masks to Extract Bits from an Expression.

---

*A Discipline of Programming, Prentice-Hall, Inc., Englewood Cliffs, N.J., 1976, pp. 209–210.

116   Types and operators   CHAPTER 4

4.1 INTRODUCTION

In the previous chapters, we used data of type *int, char,* and *double*. In this chapter, these types are presented in more detail. We show, for example, how to vary the use of type *int* with qualifiers: *short, long,* and *unsigned*. These qualifiers add a welcome flexibility to the use of integers in C programs.

Type *char* has many facets not yet considered. For example, it is possible to introduce a character constant like '!' in a program. This character constant can be used to scan the character table used by your local C compiler. We show how to scan the character table your system uses and to print out both the order used to store these characters and their corresponding machine codes. We also distinguish between character constants and string constants like "Eureka!". This will lead us to a closer look at how C stores strings and how they are located in memory using pointers.

We also begin a more detailed examination of floating-point numbers. There is always the nagging question of how these numbers can be formatted and how they can be manipulated in a C program. We discuss ways to explore the sizes of these types on your local system.

The treatment of types in this chapter is inspired by a belief that it is helpful to push your local compiler early. It is very helpful to find out as soon as possible the capabilities of your local compiler *and* the magnitudes of its data types.

This chapter also introduces the use of Boolean and shift operators. Boolean operators are useful in setting up conditions to manage the flow of control within a program. C has shift operators that can be used to manipulate the bits of an operand. We suggest how these operators can be used.

In C it is possible to use a *cast,* which is a way to force C to convert a variable of one type into another type. This is useful in functions like exp() and log(), which require an argument of type double. A cast makes it possible to use an integer argument in one of these functions. In this chapter we suggest ways to use casts.

Finally, we look more closely at various forms of the assignment statements in C. This will lead to a closer look at the order in which the parts of an expression are executed by a processor.

4.2 TYPE CHAR

Values of variables and constants of type *char* are taken from an ASCII or EBCDIC table. The 7-bit ASCII character set is more commonly used with C compilers. Our discussion is restricted to use of the ASCII table.

A value for a variable or constant of type *char* is an ASCII code. There are a total of 128 ASCII codes, which are represented in either octal or hexadecimal.

CHAPTER 4   **4.2 Type char   117**

Eight of these codes are used for cursor controls or what are known as *whitespaces* in C. For example, a tab or carriage return (cr) is a whitespace. There are 31 codes used for punctuation. Another 26 codes are used for nonprinting characters, like 28 (decimal) for an escape (esc) or 0 for a null. The remainder of the ASCII codes are used for the numerals 0 through 9 and upper- and lowercase letters.

It is possible to print out the ASCII codes and characters used by your system using a character constant. A character enclosed by single quotes, like '!', is a *character constant*. The value of a character constant is its corresponding ASCII code. For example, the ASCII code for a '!' is 33 (decimal).

In C, a variable is assigned the value of a character constant as follows:

```
char ch = '!';        /*first printable char*/
char numeral = '0';
char lc_letter = 'a';
char uc_letter = 'A';
char bell = '1007';
```

The first character constant in this list is the first printable character in the ASCII table. The string constant ch is stored in the machine, not as '!', but as

$$100\ 001\ \text{(binary)}\quad \text{or}\quad 41\ \text{(octal)}\quad \text{or}\quad 33\ \text{(decimal)}$$

If 1 is added to ch within a C program, this replaces 33 (decimal) by 34 (decimal). In other words, the addition of 1 to ch advances ch to the next code in the ASCII table, which is the code for a double quote (").

Using this idea, we can set up the following loop, which can be used to cycle through the entire ASCII table of printable characters:

```
for (i = 1; i <= 94; ++i)
   {
   printf("%5c %5d", ch + i, ch + i);
   if (i % 5 == 0)
      printf("\n\n");
   }
```

Except for the first line, this loop will print five characters and their corresponding ASCII codes in decimal on the same line. Then it skips a line and starts printing the next set of five characters and codes. We show a program to do this in Figure 4.1.

Until now, we have used

```
char bell = "\007"
```

to ring the keyboard bell with a printf(). This has been done by using, for example,

118 Types and operators

CHAPTER 4

```
#include <stdio.h>

buildtable()
        {
                char ch = ' ';
                int i;

                printf("\n\n %40s", "Printable ASCII char and code:");
                printf("\n\n");
                for (i = 1; i <= 80; ++i) printf("-"); printf("\n\n");
                for (i = 1; i <= 94; ++i)
                        {
                        printf("%5c %5d", ch + i, ch + i);
                        if (i % 5 == 0)
                                    printf("\n\n");
                        }
        }

main()
        {

                buildtable();

        }


RUN C41


        Printable ASCII char and code:

--------------------------------------------------------------------------------

    !    33    "    34    #    35    $    36    %    37

    &    38    '    39    (    40    )    41    *    42

    +    43    ,    44    -    45    .    46    /    47

    0    48    1    49    2    50    3    51    4    52

    5    53    6    54    7    55    8    56    9    57

    :    58    ;    59    <    60    =    61    >    62

    ?    63    @    64    A    65    B    66    C    67

    D    68    E    69    F    70    G    71    H    72

    I    73    J    74    K    75    L    76    M    77

    N    78    O    79    P    80    Q    81    R    82
```

Figure 4.1 Printing ASCII Characters and Codes

S	83	T	84	U	85	V	86	W	87
X	88	Y	89	Z	90	[	91	\	92
]	93	^	94	_	95	`	96	a	97
b	98	c	99	d	100	e	101	f	102
g	103	h	104	i	105	j	106	k	107
l	108	m	109	n	110	o	111	p	112
q	113	r	114	s	115	t	116	u	117
v	118	w	119	x	120	y	121	z	122
{	123	|	124	}	125	~	126		

Figure 4.1 *concluded*

$$\text{printf(bell, bell, bell);}$$

which rings the keyboard bell three times. In **C**, zero or more characters enclosed by double quotes make up a string constant. We discuss string constants in detail in the next section. For now, notice, for example, that ''!'' is a string constant, whereas '!' is a character constant. Why? Double quotes are used for a string constant like ''!'' and single quotes are used to surround the exclamation point in a character constant like '!'. If we use

$$\text{char ping } = \text{ '\textbackslash007'}$$

then

$$\text{for (i } = \text{ 1; i } <= \text{ 20; } ++\text{i)}$$
$$\text{printf(''\%c'', ping);}$$

will ring the keyboard bell 20 times. The slash in '\007' is an escape character used by **C** to specify the octal code for an ASCII character. For example, '\101' is a way of specifying the 'A' character constant. The leading zeros of '\007' for the keyboard bell are optional. We can also use '\7' for the keyboard bell.

The ASCII codes in octal and hex can be printed out using the conversion character o (oh) for *o*ctal or x for he*x*adecimal. For example,

$$\text{printf(''\%12c \%12d \%12o \%12x'', ch, ch, ch, ch);}$$

120   Types and operators   CHAPTER 4

will print out the ASCII codes for the string constant ch in decimal, octal, and hex. Carrying out this idea in a **C** program is left as an exercise.

In addition to the use of three octal digits in a string constant like '\101', there are also some special uses of the backslash to set up string constants for whitespaces, the null, and hard-to-print characters (single and double quotes and the backslash). These special cases are summarized in Table 4.1.

TABLE 4.1   Special String Constants

Constant	Character	Octal Code	Hex Code	Decimal Code
'\0'	Null	0	0	0
'\b'	Backspace	10	8	8
'\t'	Tab	11	9	9
'\n'	cr + lf			
'\f'	Form feed	14	C	12
'\r'	cr	15	F	13
'\'''	Double quote	42	22	34
'\''	Single quote	47	27	39
'\\'	backslash	134	5C	92
'\ddd'	?	ddd		

Note: '\n' reads "newline";
          '\ddd' represents three octal digits following the backslash.

We use '\\' to print a copy of cp34 in Figure 2.2. This is buried inside a puts() as follows:

puts(''\\'')

This will print a single backslash, and

puts(''\\\\\\\\'')

will print a succession of backslashes. How many? We can also use, for example,

char bkslash = '\\';

to set up a string constant. Then we can use, for example,

for (i = 1; i <= 30; ++i)
printf(''%c'', bkslash);

to print a success of backslashes. How many?

4.3 STRING CONSTANTS

In C, a *pointer* is an address of a memory location. An asterisk (*) prefix is used to identify a pointer. It is possible to set up a string constant using a pointer in a type char declaration. For example, we can use the following declaration:

char *s = "Oh! C!";

This makes *s point* to the beginning of a byte row in memory that is used to store the character codes for "Oh! C!". The *s*-pointer identifies the location of the leading byte of this byte row. The leading byte is used to hold the uppercase 'O' in this string constant.

This string constant has a hidden character, a null, that the C compiler inserts at the end of every string. That is, C stores "Oh! C!" in memory as shown in Figure 4.2. This means a string constant like "!" uses two bytes, one for the character and another for the null. The C compiler uses the null to determine when it has reached the end of a string. By contrast, the character constant '!' uses only one byte.

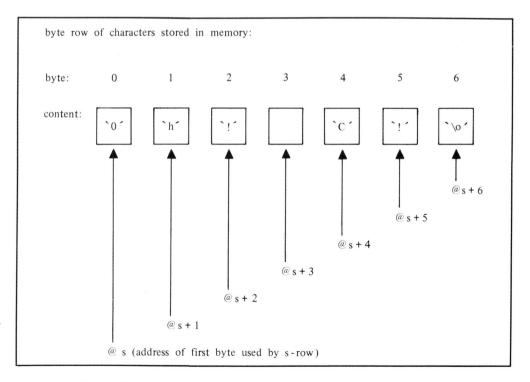

Figure 4.2 Byte Row of Characters

122   Types and operators   CHAPTER 4

In effect, a string constant sets up an array of contiguous bytes, or a byte row, in computer memory, one byte for each character in the string constant. If a string constant has n characters, the corresponding byte row will have $n + 1$ bytes. The extra byte is for the null. The string constant "Oh! C!" has six characters. This means s identifies a byte row with 7 bytes.

The entire string constant can be printed out using

$$printf("\%s", s);$$

or

$$puts(s);$$

The individual bytes of a string constant can be printed. For example,

$$printf("\%10c \%10c \%10c", s[0], s[1], s[2]);$$

will print

$$0 \qquad\qquad h \qquad\qquad\qquad !$$

We show a program to illustrate these ideas in Figure 4.3.

A string can be brought in from the keyboard using a gets(s). The gets() function is a standard **C** library function. It will accept a string with spaces between characters, whereas a scanf() will use a space as a string constant terminator. The gets() uses a return as the terminator of a string constant taken from the input stream.

4.3.1 New For-Loop

Until now we have used an upper bound on the index variable in a for-loop to control repeated execution of the for-loop. For example, we use

```
for (i = 0; i <= 80; ++i)
    printf("_");
```

to draw a line. The upper bound on i used in this for-loop is 80. In the program of Figure 4.3, the following for-loop is used:

```
for (i = 0; x[i] != '\0'; ++i)
    {
    printf("\t\t x[ %1d ] = %5c", i, x[i]);
    printf("\n\n");
    }
```

Continued execution of this loop depends on

$$x [i] != '\backslash 0'$$

```
#include "newlib.h"                    /*streamlined library*/

printchar(x)
char *x;
      {
      int i;

      printf("\n\n %20s", "string:");
      printf("\n\n");
      drawline();
      printf("\n\n\t %s", x);
      printf("\n\n\t %s", "separate characters of string:");
      printf("\n\n");
      drawline();
      printf("\n\n");
      for (i = 0; x[i] != ´\0´; ++i)
            {
            printf("\t\t x[ %1d ] = %5c", i, x[i]);
            printf("\n\n");
            }
      }

main()
      {
      char *s = "Eureka!";

      printchar(s);

      }


RUN  C43

         string:

---------------------------------------------------------------------

         Eureka!

         separate characters of string:

---------------------------------------------------------------------

                  x[ 0 ] =     E

                  x[ 1 ] =     u

                  x[ 2 ] =     r

                  x[ 3 ] =     e

                  x[ 4 ] =     k

                  x[ 5 ] =     a

                  x[ 6 ] =     !
```

Figure 4.3 Printing String Constants

124   Types and operators   CHAPTER 4

being true. That is, as long as x[i] does not equal (!=) a null, execution of the for-loop continues. In effect, this for-loop hunts for the null, which marks the end of the string constant.

4.3.2 Streamlined Local Library

Using

$$\#include \ \ ''lib.h''$$

slows down the compiling of a source text by **C**. The local library lib.h given in Appendix C is bulky. Until now we have relied on the use of the noise words begin/end in lib.h. This means the **C** preprocessor must replace each instance of a *begin* by { and *end* by }. This takes time. So we have used braces instead in the source text for Figure 4.3.

For the most part, we need only the drawline() function and

$$\#include \ <std.h> \qquad /*standard \ header*/$$
$$\#include \ <stdio.h> \quad /*standard \ i/o*/$$

in most programs. So we have reduced lib.h down to a local library newlib.h with minimal entries. We show this streamlined local library in Figure 4.4.

```
#include <stdio.h>

#define drawline() {                         \
                printf("----------------------------------------");  \
                printf("----------------------------------------");  \
                }
```

Figure 4.4   Streamlined Local Library

4.3.3 Making Copies of Pointers

It is possible to make a copy of a pointer; for example, we can use the following declaration:

$$char \ *my\_tea \ = \ ''Aha! \ Ada!'';$$
$$char \ *x;$$

This declares my_tea (short for my_cup_of_tea) to be a pointer. It points to the string constant ''Aha! Ada!'' stored in memory. We know my_tea points to the first byte of the byte row used to hold this string constant.

CHAPTER 4   4.3 String constants   125

This declaration also makes *x* a pointer type. We can make *x* point to the string pointed to by my_tea by using the following assignment:

$$x = my\_tea$$

In what follows, we show a program to illustrate this idea. To do this, we introduce the function

duplicate_string (row)
char *row;
{
.
.
.
}

This function illustrates how a pointer can be used as an argument in a function call. This is another form of a *call by reference* introduced in Chapter 3. We show this function in the program in Figure 4.5.

```
#include "newlib.h"                      /*streamlined library*/

duplicate_string(row)                    /*call by reference*/
char *row;
     {
     char *x;

     x = row;                            /*make copy of pointer*/
     printf("\n\n %40s", "original string:");
     printf("\n\n\t %s", row);
     printf("\n\n");
     drawline();
     printf("\n\n %40s", "copy of string:");
     printf("\n\n\t %s", x);
     printf("\n\n");
     drawline();
     }

main()
     {
     char *my_tea = "A way a lone a loved a last a long the...";

     duplicate_string(my_tea);
     for (1) {
             printf("\n\n Enter string: ");scanf("%s", my_tea);
             duplicate_string(my_tea);
             }
     }
```

Figure 4.5 Pointing to Strings

126 Types and operators

CHAPTER 4

```
RUN C45

                        original string:

        A way a lone a loved a last a long the...

--------------------------------------------------------------------

                        copy of string:

        A way a lone a loved a last a long the...

--------------------------------------------------------------------

 Enter string: Eureka!

                        original string:

        Eureka!

--------------------------------------------------------------------

                        copy of string:

        Eureka!

--------------------------------------------------------------------

 Enter string: Tumty-tumty-tum-toes!

                        original string:

        Tumty-tumty-tum-toes!

--------------------------------------------------------------------

                        copy of string:

        Tumty-tumty-tum-toes!

--------------------------------------------------------------------

 Enter string: ^C
```

Figure 4.5 *concluded*

4.3.4 Changing a String Constant

The program in Figure 4.5 allows the user to change the string pointed to by the pointer. This is done with

scanf("%s", my_tea);

CHAPTER 4   **4.3 String constants   127**

Notice that the length of the byte row pointed to by *s* can be varied. For example, using a scanf() in terms of

''Eureka!''

makes *s* point to a byte row with 8 bytes, and using scanf() in terms of

''Tumty-tumty-tum-toes!''

makes *s* point to a byte row that is considerably longer than the row used for ''Eureka!''. How many bytes are used by this new byte row?

4.3.5 Bug Clinic: Spaces in a String Constant

If we use

char *my_tea = ''Oh! C!'';

the space between '!' and 'C' is taken as part of the string constant because it is inside the surrounding double quotes. However, if the use

scanf(''%s'', my_tea);

in terms of

Oh! C!

typed at a keyboard, then only the ''Oh!'' is used as the string constant pointed to by *s*. Why? The space is used as a delimiter to separate the pieces of the input stream. Use a gets(s), instead, to assign ''Oh! C!'' to *s*.

4.3.6 Refinement: Selecting Characters of a Substring

The program in Figure 4.3 demonstrates how to get at the individual characters of a string constant. However, this program is quite limited. Why? It is written in terms of a single string constant

''Eureka!''

The program needs to be refined so that the user can enter a string from a keyboard by using an array of characters like ch[80] instead of a pointer like *ch. This will reserve 80 bytes for the ch-string. In addition, the printchar() needs to be improved as follows:

1. Add to the formal parameter list parameters to select the characters of a substring of the string pointed to by *x*.

2. Print out the substring.

128 Types and operators   CHAPTER 4

These refinements of printchar() imply the need for a new function, which we can call *length*. That is, add to the program in Figure 4.3 the following function:

```
length (string)
char string[80];
    {
    int count  =  0;      /*use to count characters*/
    int i;                /*index used in for-loop*/
    /*scan string inside a for-loop that increments
    count each time it is found that string[i] does
    not equal a null. Then return the value of count.*/
    }
```

Then the main block of the program in Figure 4.3 will have the following form:

```
main()
    {
    char s[80];
    int low, high;      /*bounds on substring*/
    /*enter string, low, high in main() */
    printf("%s %d", "length = ", length(s));
    /*prompt for substring to be printed*/
    printchar(s, low, high);
    }
```

These changes in Figure 4.3 are left as an exercise.

4.4 TYPE INT QUALIFIERS: SHORT, LONG, UNSIGNED

The possible qualifiers for type int are shown in Table 4.2. The size of the scale used for short and long depends on the C compiler and the particular computer

TABLE 4.2   Type Int Qualifiers

Form	Simplified Form	PDP-11 Bits	VAX-11 Bits
Int		16	32
Short int	Short	16	16
Long int	Long	32	32
Unsigned int	Unsigned	16	32
Unsigned short int	Unsigned short	16	16
Unsigned long int	Unsigned long	32	32

CHAPTER 4   **4.4 Type int qualifiers: short, long, unsigned   129**

system used. The number of bytes these qualifiers use can be determined using the *sizeof* operator. The program given in Figure 4.6 can be used to determine the number of bytes used by short and long on your system. The sample run shown is from PDP 11/70. We demonstrate the use of type *long* in a program to print powers of 2. This program will print both 2^n and 2^{-n} for n in the range from 0 to 30. We show this in Figure 4.7.

```
#include "newlib.h"                          /*see Figure 4.4*/

bytecount()
      {
      printf("\n\n %40s", "byte count for type int qualifiers:");
      printf("\n\n %30s %20s \n\n", "type", "no. of bytes");
      drawline();
      printf("\n\n\t %20s %20d", "int", sizeof(int));
      printf("\n\n\t %20s %20d", "short", sizeof(short));
      printf("\n\n\t %20s %20d", "long", sizeof(long));
      printf("\n\n\t %20s %20d", "unsigned", sizeof(unsigned));
      printf("\n\n\t %20s %20d", "unsigned short", sizeof(unsigned short));
      printf("\n\n\t %20s %20d", "unsigned long", sizeof(unsigned long));
      printf("\n\n");
      drawline();
      }

main()
      {
            bytecount();
      }


RUN  C46

      byte count for type int qualifiers:

                       type        no. of bytes

      -----------------------------------------------------------------

                        int              2

                      short              2

                       long              4

                   unsigned              2

             unsigned short              2

              unsigned long              4

      -----------------------------------------------------------------
```

Figure 4.6   Counting Bytes with Sizeof Operator

130 Types and operators

CHAPTER 4

```
#include "newlib.h"                          /*see Figure 4.4*/

long power( b,n )
long b;
int n;
        {
        int i;
        long p = 1;

        for (i = 1; i <= n; ++i)
                {
                p = p * b;
                }

        return( p );
        }


printheading()
        {
        printf("\n\n %40s \n\n", "Powers of 2");
        printf("%20s %5s %15s \n\n", "2^n", "n", "2^(-n)");
        drawline();
        printf("\n\n");
        }

main()
        {
        long x,base = 2;
        double y;
        int j;

        printheading();
        for (j = 0;j <= 30; ++j)
                {
                x = power( base, j );
                y = 1.0 / (double)x;
                printf("%20ld %5d %5s %.20f \n", x, j, " ", y);
                }
        }


RUN C47

                            Powers of 2

        2^n       n           2^(-n)

------------------------------------------------------------------

                 1        0       1.00000000000000000000
                 2        1       0.50000000000000000000
```

Figure 4.7 Powers of 2 with Type Long

CHAPTER 4   4.4 Type int qualifiers: short, long, unsigned   131

4	2	0.25000000000000000000
8	3	0.12500000000000000000
16	4	0.06250000000000000000
32	5	0.03125000000000000000
64	6	0.01562500000000000000
128	7	0.00781250000000000000
256	8	0.00390625000000000000
512	9	0.00195312500000000000
1024	10	0.00097656250000000000
2048	11	0.00048828125000000000
4096	12	0.00024414062500000000
8192	13	0.00012207031250000000
16384	14	0.00006103515625000000
32768	15	0.00003051757812500000
65536	16	0.00001525878906250000
131072	17	0.00000762939453125000
262144	18	0.00000381469726562500
524288	19	0.00000190734863281250
1048576	20	0.00000095367431640625
2097152	21	0.00000047683715820313
4194304	22	0.00000023841857910156
8388608	23	0.00000011920928955078
16777216	24	0.00000005960464477539
33554432	25	0.00000002980232238770
67108864	26	0.00000001490116119385
134217728	27	0.00000000745058059692
268435456	28	0.00000000372529029846
536870912	29	0.00000000186264514923
1073741824	30	0.00000000093132257462

Figure 4.7   *concluded*

4.4.1 Bug Clinic: Casts

In C, it is possible to *cast* (or convert) an expression to another data type. This is done with a cast operator, which has the following construction:

(new type) (expression)

For example, if x is of type int, then

(double)x

coerces (forces) C to make x type double. Some other examples of casts are as follows:

log((double(i)
y = 2.0 / (double)x;
printf("%f", 1.0 / (double)5.0);
printf("%d", (int)y);
term = (int)((short)10 * i + j);

132   Types and operators   CHAPTER 4

In the program in Figure 4.7 the following cast is used:

$$y = 1.0 \ / \ (double)x;$$

which makes the value of *x*, which is type long, a type double value. This is used to advantage in this program to print out the reciprocals of powers of 2, which have a "%.20f" format. In some cases, **C** will volunteer type conversions of operands in arithmetic expressions and assignments. These cases are shown in Table 4.3.

TABLE 4.3   Usual Arithmetic Conversions

Operands			*Result Type from*
x (y)			
Type *(Type)*		*Conversions by* **C**	*x op y*
Automatic conversions			
Char		*x* converted to int	
Short		*x* converted to int	
Float		*x* converted to double	
Hierarchical conversions			
First			
double (long, unsigned, or int)		*y* is converted to double	Double
Then			
long (unsigned, or int)		*y* is converted to long	Long
Then			
unsigned (int)		*y* is converted to unsigned	Unsigned
Then			
int (int)		None	Int

4.4.2 Formatting a Variable of Type Long

In the program in Figure 4.7, we use the following printf() statement:

printf("%20 ld %5d %5s %.20f \n", x, j, " ", y);

variable of type long

lowercase *l* ("ell"), which is a qualifier
used with the conversion specifier *d* to tell
C that the corresponding output is type long

CHAPTER 4   **4.4 Type int qualifiers: short, long, unsigned   133**

A lowercase *l* ("ell") is used in a printf() control string as a prefix before a *d* for a decimal format for a type long argument. This specifies that the corresponding output argument is of type long. A lowercase *l* can also be used as follows:

"%lo"	to specify an octal argument of type long
"%lx"	to specify a hex argument of type long
"%lu"	to specify an unsigned argument of type long
"%ld"	to specify an argument of type long

4.4.3 Refinement: Varying the Double Format

The program in Figure 4.7 uses a "%.20f" to format a reciprocal of a power of 2. This is adequate up to 2^{20}. However, notice that the next reciprocal power of 2 is rounded off. That is, the following gets printed by the program:

2^21	21	2^(-21)
2097152	21	0.00000047683715820313

This gives 2^{-21} with its twentieth digit to the right of the decimal rounded to 3. That is, this power of 2^{-21} is given exactly as follows:

2^21	21	2^(-21)
2097152	21	0.000000476837158203125

It does not hurt to push your machine, to see the outer limits of its computational powers. To do this in the preceding example, change "%.20f" to "%.30f" and see how much more accuracy your machine can produce using type double with reciprocals of powers of 2. You can spot where its accuracy starts dropping off by the following fact: *every negative power of 2 ends in 5.*

For example, you should be able to produce the following result:

2^30	30	2^(-30)
1,073,741,824	30	0.000 000 000 931 322 574 615 478 515 625

4.4.4 Further Refinement: Varying the Base Used

The program in Figure 4.7 is limited to producing powers of 2 tables. This limitation is not necessary and probably not desirable. It can be eliminated by prompting the user for a value of the *base* variable. This refinement is left as an exercise.

4.4.5 Another Refinement: Varying the Range of Exponents

The program in Figure 4.7 is limited to exponents in the range from zero to 30.

134 Types and operators   CHAPTER 4

Variables *low* and *high* should be introduced to allow the user to select the beginning and ending values of the exponent *j* in main(). This refinement is also left as an exercise.

4.4.6 Example with Type Short

There is no guarantee that type *short* will specify a variable that takes fewer bytes than type *int*. In fact, on a PDP 11/70, type short and type int both use 2 bytes or 16 bits. However, on a VAX-11, type short uses 2 bytes and type int uses 4 bytes. This is significant. Why? On a VAX-11, type short can be used to cut down on the storage used for many integer variables. This can contribute to a significant savings in the storage required by a large-scale C program.

In Figure 4.8, we illustrate the use of type short in a program to print a table of squares. This program is the C equivalent of a Pascal program given by Flanders (1984, pp. 68–69). Unlike Pascal, C gives a programmer the ability to *select* how many bytes a variable will use.

```
#include "newlib.h"                        /*see Figure 4.4*/

buildtable( low,high )
short low,high;
        {
        short i,j;
        int term;

        printf("\n\n %40s \n\n", "Table of squares");
        drawline();
        printf("\n\n %10s", " ");
        for (j = low; j <= high; ++j)
                printf("%5d", j);
        printf("\n\n");
        for (i = low;i <= high; ++i)
                {
                printf("%5d %5s", i, " ");
                for (j = low; j <= high; ++j)
                        {
                        term = (int)((short)10 * i + j);
                        printf("%5d", sqr(term));
                        }
                printf("\n\n");
                }
        }

sqr( x )
int x;
        {
                return( x * x );
        }
```

Figure 4.8 Using Type Short to Save Storage

CHAPTER 4   **4.4 Type int qualifiers: short, long, unsigned   135**

```
main()
        {
        short a = 0,b = 9;

        buildtable( a,b );
        }
```

RUN C48

Table of squares

		0	1	2	3	4	5	6	7	8	9
0		0	1	4	9	16	25	36	49	64	81
1		100	121	144	169	196	225	256	289	324	361
2		400	441	484	529	576	625	676	729	784	841
3		900	961	1024	1089	1156	1225	1296	1369	1444	1521
4		1600	1681	1764	1849	1936	2025	2116	2209	2304	2401
5		2500	2601	2704	2809	2916	3025	3136	3249	3364	3481
6		3600	3721	3844	3969	4096	4225	4356	4489	4624	4761
7		4900	5041	5184	5329	5476	5625	5776	5929	6084	6241
8		6400	6561	6724	6889	7056	7225	7396	7569	7744	7921
9		8100	8281	8464	8649	8836	9025	9216	9409	9604	9801

Figure 4.8   *concluded*

In the program in Figure 4.8, the variables low, high, i, and j are of type short. The variables i and j are used as index variables, which require minimal storage in this example. The variables low and high are the boundary values on the index variables. If the values of low and high were pushed past 32767, these variables would need to be changed to type long.

You might wonder if the following casts are necessary:

$$\text{term} = \text{(int) ((short)10 * i + j)};$$

The inner cast, (short)10, makes 10 type short, and the outer cast

$$\text{(int) (expression)}$$

converts the expression to type int. It is left as an exercise to determine if this program will produce the same results without these casts.

136 Types and operators CHAPTER 4

4.4.7 Refinement: Selecting the Boundary Values

The program in Figure 4.8 is limited because it always produces the same table of squares. This makes this program fairly useless. This can be changed by letting the user select the values of *a* and *b* before buildtable() is called. This refinement is left as an exercise.

4.5 TYPE FLOAT AND DOUBLE

A *fixed-point number* is a number of the form

$$\text{whole number . fraction part}$$

Until now we have worked with fixed-point numbers using the "%f" format with numbers of type double. A number *x* of the form

$$x = m \cdot b^c$$

is called a *floating-point number*. The coefficient *m* is called the *mantissa*. The letter *b* represents the radix or *base*. The letter *c* represents the exponent or *characteristic* of the number. For example, a fixed-point number like 0.35 can be represented as a floating-point number as follows:

$$0.35 = 35 \times 10^{-2}$$

The C language provides an e-format to represent fixed-point numbers in floating-point form. A number *x* written in e-format has the following form:

$$x = \text{(fixed point number) e (characteristic)}$$

The base used for e-format is 10. For example, the fixed-point number 0.161803 can be formatted as follows:

$$0.161803 = 1.618\text{e-}1$$

An e-format specifier has the following form:

$$\text{"%(fixed point format)e"}$$

For example, we can use "%e" to produce

$$4181.0/33.0 = 1\text{e}+02$$

or "%1.3e" to produce

$$4181.0/33.0 = 1.267\text{e}+02$$

A program to illustrate some uses of the f- and e-formats is given in Figure

4.9. In the sample run, notice that ''%1.20f'' and ''%3.20f'' both produce errone-ous results for the fraction

$$4.181.0/33.0 = 126.6969 \ldots$$

As a rule it is better to use a format like ''%.3f'' to print out a fixed-point result. This gives C latitude in setting up the whole-number part of the fixed-point num-ber to be printed. It is possible to force C to print a type double result by using ''%1f'' as the format in a printf() control string. Experimenting with this format is left as an exercise.

```
#include "newlib.h"

fpoint_nos()
     {
     float x = 377.0, y = 233.0;
     double a = 377.0, b = 233.0;
     double two30 = 1073741824.0; two40 = 1099511627776.0;
     printf("\n\n %40s \n\n", "Sample floating point nos.");
     printf("%20s %20s %30s \n\n", "expression", "format", "value");
     drawline();
     printf("\n\n %20s %20s %.20f", "377.0 / 233.0", "%.20f", x / y);
     printf("\n\n %20s %20s %.20e", "377.0 / 233.0", "%.20e", x / y);
     printf("\n\n %20s %20s %e", "2.0/999999.0", "%e", 2.0/999999.0);
     printf("\n\n %20s %20s %1.0e", "2.0/999999.0", "%1.0e", 2.0/999999.0);
     printf("\n\n %20s %20s %e", "33.0/99.0", "%e", 33.0/99.0);
     printf("\n\n %20s %20s %1.0e", "33.0/99.0", "%1.0e", 33.0/99.0);
     printf("\n\n %20s %20s %1.20f", "33.0/99.0", "%1.20f", 33.0/99.0);
     printf("\n\n %20s %20s %e", "4181.0/33.0", "%e", 4181.0/33.0);
     printf("\n\n %20s %20s %.3e", "4181.0/33.0", "%.3e", 4181.0/33.0);
     printf("\n\n %20s %20s %1.3e", "4181.0/33.0", "%1.3e", 4181.0/33.0);
     printf("\n\n %20s %20s %2.3e", "4181.0/33.0", "%2.3e", 4181.0/33.0);
     printf("\n\n %20s %20s %3.5e", "4181.0/33.0", "%3.5e", 4181.0/33.0);
     printf("\n\n %20s %20s %f", "4181.0/33.0", "%f", 4181.0/33.0);
     printf("\n\n %20s %20s %.3f", "4181.0/33.0", "%.3f", 4181.0/33.0);
     printf("\n\n %20s %20s %1.20f", "4181.0/33.0", "%1.20f", 4181.0/33.0);
     printf("\n\n %20s %20s %3.20f", "4181.0/33.0", "%3.20f", 4181.0/33.0);
     printf("\n\n %20s %20s %.20f", "1/(2^30)", "%.20f", 1.0/two30);
     printf("\n\n %20s %20s %.20f", "1/(2^40)", "%.20f", 1.0/two40);
     printf("\n\n");
     drawline();
     }

main()
     {
          fpoint_nos();
     }
```

Figure 4.9 Type Float and Double

138 Types and operators CHAPTER 4

```
RUN C49

              Sample floating point nos.

          expression          format          value

 ----------------------------------------------------------------

            377.0 / 233.0      %.20f    1.6180257510729614000

            377.0 / 233.0      %.20e    1.6180257510729614e+00

            2.0/999999.0       %e       2e-06

            2.0/999999.0         %1.0e 2e-06

              33.0/99.0           %e 3e-01

              33.0/99.0         %1.0e 3e-01

              33.0/99.0      %1.20f 0.33333333333333334000

            4181.0/33.0           %e 1e+02

            4181.0/33.0         %.3e 1.267e+02

            4181.0/33.0        %1.3e 1.267e+02

            4181.0/33.0        %2.3e 1.267e+02

            4181.0/33.0        %3.5e 1.26697e+02

            4181.0/33.0           %f 127

            4181.0/33.0         %.3f 126.697

            4181.0/33.0      %1.20f 26.69696969696970000000

            4181.0/33.0      %3.20f 26.69696969696970000000

              1/(2^30)       %.30f 0.00000000093132257462

              1/(2^40)       %.30f 1.00000000000000000000

 ----------------------------------------------------------------
```

Figure 4.9 *concluded*

4.6 BOOLEAN OPERATORS

The Boolean operators (in English!) are

> **and** (for conjunction)
> **or** (for disjunction)
> **not** (for negation)

CHAPTER 4   **4.7 Bitwise operators   139**

They are named after George Boole (1815–1864), who first suggested, in 1847, how they might be used in an algebra of logic. In C, these operators are represented as follows:

$$\&\& \quad \text{for 'and'}$$
$$\| \quad \text{for 'or'}$$
$$! \quad \text{for 'not'}$$

The truth value of these operators is measured in terms of whether expressions evaluated by these operators are zero or not. The truth tables for these operators are given in Table 4.4. These operators are useful in setting up conditional execution of a statement. We illustrate their uses in the discussion of control structures in Chapter 5.

TABLE 4.4   Boolean Operators

p	&&	q		p	||	q		! p	
not 0	1	not 0		not 0	1	not 0		0	not 0
not 0	0	0		not 0	1	0		1	0
0	0	not 0		0	1	not 0			
0	0	0		0	0	0			

Examples
```
int x,y,z;
x = y = z = 2;
```

x && (y + z)	gives a truth value of 1
(x - y) && z	gives a truth value of 0
(x - y) || z	gives a truth value of 1
!x	gives a truth value of 0
!(x - y)	gives a truth value of 1

Note: p and q are expressions.

4.7 BITWISE OPERATORS

The bitwise operators available in C are given in Table 4.5. These operators bring C down to the assembler level, where the bits of an operand can be manipulated. They offer powerful tools to a C programmer.

For example, it is possible to use the & **(and)** and | **(or)** to extract the bits of an operand. This is done with a mask. The term *mask* refers to a number with target bits that are either set or unset. A target bit of a mask is compared with the

140 **Types and operators**

CHAPTER 4

TABLE 4.5   Bitwise Operators

Operation	Name	Function
~	1's complement	Throw switches
&	and (binary)	A bit in the result is set only when bits in the same position of the operands are both 1
|	or (binary)	A bit in the result is set when either bit (or both bits) in the same place in the operands is 1
^	xor (exclusive or)	A bit in the result is set when either bit in the same place in the operands is 1, but not both
<<	Shift left	Move all bits to left by one (effect: multiply by 2)
>>	Shift right	Move all bits to right by one (effect: divide by 2)

bit of an operand using the & or the | operator. In what follows, we illustrate how a mask can be used in a C program.

We start with the extract() function in Figure 4.10 to print the bits of an expression. This function is made almost system independent by using

$$mask \; != \; 0$$

in the for-loop. The same function can be used on either a 16- or 32-bit machine. Why? On a 16-bit machine, values of variables of type *int* are stored in 16-bit strings. Using

$$mask \; = \; 1$$

we get the following result on a 16-bit machine like a PDP-11:

$$mask \; = \; 0 \; 000 \; 000 \; 000 \; 000 \; 001 \; (base \; 2)$$

Each time the statement

$$mask \; = \; mask \; << \; 1;$$

is executed, the content of each nonzero bit is *moved* to the adjacent bit on the left. After the first shift left on the preceding mask, we get

$$mask \; = \; 0 \; 000 \; 000 \; 000 \; 000 \; 010 \; (base \; 2)$$

If we repeat this shift-left operation 15 times, we get

$$mask \; = \; 1 \; 000 \; 000 \; 000 \; 000 \; 000 \; (base \; 2)$$

The next shift left will make the 1 in bit 15 drop off the edge of the world. Then the mask will be zero.

CHAPTER 4   **4.7 Bitwise operators 141**

```
extract(expr)

int expr;

    {

    int i;

    int mask;

    mask = 1;
    printf("%70s", " ");
    for (i = 0; mask != 0; ++i)

        {

        if (expr & mask)

                printf("\b\b\b\b\b\b %2d",1);

        else

                printf("\b\b\b\b\b\b %2d",0);

        mask = mask << 1;

        }

    }
```

Figure 4.10   Extract() Function

On a 32-bit machine like a VAX-11, values of variables of type *int* will probably be stored in a 32-bit string. Then the shift-left operation in the extract() function will be repeated 32 times before the mask becomes zero.

The extract() function also uses printer gymnastics to make the least significant bit of the *expr* variable appear on the right. This is the way the Digital Equipment Corporation organizes the bit strings on both its PDP-11 and VAX-11 systems. That is, bit zero is the *rightmost* bit. This is the least significant bit (or lsb) printed by the extract() function. Bit 15 is the most significant bit (or msb); it is the *leftmost* bit for a computer word on a PDP-11.

How is this done? The cursor is first moved 70 columns to the right. Then six backspaces are printed with "\b\b\b\b\b\b" each time through the for-loop. This puts spaces between the digits printed. To use the extract() function on a 32-bit machine, drop two backspaces.

142   Types and operators   CHAPTER 4

Finally, notice that the extract() function in Figure 4.10 uses a new control structure:

> if (condition)
>> statement;
>
> else
>> statement;

This control structure is explained in detail in Chapter 5. For now, notice that if the condition is true the processor will execute the first statement (immediately after the condition). If the condition is false, the statement following the *else* is executed.

A program to illustrate the use of the extract function is given in Figure 4.11.

4.7.1 Refinement: Specifying Bit Zero

In effect, the program in Figure 4.11 prints out the binary equivalent of integers entered at a keyboard. This program can be improved by specifying bit zero for each run as follows:

> 0 000 000 000 001 000
>> bit zero

This refinement is left as an exercise.

```
#include "newlib.h"

extract(expr)
int expr;
    {
    int i;
    int mask;

    mask = 1;
    printf("%70s", " ");
    for (i = 0; mask != 0; ++i)
        {
        if (expr & mask)
            printf("\b\b\b\b\b\b %2d", 1);
        else
            printf("\b\b\b\b\b\b %2d", 0);
        mask = mask << 1;
        }
    }
```

Figure 4.11   Extracting Bits

CHAPTER 4   **4.7 Bitwise operators   143**

```
main()
        {
        int x;

        for (1)
                {
                printf("%20s", "Enter integer:");
                scanf("%d", &x);
                printf("\n\n");
                extract( x );
                printf("\n\n");
                drawline();
                printf("\n\n");
                }


        }
RUN C411

    Enter integer:8

                    0 0 0 0 0 0 0 0 0 0 0 0 1 0 0 0

------------------------------------------------------------------------

    Enter integer:7

                    0 0 0 0 0 0 0 0 0 0 0 0 0 1 1 1

------------------------------------------------------------------------

    Enter integer:32767

                    0 1 1 1 1 1 1 1 1 1 1 1 1 1 1 1

------------------------------------------------------------------------

    Enter integer:32768

                    1 0 0 0 0 0 0 0 0 0 0 0 0 0 0 0

------------------------------------------------------------------------

    Enter integer:^C
```

Figure 4.11   *concluded*

4.7.2 Refinement: Printing a PDP-11 or IBM-370 Bit String

On an IBM 360/370 computer system, bit strings are read from left to right. That is, bit zero is the *leftmost* bit of an IBM 360/370 bit string. The program in Figure

144 Types and operators   CHAPTER 4

4.11 can be improved by giving the option of printing a bit string in IBM or PDP-11/VAX-11 format. This can be done with a switch statement inside the extract() function. Printing out a bit string with bit zero is actually easier than it may sound. Why? Printing *normally* starts on the left end of an output line. This refinement is left as an exercise.

4.7.3 Refinement: Returning a Value from Extract()

The extract() function in Figure 4.10 can be simplified by eliminating its use of the printf() function and by returning a value (the bit that has been stripped off the *expr* variable). This can be done as follows:

```
extract (expr, mask)
int expr, mask;
    {
    if (expr & mask)
        return(1);
    else
        return(0);
    }
```

The changes to the mask can be done outside this function. It will also ''shift'' to another function the problem of determining whether a PDP-11/VAX-11 or IBM 360/370 format is required by the user. This refinement is also left as an exercise.

4.7.4 Another Use of the Shift-Left Operator

The shift-left operator ($<<$) produces the same result we would obtain if we multiplied an expression by 2. For example,

$$((mask <<1) <<1) <<1$$

is the same as

$$mask * 8$$

or

$$mask * 2 * 2 * 2$$

Why bother with shift operators? It takes less time to execute a shift left. A times operation (*) can take three times as long as a shift-left operation for the processor to execute.

Using a shift-left operation, we can rewrite the power() function in Figure 4.7. We show how to do this in Figure 4.12.

CHAPTER 4   4.7 Bitwise operators   145

```
#include "newlib.h"                    /*see Figure 4.4*/

long powers_of2( n )
int n;
        {
        static long p = 1;

        p = p << 1;
        return( p );
        }


printheading()
        {
        printf("\n\n %40s \n\n", "Powers of 2");
        printf("%20s %5s %15s \n\n", "2^n", "n", "2^(-n)");
        drawline();
        printf("\n\n");
        }

main()
        {
        long x;
        double y;
        int j;

        printheading();
        for (j = 0;j <= 20; ++j)
                {
                x = powers_of2( j );
                y = 1.0 / (double)x;
                printf("%20ld %5d %5s %.20f \n", x, j, " ", y);
                }
        }


RUN C412

                        Powers of 2

            2^n      n          2^(-n)

-----------------------------------------------------------------

               2     0     0.50000000000000000000
               4     1     0.25000000000000000000
               8     2     0.12500000000000000000
              16     3     0.06250000000000000000
              32     4     0.03125000000000000000
              64     5     0.01562500000000000000
             128     6     0.00781250000000000000
             256     7     0.00390625000000000000
```

Figure 4.12 Computing Powers of 2 with $<<$

146 Types and operators

CHAPTER 4

```
    512     8     0.00195312500000000000
   1024     9     0.00097656250000000000
   2048    10     0.00048828125000000000
   4096    11     0.00024414062500000000
   8192    12     0.00012207031250000000
  16384    13     0.00006103515625000000
  32768    14     0.00003051757812500000
  65536    15     0.00001525878906250000
 131072    16     0.00000762939453125000
 262144    17     0.00000381469726562500
 524288    18     0.00000190734863281250
1048576    19     0.00000095367431640625
2097152    20     0.00000047683715820313
```

Figure 4.12 *concluded*

4.7.5 Shift-Right Operator

The shift-right operator does not necessarily perform the inverse of the shift-left operation. By rights, a statement like

$$x = expr >> 1;$$

should produce the same result as the following:

$$x = expr / 2;$$

The implementation of the shift-right operator ($>>$) may vary, depending on the system used by C. We illustrate the use of this operator in a program in Figure 4.13. The sample run was obtained on a PDP-11/70. The PDP-11 is a 16-bit machine. With signed numbers, bit 15 is used to determine the sign of an integer. For example, for a variable of type int, the following value

$$0\ 100\ 000\ 000\ 000\ 000\ (\text{base 2})$$

equals 16,384 (decimal) or 2^{14}, whereas

$$1\ 000\ 000\ 000\ 000\ 000\ (\text{base 2})$$

equals -32,768. This explains the result in the first row of the table printed in Figure 4.13. If we let x be a variable of type int and set x equal to 16,384, a shift left produces a negative number on a PDP-11. On a wonderful 32-bit system like a VAX-11, we can shift left a variable of type int with the value

$$7\text{ffffffff (hex)} = 2,187,483,647 = 2^{31} - 1$$

to produce a negative number. Which number?

CHAPTER 4   **4.7 Bitwise operators   147**

The second row of the table in Figure 4.13 illustrates the use of the shift-left operator << with an unsigned expression. The remaining rows of this table illustrate the use of the shift-right operator >>.

```
#include "newlib.h"

shift_no()
        {
        int y = 16384, a = 8;
        unsigned x = 16384, b = 8;

        printf("%40s", "Use of shift operators");
        printf("\n\n %20s %10s %20s", "operand", "shift", "decimal");
        printf("%10s %10s", "octal", "hex");
        printf("\n\n");
        drawline();
        printf("\n\n");
        printf("%20s %10s", "(int)16384", "op << 1");
        printf("%20d %10o %10x", y << 1, y << 1, y << 1);
        printf("\n\n");
        printf("%20s %10s", "(unsigned)16384", "op << 1");
        printf("%20u %10o %10x", x << 1, x << 1, x << 1);
        printf("\n\n");
        printf("%20s %10s", "(int)8", "op >> 1");
        printf("%20d %10o %10x", a >> 1, a >> 1, a >> 1);
        printf("\n\n");
        printf("%20s %10s", "(unsigned)8","op >> 1");
        printf("%20u %10o %10x", b >> 1, b >> 1, b >> 1);
        }

main()
        {
            shift_no();
        }


RUN C413

            Use of shift operators

        operand        shift            decimal     octal       hex

    --------------------------------------------------------------------

            (int)16384     op << 1        -32768      100000      8000

        (unsigned)16384    op << 1         32768      100000      8000

               (int)8      op >> 1             4           4         4

           (unsigned)8     op >> 1             4           4         4
```

Figure 4.13   Shift Operators

148   Types and operators   CHAPTER 4

4.7.6 Refinement: Generalized Shift-no() Function

We can improve the shift_no() function in Figure 4.13 by establishing a formal parameter list for this function. We should let the user call this function with an expression and then use the function merely to return the bits of the expression either shifted left or right, depending on the value of a choice variable included in the function parameter list. Then the function heading for shift_no() will have the following form:

$$shift\_no(expr, choice)$$
$$int\ expr,\ choice;$$

This refinement is left as an exercise.

4.8 COMPRESSION OF ASSIGNMENT STATEMENTS

In **C** it is possible to compress an assignment statement. With notable exceptions, the statement

$$expression_1\ =\ expression_1\ op\ expression_2$$

is the same as

$$expression_1\ op\ =\ expression_2$$

For example,

$$mask\ <<\ =\ 1$$

can be used instead of the following statement used in the extract() function in Figure 4.10.

$$mask\ =\ mask\ <<\ 1$$

Again, for example, we can use the following compressions of assignment statements:

$$x\ =\ x\ +\ 10 \qquad \text{is the same as } x\ +\ =\ 10;$$
$$x\ =\ x\ *\ (a+2) \qquad \text{is the same as } x\ *\ =\ (a+2);$$
$$x\ =\ x\ \%\ 2001 \qquad \text{is the same as } x\ \%\ =\ 2001;$$

Table 4.6 summarizes the various forms of op= available in **C**.

4.8.1 Nested Assignments

In **C** it is possible to nest assignment statements within a single statement. Doing

CHAPTER 4   **4.8 Compression of assignment statements**   **149**

TABLE 4.6   Op= Forms in C

Assignment	*Compressed Form*
x = expression	None
x = x + expression	x += expression
x = x - expression	x -= expression
x = x * expression	x *= expression
x = x / expression	x /= expression
x = x % expression	x %= expression
x = x >> expression	x >>= expression
x = x & expression	x &= expression
x = x ^ expression	x ^ = expression
x = x | expression	x |= expression

this requires a complete mastery of the precedence of operators used in C. For example, we write the following statement:

$$+ + x = + + x * 5$$

In this statement, the $+ +$ operator has the highest precedence. The $+ +$ operator is also right associative. The $+ +$ operator on the right gets evaluated first; then the $+ +$ operator on the left gets evaluated. Then the times operation (*) is carried out. Finally, the result is assigned to x. So we can make an invariant assertion about the preceding statement. That is, the statement

$$+ + x = + + x * 5$$

produces the same result as

$$x = (+ + (+ + x)) * 5$$

However, the statement

$$+ + x = + + x * 5$$

is not the same as

$$+ + x * = 5$$

In Figure 4.14, we show a program that will allow us to test our invariant assertion.

4.8.2 Refinement: Another Invariant Assertion

An *invariant assertion* is a claim about something (in a program). We should make a claim about the following statement:

150   Types and operators   CHAPTER 4

$$++x * = 5;$$

How can we do this? The output from the program in Figure 4.14 hints at what
C does with this statement. However, this statement should be analyzed using the
precedence levels for the operators shown in Table 4.7. The determination of an
invariant assertion for the preceding statement is left as an exercise.

```
#include "newlib.h"

/*invariant assertion:                                                      */
/*
        */
/*      ++x = ++x * 5 will always equal x = (++(++x)) * 5
        */
/*
        */
compression(operand)
int operand;
        {
        int x, copy;

        x = operand;
        copy = operand;
        ++x = ++x * 5;
        ++copy *= 5;

        printf("\n\n %20s %20d", "++x = ++x * 5", x);

        x = operand;
        x = (++(++x)) * 5;
        printf("\n\n %30s %20d", "(++(++x)) * 5 gives", x);
        printf("\n\n whereas");
        printf("\n\n %20s %20d", "++x *= 5 gives", copy);
        }

main()
        {
        int entry;

        for (1)
                {
                printf("\n\n %20s", "Enter integer: ");
                scanf("%d", &entry);
                compression(entry);
                printf("\n\n");
                drawline();
                }
        }
```

Figure 4.14 Compressed Assignments

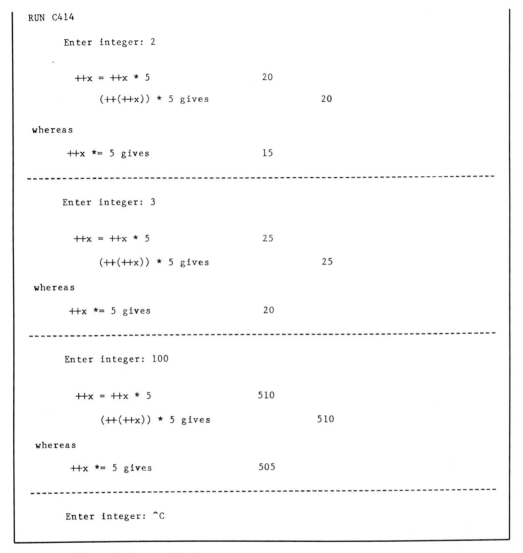

Figure 4.14 *concluded*

4.9 SUMMARY

There are four fundamental data types in C: *char, int, float,* and *double.* There is flexibility in the use of these types, thanks to the use of qualifiers *(short, long* and *unsigned)* and casts. An experienced C programmer can use these qualifiers to expand *and* shrink the amount of storage used by variables in a C program.

152 Types and operators   CHAPTER 4

TABLE 4.7 Operator Precedence Levels

Level	Operators	Associativity
1	() []	Left to right
2	! + + -- - (unary)	Right to left
	& (address)	
3 (arithmetic)	* / %	Left to right
4 (arithmetic)	+ - (subtraction)	Left to right
5	<< (shift left)	Left to right
	>> (shift right)	
6 (inequalities)	< <=	Left to right
	> >=	
7	== (equal) != (not equal)	Left to right
8 (bit op)	& (and)	Left to right
9 (bit op)	^ (not)	Left to right
10 (bit op)		(or)	Left to right
11	&& (logical and)	Left to right
12	|| (logical or)	Left to right
13	= (assigns) + = -= *=	Right to left
	/= %= >>= <<= &=	
	^= |=	

There are also a medley of operators available in C. The majority of these operators have been presented in this chapter. Most of the C operators are given in Table 4.6, with an indication of two things about *each* operator:

1. Precedence level of an operator.
2. Associativity of each operator.

In a C statement with a mixture of operators, the evaluation of a statement starts with the operator(s) with the highest precedence. Either round or square brackets have the highest precedence. An expression inside parentheses will be evaluated first. If expressions are nested inside parentheses, then the innermost expression gets evaluated first. After the question of precedence, comes the question of the direction to scan an expression with operators with the *same* precedence. This is the associativity question.

For example, parentheses are left associative. An expression with more than one set of parentheses will be scanned from left to right. The + + operator is right associative. When this operator is used more than once in the same expression, the

CHAPTER 4   **Review terms and symbols   153**

expression is evaluated from right to left. It takes practice to become skillful in judging how a statement in C will be evaluated, in knowing which parts of an expression will get executed first. Precedence level and associativity determine the order in which the parts of an expression will be evaluated.

REVIEW TERMS AND SYMBOLS

Term	*Meaning*
Bitwise operator	& (and), ˆ (exclusive OR),	(inclusive OR)
Boolean operator	&& (and), || (or), ! (not)
byte row	contiguous bytes used to store characters
cast	coerce C to convert one type to another
char	ASCII or EBCDIC character/code
character constant	character surrounded by single quotes
characteristic	exponent of floating-point number
fixed-point number	(whole part) . (fraction part)
floating-point number	$m \cdot b^c$
fundamental data types	char, int, float, double
IBM 360/370 bit string	lsb (bit 0) is leftmost bit
l (''ell'')	qualifier for *d, o, x,* or *u* conversion characters used with arguments of type long
long	extended precision integer
lsb	least significant bit
mask	number with target bits set/unset used to extract bits of an operand
o	*o*ctal conversion character
operator	see Table 4.6
operator associativity	direction to start evaluating expression with more than one operator with the same precedence
operator precedence	determines order of evaluation of an expression with more than one operator (priority, succession used to evaluate an expression)
PDP-11/VAX-11 bit string	lsb (bit zero) is rightmost bit
pointer	address
shift-left operator	multiply by 2 operator
shift-right operator	divide by 2 operator
short	less storage for a type int variable on *some* systems (cf. VAX-11)
string constant	characters surrounded by double quotes
u	*u*nsigned conversion character
unsigned	natural numbers plus zero
whitespace	cursor control characters
x	he*x* conversion character

154   Types and operators   CHAPTER 4

EXERCISES

1. What is the difference between a variable x with type unsigned short and a variable y with type unsigned long?
2. If x is a floating-point number with no fractional part, what format would be used to print out x without zeros after the decimal point?
3. Is it possible to print the integer 233 using a floating-point format? If so, give the printf() statement to use to do this.
4. Is it possible to print the floating-point number 2.718281828 as an integer? If so, give the printf() statement to use to do this.
5. Assume x is a variable of type long with nine digits. Give the printf() statement to use to print x in the following cases:
   a. x displayed as a base 10 integer
   b. x displayed in octal
   c. x displayed in hex
   d. $x * 2$ in octal
   e. 5.0 divided by x
   f. Reciprocal of x
6. Show how the shift-left/right operators can be used to rewrite the following expressions:
   a. x *= 16
   b. x = x * 20 + 1
   c. x /= 16
   d. x /= 20
   e. x = (x*4) + (x/2)

7. In **C**, what is the meaning of *to cast*?
8. Show how to cast (and, if necessary, rewrite) the following expressions to obtain the result indicated in parentheses:
   a. 92 + 'a'   (to obtain an integer)
   b. "Aha!" pointed to by x (to obtain a sum that is type short)
   c. (2.7 / 1984) * 2   (to obtain a type double result)
   d. x * y   (to obtain a result of type long when x is of type short, y of type int)
   e. ++x/33.0   (to obtain a double result when x is type int)
9. Give equivalent **C** statements for the following assignments:
   a. ++x *= 5;
   b. y = (++ (++ (++y))) * 2;
   c. a %= ++a;
   d. x + = (--(++x));

   e. x = x * 25 + 2;
   f. x = x * (x * 5));

10. In Exercise 9, you made six invariant assertions! Write a function assert() with a formal parameter list that can be used for text values for your assertions. Put each of the

CHAPTER 4   Exercises   155

original statements and your assertions into assert(). Then write a C program to test your assertions.

11. Write a program to print the printable characters on your system forward and backward.

12. Write a function code_sum() to compute the sum of the character codes between two given characters. Let the user enter the beginning and ending characters to initialize two character constants x and y. Write a program to test code_sum() using the following entries:

   a. '!' to 'z'
   b. '0' to '9'
   c. '9' to '9'
   d. 'a' to 'z'
   e. 'A' to 'Z'

13. Write a function select_char() to select and print characters between two given characters. Let the user enter the beginning and ending characters for the subinterval of your system character table to be printed. Write a C program to test select_char() using the entries of parts a through e in Exercise 12.

14. Write a function and() to extract the bits of an operand after it has been operated on by the bitwise & operator using a mask supplied by the user. Allow the user to call this function with a number and a mask. Make and() return a number that results from the operand & mask operation. Write a program to print out the user-supplied operand as a binary number.

15. Refine the program in Exercise 14 so that the user can specify any of the following formats for the value returned by the and() function:

   a. Binary
   b. Octal
   c. Hex
   d. Binary and octal
   e. Binary and hex
   f. Binary, octal, and hex

16. Write a function super_sum() that computes the sum of the codes used for the characters of two strings supplied by the user. Write a program to test super_sum() using the following string constants:

   a. "Aha!" and "Ada!"
   b. "Oh!" and "C!"
   c. "tumty-tum" and "Tumty-tum-toes!"

17. What is printed by the following statements?

   a. puts("\\\\\\\\");
   b. printf("\loc", \007\);
   c. printf("\n\n\b\b\b");
   d. printf("\t\t\t %10s", "Yes!");

18. How many bytes are used to store the string constants in the following declarations?

   a. char *x = "A way a lone a long . . .";
   b. char * y = "Tumty-tumty-tum-toes!";

19. What are the whitespaces used by C?

156 **Types and operators** CHAPTER 4

20. Carry out the refinement of the program in Figure 4.3 described in Section 4.3.6. Give a sample run.
21. Carry out the refinement of the program in Figure 4.7 described in Section 4.4.4. You may need to decrease the upper bound of the loop to accommodate larger bases. Give a sample run.
22. Carry out the refinement of the program in Exercise 21 described in Section 4.4.5. Give a sample run.
23. Carry out the refinement of the program in Figure 4.8 described in Section 4.4.7. Give a sample run.
24. Show the result of using the %lf format in the program in Figure 4.9. Give a sample run.
25. Carry out the refinement of the program in Figure 4.11 described in Section 4.7.1.
26. Carry out the refinement of the program in Exercise 25 as described in Section 4.7.2. Give a sample run.
27. Carry out the refinement of the program in Exercise 26 as described in Section 4.7.3. Give a sample run.
28. Carry out the refinement of the program in Figure 4.13 described in Section 4.7.6. Give a sample run.

LAB PROJECTS

1. Write a program to encode a message using the following technique:
   a. Enter message (allow up to 512 characters).
   b. Use a function compress() to remove the spaces from the entered string constant.
   c. Print out the ASCII codes for the message in groups of 10 separated by two spaces.
      Give a sample run, using the strings in Exercises 18a and 18b as messages to encode.
2. Write a function decode() that accepts character codes and prints out the corresponding characters. Use decode() to print out the plain text for the enciphered text produced by the program in Lab Project 1.

SELECTED SOLUTIONS

Exercise 10

```
#include "lib.h"
int xbuf = 0,ybuf = 0,abuf = 0;

assert()
        {
        int x,y,a;

        x = xbuf;
        ++x *= 5;
        printf("%s %d\n", "++x *= 5 gives: ", x);
        x = xbuf;
        x = ++x * 5;
```

Exercise 10 *concluded*

```
        printf("%s %d\n", "x = ++x * 5 gives: ", x);
        y = ybuf;
        y = (++(++(++y))) * 2;
        printf("%s %d\n", "y = (++(++(++y))) * 2 gives: ", y);
        y = ybuf;
        ++(++(++y)) *= 2;
        printf("%s %d\n", "++(++(++y)) *=2 gives: ", y);
        a = abuf;
        a %= ++a;
        printf("%s %d\n", "a %= ++a gives: ", a);
        a = abuf;
        a = a % ++a;
        printf("%s %d\n", "a = a % ++a gives: ", a);
        x = xbuf;
        x += (--(++x));
        printf("%s %d\n", "x += (--(++x)) gives: ", x);
        x = xbuf;
        x = x + (--(++x));
        printf("%s %d\n", "x = x + (--(++x)) gives: ", x);
        x = xbuf;
        x = x * 25 + 2;
        printf("%s %d\n", "x = x * 25 + 2 gives: ", x);
        x = xbuf;
        x = (x *= 25) + 2;
        printf("%s %d\n", "x = (x *=25) + 2 gives: ", x);
        x = xbuf;
        x = x * (x * 5);
        printf("%s %d\n", "x = x * (x * 5) gives: ", x);
        x = xbuf;
        x *= (x * 5);
        printf("%s %d\n", "x *= (x * 5) gives:", x);
        }

main()
        {
        printf("Enter values.  x,y,a -:> ");
        scanf("%d,%d,%d", &xbuf, &ybuf, &abuf);
        printf("\n");
        assert();
        }

RUN CE410

Enter values.  x,y,a -:> 2 4 3

++x *= 5 gives:  15
x = ++x * 5 gives:  15
y = (++(++(++y))) * 2 gives:  6
++(++(++y)) *=2 gives:  6
a %= ++a gives:  0
a = a % ++a gives:  0
x += (--(++x)) gives:  4
x = x + (--(++x)) gives:  4
x = x * 25 + 2 gives:  52
x = (x *=25) + 2 gives:  52
x = x * (x * 5) gives:  20
x *= (x * 5) gives:  20
```

Exercise 13

```
#include "lib.h"

select_char(low,up)
char low, up;
        {
        char a;

        for (a = low;a <= up;++a)
          printf("%c", a);
        printf("\n");
        }

main()
        {
        char c[20];

        for (1)
          {
          printf("\nEnter begining char, ending char-:> ");
          scanf("%s",c);
          printf("\nThe characters between are:\n");
          select_char(c[0],c[2]);
          /*skip the ´,´ and send the 1st and 3rd char. to code_sum()*/
          {
        }


RUN CE413

Enter begining char, ending char-:> !,z

The characters between are:
!"#$%&´()*+,-./0123456789:;<=>?@ABCDEFGHIJKLMNOPQRSTUVWXYZ[\]^_`abcdefghijklmno
pqrstuvwxyz

Enter begining char, ending char-:> 0,9

The characters between are:
0123456789

Enter begining char, ending char-:> 9,9

The characters between are:
9

Enter begining char, ending char-:> a,z

The characters between are:
abcdefghijklmnopqrstuvwxyz

Enter begining char, ending char-:> A,Z

The characters between are:
ABCDEFGHIJKLMNOPQRSTUVWXYZ


Enter begining char, ending char-:> ^C
```

CHAPTER 4   Selected solutions   159

Exercise 14

```
#include "lib.h"

and(no,mask)
int no,mask;

        {
        int a;

        a = no & mask;
        return (a);
        }

binary(x)
int x;

        {
        int a, mask = 1;

        printf("                    ");
        for (a = 0;mask != 0;++a)
          {
          if (a == 7)
            printf(" ");
          if (x & mask)
            printf("1\b\b");
          else
            printf("0\b\b");
          mask = mask << 1;
          }
        printf("\n");
        }

main()
        {
        int x,y;

        printf("\nEnter number,mask-:> ");
        scanf("%d,%d", &x, &y);
        printf("\n");
        printf("The & operation produces: ");
        binary(and(x,y));          /*print out the binary result of x & y */
        }


RUN CE414

Enter number,mask-:> 32767,233

The & operation produces:              1001011 100000000
```

160 Types and operators

CHAPTER 4

Exercise 20

```c
#include "lib.h"

length(string)
char string[80];
        {
        int count = 0;             /*used to count characters*/
        int i;

        for (i = 0;string[i] !=´´; ++i)
          count += 1;
        return(count);
        }

printchar(x,low,high)
char x[80];
int low,high;
        int i;

        printf("\n\n %20s", "string:");
        printf(" %s\n\n", x);
        drawline();
        printf("\n\n%20s", "substring: ");
        for (i = low;i <= high; ++i)
          printf("%c", x[i]);
        printf("\n\n");
        drawline();
        printf("\n\n\t %s", "separate characters of string:");
        printf("\n\n");
        printf("\n\n");
        for (i = 0; x[i] != ´\0´; ++i)
                {
                printf("\t\t x[ %ld ] = %5c", i, x[i]);
                printf("\n\n");
                }
        }

main()
        {
        char s[80];
        int low,high;               /*bounds on substring*/

        printf("\nEnter string-:> ");
        gets(s);
        printf("\nEnter bounds on substring.  low,high-:> ");
        scanf("%d,%d", &low, &high);
        printf("\n\n");
        printf("length= %d", length(s));
        printf("\n\n");
        printchar(s,low,high);

        }
```

CHAPTER 4   **Selected solutions   161**

Exercise 20   *concluded*

```
RUN CE420

Enter string-:> Hello world

Enter bounds on substring.  low,high-:> 1,5


length= 11



        string: Hello world
--------------------------------------------------------------------------


        substring: ello
--------------------------------------------------------------------------


    separate characters of string:


            x[ 0 ] =      H

            x[ 1 ] =      e

            x[ 2 ] =      l

            x[ 3 ] =      l

            x[ 4 ] =      o

            x[ 5 ] =

            x[ 6 ] =      w

            x[ 7 ] =      o

            x[ 8 ] =      r

            x[ 9 ] =      l

            x[ 10 ] =     d
```

162   Types and operators

CHAPTER 4

Exercise 21

```
#include "lib.h"

long power( b,n )
long b;
int n;
        {
        int i;
        long p = 1;

        for (i = 1; i <= n; ++i)
                p = p * b;
        return( p );
        }


printheading(bs)
long bs;
        {
        printf("\n\n %40s %ld\n\n", "Powers of", bs);
        printf("%20ld^n    n %15ld^(-n)\n", bs, bs);
        drawline();
        printf("\n\n");
        }

main()
        {
        long x,base;
        double y;
        int j;

        printf("Enter the base-:> ");
        scanf("%ld", &base);
        printf("\n\n\n");
        printheading(base);
        for (j = 0;j <= 15; ++j)
                {
                x = power( base, j );
                y = 1.0 / (double)x;
                printf("%20ld %5d %5s %.20f \n", x, j, " ", y);
                }
        }


RUN CE421

Enter the base-:> 4
```

CHAPTER 4

Exercise 21 *concluded*

```
                        Powers of 4

            4^n    n              4^(-n)
--------------------------------------------------------------------------

              1    0     1.00000000000000000000
              4    1     0.25000000000000000000
             16    2     0.06250000000000000000
             64    3     0.01562500000000000000
            256    4     0.00390625000000000000
           1024    5     0.00097656250000000000
           4096    6     0.00024414062500000000
          16384    7     0.00006103515625000000
          65536    8     0.00001525878906250000
         262144    9     0.00000381469726562500
        1048576   10     0.00000095367431640625
        4194304   11     0.00000023841857910156
       16777216   12     0.00000005960464477539
       67108864   13     0.00000001490116119385
      268435456   14     0.00000000372529029846
     1073741824   15     0.00000000093132257462
```

164   Types and operators

CHAPTER 4

Exercise 26

```c
#include "lib.h"

extract(expr,choice)
int exprm,choice;
            {
      int i;
      int mask;

      mask = 1;
      switch (choice)
        {
        case 1: /*PDP-11/VAX-11 format*/
          printf("%70s", " ");
          for (i = 0; mask != 0; ++i)
              {
              if (expr & mask)
                      printf("\b\b\b\b\b\b %2d", 1);
              else
                      printf("\b\b\b\b\b\b %2d", 0);
              mask = mask << 1;
              }
          printf("\n%67c", ^^^i);
          printf("\n%67s\n", "Bit Zero");
          break;
        case 2: /*IBM 36/370 format*/
          printf("%20s"," ");
          for (i = 0; mask != 0; ++i)
            {
            if ( expr & mask)
              printf(" 1");
            else
              printf(" 0");
            mask = mask << 1;
            }
          printf("\n%23s \n%23s", "^", "Bit Zero");
          break;
        }
      }
main()
      {
      int x,choice;

      for (1)
              {
              printf("%20s", "Enter integer:");
              scanf("%d", &x);
              printf("\n 1)PDP-11/VAX-11 or 2)IBM 360/370 format? (1/2)-:> ");
              scanf("%d", &choice);
              printf("\n\n");
              extract( x, choice );
              printf("\n\n");
              drawline();
```

CHAPTER 4   Selected solutions   165

Exercise 26   *concluded*

```
                    printf("\n\n");
                    }
          }
RUN CE426

     Enter integer:233

1)PDP-11/VAX-11 or 2)IBM 360/370 format? (1/2)-:> 1

                    0  0  0  0  0  0  0  0  1  1  1  0  1  0  0  1
                                                                ^
                                                    Bit Zero


------------------------------------------------------------------------

     Enter integer:233

1)PDP-11/VAX-11 or 2)IBM 360/370 format? (1/2)-:> 2

                    1  0  0  1  0  1  1  1  0  0  0  0  0  0  0  0
                    ^
                    Bit Zero

------------------------------------------------------------------------

     Enter integer:32767

1)PDP-11/VAX-11 or 2)IBM 360/370 format? (1/2)-:> 1

                    0  1  1  1  1  1  1  1  1  1  1  1  1  1  1  1
                                                                ^
                                                    Bit Zero


------------------------------------------------------------------------

     Enter integer:32767

1)PDP-11/VAX-11 or 2)IBM 360/370 format? (1/2)-:> 2

                    1  1  1  1  1  1  1  1  1  1  1  1  1  1  1  0
                    ^
                    Bit Zero

------------------------------------------------------------------------

     Enter integer:^C
```

166 Types and operators

CHAPTER 4

Lab Project I

```
#include " newlib.h"

print_text(script3)
   char script3[40];

      {
         int i;
         int j;
         int set = 1;
         int column = 1;
         char ch3[40];

         printf("\n\n %30s \n","Encoded text:");
         drawline();
         printf("\n");
         for (i = 0; script3[i] > ´\32´; ++i)
            {
               printf("%2d",(script3[i]));
               set = (i + 1) % 10;
               if (set == 0)
                  {
                     printf("%s","  ");
                     column = j % 2;
                     if (column == 0)
                        printf("\n\n");
                     ++j;
                  }
            }
      }


compress(script1,script2)
   char script1[80];
   char script2[80];

      {
         int j = 0;
         int i;
         char ch4[80];

         for (i = 0; script1[i] != ´\0´;++i)
            if ( script1[i] != ´\ ´)
               {
                  script2[j] = script1[i];
                  ++j;
               }

      }

build_string(script)
   char script[80];
      {
```

CHAPTER 4   **Selected solutions 167**

Lab Project 1   *concluded*

```
        int i;
        int j;

        printf("\n\nEnter string: using caps,completing the line with
    spaces:\n>");
                scanf("%80c",script);

        }

main ()

    {
        char text1[80];
        char text2[80];
        int letter;
        char ch[80];
        char ch2[80];
        int i;

        build_string(text1);

        compress(text1,text2);

        print_text(text2);

    }


RUN CL41

Enter string: using caps,completing the line with spaces:
>A WAY A LONE A LONG...



                Encoded text:
-----------------------------------------------------------------------
65876589657679786965  76797871464646


RUN CL41

Enter string: using caps,completing the line with spaces:
>TUMTY-TUMTY-TUM-TOES!



                Encoded text:
-----------------------------------------------------------------------
84857784894584857784  89458485774584796983

33
```

168 Types and operators

CHAPTER 4

RELATED READINGS

Boole, G., *Studies in Logic and Probability*. La Salle, Ill.: Open Court Publishing Co., 1952, pp. 9–49, for 1847 work.

Flanders, H., *Scientific Pascal*. Reston, Va.: Reston Publishing Co., 1984, Chapter 2.

5

Control Structures

A robust program is like a large, amiable dog—not easily ruffled, slow to take offense and difficult to divert from its chosen course. Unfortunately most programs tend to be like toy poodles—very finicky about their food, demanding only the very best and its tastiest tit-bits, very quick-tempered, easily upset and generally more trouble than they are worth.

A. R. Brown and W. A. Sampson*

AIMS

- Introduce the Canonical Control Structures of Structured Programming.
- Show the Use of the Boolean Operators to Construct Boolean Expression Used to Control the Selection of a Statement to Be Executed or the Number of Iterations of an Action.
- Introduce the Use of Random Number Generators.
- Show How to Begin Creating Form Letters.
- Suggest Approaches to Gries's Coffee Can Problem.
- Introduce a Chop() Function to Truncate the Fractional Part of a Floating-Point Number.

---

*Program Debugging, Elsevier North-Holland, Inc., New York, 1973, p. 35.

170   Control structures   CHAPTER 5

5.1 INTRODUCTION

A *control structure* is a programming facility that makes it possible to select, repeat, or perform conditionally actions specified by a program. A control structure
makes it possible to write robust programs that can deal with exceptions, programs
that are not so finicky. Three types of control structures are used in structured programming. These are shown in Table 5.1. They are known as the *canonical control structures* used in structured programming. Table 5.1 provides references to
our more recent uses of some of these structures. We take time in this chapter to
look more closely at how these structures can be used to control the execution of
a program.

   In this chapter, we make extensive use of the Boolean operators

$$\&\& \quad \textbf{(and)}$$
$$|| \quad \textbf{(or)}$$
$$! \quad \textbf{(not)}$$

to set up conditions to control execution of parts of a program. These conditions
make it possible to set up companion assertions that can be used to test the correctness of a program. The trick is to look for a basis for predicting output relative to
the Boolean conditions used in the control structures.

   There is one control structure in **C** that we avoid, the *goto*. A

$$\text{goto label}$$

is an unconditional branch to a section of a program identified by *label*. The use
of goto's contribute to the unreadability of a program. Dijkstra (1968) suggests
that the readability of a program is inversely proportional to the number of goto's
in a program. It is possible to use canonical control structures instead of goto's.
We encourage this approach to **C** programming.

TABLE 5.1   Control Structures

Type	Example(s)	Used in:
Sequential control	Any block	Figs. 4.8, 3.16
Selection control	If	Fig. 4.11
	Switch	Fig. 3.13
	Break	Fig. 3.13
Iteration control	For	Figs. 4.12, 4.11
	While	None
	Do	None

CHAPTER 5   **5.2 Sequential control   171**

To illustrate the uses of control structures, we introduce some new functions. Among these, we introduce the use of random-number generators to make "chance" selections of characters in a string. This will lead us to a program to pick coffee beans randomly from a pot. This is known as the coffee can problem, which was suggested by Gries (1981).

We also deal more with string handling in this chapter. We introduce the use of getchar(), a standard C function used to pull characters from an input stream. This function is useful, since it allows us to pick and choose the characters of a string we enter from a keyboard. We also introduce an insert_word() function useful in constructing texts like form letters.

5.2 SEQUENTIAL CONTROL

A sequential control structure is a sequence of zero or more statements bracketed by braces { }. This is what we have been calling a block or compound statement. This is the simplest structure used to control flow of execution within a program.

In C, each block can have its own local variables. In addition, blocks can be nested as follows:

```
{                                           /*outer block*/
int i, j;
      .
      .
      .
i = exp(j) + 5;
if (i % 2 = = 1)
      {                                     /*inner block*/
            .
            .
            .
      }
      .
      .
      .
}
```

In this fragment, execution of the statements in the inner block depends on the following Boolean condition:

$$i \% 2 = = 1$$

Why is this a Boolean condition? Its evaluation produces either a zero or a one as

172 Control structures   CHAPTER 5

its truth value. If i % 2 does have a remainder of 1, then the expression is true
and execution begins inside the inner block. Otherwise, the processor transfers
control around the inner block and continues its execution in the outer block. The
braces serve to mark the boundaries of the sequence of statements associated with
the Boolean condition of the if-statement.

5.3 SELECTION CONTROL STRUCTURES

The syntax diagram for an if-statement is shown in Figure 5.1. The else-part of
the if-statement is optional. Notice that an *else* is always immediately preceded by
a semicolon (;) provided that the if-statement is not a block. Also notice that the
statement following the *else* can be another if-statement. The Boolean expression
of an if-statement is used to *select* an action. How? The statement immediately
after the Boolean condition gets executed, if the Boolean expression is true. Otherwise, the else-statement gets executed.

For example, we can use an if-statement to determine what to do next based
on the temperature. We illustrate this idea in Figure 5.2, where the choice() function consists of a chain of if-statements, with various alternatives. In general, an
if-statement has the following structure:

$$\text{if expression}_1$$
$$\text{statement}_1;$$
$$\text{else}$$
$$\text{if expression}_2$$
$$\text{statement}_2;$$
$$\text{else}$$
$$\text{if expression}_3$$
$$\text{statement}_3;$$
$$.$$
$$.$$
$$.$$
$$\text{else}$$
$$\text{if expression}_k$$
$$\text{statement}_k;$$
$$\text{else}$$
$$\text{default statement};$$

The default statement

$$\text{printf(''check your thermometer!'');}$$

is executed if each of the preceding expressions produces a truth value of false. In

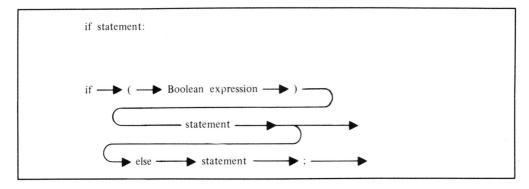

Figure 5.1 Syntax Diagram for the If-Statement

```
#include <std.h>
#include <stdio.h>

choice(temp)
int temp;
            {
            if (temp > 90)
                    printf("Try waterskiing!");
            else
                if ((temp > 75) && (temp < 85) && !(temp == 80))
                    printf("Aha! Try biking!");
                else
                    if ((temp >= 30) && (temp < 80))
                        printf("Try walking!");
                    else
                        if ((temp > 10) && (temp < 30))
                                printf("Try ice skating!");
                        else
                            if (((temp < 10) && (temp > -30)) || (temp == -3))
                                printf("Time to write C program........");
                            else
                                printf("Check your thermometer!");
            }

main()
            {
            int t,i;

            for (i = 0;i <= 6; ++i)
                        {
                        printf("%40s", "Enter temp as integer:");
                        scanf("%d", &t);
                        printf("\n\n");
                        choice(t);
                        printf("\n\n----------------------------------------\n\n");
                        }
            }
```

Figure 5.2 Selecting an Action with an If-Statement

174 Control structures   CHAPTER 5

```
RUN C52

                    Enter temp as integer:92

Try waterskiing!

-------------------------------------------

                    Enter temp as integer:80

Check your thermometer!

-------------------------------------------

                    Enter temp as integer:76

Aha! Try biking!

-------------------------------------------

                    Enter temp as integer:35

Try walking!

-------------------------------------------

                    Enter temp as integer:15

Try ice skating!

-------------------------------------------

                    Enter temp as integer:2

Time to write C program........

-------------------------------------------

                    Enter temp as integer:-45

Check your thermometer!

-------------------------------------------
```

Figure 5.2   *concluded*

CHAPTER 5   **5.3 Selection control structures 175**

the choice() function, statement₂ (it follows the first else) is the beginning of a
second if-statement.

In Figure 5.2, notice that the following condition is used in the second if-
statement:

$$\text{if ((temp} > 75) \;\&\&\; (\text{temp} < 85) \;\&\&\; !(\text{temp} == 80))$$

This is another way of saying (in English!) the following:

$$\text{if (temp} > 75)$$
$$\text{and (temp} < 85)$$
$$\text{and the temp is not } 80$$

If we enter temp $= 80$, the preceding condition results in a truth value of false
(or zero). This can be reasoned as follows:

Enter temp	*Expression*	*Truth value*
80	$x > 75$	1
80	$x < 85$	1
80	$!(x == 80)$	
	$= !(1)$	
	$= 0$	0

The $\&\&$ operator will always produce a value of false or zero if one of its operands (expressions) is false.

The Boolean operator $\|$ represents an *inclusive or*. It produces a truth value
of true (or 1) if at least one of its operands is true.

5.3.1 Nested If-Statements

In the construction

$$\text{if (expression)}$$
$$\text{statement}_1;$$
$$\text{else}$$
$$\text{statement}_2$$

it is possible for statement₁ also to be an if-statement. For example, we can construct the following statement:

```
if (code == 007)
  if (weight > 175)
    if (character == '!')
      printf("send the message.")
    else
      scanf("%d %d %c", &code, &weight, &character);
```

176 Control structures CHAPTER 5

This nests if-statements three deep. What about the else? Which if-statement does it belong to? The else belongs to the innermost if-statement, not the first or second if-statement in this example. In general, the else always belongs to the nearest if-statement. This gives rise to the pit stop of selection control structures:

```
* * * * * * * * * * * * * * * * * *
*                                 *
* Pit stop of selection control: Each else  *
* belongs to the nearest if        *
*                                 *
* * * * * * * * * * * * * * * * * *
```

We can also make the following assertion about the preceding if-statement:

```
if ((code = = 007) && (weight > 175) && (character = = '!'))
    printf("send the message.")
else
        scanf("%d %d %c", &code, &weight, &character);
```

This assertion is false. Why? Verifying this is left as an exercise.

5.3.2 Switch Statement

The *switch* statement offers a way to simplify certain if/else statements. Its syntax diagram is shown in Figure 5.3. For example, we can have the following switch statement:

```
int C ;
        .
        .
        .
switch (C) {
    case 'A' : case 'a' :
            + +c;
        .   break;
    case 'b':
    case 'c':
    case 'd':
    case 'e':
            break;
    case 5 : case 233 :
            printf("Eureka!");
            break;
```

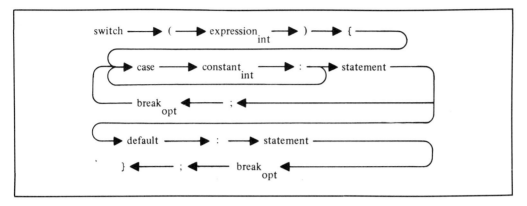

Figure 5.3 Syntax Diagram for the Switch Statement

```
                case 'm':
                case 25 :
                case '2' :
                        printf("Oh oh . . ."); break;
                default:
                        printf("Try again.");
                        break;
        }
```

C will coerce the case constant to be an integer. For example, '2' will be coerced to its corresponding character code [*example:* 32 (hex) in the ASCII table]. This is not the same case as

case 2 :

which tests for the integer 2.

Notice that switch statements can be nested. How? Use, for example, the following construction:

```
                case 'e' :
                        switch (ch) {
                                case 1 :
                                case '1' :
                                case '{' :
                                        break;
                                case '}' :
```

178 Control structures   **CHAPTER 5**

```
                        printf("Aha!");
                        break;
            default :
                        printf("default reached.");
                        break;
        }
        break;
case 5 : case 233 :

                .

                .

                .
```

The *break* statement prompts the processor to exit from the switch statement. Without this statement, the processor would continue executing the switch statement cases. (This may be desirable.) The break statement is optional. It is used to terminate processing within a switch statement. This statement can also be used to exit from *for, while,* and *do* loops.

The counterpart of a break is a *continue* statement. It is used inside a loop to terminate the current iteration and begin the next. For example, we use the following construction:

```
for (i = 0; scanf("%d", &c); + + i)
    switch (c) {
        case 'a' :
        case 'A' : continue;
        case 5 :   break;
        case '5' :
                    switch (i) {
                        case 9 : continue;
                        case 120 : break;
                    }
    }
```

In both cases, the continue statement will cause processing within the for-loop to continue after i and c have been given new values. Testing the use of the *continue* in a statement like this is left as an exercise.

5.4 ITERATION CONTROL STRUCTURES

A statement can be iterated (repeated, put inside a loop) using a *for* or *while* or *do* statement. We have already made extensive use of the *for*-loop. We can set up the equivalent of a *while*-loop using the following construction with a for-loop:

For-loop	Equivalent while-loop

i = 0;
for (i <= max) {
.
.
.
++i;
}
	i = 0;
	while (i <= max) {
	.
	.
	.
	++i;
	}

In other words, the value of *i* gets incremented somewhere inside both loops. Processing of the for-loop continues *while* the expression

$$i <= max$$

remains true. We look, next, at how this same construction can be written explicitly as a while-loop.

5.4.1 While Statement

The syntax diagram for a while-loop is given in Figure 5.4. We illustrate the use of a while-loop in an atou() function, which converts lowercase letters to uppercase. The atou() function is given in Figure 5.5. For example, if

$$s\ [0] = 't'$$

its corresponding ASCII code (in decimal) is 116. The bias variable is evaluated as follows:

$$\begin{aligned} bias &= 'A' - 'a' \\ &= 65 - 97 \\ &= -32 \end{aligned}$$

Then

$$\begin{aligned} s\ [0] &= 't' + bias \\ &= 116 - 32 \\ &= 84\ (\text{ASCII code for 'T'}) \end{aligned}$$

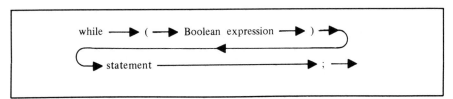

Figure 5.4 Syntax Diagram for the While Statement

180 Control structures

CHAPTER 5

```
atou(s)

char *s;

    {

    int bias, i = 0;

    bias = ´A´ - ´a´;

    while ((s[i] != ´\0´)

            && (s[i] >= ´a´)

                && (s[i] <= ´z´))

        {

        s[i] = s[i] + bias;

        ++i;

        }

    }
```

Figure 5.5 Atou() Function

The Boolean expression

$$(s[i] \ != \ '\backslash 0')$$
$$\&\& \ (s[i] >= 'a')$$
$$\&\& \ (s[i] <= 'z')$$

checks three expressions:

1. End of string, if s[i] = '\0'
2. s[i] >= 'a'
3. s[i] <= 'z'

Before the statement of the atou() while-loop to be executed, it is necessary for all three of these expressions to be true. The index i on s[i] is incremented inside the while-loop.

We show a program to illustrate the use of the atou() function in Figure 5.6.

CHAPTER 5   **5.4 Iteration control structures**

```
#include <std.h>
#include <stdio.h>

atou(s)
char *s;
        {
        int bias, i = 0;

        bias = ´A´ - ´a´;
        while ((s[i] != ´\0´) && (s[i] >= ´a´) && (s[i] <= ´z´)) {
                s[i] = s[i] + bias;
                ++i;
                }
        }

main()
        {
        char *target;
        int yes = 1;

        while (yes == 1) {
                printf("Enter string in lower case:");
                scanf("%s", target);
                atou(target);
                printf("\n\n %30s %20s", "new word:", target);
                printf("\n\n %40s", "Do you wish to continue--1=Y,0=N:");
                scanf("%d", &yes);
                printf("\n\n -------------------------------- \n\n");
                }
        }

RUN C56

Enter word in lower case:tumty!


                      new word:                TUMTY!

        Do you wish to continue--1=Y,0=N:1


-----------------------------------

Enter word in lower case:tumty!-ti-tumty!-tum-tumtoes!


                      new word: TUMTY!-ti-tumty!-tum-tumtoes!

        Do you wish to continue--1=Y,0=N:0


-----------------------------------
```

Figure 5.6   Program to Convert to Uppercase

182 Control structures

CHAPTER 5

5.4.2 Refinement: Allowing for Other Characters

The sample run in Figure 5.6 demonstrates a weakness in the atou() function. It stops when it encounters a nonlowercase character that is not a '\0' to mark the end of the string. This can be remedied by using only the first of the three expressions,

$$s[i] \; ! = \; '\backslash 0'$$

to control the while-loop. The remaining two expressions can be made part of an if-statement to determine when to convert a character to lowercase. This refinement is left as an exercise.

5.4.3 Nested While-Loops

While-loops can be nested. We illustrate this idea by setting up a prefix() function, which will be used to determine all possible three-letter prefixes of a word. We show this function in the program in Figure 5.7.

5.4.4 Refinement: Determining the Range of Prefixes

The program in Figure 5.7 should be modified to allow the user to specify a subinterval of

"abcdefghijklmnopqrstuvwxyz"

which can be used to construct prefixes. For example, the user should be able to specify all prefixes constructed using

"a e i o u"

This will mean expanding the argument list of prefix() to allow the user to pass to the function specifications of the subinterval to be used. This problem can be simplified by passing the address of the i-string constant in the function call.

This refinement is left as an exercise.

5.4.5 Refinement: Specifying the Target Word

The program in Figure 5.7 should allow the user to choose the target word used to attach prefixes. This means expanding the main() function. This refinement is left as an exercise.

5.4.6 Bug Clinic: The '\0' Sentinel

When the "%s" format is used in a printf() or scanf(), a '\0' is used by C to detect

```
#include <stdio.h>

prefix(s)
char *s;
      {
      char *i = "abcdefghijklmnopqrstuvwxyz";
      char *j, *k, *target;
      int count = 0;
      int a = 0, b = 0, c = 0;

      j = i; k = i;                        /*now j and k point to i string*/

      while (a <= 25) {
        while (b <= 25) {
          while (c <= 25) {
                target[0] = i[a]; target[1] = j[b]; target[2] = k[c];
                target[3] = '\0';
                printf("%s %c %s %s", target, '-', s, "  ");
                ++c;
                ++count;
                if (count % 5 == 0)
                        printf("\n\n");
          }
        c = 0;
        ++b;
        }
      b = 0;
      ++a;
      }

      }

main()
      {
      char *target = "music";

      prefix(target);
      }


RUN C57

aaa - music    aab - music    aac - music    aad - music    aae - music

aaf - music    aag - music    aah - music    aai - music    aaj - music

aak - music    aal - music    aam - music    aan - music    aao - music

aap - music    aaq - music    aar - music    aas - music    aat - music

aau - music    aav - music    aaw - music    aax - music    aay - music

aaz - music    aba - music    abb - music    abc - music    abd - music

abe - music    abf - music    abg - music    abh - music    abi - music

abj - music    abk - music    abl - music    abm - music    abn - music

abo - music    abp - music    abq - music    abr - music^C
```

Figure 5.7 Nested While-Loops

184 Control structures

CHAPTER 5

the end of a string. This explains the use of

$$target[3] \ = \ '\backslash 0';$$

in Figure 5.7, which allows us to use a printf() to print each prefix as a string.

5.4.7 Bug Clinic: Controlling the Output on a Line

The statement

$$\text{if ((count \% 5 = = 0) \&\& (count != 0))}$$
$$\text{printf(''\backslash n\backslash n'');}$$

inhibits printing on the next line while the count is not a multiple of 5. The use of this idea in Figure 5.7 is still imperfect. Why? It prints four entries on the first line and five entries on the remaining lines. This can be remedied by adjusting the initial value of count. This correction is left as an exercise.

5.4.8 Infinite While-Loops

The construction

$$\text{while (1)}$$
$$\text{statement;}$$

results in an infinite while-loop. This is equivalent to writing

$$\text{while (1 > 0)}$$
$$\text{statement;}$$

We illustrate this in terms of the use of a chop() function, which truncates the fraction part of a floating-point number, leaving an integer result. The chop() function given in Figure 5.8 illustrates the use of the assignment statement to perform a conversion. The statement

$$\text{trunk} \ = \ \text{x};$$

is equivalent to

$$\text{trunk} \ = \ \text{(int) x};$$

That is, the C compiler handles the conversion of the type *double* variable x to type *int*. It leaves the trunk variable with the integer part of x. For example, if

$$x \ = \ 2.71828$$

then

CHAPTER 5   **5.4 Iteration control structures** **185**

```
chop(x)

double x;

    {

    int trunk;

    trunk = x;              /*conversion to int*/

    return(trunk);

    }
```

Figure 5.8   Chop() Function

leaves
$$trunk = x$$
$$trunk\ equal\ to\ 2$$

We illustrate this idea in a program in Figure 5.9.

Some **C** compilers have a trunc() function in one of their companion libraries (stdio.h, for example). Apparently, this is not common. To avoid this, we have used chop() rather than trunc(), which will do the same thing. The chop() function is useful in constructing a random-number generator besides rand(), which is usually part of the standard **C** library. We show how to do this later.

5.4.9 Do-Loops

The syntax diagram for a do-loop is given in Figure 5.10. A do-loop in **C** is like a repeat loop in Pascal. It will always execute the do-loop statement at least once. Why? It checks the truth value of the Boolean expression after it has executed the loop statement. There is one important difference between a do in **C** and a repeat loop in Pascal. That is, execution of the do-loop will continue if the Boolean expression following the *do-while* is true. This distinguishes a **C** do-loop from a Pascal repeat loop, which only continues execution if the repeat-loop condition is false.

We illustrate the use of a do-loop in an insert_word() function in Figure 5.11. This function can be used to insert target words into a form letter. The *s* variable points to the location of the form letter. The target variable points to the location of the word to be inserted. This function relies on the use of an asterisk, '*', as a sentinel in the form letter. This signals a place to insert the target word. We use '!' as a sentinel to mark the end of the target word.

```
#include <std.h>
#include <stdio.h>

chop(x)
double x;
      {
      int trunk;

      trunk = x;
      return(trunk);
      }

main()
      {
      double a,y;
      double r;

      while (1) {
      printf("\n\n Enter a and y:    ");
      scanf("%f %f", &a, &y);
      printf("\n\n %10s %.5f", "a / y = ", (a / y));
      printf("\n\n %20s %5d", "trunc(a / y) = ", chop (a / y));
      r = a / y - chop( a / y);
      printf("\n\n %20s %.5f", "a/y - trunc(a/y) = ", r);
      }

      }

RUN C59

 Enter a and y:   610.0 377.0


   a / y =   1.61804

       trunc(a / y) =      1

   a/y - trunc(a/y) =  0.61804

 Enter a and y:   377.0 610.0


   a / y =   0.61803

       trunc(a / y) =      0

   a/y - trunc(a/y) =  0.61803

  Enter a and y:   28657.0 233.0

 a / y =   122.99142

       trunc(a / y) =    122

   a/y - trunc(a/y) =  0.99142

  Enter a and y:   ^C
```

Figure 5.9 Program to Print Truncated Floating-Point Numbers

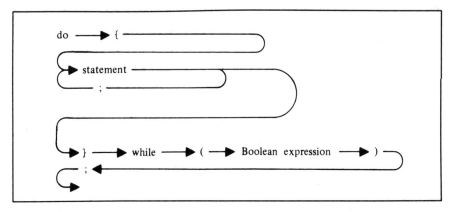

Figure 5.10 Syntax Diagram for a Do-Loop

```
insert_word(s, target)
char *s, *target;
    {
    int i = 0, j = 0;

    do
        if (s[i] == '*') {
            while (target[j] != '!') {
            s[i] = target[j];
            ++i;  ++j;
            }                       /*end while*/
        j = 0;
        }                           /*end if*/
    while (s[i++] != '!');
    }                               /*end insert_word()*/
```

Figure 5.11 Insert_word() Function

188 Control structures

CHAPTER 5

Notice how the Boolean expression

$$s[i++] \,!= \text{ '!'}$$

is used to control the execution of the do-loop. First i is incremented by 1. Then the truth of this expression is checked. If we have not reached the end of the s string, execution of this do-loop continues.

We show a program to illustrate the use of the insert_word() function in Figure 5.12.

5.4.10 Refinement: Adjusting Spaces in the Form Letter

The program in Figure 5.12 makes no provision for eliminating spaces not filled by the target word. This problem can be eliminated by doing the following things:

1. Determine the length of the target word using

$$x = \text{strlen (target)};$$

```
#include <std.h>
#include <stdio.h>

buildform(s)
char *s;
        {
        int i = 0;

        do
          {
          s[i] = getchar();
          ++i;
          }
        while (s[i-1] != '!');
        }


printcopy(s)
char *s;

        {
        int i=0;

        while (s[i] != '!')
          {
          printf("%c", s[i]);
          ++i;
          }
        }
```

543   **Figure 5.12** Program to Build a Form Letter

CHAPTER 5   **5.4 Iteration control structures**   189

```
                insert_word(s,target)
                char *s,*target;
                        {
                        int i = 0,j = 0;

                        do
                                if (s[i] == '*') {
                                        while (target[j] != '!') {
                                        s[i] = target[j];
                                        ++i; ++j;
                                        }
                                j = 0;
                                --i;                    /*move pointer back one char*/
                                }
                            while (s[i++] != '!');
                        }

                main()
                        {
                        char letter[212], word[10];

                        while (1) {
                        printf("\n\n %20s \n\n", "Enter text:");
                        buildform(letter);
                        printcopy(letter);
                        printf("\n\n %20s", "Enter word: ");
                        scanf("%s", word);
                        printf("\n\n");
                        insert_word(letter,word);
                        printf("\n\n");
                        printcopy(letter);
                        }
                }


    RUN F512

            Enter text:

        Tom went walking with *            . Of course, you
    know that *           is the riverman's daughter.!
            Tom went walking with *            . Of course, you
    know that *           is the riverman's daughter.

            Enter word: Goldberry!




    Tom went walking with Goldberry    . Of course, you
    know that Goldberry  is the riverman's daughter.

            Enter text:
```

Figure 5.12 *concluded*

190 Control structures   CHAPTER 5

2. Copy the *s* string to a copy string. When an asterisk (*) is encountered, only copy $x + 1$ spaces following the asterisk into the copy string.

The strlen() function is usually part of the standard **C** library. If it is not, then the strlen() function given in Figure 5.13 can be used. Then the copy string can be used to produce the form letter without the extra spaces. This refinement is left as an exercise.

5.4.11 Refinement: Allowing More Than One Target Word

The insert_word() function in Figure 5.12 is set up for one target. This can be changed by adding a provision for a second or third target to be inserted into a text. The following scheme can be used for three target words:

Sentinel	**target*
*	*target_1 = ''Goldberry''
**	*target_2 = ''Withywindle''
***	*target_3 = ''J.R.R. Tolkien''

For example, we can enter the following text:

> Tom went walking with *   on
> up the **   . This is from
> a story told by ***

This refinement of insert_word() is left as an exercise.

5.4.12 Bug Clinic: Choice of Sentinel

In the buildform() function in Figure 5.13, the following while-loop is used:

```
s[0] = getchar();
while (s[i] != '!') {
    ++i;
    s[i] = getchar();
}
s[i] = '!'; ++i; s[i] = '\0';
```

The getchar() is a standard **C** function that can be used to pull a single character from the input stream. This while-loop depends on the following Boolean expression:

$$s[i] \; != \; '!'$$

CHAPTER 5   **5.5 Application: random numbers   191**

```
                    strlen(s)

                char *s;

                    {

                int  i = 0;

                while (s[i] != ´\0´)

                        ++i;

                return(i);

                    }
```

Figure 5.13   Strlen() Function

Since the exclamation point is a commonly used character in texts, this does not make a good sentinel. A control x ('\30') would be a good choice for a sentinel. This refinement is left as an exercise.

5.5 APPLICATION: RANDOM NUMBERS

Events are *random* if they are equally likely. For example, the roll of a *perfectly* balanced die will produce random numbers in the range from 1 to 6. *Almost* random numbers can be produced by a computer in various ways. One of the best discussions of the methods that can be used to produce *almost* random numbers is given by Knuth (1981).

For example, most C compilers have an accompanying rand() function. It will produce integers in the range from 0 to the upper limit of type int. In Figure 5.14, we show a program to produce sample rand() values. This function will usually produce the *same* set of integers each time this program is run. Why? The rand() depends on the use of a seed, which is fixed. In a smart rand() function, it will be possible to vary the seed from a keyboard, or the system time will be used as the seed each time the program is run.

It is better not to depend on the built-in rand() function. Instead, we can construct random-number functions of our own. For example, we can use the rnd() function shown in Figure 5.15. For example, if we use

$$seed = 2.71828;$$

as the initial value of seed, then the numbers shown in Table 5.2 are produced.

192   Control structures   CHAPTER 5

```
#include <std.h>
#include "newlib.h"

samples(limit)
int limit;
        {
        int count = 0;

        while (count < limit) {
                printf("%d %s", rand(), "   ");
                ++count;
                if (count % 6 == 0)
                        printf("\n\n");
                }
        }

main()
        {
        int no;

        while (1) {
                printf("\n\n %30s", "No. of samples you wish:");
                scanf("%d", &no);
                printf("\n\n %50s \n\n", "Sample random numbers:");
                drawline();
                samples(no);
                }
        }

RUN C514

        No. of samples you wish:40


                            Sample random numbers:

------------------------------------------------------------------------
0     21468     9988     22117     3498     16927

16045     19741     12122     8410     12261     27052

5659     9758     21087     25875     32368     26233

15212     17661     20496     8191     23065     23471

32096     10781     14596     23212     24244     5661

514     25643     1350     19576     8051     18234

16882     13023     5983     21166

        No. of samples you wish:^C
```

Figure 5.14   How to Use the Rand() Function

CHAPTER 5   **5.5 Application: random numbers   193**

```
double rnd()

    {

    double sqr();

    seed = sqr(seed + 3.1415926535);

    seed = seed - chop(seed);

    return(seed);

    }
```

Figure 5.15   Rnd() Function

TABLE 5.2   Sample Rnd() Values

Seed	sqr(seed + 3.14159)	seed − chop(seed)
2.71828	34.33807642	0.338076420
0.33807642	12.10807839	0.10807839
0.10807839	10.56034464	0.56034464
0.56034464	13.70432008	0.70432008
0.70432008	14.79102434	0.79102434
0.79102434	15.46545555	0.46545555

Ideally, the seed variable should be of both storage classes external and static of type double. This will allow the seed variable to be used across function boundaries. It should also be possible for the user to initialize the value of seed. We can use the rnd() function to simulate the rolls of a die, for example, using the following expression:

$$chop(6 * rnd()) + 1$$

The fraction produced by rnd() is multiplied by 6, first. The expression

$$chop(6 * rnd())$$

then produces an integer in the range from 0 to 5. By adding 1 to this expression, we shift this range to the 1 to 6 interval. We show a program to implement this idea in Figure 5.16.

194 **Control structures** CHAPTER 5

```
static double seed = 0.0;
#include <math.h>
#include "newlib.h"

init(x)
double x;
      {
      seed = x;
      }

chop(x)
double x;
      {
      int trunk;

      trunk = x;                   /*assigns integer part of x to trunk*/
      return(trunk);
      }

double rnd()
      {
      double sqr();

      seed = sqr(seed + 3.1415927);
      seed = seed - chop(seed);
      return(seed);
      }
main()
      {

      printf("\n\n %50s \n\n", "Simulated rolls of a die:");
      drawline();
      printf("\n\n");
      init(2.71828);
      for (1)
            {
            printf("%5d", chop(6.0 * rnd()) + 1);
            }
      }



RUN C516

                        Simulated rolls of a die:

----------------------------------------------------------------------------

   3    1    4    5    6    2    1    1    2    6    6    4    6    1    2    6
   3    4    2    6    3    2    5    3    3    4    3    4    5    5    5    4
   4    3    5    1    5    4    6    1    3    1    6    1    6    1    6    3
   1    4    5    5    2    6    6    2    6    1    3    1    3    2    1    4
```

Figure 5.16 Program to Produce Random Numbers

CHAPTER 5

```
3   5   5   2   1   6   1   6   2   2   2   4   3   3   2   3
2   6   2   1   5   4   2   5   6   2   2   5   1   5   4   4
2   4   2   1   2   1   6   1   5   4   5   5   1   1   5   4
3   1   6   6   1   3   5   4   2   6   5   3   4   4   5   4
6   4   5   5   5   4   4   1   1   4   1   6   2   5   4   3
4   6   6   2   1   2   3   1   4   4   2   2   1   6   6   1
6   6   5   2   2   1   6   4   1   4   5   3   2   5   4   2
2   2   6   4   6   1   4   5   1   1   1   6   6   4   4   6
3   6   3   6   5   5   4   5   4   3   5   5   5   5   4   4
2   4   3   5   4   5   4   1   5   2   6   3   4   2   2   5
1   3   2   2   5   2   4   2   6   1   6   1   2   3   3   6
1   4   6   4   5   2   4   2   5   3   3   1   4   1   3   4
2   1   2   6   6   6   2   2   2   ^C
```

Figure 5.16 *concluded*

5.5.1 Refinement: Choosing the Upper and Lower Bounds

The program in Figure 5.16 can be improved by allowing the user to choose the upper and lower bounds of the random numbers produced. This can be done as follows:

$$no = chop ((max - min + 1) * rnd());$$
$$no = no + min;$$

Both *max* and *min* are of type int or long. Implementing this idea is left as an exercise.

5.5.2 The Gries Coffee Can Problem

Gries (1981) suggests the following problem:

We start with a coffee can containing some white and some black beans. In addition, we have a reserve supply of black beans not in the coffee can. Then randomly choose a pair of beans from the coffee can. If the pair are the same color, delete both beans and put a black bean back into the can. If the beans chosen are not the same color, then delete the black bean and replace the white bean.

We can simulate this idea by using a string of the form

"bbwwbwbbwwwwb"

where a lowercase *b* represents a black bean, a *w* a white bean. In Figure 5.17 we show a select() function to simulate the actions described by Gries.

196 Control structures   CHAPTER 5

```
        select(coffee_can,max)
char *coffee_can;
int max;
    {
    int  count, i, j;

    do {
    i = chop(max * rnd());
    j = chop(max * rnd());
    if (coffee_can[i] == coffee_can[j]) {
            coffee_can[i] = ´ ´;
            coffee_can[j] = ´b´;
            }
    else
            if (coffee_can[i] == ´w´)
                    coffee_can[j] = ´ ´;
            else
                    coffee_can[i] = ´ ´;
    count = 0;   i = 0;
    while (coffee_can[i] != ´\0´)
            if (coffee_can[i++] != ´ ´)
                    ++count;
    }
    while (count > 1);
    }
```

Figure 5.17 Select() Function

CHAPTER 5   **5.5 Application: random numbers   197**

5.5.3 Bug Clinic: A '=' is not the same as '= ='

Notice that a test of equality is handled in C using a double equal sign (= =). For example, the following if-statement checks if a bean is white:

```
if (coffee_can[i]  = =  'w')
    coffee_can[j]  = '  ';
else
    coffee_can[i]  = '  ';
```

The single equal sign (=) is used in C to make an assignment.

5.5.4 Simulating the Gries Coffee Can

In Figure 5.18, we show a program that brings together several of the functions presented so far. This program simulates the selection of pairs of beans from a coffee can. The use of *limit* in main() is crucial. Why? This variable is assigned the length of the input string using

$$limit = strlen(pot);$$

In effect, the *limit* variable gets the count of the initial number of beans in the can. Then

$$i = chop(max * rnd());$$
$$j = chop(max * rnd());$$

gets values of i and j in the interval

$$0 , . . ., max - 1$$

Notice that the limit variable supplies max with its value. Then i and j can be used to select characters in the coffee_can string.

5.5.5 Bug Clinic: Improving the Select() Function

The select() function in Figure 5.18 is imperfect. It does not accurately simulate the situation described by Gries. Why? First, although i and j are randomly selected, they can be equal. It is possible to pick up the same bean twice in one pick.

To avoid picking up the same bean twice in one pick, it will be necessary to guarantee that i and j are not equal. This can be done in a while-loop.

Second, it may happen that coffee_can[i] or coffee_can[j] is a space. It will be necessary to check whether a space has been ''picked.'' If a space has been picked, it will be necessary to go back to the coffee can to get a nonspace.

These two improvements of the select() function are left as an exercise.

198 Control structures

CHAPTER 5

```
static double seed=0.0;

#include <math.h>
#include "newlib.h"

/*------------------------------------------------------------------*/

init(x)
double x;
        {
        seed = x;
        }

/*------------------------------------------------------------------*/

chop(x)
double x;
        {
        int trunk;

        trunk = x;
        return(trunk);
        }

/*------------------------------------------------------------------*/

double rnd()
        {
        double sqr();

        seed = sqr(seed + 3.1415927);
        seed = seed - chop(seed);
        return(seed);
        }

/*------------------------------------------------------------------*/

select(coffee_can,max)
char *coffee_can;
int max;
        {
        int count, i, j;

        do {
                i = chop(max * rnd());
                j = chop(max * rnd());
                if (coffee_can[i] == coffee_can[j]) {
                        coffee_can[i] = ´ ´;
                        coffee_can[j] = ´b´;
                        }
                else
```

Figure 5.18 Gries's Coffee Can Problem

CHAPTER 5   **5.5 Application: random numbers   199**

```
                              if (coffee_can[i] == ´w´)
                                      coffee_can[j] = ´ ´;
                              else
                                      coffee_can[i] = ´ ´;

                count = 0; i = 0;
                while (coffee_can[i] != ´\0´)
                        if (coffee_can[i++] != ´ ´)
                                ++count;
                }
        while (count > 1);
        }

/*-------------------------------------------------------------------------*/

main()
        {
        char *pot;
        int limit;

        init(2.71828);
        for(1)
                {
                printf("\n\n %20s", "Enter beans (b/w): ");
                scanf("%s", pot);
                limit = strlen(pot);
                printf("\n\n");
                select(pot,limit);
                printf("\n\n");
                drawline();
                printf("\n\n %40s", "Bean left in coffee can:   ");
                printf("%s \n\n", pot);
                drawline();
                printf("\n\n");
                }
        }


RUN C518

  Enter beans (b/w): bbbbbw




----------------------------------------------------------------------------

              Bean left in coffee can:    b
```

Figure 5.18   *continued*

200 Control structures

CHAPTER 5

```
------------------------------------------------------------------

Enter beans (b/w): bwbwwbw




------------------------------------------------------------------

          Bean left in coffee can:     w
------------------------------------------------------------------


Enter beans (b/w): ^C
```

Figure 5.18 *concluded*

5.5.6 Assertions about the Bean That Is Left

It is important to make a claim about the color of the bean that is left in the Gries coffee can problem. A way to gain insight into what happens when the corrected program in Figure 5.18 is executed is to consider extreme cases. For example, consider the following cases (the underlined letter indicates a bean that has been put in the can after a pair has been picked):

	Case 1			*Case 2*	
Pick	*Beans*	*Action*	*Pick*	*Beans*	*Action*
	wwwwb			bbbbw	
wb	wwww<u>w</u>	Restore w	bw	bbb<u>w</u>	Restore w
ww	ww<u>b</u>	Add b	bw	bb<u>w</u>	Restore w
wb	w<u>w</u>	Restore w	bw	b<u>w</u>	Restore w
ww	<u>b</u>	Add b	bw	<u>w</u>	Restore w

	Case 3			*Case 4*	
Pick	*Beans*	*Action*	*Pick*	*Beans*	*Action*
	wwwb			bbbw	
wb	ww<u>w</u>	Restore w	bw	bb<u>w</u>	Restore w
ww	w<u>b</u>	Add b	bw	b<u>w</u>	Restore w
wb	<u>w</u>	Restore w	bw	<u>w</u>	Restore w

CHAPTER 5   5.6 Summary   201

	Case 5			Case 6	
Pick	*Beans*	*Action*	*Pick*	*Beans*	*Action*
	wwwwbb			wwbbbb	
wb	wwwwb	Restore w	wb	wwbbb	Restore w
wb	wwww	Restore w	wb	wwbb	Restore w
ww	wwb	Add b	wb	wwb	Restore w
wb	ww	Restore w	wb	ww	Restore w
ww	b	Add b	ww	b	Add b

That is, we need to establish a relation between the coffee can rules governing replacement or addition and the initial number of beans of each color. In cases 1 and 2, there is an odd number of each color. One case leaves a black bean (case 1), whereas the second case leaves a white bean. Does the color that dominates make a difference? No. Consider case 3. There are more white than black and white wins. In case 1, there were more white, but black won. Make a claim about this in terms of what you know about Gries's rules.

Cases 4 and 5 illustrate the use of an even number of each color. Can we always expect a black bean to be left if we start with an even number of each color of bean? Make a claim about this.

Test your assertions by running the modified version (based on the bug clinic in Section 5.5.5) of the program in Figure 5.18.

5.6 SUMMARY

Control structures regulate the flow of processor control during the execution of a program. There are three types of canonical control structures:

1. Sequential (a block)
2. Selection (if and switch)
3. Iteration (for, while, and do)

Boolean expressions are used to determine the selection of a statement to be executed or the repeated execution of a statement. The term *statement* refers to either an atomic statement or a block. A *block* is a sequential control structure.

A double equal (= =) can be used to construct a Boolean expression to test for equality. The *and* (&&), *or* (||), and *not* (!) operators are also used to construct Boolean expressions. A Boolean expression returns a single value, zero or one.

Control structures can be nested. We illustrated the use of nested while-loops in Figure 5.7.

202 **Control structures** CHAPTER 5

The chop() function in Figure 5.8 is useful in constructing a random-number generator. It uses a forced conversion from type double to type int in

$$trunk \ = \ x$$

The rnd() function in Figure 5.14 depends on the use of a seed that is put in the static storage class external to any function. This allows seed to retain its value after one or more functions use seed. For example, in Figure 5.15, the init() function is used to initialize seed. The rnd() function in this same program uses seed to produce a set of random numbers. By making *seed* static and external, we make a variable that is private and available *only* to functions declared after seed in the same source file.

REVIEW TERMS AND SYMBOLS

Term	*Meaning*
Boolean expression	returns value of 1 or 0
break	transfers control to end of a block
canonical	standard
canonical control structure:	
sequential	block
selection	if and switch
iteration	for, while, and do
chop()	truncate fraction part of a floating-point number
continue	stops current iteration and begins next iteration of a loop
do	execute loop statement before checking condition the first time through the loop
else	belongs to nearest if
inclusive or	||
iterate	repeat
sequential control	execution within a block
strlen()	computes length of string, not including the trailing '\0'
switch	case statement
test for equality	==
while	test condition first before while-loop statement is executed
while(1) statement	infinite while-loop

EXERCISES

1. How does a *while* statement differ from a *do* statement?

2. Assume that x = 'a', y = 3, z = 125, and k = 97, and give the values of the following Boolean expressions:

CHAPTER 5   **Exercises   203**

    a. $(x > y)$ && ! $(x - y == 0)$
    b. $(x > y)$ || ! $(x - z == 0)$
    c. $(x > y)$ || ! $(x - 'a' == 0)$
    d. $!(y + k > z)$ || $(x != 'a')$

3. Write a program to illustrate the use of the first switch statement used in Section 5.3.2. Prompt the user to feed appropriate values that can be tested by the switch statement.
4. Write a program to illustrate the use of nested switch statements using the third switch statement given in Section 5.3.2.
5. Write a program to carry out the refinement of Figure 5.6 specified in Section 5.4.2. Give a sample run.
6. Test the assertion that

```
if (expression1 && expression2 && expression3)
        statement;
```

  is equivalent to

```
            if expression1
                if expression2
                    if expression3
                        statement;
```

  Write a program to do this using the sample if-statement given at the end of Section 5.3.1.
7. Test the use of the continue statement in the following statement:

```
for (i = 0; i <= max; ++i)  {
    x  =  rand();
    if (x % 2 == 0)
            continue;
    else
            printf("%5d", x);
}
```

  Write a program to do this and comment on the output.
8. Write a program to carry out the refinement specified in Section 5.4.4 for the program in Figure 5.7. Give a sample run.
9. Carry out the refinement specified in Section 5.4.5 for the program in Figure 5.7. Give a sample run.
10. Carry out the correction specified in Section 5.4.7 for the program in Figure 5.7. Give a sample run.
11. Carry out the refinement specified in Section 5.4.10 for the program in Figure 5.12. Give a sample run.
12. Carry out the refinement specified in Section 5.4.11 for the program in Figure 5.12. Give a sample run.
13. Carry out the suggestion specified in Section 5.4.12 for the buildform() function in Figure 5.12. Give a sample run.
14. Refine the program in Figure 5.16 as follows:
    a. Allow the user to choose the upper and lower bounds of the random numbers that are printed.

204 Control structures   CHAPTER 5

    b. Give a sample run for the numbers in the following intervals:
      (i) 5 to 50
      (ii) 25 to 99
    Hint: See the suggestion in Section 5.5.1.
15. Carry out the corrections specified in Section 5.5.5 for the program in Figure 5.18 (the coffee can problem). Modify the output so that it produces a display like the following:

Coffee can contents		*Example*
Pick:	bb	bbwbwb
New contents:		bwbwb
Pick:	wb	
New contents:		bw wb
Pick:	bw	
New contents:		w wb
etc.		

16. Make an invariant assertion about the bean that will be left when Gries's rules are followed in the coffee can problem. Test your assertion with sample runs of the program in Exercise 15.

LAB PROJECTS

1. Write a program to play a guessing game that works as follows:
    a. Randomly generate a number the machine knows, but you do not.
    b. Prompt for guesses for the number the computer is "thinking about."
    c. Print

Eureka! you guessed correctly
after _____ guesses

    (In other words, keep track of how many guesses are used. Print the tally when a correct guess is made.)
    d. Print

"You're low"

    if the guess is less than the actual number and

"You're high"

    if the guess is greater than the actual number.
2. *Modified Coffee Can Problem:* Add to the program in Figure 5.18 the following conditions:
    a. If two pairs in succession are matching pairs and have the same color, then put two black beans in the can instead of one black bean when the second matching pair is picked.
    b. If two pairs in succession are not matching pairs, then put two white beans in the can instead of a black bean when the second nonmatching pair is picked.
    c. Follow Gries's rules, otherwise.

CHAPTER 5

d. Then stop when two beans are left in the can.
e. And make an assertion about the remaining two beans after following the modified coffee can rules.
3. Knuth (1981) suggests using

$$(a \text{ x} + b) \text{ mod } c$$

to produce random numbers on the computer. The initial value of x is the seed. Then let newx be defined in terms of the remainder produced by the preceding expression. That is, use

$$newx = (a * oldx + b) \text{ mod } c$$

The values for a, b, and c should be chosen with care. Try using

$$a = 637$$
$$b = 3109$$
$$c = 9423$$

A good starting value for x is the system time, if it is available. The number b should have no factor in common with c. The multiplier a should be in the range

$$0.01 <= a <= 0.99c$$

Knuth suggests choosing c to be the word size of the machine. It is also a good idea to choose c to be a prime number. On a 16-bit machine, try $c = 65,521$ (a prime). On a 32-bit machine, try $c = 10,006,721$, the largest prime recorded in Lehmer (1914). Write a program to test the use of this new random-number generator to simulate 100 rolls of a balanced 20-faced die.

206 Control structures   CHAPTER 5

SELECTED SOLUTIONS

Exercise 5

```
#include <std.h>
#include <stdio.h>

atou(s)
char *s;
        {
        int bias, i = 0;

        bias = ´A´ - ´a´;
        while (s[i] != ´\0´)
          {
          if  (s[i] >= ´a´ && s[i] <= ´z´)
                s[i] = s[i] + bias;
          ++i;
          }
        }

main()
        {
        char *target;
        int yes = 1;

        while (yes == 1) {
                printf("Enter string in lower case:");
                scanf("%s", target);
                atou(target);
                printf("\n\n %30s %20s", "new word:", target);
                printf("\n\n %40s", "Do you wish to continue--1=Y,0=N:");
                scanf("%d", &yes);
                printf("\n\n --------------------------------- \n\n");
                }
        }


RUN CE55

Enter string in lower case:tumty tumty tum toes


                              new word:            TUMTY

        Do you wish to continue--1=Y,0=N:

    -----------------------------------

Enter string in lower case:

                              new word:            TUMTY

        Do you wish to continue--1=Y,0=N:

    -----------------------------------
```

CHAPTER 5   Selected solutions   207

Exercise 5   *concluded*

```
Enter string in lower case:

                    new word:                TUM

        Do you wish to continue--1=Y,0=N:

-----------------------------------

Enter string in lower case:

                    new word:                TOES

        Do you wish to continue--1=Y,0=N:1


-----------------------------------

Enter string in lower case:hello mom


                    new word:                HELLO

        Do you wish to continue--1=Y,0=N:

-----------------------------------

Enter string in lower case:

                    new word:                MOM

        Do you wish to continue--1=Y,0=N:0


-----------------------------------
```

208 Control structures   CHAPTER 5

Exercise 8

```
#include "lib.h"
char *word = "music";

prefix(i)
char i[80];
        {
        char *j, *k, *target;
        int count = 0;
        int a = 0, b = 0, c = 0;

        j = i; k = i;                           /*now j and k point to i string*/

        while (a < strlen(i)) {
          while (b < strlen(i)) {
            while (c < strlen(i)) {
                target[0] = i[a]; target[1] = j[b]; target[2] = k[c];
                target[3] = '\0';
                printf("%s%c%s    ",target, '-', word);
                ++c;
                ++count;
                if (count % 5 == 0)
                        printf("\n\n");
            }
          c = 0;
          ++b;
          }
        b = 0;
        ++a;
        }

        }

main()
        {
        char range[80];

        printf("enter substring for constructing prefixes :");
        scanf("%s", range);
        printf("\n\n");
        prefix(range);
        }


RUN CE58

enter substring for constructing prefixes :abrt


aaa-music    aab-music    aar-music    aat-music    aba-music

abb-music    abr-music    abt-music    ara-music    arb-music

arr-music    art-music    ata-music    atb-music    atr-music

att-music    baa-music    bab-music    bar-music    bat-music
```

CHAPTER 5   **Selected solutions   209**

Exercise 8   *concluded*

```
bba-music    bbb-music    bbr-music    bbt-music    bra-music

brb-music    brr-music    brt-music    bta-music    btb-music

btr-music    btt-music    raa-music    rab-music    rar-music

rat-music    rba-music    rbb-music    rbr-music    rbt-music

rra-music    rrb-music    rrr-music    rrt-music    rta-music

rtb-music    rtr-music    rtt-music    taa-music    tab-music

tar-music    tat-music    tba-music    tbb-music    tbr-music

tbt-music    tra-music    trb-music    trr-music    trt-music

tta-music    ttb-music    ttr-music    ttt-music^C
```

Exercise 11

```c
#include <std.h>
#include <stdio.h>
char result[212] = " ";              /*resultant string*/

buildform(s)
char *s;
      {
      int i = 0;

      do
        {
        s[i] = getchar();
        ++i;
        }
      while (s[i-1] != '!');
      }


printcopy(s)
char *s;
      {
      int i = 0;

      while (s[i] != '!')
        {
        printf("%c", s[i]);
        ++i;
        }
      }
```

210 Control structures   CHAPTER 5

Exercise 11   *concluded*

```
insert_word(s,target)
char *s,*target;
        {
        int i = 0,j = 0,k = 0;

        do {
                if (s[i] == '*')
                        {
                        while (target[j] != '!') {
                          result[k] = target[j];
                          ++k; ++j;
                          }
                        j = 0;
                        }
                else {
                        result[k] = s[i];
                        ++k;
                        }
                }
            while (s[i++] != '!');
        }

main()
        {
        char letter[212], word[10];

        while (1) {
                printf("\n\n %20s \n\n", "Enter text:");
                buildform(letter);
                printcopy(letter);
                printf("\n\n %20s", "Enter word: ");
                scanf("%s", word);
                printf("\n\n");
                insert_word(letter,word);
                printcopy(result);
                }
        }


RUN CE511

        Enter text:

Dave discovered the * about the computer!
Dave discovered the * about the computer

        Enter word: truth!


Dave discovered the truth about the computer

        Enter text:
```

CHAPTER 5

Selected solutions 211

Exercise 12

```
                #include <std.h>
                #include <stdio.h>

                buildform(s)
                char *s;
                        {
                        int i = 0;

                        do
                          {
                          s[i] = getchar();
                          ++i;
                          }
                        while (s[i-1] != '!');
                        }


                printcopy(s)
                char *s;
                        {
                        int i = 0;

                        while (s[i] != '!')
                          {
                          printf("%c", s[i]);
                          ++i;
                          }
                        }

                insert_word(s,t1,t2,t3)
                char *s,*t1,*t2,*t3;
                        {
                        int i = 0,j = 0;

                        do
                                if (s[i] == '*') {
                                  if (s[i+1] == '*')
                                    if (s[i+2] == '*')
                                      while (t3[j] != '!')
                                        {
                                        s[i] = t3[j];
                                        ++i; ++j;
                                        }
                                    else
                                      while (t2[j] != '!')
                                        {
                                        s[i] = t2[j];
                                        ++i; ++j;
                                        }
                                  else
                                    while (t1[j] != '!')
                                      {
```

212 Control structures

Exercise 12 *concluded*

```
                              s[i] = tl[j];
                              ++i; ++j;
                              }
                        j = 0;
                        --i;                 /*move pointer back one char*/
                        }
                  while (s[i++] != '!');
            }

main()
      {
      char letter[212], word1[10], word2[10], word3[10];

      while (1) {
            printf("\n\n %20s \n\n", "Enter text:");
            buildform(letter);
            printcopy(letter);
            printf("\n\nEnter target * -:> ");
            scanf("%s", word1);
            printf("\n");
            printf("Enter target ** -:> ");
            scanf("%s", word2);
            printf("\n");
            printf("Enter target *** -:> ");
            scanf("%s", word3);
            printf("\n");
            insert_word(letter,word1,word2,word3);
            printf("\n\n");
            printcopy(letter);
            }
      }

RUN CE512

        Enter text:

A *    a **    a ***    a loved along...!
A *    a **    a ***    a loved along...

Enter target * -:> way!

Enter target ** -:> lone!

Enter target *** -:> last!


A way  a lone  a last  a loved along...

        Enter text:

^C
```

CHAPTER 5

Exercise 15

```c
#include <math.h>
#include "lib.h"

/*-----------------------------------------------------------------------*/

chop(x)
double x;
        {
        return( (int)x );
        }

/*-----------------------------------------------------------------------*/

double rnd()
        {
        static double seed=2.71829;
        double sqr();

        seed = sqr(seed + 3.1415927);
        seed = seed - chop(seed);
        return(seed);
        }

/*-----------------------------------------------------------------------*/

select(coffee_can,max)
char *coffee_can;
int max;
        {
        int count, i, j;

        do {
                do {
                  do
                    i = chop(max * rnd());
                  while (coffee_can[i] == ' ');
                  do
                    j = chop(max * rnd());
                  while (coffee_can[j] == ' ');
                }
                while (i == j);
                        /*make sure we haven't picked the same one*/
                        /*and they are not spaces.*/
                printf("Coffee can contents:  %s\n", coffee_can);
                printf("Pick   %c%c\n", coffee_can[i], coffee_can[j]);
                if (coffee_can[i] == coffee_can[j]) {
                        coffee_can[i] = ' ';
                        coffee_can[j] = 'b';
                        }
                else
                        if (coffee_can[i] == 'w')
                                coffee_can[j] = ' ';
```

214 **Control structures**   CHAPTER 5

Exercise 15 *continued*

```
                else
                        coffee_can[i] = ´ ´;

            printf("New contents:          %s\n\n", coffee_can);
        count = 0; i = 0;
        while (coffee_can[i] != ´\0´)
                if (coffee_can[i++] != ´ ´)
                        ++count;
        }
    while (count > 1);
    }

/*----------------------------------------------------------------------*/

main()
        {
        char *pot;
        int limit;

        for(1)
                {
                printf("\n\n %20s", "Enter beans (b/w): ");
                scanf("%s", pot);
                limit = strlen(pot);
                printf("\n\n");
                select(pot,limit);
                printf("\n\n");
                drawline();
                printf("\n\n %40s", "Bean left in coffee can:  ");
                printf("%s \n\n", pot);
                drawline();
                printf("\n\n");
                }
        }


RUN CE515

  Enter beans (b/w): bbwbwb


Coffee can contents:  bbwbwb
Pick    wb
New contents:         bwbwb

Coffee can contents:  bwbwb
Pick    bw
New contents:         bw wb

Coffee can contents:  bw wb
Pick    bw
New contents:         bw w
```

CHAPTER 5   **Selected solutions   215**

Exercise 15   *continued*

```
Coffee can contents:   bw w
Pick    ww
New contents:             bb

Coffee can contents:   bb
Pick    bb
New contents:              b


-------------------------------------------------------------------------------


              Bean left in coffee can:     b


-------------------------------------------------------------------------------



   Enter beans (b/w): wwwbbwbwwbb


Coffee can contents:  wwwbbwbwwbb
Pick    bw
New contents:         wwwbbwbwwb

Coffee can contents:  wwwbbwbwwb
Pick    ww
New contents:         wbwbb bwwb

Coffee can contents:  wbwbb bwwb
Pick    ww
New contents:         bbwbb b wb

Coffee can contents:  bbwbb b wb
Pick    wb
New contents:         bbw b b wb

Coffee can contents:  bbw b b wb
Pick    wb
New contents:         b w b b wb

Coffee can contents:  b w b b wb
Pick    bw
New contents:         b w b   wb

Coffee can contents:  b w b   wb
Pick    wb
New contents:         b w b   w
```

216   Control structures

CHAPTER 5

Exercise 15   *concluded*

```
Coffee can contents:  b w b   w
Pick   bw
New contents:           w b   w

Coffee can contents:    w b   w
Pick   wb
New contents:           w     w

Coffee can contents:    w     w
Pick   ww
New contents:                 b


------------------------------------------------------------------------


        Bean left in coffee can:        b

------------------------------------------------------------------------



   Enter beans (b/w): ^C
```

CHAPTER 5   Selected solutions   217

Lab Project 2

```
#include <math.h>
#include "lib.h"

/*-------------------------------------------------------------------*/

chop(x)
double x;
        {
        return( (int)x );
        }

/*-------------------------------------------------------------------*/

double rnd()
        {
        static double seed=2.71829;
        double sqr();

        seed = sqr(seed + 3.1415927);
        seed = seed - chop(seed);
        return(seed);
        }

/*-------------------------------------------------------------------*/

select(coffee_can,max)
char *coffee_can;
int max;
        {
        int count, i, j;
        char prevpair = 'n';

        do {
                do {
                  do
                    i = chop(max * rnd());
                  while (coffee_can[i] == ' ');
                  do
                    j = chop(max * rnd());
                  while (coffee_can[j] == ' ');
                }
                while (i == j);
                        /*make sure we haven't picked the same one*/
                        /*and they are not spaces.*/
                printf("Coffee can contents:  %s\n", coffee_can);
                printf("Pick   %c%c\n", coffee_can[i], coffee_can[j]);
                if (coffee_can[i] == coffee_can[j])
                  if (prevpair == 'n') {
                    prevpair = coffee_can[i];
                    coffee_can[i] = ' ';
                    coffee_can[j] = 'b';
                    }
```

218 Control structures CHAPTER 5

Lab Project 2 *continued*

```
                    else
                      if (prevpair == coffee_can[i]) {
                        coffee_can[i] = 'b';
                        coffee_can[j] = 'w';
                        }
                      else {
                        prevpair = coffee_can[i];
                        coffee_can[i] = 'w';
                        coffee_can[j] = 'w';
                        }
                  else {
                    prevpair = 'n';
                    if (coffee_can[i] == 'w')
                      coffee_can[j] = ' ';
                    else
                      coffee_can[i] = ' ';
                  }

              printf("New contents:        %s\n\n", coffee_can);
          count = 0; i = 0;
          while (coffee_can[i] != '\0')
                if (coffee_can[i++] != ' ')
                      ++count;
          }
      while (count > 1);
      }

/*----------------------------------------------------------------------*/

main()
      {
      char *pot;
      int limit;

      for(1)
              {
              printf("\n\n %20s", "Enter beans (b/w): ");
              scanf("%s", pot);
              limit = strlen(pot);
              printf("\n\n");
              select(pot,limit);
              printf("\n\n");
              drawline();
              printf("\n\n %40s", "Bean left in coffee can:  ");
              printf("%s \n\n", pot);
              drawline();
              printf("\n\n");
              }
      }
```

CHAPTER 5   **Selected solutions   219**

Lab Project 2   *continued*

```
RUN CL52

   Enter beans (b/w): bbwwwbbwbwbb


Coffee can contents:  bbwwwbbwbwbb
Pick   wb
New contents:         b wwwbbwbwbb

Coffee can contents:  b wwwbbwbwbb
Pick   bw
New contents:         b wwwb wbwbb

Coffee can contents:  b wwwb wbwbb
Pick   wb
New contents:           wwwb wbwbb

Coffee can contents:    wwwb wbwbb
Pick   wb
New contents:           wwwb wbwb

Coffee can contents:    wwwb wbwb
Pick   bw
New contents:           wwwb w wb

Coffee can contents:    wwwb w wb
Pick   ww
New contents:           wb b w wb

Coffee can contents:    wb b w wb
Pick   wb
New contents:           wb   w wb

Coffee can contents:    wb   w wb
Pick   ww
New contents:           bb     wb

Coffee can contents:    bb     wb
Pick   bw
New contents:           b      wb

Coffee can contents:    b      wb
Pick   bb
New contents:                  wb

Coffee can contents:           wb
Pick   wb
New contents:                  w
```

Lab Project 2 *concluded*

```
                    Bean left in coffee can:          w
-----------------------------------------------------------------------



    Enter beans (b/w): bwbwwwbbb


Coffee can contents:  bwbwwwbbb
Pick    bb
New contents:         bwbwwwb b

Coffee can contents:  bwbwwwb b
Pick    bw
New contents:         bwbwwwb

Coffee can contents:  bwbwwwb
Pick    wb
New contents:         bwbwww

Coffee can contents:  bwbwww
Pick    wb
New contents:          wbwww

Coffee can contents:   wbwww
Pick    bw
New contents:          w www

Coffee can contents:   w www
Pick    ww
New contents:          w w b

Coffee can contents:   w w b
Pick    ww
New contents:          b w b

Coffee can contents:   b w b
Pick    wb
New contents:            w b

Coffee can contents:     w b
Pick    wb
New contents:            w



-----------------------------------------------------------------------
                    Bean left in coffee can:     w

-----------------------------------------------------------------------



    Enter beans (b/w): ^C
```

CHAPTER 5

RELATED READINGS

Dijkstra, E. "Go to Statement Considered Harmful," ACM Communications (1968), vol. 11, No. 3.

Gries, David, *Science of Programming*. New York: Springer-Verlag, New York, Inc., 1981.

Knuth, Donald E., *The Art of Computer Programming,* Vol. 2, Seminumerical Algorithms. Reading, Mass.: Addison-Wesley Publishing Co., 1981.

Lehmer, Derrick N., *List of Prime Numbers from 1 to 10,006,721*. Ann Arbor, Mich.: University Microfilms International, 1914.

6

Arrays

Yea, from the table of my memory I'll wipe away all trivial fond records. Hamlet, Act 5, scene 5, line 98.

An array is a homogenous structure; it consists of components which are all of the same type, called the base type. The array is also a so-called random-access structure; all components can be selected at random and are equally accessible.

*N. Wirth**

AIMS
- Introduce Methods of Building and Using Arrays in C.
- Distinguish between Array Names That Are Pointer Constants and Pointer Variables.
- Distinguish between the Address of an Array Cell and the Content of an Array Cell.
- Introduce External Function Libraries.
- Suggest a Method for Measuring Randomness.
- Use Arrays to Compute Large Products.
- Use Arrays to Sort a Set of Numbers.
- Suggest Ways to Set up Multidimensional Arrays.

**Algorithms* + *Data Structures* = *Programs,* Prentice-Hall, Inc., Englewood Cliffs, N.J., 1976.

CHAPTER 6   6.1 Introduction   223

6.1 INTRODUCTION

A row of objects of the same type is a *linear data structure*. A single-dimensional array is a linear data structure. The objects of an array are stored in cells. A *cell* is a primary memory location inside a processor. An example of an array of integers relative to main memory is shown in Figure 6.1. The initial cell[0] location is pointed to by the array name. An array name is a pointer constant. Its *fixed* value is the address of the initial array cell. We can use

$$\text{cell} + 2 \quad \text{or} \quad \text{cell}[2]$$

to address (locate) the third array cell. Why is this the third array cell? The first three array cells are cell[0], cell[1], and cell[2].

The array in Figure 6.1 is an example of a one-dimensional array. Each cell[i] points to a single object rather than a row of objects. For example, cell[7] in Figure 6.1 points to one integer, 21.

All array elements (objects) are of the *same* type. In Figure 6.1, each array element is of type int. For this reason, an array is called a *homogenous data structure*. Array elements can be accessed directly using an array selector. An array name provides the *base address* or beginning address for the first cell of an array. An *array selector* provides a value that is added to the base address to compute the *effective address* or actual location of an array cell.

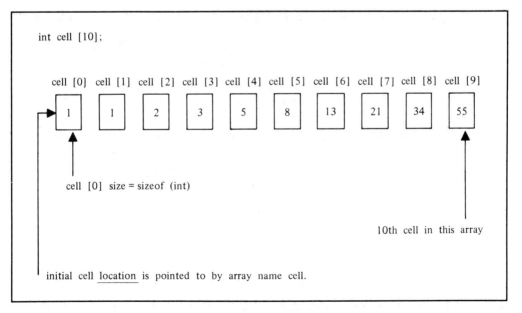

Figure 6.1   Array of Integers

For example, if we use *i* as an array selector of type int, then

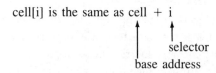

provides the effective address of a desired cell. Since array elements can be accessed directly using selectors, an array is also a *direct-access* or what Niklaus Wirth (1976) calls a *random-access data structure*.

A syntax diagram for one-dimensional array declarations is given in Figure 6.2. Examples of one-dimensional array declarations in **C** are given next:

```
int x[1000];            /* array with 1000 cells */
int a[5], b[5], c[20];
double box[10];         /* array with 10 cells set aside
                           for type double values */
char ch[80];            /* array with 80 cells set aside
                           for characters */
char *ptr_<[10];        /* array with 10 cells set aside
                           for pointers to objects of
                           type char */
int *ptr_i[50];         /* array with 50 cells set aside
                           for pointers to objects of
                           type int */
```

Each declaration specifies the following things:

1. Type of object in *each* array cell.
2. Size of an array cell determined by the type declaration for the array.
3. Number of cells in an array (this *size* declaration must always be of type int).
4. Storage class for array cells (within a function the default storage class *auto;* arrays in the extern and static storage class can be initialized; the register storage class cannot be used for arrays).

Examples of array declarations with initial values put into one or more cells are given next:

1. Arrays in extern storage class:
    int x[5] = {2, 3};

CHAPTER 6

6.1 Introduction

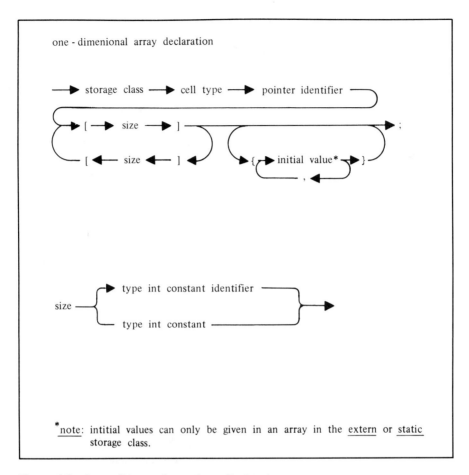

Figure 6.2 Syntax Diagram for an Array Declaration

```
        int box[4] = {1, 1, 2, 3};
        char ch[5] = {'a', 'b', 'c', '!', '*'};
        double nos[2] = {1.61803, 2.71828};
        int *ptr[2] = {x, x+1};
```
2. Arrays in static storage class:
```
        static int x[5] = {1, 1, 2, 3, 5};
        static char ch[3] = {'A', '2', '!'};
        Static double x[50] = {2.71828};
```

What happens as a result of the first of these declarations is shown in Figure 6.3. Notice here what C does with the trailing cells of an array that are *not* initialized. They are filled with zeros.

226 Arrays

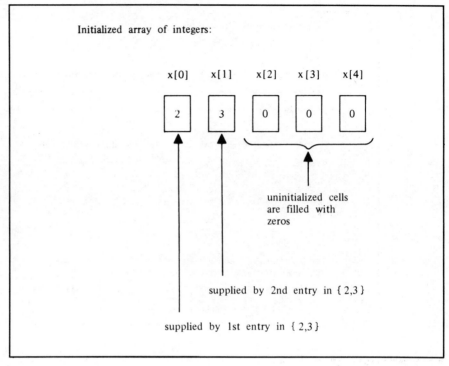

Figure 6.3 Initialized Array

It is also possible to set up array declarations where the number of cells is not specified *explicitly*. The array size is determined by the number of initial values that are specified. For example, we can have the following initialized arrays:

```
static int x[ ] = {1, 3, 4, 7, 11, 18, 29}
static char ch[ ] = "Hello, world!";
static char ch[ ] = {'r', 'i', 'v', 'c', 'r'};
```

Finally, it is possible to pass the base address of an array in a function call. For example, we can use the following scheme:

```
copy_array (x, size)
int x[ ];          /*identifies base address*/
int size;          /*array dimension*/
    {
```

CHAPTER 6   **6.2 Constructing arrays   227**

```
                                }
                        main()
                            {
                        int  box[10];

                            .

                            .

                            .

                        copy_array (box,  10);
                            .

                            .

                            .

                            }
```

In this chapter, we show how to build arrays using an input stream to supply values for array cells. We also show how to construct arrays of random numbers and how to print array contents. Arrays of numbers and characters are considered. Finally, we show how to set up and use function libraries.

6.2 CONSTRUCTING ARRAYS

In Figure 6.4, we give a build_array() function to build arrays of integers taken from an input stream. You might wonder why we use

scanf("%d %d", &x[i], &yes);

instead of

scanf("%d %d", &x[i+ +], &yes);

By incrementing i separately, we avoid the possibility of i running past max (the upper bound on i). As a rule, an error will result if an attempt is made to select an array cell past the declared dimension of an array.

Notice that we also use

return (i-1)

to return the number of array elements entered by the user. We do not use

return (i);

Why? First, the final allowable value of i as a *selector* is max. However, i itself can be incremented past max. This shuts down the while-loop in Figure 6.4. The final value of i will be in the following range:

$$0 <= i <= max + 1$$

228 Arrays   CHAPTER 6

```
build_array(x, n)

int x[];                              /*array of integers*/

int n;                                /*no. of array cells*/

    {

    int i = 0;                        /*array selector*/

    int max = n;                      /*upperbound on i*/

    int yes = 1;                      /*control variable*/

    while ((yes != 0) && (i <= max)) {

        printf("\n\n ---->");

        scanf("%d %d", &x[i], &yes);

        ++i;

        }

    return(i - 1);                    /*why i - 1?*/

    }
```

Figure 6.4 Build_array() Function

We need to decrement *i* to return a value of *i* that indicates the upper bound on *i* in the array that has been built. For example, we can have the final values of *i*, when max = 5, shown in Table 6.1. In effect, the value of *i* returned by the build_array() function is *k*, there will be *k* cells in the array that has been built.

In Figure 6.5, we show a program that uses the build_array() function. This program also introduces a print_array() function. The statement

$$printf("\%10d", x[i]);$$

is equivalent to

$$printf("\%10d", x + i);$$

It is left as an exercise to verify this. We can put the functions in Figure 6.5 into an external library. We show how to do this next.

CHAPTER 6   6.2 Constructing arrays   229

TABLE 6.1   Sample Array Sizes

Number of Cells (max = 5)	Cells	i	i - 1
1	x[0]	1	0
2	x[0], x[1]	2	1
3	x[0], x[1], x[2]	3	2
4	x[0], x[1], x[2], x[3]	4	3
5	x[0], x[1], x[2], x[3], x[4]	5	4

```
#include "newlib.h"

build_array(x, n)
int n;                                  /*upper bound on array x*/
int x[];                                /*array of integers*/
       {
       int i = 0;                       /*init. index value*/
       int max = n;                     /*init. with upper bound on index*/
       int yes = 1;                     /*control variable*/

       while ((yes != 0) && (i <= max)) {
               printf("\n\n ---->");
               scanf("%d %d", &x[i], &yes);
               ++i;
               }
       return(i - 1);
       }

print_array(x, n)
int x[], n;
       {
       int i = 0;

       while (i <= n) {
               printf("%10d", x[i]);
               ++i;
               if (i % 6 == 0)
                       printf("\n\n");
               }
       printf("\n");
       }

main()
       {
       int box[50];
       int limit;
```

Figure 6.5   Constructing an Array Using the Input Stream

230 Arrays CHAPTER 6

```
        printf("\n\n %s \n\n", "Enter int, 1 to continue, int,0 to stop");
        drawline();
        printf("\n\n");
        limit = build_array(box, 49);
        printf("\n\n %40s \n\n", "Copy of array:");
        drawline();
        printf("\n\n %10s %10d \n\n", "limit =", limit);
        print_array(box, limit);
        }
```

RUN C65

 Enter int, 1 to continue, int,0 to stop

 ---->233 1

 ---->144 1

 ---->8 1

 ---->610 1

 ---->3 1

 ---->0 1

 ---->1 1

 ---->21 1

 ---->0 0

                              Copy of array:

 ----

     limit =   8

          233   144   8   610   3   0

            1   21   0

Figure 6.5 *concluded*

CHAPTER 6   6.3 Library of functions   231

6.3 LIBRARY OF FUNCTIONS

In Figure 6.6 we show the source text for a separate file containing a function library. This library can be referenced as a source text in a program by using

#include ''C66.h''

This will tell the **C** preprocessor to make the source text in Figure 6.6 available to a second source text that includes it. The library in Figure 6.6 brings together functions from Figure 5.16 (random numbers), as well as functions from Figure 6.5. We show a program that uses two of these functions in Figure 6.7. In the next section we show how the rnd() function in Figure 6.6 can be used to build an array of random numbers.

```
static double seed = 0.0;

init(x)                                  /*from Figure 5.16*/
double x;
        {
        seed = x;
        }

chop(x)                                  /*from Figure 5.16*/
double x;
        {
        int trunk;

        trunk = x;              /*assigns integer part of x to trunk*/
        return(trunk);
        }

double rnd()
        {                                /*from Figure 5.16*/
        double sqr();

        seed = sqr(seed + 3.1415927);
        seed = seed - chop(seed);
        return(seed);
        }

build_array(x, n)                        /*from Figure 6.5*/
int x[];                                 /*array of integers*/
int n;                                   /*upper bound on array index*/
        {
        int i = 0;                       /*init. index value*/
        int max = n;                     /*init. with upper bound on index*/
        int yes = 1;                     /*control variable*/
```

Figure 6.6   External Function Library

232 Arrays CHAPTER 6

```
        while ((yes != 0) && (i <= max)) {
                printf("\n\n ---->");
                scanf("%d %d", &x[i], &yes);
                ++i;
                }
        return(i - 1);                          /*why i - 1?*/
        }

print_array(x, n)                               /*from Figure 6.5*/
int x[], n;
        {
        int i = 0;

        while (i <= n) {
                printf("%10d", x[i]);
                ++i;
                if (i % 6 == 0)
                        printf("\n\n");

                        }
                printf("\n");
                }
```

Figure 6.6 *concluded*

6.4 ARRAYS OF RANDOM NUMBERS

To build an array of random numbers, we need to use the init() function to initialize the value of the static double variable *seed* declared in Figure 6.6. In Figure 6.8 we show a program that includes a fill_cells() function, which allows the user to choose between an array of random numbers or an array of integers taken from an input stream. The fill_cells() function will produce random numbers in the range from 0 to 99. This function uses all the functions given in Figure 6.6, although the functions being referenced are hidden. This function also uses a new form of the return statement:

$$return(build\_array(x, n));$$

The execution of this statement begins with a transfer of control to the build_array function, which constructs an array of integers taken from an input stream and then returns (i - 1). It is this value of i - 1 that is returned by the fill_cells() function. We show a program that uses the fill_cells() function in Figure 6.9.

6.4.1 Refinement: Simplifying Fill Cells()

The fill_cells() function in Figure 6.9 should be simplified. This can be done by setting up a separate function [call it buildtable()] to build a table (array) of random numbers. The following lines of code can be used to do this:

CHAPTER 6　　　　　　　　　　　　　　　　6.4 Arrays of random numbers　233

```
#include "c66.h"
#include "newlib.h"

main()
        {
        int box[50];
        int limit;

        printf("\n\n %s \n\n", "Enter int, 1 to continue, int,0 to stop");
        drawline();
        printf("\n\n");
        limit = build_array(box, 49);
        printf("\n\n %40s \n\n", "Copy of array:");
        drawline();
        printf("\n\n %10s %10d \n\n", "limit =", limit);
        print_array(box, limit);
        }


RUN C67

 Enter int, 1 to continue, int,0 to stop

 ------------------------------------------------------------------------------


 ---->1221 1


 ---->23 1


 ---->1 0


                              Copy of array:

 ------------------------------------------------------------------------------


    limit =              2

        1221          23            1
```

Figure 6.7　Program That Uses External Functions

```
            scanf("%f", & newseed);
            init (newseed);
            while (i < max)  {
                x[i] = chop(100 * rnd());
                ++i;
            }
            return(i - 1);
```

234 Arrays

CHAPTER 6

```c
fill_cells(x, n)
int x[], n;

    {
    int i = 0, max = n;

    double newseed;

    char ans;

    printf("Enter r for random nos, k for kb entries:  ");

    ans = getchar();

    if (ans == 'r') {

        printf("\n\n seed:  ");

        scanf("%f", &newseed);

        init(newseed);          /*crucial step!*/

        while (i <= max) {

            x[i] = chop(100 * rnd());

            ++i;

            }

        return(i - 1);

        }

    else

        {

        printf("Enter x[i] 1 to continue, x[0] 0 to stop:  ")'

        return(build_array(x, n));

        }

    }
```

Figure 6.8 Fill_cells() Function

CHAPTER 6   **6.4 Arrays of random numbers** 235

```
#include "c66.h"
#include "newlib.h"


fill_cells(x, n)
int x[], n;
        {
        int i = 0, max = n;
        double newseed;
        char ans;

        printf("Enter r for random nos, k for kb nos for array:    ");
        ans = getchar();
        if (ans == 'r') {
                printf("\n\n Enter seed for random number generator:   ");
                scanf("%f", &newseed);
                init(newseed);
                while (i < max)
                        x[i++] = chop(100 * rnd());

                return(i - 1);
                }
        else
                {
                printf("\n\n");
                printf("Enter x[i] 1 (to continue), x[i] 0 (to stop) \n\n");
                return(build_array(x, n));
                }
        }
main()
        {
        int box[50];
        int limit;

                printf("\n\n");
                limit = fill_cells(box, 49);
                printf("\n\n %40s \n\n", "Copy of array:");
                drawline();
                printf("\n\n %10s %10d \n\n", "limit =", limit);
                print_array(box, limit);
        }

RUN C69

Enter r for random nos, k for kb nos for array:    r


 Enter seed for random number generator:  1.61803


                        Copy of array:
```

565   **Figure 6.9** Constructing an Array of Random Numbers

236 Arrays   CHAPTER 6

```
limit =          48

   65        40        58        92        50        32

   98         6        29        78        42        71

   86         4        15        87        16        91

   45        96        86         7        36        31

   95        79        53        51        34        19

   10        53        49        25        55        63

   28        76        26        63        28        73

    0        91        42        69        70        80

   55
```

Figure 6.9 *concluded*

Then the fill_cells() function can be used to transfer control to the buildtable() function. Carrying out this idea is left as an exercise.

6.4.2 Refinement: Choose the Range of Random Numbers

The buildtable() function in Section 6.4.1 is limited to building tables of random numbers in the range from 0 to 99. This comes from the use of the following assignment:

$$x(i) = chop(100 * rnd());$$

This can be changed to advantage as follows:

$$x[i] = chop(bound * rnd());$$

Notice that this still leaves the lower bound on the table of random numbers unchanged. The lower bound is still zero. The new build_rtable() function can be revised to allow the user to choose the upper *and* lower bound on the random numbers put into a table. A suggestion on how to do this is given in Section 5.5.1. This refinement is left as an exercise.

6.4.3 Application: Measuring Randomness

A good random-number generator will produce a fairly uniform distribution of

CHAPTER 6   **6.4 Arrays of random numbers   237**

numbers. For example, if we produce a table of 10,000 random integers in the
range from 1 to 10, we should produce a distribution like the following:

Random number	Sample frequency	Ideal frequency
1	990	1000
2	1005	1000
3	986	1000
4	994	1000
5	1006	1000
6	1001	1000
7	1010	1000
8	999	1000
9	995	1000
10	1014	1000

This says nothing about *where* a particular random number occurs in a random-
number table. This only counts the number of occurrences of a particular random
number in a table. In Figure 6.10 we show a get_freq() function, which can be
used to count sample frequencies in a random-number table. This function uses a
random number as the selector of an array cell used to hold the frequency of the
random number. For example, if a sample equals 8, then

$$x[8] \; = \; x[8] \; + \; 1;$$

The get_freq() function is limited to tables of random numbers in the range from
1 to 10. This limitation will be taken care of in a refinement. Before the *x* array

```
            get_freq(x, n)

            int x[], n;

                {

                int i = 0, max = n, no;

                while (i <= max)  {

                    no = chop(10 * rnd()) + 1;

                    x[no] = x[no] + 1;

                    ++i;

                }

            }
```

Figure 6.10   Get_freq() Function

238 Arrays CHAPTER 6

in the get_freq() function is used, it is necessary to guarantee that the cells of the x array do not contain stray garbage. We can guarantee that the x array is "empty" (all cells will contain zeros) by setting up an init_array() function. In Figure 6.11 we show a program to carry out this idea.

6.4.4 Refinement: Choosing the Range for get_freq()

The get_freq() function in Figure 6.11 can be improved by allowing the user to choose the range of numbers produced by this function. The suggestions in Section 6.4.2 carry over to the improvement of get_freq().

This refinement requires special care. Why? The upper bound on the range of numbers (the largest value of the *no* variable) must always be less than or equal to the dimension of the x array. This is an instance of a need for *exception handling*. That is, when the user chooses a value for *bound* in

$$no = chop(bound * rnd()) + 1;$$

it will be necessary to check the truth of the expression

$$bound <= max$$

Go back to the user for another value of *bound* if this condition is not satisfied. In general, *exception handling* is a practice of using a control structure to prevent a user from asking a program to do things that are not allowed. This will prevent a program from crashing. Exception handling makes a program more robust.

Rather than introduce a new variable called bound, the variable *limit* in Figure 6.11 can be used in place of bound. This refinement is left as an exercise.

6.4.5 Refinement: Quantifying Spike Stars

The program in Figure 6.11 prints a frequency polygon to give a graphical interpretation to the printed frequencies. Each star (*) in the frequency polygon spikes represents 10 occurrences of a sample in the table. This is done using the following lines of code:

```
newmax = x[i] / 10;
for (j = 0; j <= newmax; ++j)
    printf("%1c", '*');
```

The user should be given the opportunity to do the following things:

1. Choose the number of occurrences of a sample that a star represents.
2. Choose whether or not to display a frequency polygon.
3. Choose the symbol used to print a frequency polygon.

These refinements are left as an exercise.

```
#include "newlib.h"
#include "c66.h";

init_array(x, n)
int x[], n;
        {
        int i = 0, max = n;

        while (i <= max)
                x[i++] = 0;
        }

get_freq(x, n)
int x[],n;
        {
        int i = 0, max = n, no;

        while (i <= max) {
                no = chop(10 * rnd()) + 1;
                x[no] = x[no] + 1;
                ++i;
                }
        }

show_freq(x, n)
int x[],n;
        {
        int i = 1, max = n, newmax,j;

        printf("\n\n");
        printf("%10s %10s %30s", "random", "frequency", "frequency");
        printf("\n\n %10s %10s %30s", "number", "count", "polygon");
        printf("\n\n n.b.: each star represents 10 occurrences of a rnd no.");
        printf("\n\n");
        drawline();
        printf("\n\n");
        while (i <= max) {
                printf("%10d %10d %5s", i, x[i], "|");
                newmax = x[i] / 10;
                for (j = 0; j <= newmax; ++j)
                        printf("%1c", '*');
                ++i;
                printf("\n\n");
                }
        }

main()
        {
        int count[10];
        int limit;                      /*rnd range: 1 ... limit*/
        double newseed;                 /*seed for rnd generator*/
        printf("\n\n Enter floating pt seed for rnd nos: ");
        scanf("%f", &newseed);
        init(newseed);
        printf("\n\n Enter limit in rnd range 1 ... limit:  ");
        scanf("%d", &limit);
        init_array(count, 9);
        get_freq(count, limit);
        show_freq(count, 9);
        }
```

Figure 6.11 Measuring Randomness

240 **Arrays**

CHAPTER 6

```
RUN C611

Enter floating pt seed for rnd nos:  2.71828

Enter limit in rnd range 1 ... limit:  3000
```

random number	frequency count	frequency polygon
1	324	|********************************
2	324	|********************************
3	307	|******************************
4	316	|*******************************
5	256	|*************************
6	316	|*******************************
7	287	|***************************
8	278	|**************************
9	293	|*****************************
10	300	|******************************

Figure 6.11 *concluded*

6.5 POINTER CONSTANTS AND POINTER VARIABLES

An array name is a constant pointer. The base address represented symbolically by an array name cannot be changed. In **C**, it is also possible to set up variable pointers. These are pointers with addresses that can be changed. For example, the following declaration includes both constant and variable pointers:

$$\text{int box[50], a;}$$
$$\text{int *ptr, *q, *buff;}$$

Then *box* is a constant pointer. It is illegal to write

$$\text{box = ptr; /*illegal assignment!*/}$$

The variable *ptr* is a variable pointer. It is legal, for example, to make the following assignments:

CHAPTER 6   **6.5 Pointer constants and pointer variables   241**

ptr = box;   /*assigns box-address to ptr*/
q = &a;   /*assigns a-address to q*/
buff = ptr;   /*copies ptr-address into buff*/
ptr = ptr+1;   /*advances ptr to next box cell*/

In either case, a pointer identifier represents a memory address.

A star (*) prefix for a pointer is used to access the content at a memory location. For example,

ptr   is an address of a memory cell;
*ptr   is the content of the cell pointed to by ptr;

We can use, for example,

* (ptr + 0) to access box[0]
* (ptr + 1) to access box[1]
* (ptr + 2) to access box[2]

In Figure 6.12 we give an example of a show_addresses() function to illustrate these ideas. This function will print out the address of each x-array element in decimal. It also illustrates two different ways to print out the content of the array cells. This is done using

printf("%20d %20d %20d", ptr + i, *(ptr + i), x[i]);

```
show_addresses(x, n)

int x[ ], n;

    {

    int i = 0;

    int *ptr;

    ptr = x;        /*now ptr points to x*/

    while (i <= n) {

        printf("%20d %20d %20d", ptr + i, *(prt + i), x[i]);

        ++i;

        printf("\n\n");

        }

    }
```

Figure 6.12   Show_addresses Function

```c
#include "c66.h"
#include "newlib.h"

show_addresses(x, n)
int x[], n;
        {
        int i = 0;
        int *ptr;                               /*makes ptr a variable pointer*/

        ptr = x;                   /*make ptr point x-address*/
        while (i <= n) {
                printf("%20d %20d %20d", ptr + i, *(ptr + i), x[i]);
                ++i;
                printf("\n\n");
                }
        }
main()
        {
        int box[50];
        int limit;

        printf("\n\n %s \n\n", "Enter int, 1 to continue, int,0 to stop");
        drawline();
        printf("\n\n");
        limit = build_array(box, 49);
        printf("\n\n %20s %20s %20s \n\n", "address", "content", "content");
        drawline();
        printf("\n\n %10s %10d \n\n", "limit =", limit);
        show_addresses(box, limit);
        }


RUN C613

 Enter int, 1 to continue, int,0 to stop

--------------------------------------------------------------------------------


 ---->12 1


 ---->23 1


 ---->144 1


 ---->55 1


 ---->21 1


 ---->34 1


 ---->1 0
```

Figure 6.13 Array Pointers and Contents

CHAPTER 6   **6.6 Arrays of pointers   243**

address	content	content
limit =	6	
6384	12	12
6386	23	23
6388	144	144
6390	55	55
6392	21	21
6394	34	34
6396	1	1

Figure 6.13 *concluded*

It is also possible to print out the addresses of the *x*-array cells in octal and hexa-decimal using ''%o'' and ''%x''. A program to illustrate the use of the show_addresses() function is given in Figure 6.13.

6.6 ARRAYS OF POINTERS

The declaration

$$\text{int *ptr[10];}$$

makes

$$\text{ptr[0], ptr[1], ptr[2], } \ldots \text{ , ptr[10]}$$

an array of pointers. For example, we can use

int a[10], b[10], c[20];
int *ptr[40];

to set up an array of pointers that can be used to point to the elements of the arrays *a, b,* and *c.* For example, we can use

ptr[0] = &a[0];
ptr[10] = &b[0];
ptr[20] = &c[0];

to point to the first element of each of the three arrays.

244 Arrays

We can also use

$$\text{char *text[row][col];}$$

to set up an array text of pointers to strings. For example, we can have the following declaration and assignments:

$$\text{char *ptr[3][12];}$$
$$\text{ptr[0] = "Eureka!";}$$
$$\text{ptr[1] = "Oh! C!";}$$
$$\text{ptr[2] = "mmm. . .";}$$
$$\text{ptr[3] = "Withywindle";}$$

These assignments and declaration are given a graphical interpretation in Figure 6.14. Each of the pointers in Figure 6.14 points to a string. We illustrate ways to use arrays of pointers in Figure 6.15.

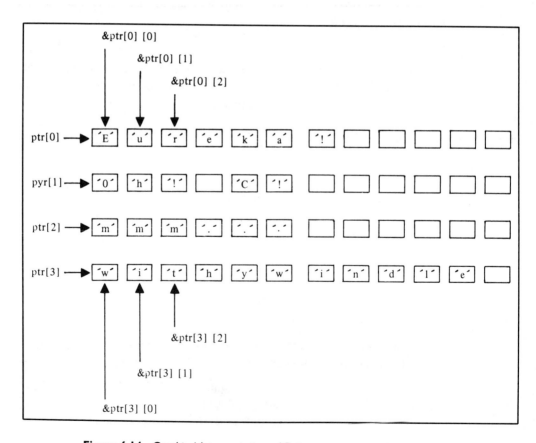

Figure 6.14 Graphical Interpretation of Pointers

CHAPTER 6   6.6 Arrays of pointers   245

```c
#include "newlib.h"

show_pointers()
        {
        static int x[10] = {144, 233, 21, 55};
        static char *y[5][25] = {
                        "Aha! Ada!!!!!!!!!!",
                        "Oh! C!...........",
                        "What? ALGOL!!!!!!!!!!!!!"
                        };
        int *ptr[20];
        int i;

        ptr[0] = &x[0];
        ptr[1] = &x[1];
        ptr[2] = &x[2];
        ptr[3] = &x[3];

        *y[3] = "Eureka!....";

        printf("\n\n %15s %15s %15s %20s", "addr(octal)",
                                           "addr(hex)",
                                           "addr(decimal)",
                                           "content");
        printf("\n\n");
        drawline();
        printf("\n\n");
        for (i = 0; i <= 3; ++i) {
           printf("%15o %15x %15d %20d", &ptr[i], &ptr[i], &ptr[i], *ptr[i]);
           printf("\n\n");
           }

        printf("\n\n\n");
        printf("%15o %15x %15d %20s", y[3], y[3], y[3], *y[3]);

        printf("\n\n");
        drawline();
        }

main()
        {
                show_pointers();
        }
```

Figure 6.15 Array of Pointers

246 **Arrays**   CHAPTER 6

```
RUN C615

        addr(octal)      addr(hex)     addr(decimal)                    content

--------------------------------------------------------------------------------

          14450            1928           6440                           144

          14452            192a           6442                           233

          14454            192c           6444                            21

          14456            192e           6446                            55


          14700            19c0           6592                     Eureka!....

--------------------------------------------------------------------------------
```

Figure 6.15 *concluded*

Next we develop functions to build and print arrays of strings like the array
y in Figure 6.15.

6.7 ARRAYS OF STRINGS: JAGGED ARRAYS

In Figure 6.16 we show a build_strings() function. Notice how the text pointers
are used in the scanf() function:

scanf("%s", text[i]);

Since the identifier *text* already represents an address, it is not necessary to use

&text[i]

to scan an input stream for the corresponding text. This function returns a value
of $i - 1$, which is a count of the number of strings. Each string in itself is an array
of varying length. The result is what is known as a *jagged array,* or rows of arrays
of varying length. In Figure 6.17 we show how the build_strings() function can
be used.

Next we show the use of arrays to find the smallest number in a list of numbers.

```
build_strings(text, r)

char *text[ROW][COL];

int r;

    {

    int i = 0, max = r, again = 1;

    while ((i <= max) && (again == 1)) {

            printf("\n\n string-----> ");

            scanf("%s", text[i]);

            printf("\n\n Again?--1 = Y, 0 = N: ");

            scanf("%d", &again);

            ++i;

            }

    return(i - 1);

    }
```

Figure 6.16 Build_Strings() Function

```
#include "newlib.h"
#define COL 15
#define ROW 10

build_strings(text, r)
char *text[ROW][COL];
int r;
        {
        int i = 0, max = r, again = 1;

        while ((i <= max) && (again == 1)) {
                printf("\n\n string-----> ");
                scanf("%s", text[i]);
                printf("\n\n Again?--1 = Y, 0 = N: ");
                scanf("%d", &again);
                ++i;
                }
        return(i - 1);
        }
```

Figure 6.17 Building an Array of Strings

```
print_strings(text, r)
char *text[ROW][COL];
int r;
        {
        int i = 0, max = r;

        while (i <= max)
                printf("\n\n %s \n\n", text[i++]);
        }

main()
        {
        char line[ROW][COL];
        int ans = 1, max = COL, limit;

        while (ans == 1) {
                limit = build_strings(line, ROW);
                print_strings(line, limit);
                printf("\n\n\n Again? --1 = Y, 0 = N:  ");
                scanf("%d", &ans);
                }
        }


RUN C617

 string----->    jim


 Again?--1 = Y, 0 = N:   1


 string----->    kath


 Again?--1 = Y, 0 = N:   1


 string----->    tumty-tumty-tum-toes!


 Again?--1 = Y, 0 = N:   0


 jim


 kath


 tumty-tumty-tum-toes!



 Again? --1 = Y, 0 = N:   0
```

Figure 6.17 *concluded*

CHAPTER 6   **6.8 Application: finding the smallest and second smallest number   249**

6.8 APPLICATION: FINDING THE SMALLEST AND SECOND SMALLEST NUMBER

A findmin() function is given in Figure 6.18. This function does not move table entries. It merely makes $n - 1$ comparisons in a table with n entries. It establishes the position p of the smallest entry in a table. We can find the smallest and second smallest entries in a table using the following technique:

1. Find the position of the smallest entry.
2. Swap x[max] and x[p].
3. Diminish max (the table size) by 1.
4. Repeat step 1.

In other words, let the machine search through $n - 1$ table entries *after* the smallest entry has been removed from the original table.

```
findmin(x, n)

int x[], n;

    {

    int i = 0, max = n, min, p;

    min = x[i]; i = 1;
    while (i <= max) {
        if (min > x[i]) {
            min = x[i];
            p = i;
        }
        ++i;
    }
    return(p);

    }
```

Figure 6.18   Find_min() Function

250 Arrays

CHAPTER 6

6.8.1 Bug Clinic: Initializing the Position Number

There is a bug in the findmin() function in Figure 6.18. This function will not always return the correct position number with

$$return(p);$$

Why? What happens if the smallest table entry is in the first (the zero-th position) of the table? The while-loop is not executed. Whatever the old (current) value of p, it is not changed. Stray values in p get returned instead of $p = 0$. To correct this problem, always initialize p each time the findmin() function is visited.

6.8.2 Using the Findmin() Function

A program to find the smallest and second smallest table entries is given in Figure 6.19. In a table with n entries, it will take $n - 1$ comparisons to find the smallest entry, and $n - 2$ comparisons will be needed to find the second smallest entry. Then

$$n - 1 + n - 2 = 2n - 3 \text{ comparisons}$$

are necessary to find the smallest and second smallest entries in a table. We can extend this method to sort an entire table. The result is a selection sort requiring the following number of comparisons:

$$(n - 1) \quad + \quad (n - 2) \quad + (n - 3) + \cdots + 3 + 2 + \quad 1$$

(smallest)   (2nd smallest)   (largest)

$$= 1 + 2 + 3 + \cdots + (n - 3) + (n - 2) + (n - 1)$$

$$= \frac{(n - 1)[(n - 1) + 1]}{2}$$

$$= \frac{n(n - 1)}{2}$$

$$= \frac{n^2}{2} - \frac{n}{2}$$

This means that the running time of a selection sort will be proportional to n^2 *for a table with n* elements. Only n swaps are made by a selection sort, which contributes little to the total running time of this sort.

```
#include "c66.h"
#include "newlib.h"

static int limit = 0;
static int box[50] = {0};

findmin(x, n)
int x[], n;
        {
        int i = 0, max = n, min;
        int p = 0;                         /* a crucial step! */

        min = x[i]; i = 1;
        while (i <= max) {
                if (min > x[i]) {
                        min = x[i];
                        p = i;
                        }
                ++i;
                }
        return(p);
        }

fill_cells(x, n)
int x[], n;
        {
        int i = 0, max = n;
        double newseed;
        char ans;

        printf("Enter r for random nos, k for kb nos for array:   ");
        ans = getchar();
        if (ans == 'r') {
                printf("\n\n Enter seed for random number generator:  ");
                scanf("%f", &newseed);
                init(newseed);
                while (i < max) {
                        x[i++] = chop(100 * rnd());
                        }
                return(i - 1);
                }
        else

                {
                printf("\n\n");
                printf("Enter x[i] 1 (to continue), x[i] 0 (to stop) \n\n");
                return(build_array(x, n));
                }
        }
main()
        {
        int buff, position;
        printf("\n\n");
        limit = fill_cells(box, 49);
        printf("\n\n %40s \n\n", "Copy of array:");
        drawline();
        printf("\n\n %10s %10d \n\n", "limit =", limit + 1);
        print_array(box, limit);
        printf("\n\n");
```

Figure 6.19 Finding Smallest and Second Smallest Entries in a Table

252 Arrays

CHAPTER 6

```
            drawline();
            printf("\n\n");
            printf("\n\n smallest no. = %5d", box[findmin(box, limit)]);
            position = findmin(box, limit);
            buff = box[limit];
            box[limit] = box[position];
            box[position] = buff;
            printf("%20s %5d","2nd smllst =",box[findmin(box, limit - 1)]);
            printf("\n\n");
            drawline();
    }
```

RUN C619

Enter r for random nos, k for kb nos for array: r

 Enter seed for random number generator: 2.71828

                            Copy of array:

----

     limit =   49

         33   10   56   71   88   19

         15   87   14   82   72   95

         81   63   25   56   72   93

         58   91   42   74   14   79

         46   0   88   22   31   93

         65   37   39   52   43   81

         66   48   13   75   18   8

         40   54   61   14   77   32

          3

----

     smallest no. =   0   2nd smllst =   3

Figure 6.19 *concluded*

CHAPTER 6   **6.8 Application: finding the smallest and second smallest number   253**

In Figure 6.20, we show a program to carry out a selection sort using the find-min() function.

6.8.3 Refinement: Defining Select()

The main() function in Figure 6.20 should be cleaned up. A select() function should be defined that does the selection sort. That is, we should use select() instead of main() to manage the use of the findmin() function to do the selection sort. Then main() can be limited to transferring control to select().

This refinement is left as an exercise.

```
#include "c66.h"
#include "newlib.h"

static int limit = 0;
static int box[50] = {0};

findmin(x, n)
int x[], n;
    {
    int i = 0, max = n, min;
    int p = 0;                          /* a crucial step! */

    min = x[i]; i = 1;
    while (i <= max) {
            if (min > x[i]) {
                    min = x[i];
                    p = i;
                    }
            ++i;
            }
    return(p);
    }

fill_cells(x, n)
int x[], n;
    {
    int i = 0, max = n;
    double newseed;
    char ans;

    printf("Enter r for random nos, k for kb nos for array:   ");
    ans = getchar();
    if (ans == 'r') {
            printf("\n\n Enter seed for random number generator:   ");
            scanf("%f", &newseed);
            init(newseed);
            while (i < max)
                    x[i++] = chop(100 * rnd());
```

Figure 6.20 Selection Sort

```c
                        return(i - 1);
                        }
        else
                        {
                        printf("\n\n");
                        printf("Enter x[i] 1 (to continue), x[i] 0 (to stop) \n\n");
                        return(build_array(x, n));
                        }
        }
main()
        {
        int buff, position;

                        printf("\n\n");
                        limit = fill_cells(box, 49);
                        printf("\n\n %40s \n\n", "Copy of array:");
                        drawline();
                        printf("\n\n %10s %10d \n\n", "limit =", limit + 1);
                        print_array(box, limit);
                        printf("\n\n");
                        drawline();
                        printf("\n\n");
                        printf("\n\n\t\tSorted Array\n\n");
                        drawline();
                        printf("\n\n");


/*                                                                      */
/*              begin selection sort:                                   */
/*                                                                      */

                        do      {
                                position = findmin(box, limit);
                                if (position != limit)
                                {
                                buff = box[limit];              /* Swapping min with */
                                box[limit] = box[position];     /* last ele. in box  */
                                box[position] = buff;
                                }
                                --limit;
                                }
                        while (limit != 0);

/*              end selection sort                                      */

                        print_array(box, 49);
                        drawline();
        }
```

Figure 6.20 *continued*

```
RUN C620

Enter r for random nos, k for kb nos for array:    r

Enter seed for random number generator:  1.61803

                        Copy of array:

-------------------------------------------------------------------------------

    limit =        49

        65        40        58        92        50        32

        98         6        29        78        42        71

        86         4        15        87        16        91

        45        96        86         7        36        31

        95        79        53        51        34        19

        10        53        49        25        55        63

        28        76        26        63        28        73

         0        91        42        69        70        80

        55        65


-------------------------------------------------------------------------------


        Sorted Array

-------------------------------------------------------------------------------

        98        96        95        92        91        91

        87        86        86        80        79        78

        76        73        71        70        69        65

        65        63        63        58        55        55

        53        53        51        50        49        45

        42        42        40        36        34        32

        31        29        28        28        26        25

        19        16        15        10         7         6

         4         0

-------------------------------------------------------------------------------
```

Figure 6.20   *concluded*

256 Arrays CHAPTER 6

6.8.4 Refinement: Counting Comparisons and Moves

Variables *compares* and *moves* of type int can be added to the program in Figure 6.20 to assess the amount of work done for tables with various sizes. The program in Figure 6.20 should also be modified so that a user can choose the table size to use in a selection sort. The following declarations can be made:

```
#define MAX  _____
main()
    {
    int box[MAX];
    int tablesize;
    .
    .
    .
    }
```

where

$$tablesize <= MAX$$

This refinement is left as an exercise.

6.9 EXTENDED PRECISION PRODUCTS WITH ARRAYS

It is possible to outstrip the ordinary ability to compute products by using arrays. For example, suppose we want to compute

$$1307674368000 \times 16$$

We can put the digits of the first factor into separate cells of an array. Then we can use repeated addition of the digits in the array cells to compute the product, *provided* we keep track of the carries.

We illustrate this idea in Figure 6.21. We use a sum array to keep track of the sums. In effect, we have

$$x = 1307674368000 = 15!$$
$$x * 16 = x+x+x+ \cdots x \ (15 \ additions)$$

The important thing is to keep track of the carries while each sum is being computed. If there is a carry, an adjustment needs to be made in the entry of the sum array that results from a carry. For example, if

$$sum[j] + x[j]$$

6.9 Extended precision products with arrays

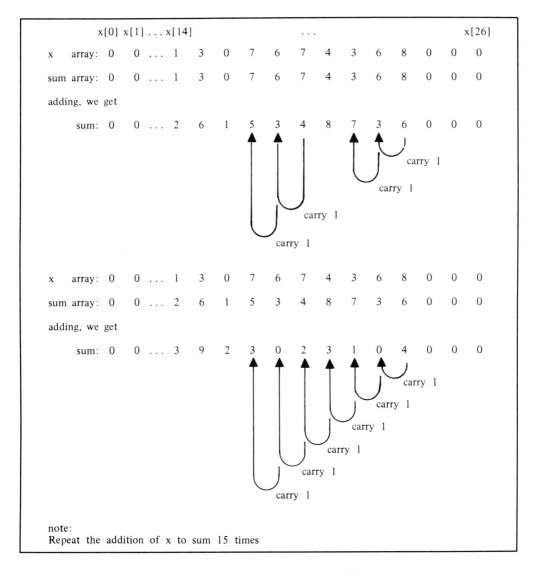

Figure 6.21 Graphical Interpretation of Repeated Addition

results in a carry like 19, then use

sum[j] = sum[j] - 10;
sum[j -1] = sum[j -1] + 1;

This will put 9 in sum[j] and the carry will be added to the adjacent cell on the left in the sum array.

258 Arrays

CHAPTER 6

We can use this idea to compute factorials, for example. The first few factorials are given as follows:

n	$n!$
0	1
1	1
2	2
3	2! x 3 = 2 x 3 = 6
4	3! x 4 = 6 x 4 = 24
5	4! x 5 = 24 x 5 = 120

A program that uses repeated addition with arrays to compute factorials is given in Figure 6.22.

6.10 MULTIDIMENSIONAL ARRAYS

The declarations

       int x[2][4]   /*2 rows, 3 columns*/
       double y[3][4]   /*3 rows, 4 columns*/
       char z[5][20]   /*5 rows, 20 columns*/

sets up three two-dimensional (rectangular) arrays (tables). In each case, the dimension inside the first pair of square brackets specifies the number of rows in the table. The dimension inside the second pair of square brackets specifies the number of columns in the table. The entries in the first row of the x table are specified by

       x[2][0] x[2][1] x[2][2] x[2][3]

For example, we can initialize the x table as follows:

       static int x[2][3] = {
                   {1, 1, 2},
                   {3, 5, 8}
                   };

This gives us the table shown in Figure 6.23.

Notice that the preceding declarations for two-dimensional arrays are consistent with the syntax diagram in Figure 6.2. In fact, the diagram in Figure 6.2 suggests the possibility of multidimensional arrays like

       int y[2][3][5]

which is a point inside 3-space (a cube). For example, we can have the following points:

CHAPTER 6   6.10 Multidimensional arrays   259

```
#include <std.h>
#include <stdio.h>
#define MAX      70

static int m=0,count=0;
static int a[MAX]=0,b[MAX]=0,sum[MAX]=0;

enquiry()
        {
        printf("How many factorials? > ");
        scanf("%d", &m);
        initialize();
        printf("\n");
        buildtable();
        printf("\n");
        }

formattable()
        {
        int k;

        printf("\n");
        printf("%3s%70s\n", "n", "n!");
        for (k=1; k<=75; k++)
                printf("-");
        printf("\n\n");
        }

initialize()
        {
        int i;

        for (i=1; i<=MAX; i++)
                a[i] = b[i] = sum[i] = 0;
        }

dofactorial()
        {
        int j,d=0;

        while (d < count)
                {
                for (j=1; j<=MAX; j++)
                        sum[j] = sum[j] + a[j];
                for (j=MAX; j>=1; j--)
                        while (sum[j] > 9)
                                {
                                sum[j] = sum[j] - 10;
                                sum[j-1] = sum[j-1] + 1;
                                }
                ++d;
                }
```

Figure 6.22 Factorials Program

260 Arrays   CHAPTER 6

```
        }
buildtable()
        {
        int newi,i;

        sum[MAX] = 0;
        a[MAX] = 1;
        formattable();
        for (newi=1; newi<=m; newi++)
                {
                count = newi;
                dofactorial();
                showfactorial();
                for (i=1; i<=MAX; i++)
                        {
                        a[i] = sum[i];
                        sum[i] = b[i];
                        }
                }
        }


showfactorial()
        {
        int selector,flag;

        flag = 1;
        printf("%2d", count);
        for (selector=1; selector<=MAX; selector++)
                if ((sum[selector] == 0)  &&  (flag == 1))
                        printf(" ");
                else
                        {
                        flag = 0;
                        printf("%1d", sum[selector]);
                        }
        printf("\n");
        }
main()
        {
        enquiry();
        }

RUN C622

How many factorials?  > 50


  n                                                                         n!
  --------------------------------------------------------------------------
```

Figure 6.22 *continued*

CHAPTER 6   6.10 Multidimensional arrays   261

```
 1                                                                              1
 2                                                                              2
 3                                                                              6
 4                                                                             24
 5                                                                            120
 6                                                                            720
 7                                                                           5040
 8                                                                          40320
 9                                                                         362880
10                                                                        3628800
11                                                                       39916800
12                                                                      479001600
13                                                                     6227020800
14                                                                    87178291200
15                                                                  1307674368000
16                                                                 20922789888000
17                                                                355687428096000
18                                                               6402373705728000
19                                                             121645100408832000
20                                                            2432902008176640000
21                                                           51090942171709440000
22                                                         1124000727777607680000
23                                                        25852016738884976640000
24                                                       620448401733239439360000
25                                                     15511210043330985984000000
26                                                    403291461126605635584000000
27                                                  10888869450418352160768000000
28                                                 304888344611713860501504000000
29                                                8841761993739701954543616000000
30                                              265252859812191058636308480000000
31                                             8222838654177922817725562880000000
32                                           263130836933693530167218012160000000
33                                          8683317618811886495518194401280000000
34                                        295232799039604140847618609643520000000
35                                      10333147966386144929666651337523200000000
36                                     371993326789901217467999448150835200000000
37                                   13763753091226345046315979581580902400000000
38                                  523022617466601111760007224100074291200000000
39                                20397882081197443358640281739902897356800000000
40                               815915283247897734345611269596115894272000000000
41                             33452526613163807108170062053440751665152000000000
42                           1405006117752879898543142606244511569936384000000000
43                          60415263063373835637355132068513997507264512000000000
44                        2658271574788448768043625811014615890319638528000000000
45                      119622220865480194561963161495657715064383733760000000000
46                     5502622159812088949850305428800254892961651752960000000000
47                   258623241511168180642964355153611979969197632389120000000000
48                 12413915592536072670862289047373375038521486354677760000000000
49                608281864034267560872252163321295376887552831379210240000000000
50              30414093201713378043612608166064768844377641568960512000000000000
```

Figure 6.22 *concluded*

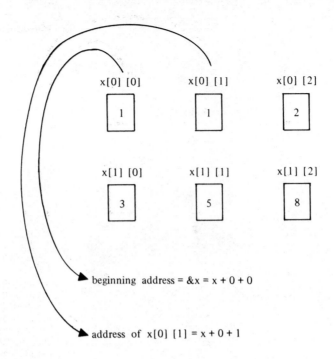

Figure 6.23 Two-Dimensional Array

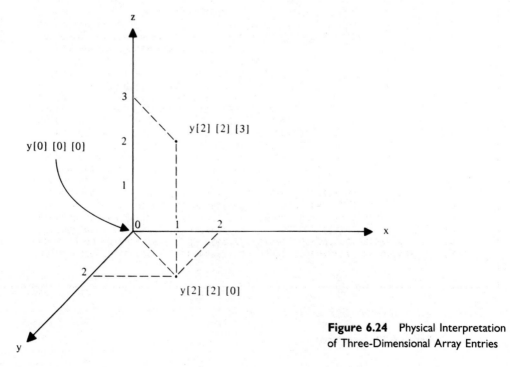

Figure 6.24 Physical Interpretation of Three-Dimensional Array Entries

CHAPTER 6   **6.10 Multidimensional arrays 263**

y[0][0][0] at the origin (corner of cube)
y[2][2][0] located on a diagonal in plane
y[2][2][3] located in space

A physical interpretation of these points is given in Figure 6.24.
The following initialization should be possible with most **C** compilers:

```
static int y[2][3][5] = {
    { {1,1,2,3,5}, {8,13,21,34,55}, {0,0,0,0,1}}
    { {0,0,1,0,1}, {0,0,0,1,0}, {0,0,0,0,1}},
};
```

To set up a function heading to use a two-dimensional array, we can use, for example, the following heading for the x array:

```
build_array (x, row)
int x[ ][3];
int row;
                {
                .
                .
                .
                }
```

The row variable can be used as an upper limit on the number of rows x can have as long as it remains less than or equal to the declared row max. If we want to vary both the rows and columns, we can use

```
build_array {x, row, col)
int x[ ][ ];
int row, col;
                {
                .
                .
                .
                }
```

Similarly, to set up a function heading for a three-dimensional array, we can use the following technique:

```
build_array (y, row)
int y[ ][3][5];
int row;
                {
```

264 Arrays

CHAPTER 6

.
.
.

}

A multidimensional array has more than one selector. A two-dimensional array has two selectors to select each array element in a table. A three-dimensional array has three selectors, and so on.

6.11 SUMMARY

A single-dimensional is a linear data structure. It is a *homogenous* data structure because all its cells contain entries of the same type. It is a *direct-access* (or random-access) data structure because each array element can be directly accessed using array selectors.

The address of an array element in the fifth position of a one-dimensional array x is given by

$$\&x[4]$$

An array name provides the address of the first entry in an array. This is the *base address*. An array element is accessed by adding an array selector value to the base address. For example,

$$x[5] \text{ which is equivalent to } x + 5$$

can be used to access the sixth element of an array x. Why the sixth element? If x is a one-dimensional array of integers, the addresses of the first six cells of x are given as follows:

Address	Content	Access with the sum	Element order
&x[0]	x[0]	x + 0	1
&x[1]	x[1]	x + 1	2
&x[2]	x[2]	x + 2	3
&x[3]	x[3]	x + 3	4
&x[4]	x[4]	x + 4	5
&x[5]	x[5]	x + 5	6

An array in the *extern* or *static* storage class can be initialized at the time it is declared. It is not necessary to initialize all cells of an array. If we use, for example,

$$\text{static int } x[10000] = \{3\};$$

this will put a 3 in x[0] and zeros in the remainder of the cells of x. The C com-

CHAPTER 6   6.11 Summary 265

piler gets very busy when an array is declared. It does the following things for *each* array declaration:

1. Assigns the array to a storage class (the default class is auto for arrays declared inside functions).
2. Establishes the beginning address of an array (as a rule, this will be a relocatable address, not the final one used by a processor).
3. Determines how much storage (in bytes) is needed for each array cell.
4. Sets aside sufficient storage for all the cells of the array.
5. Initializes (if necessary) the array cells.

An array name is a pointer constant. Its address cannot be changed. A pointer variable can have its address changed. There is a distinction between a pointer address and the content of a cell pointed to by a pointer. For example, we can have the following declaration:

        double *ptr;   /*a pointer variable*/
        double x[200];   /*array of type double*/

Then *x* is a pointer constant. We can assign this address to ptr as follows:

        ptr = x;   /*now ptr points to x*/

We can change the address in ptr as follows:

        ptr = &x[2];   /*now ptr points to x[2]*/

The content referenced by the ptr pointer variable can be accessed as follows:

        printf(''%f'', *ptr);

In other words, ptr identifies the pointer address, and *ptr identifies the pointer content.

Pointers add a welcome flexibility *and* high level of subtlety to C programming. It is possible to set up an array of pointers using a declaration like the following:

        int *newptr[15];

This says

        newptr[0], newptr[1], . . . , newptr[14]

is a row of pointers to objects that are of type int.

Finally, arrays in C are not limited to one-dimensional arrays. It is possible to identify the location of an array element with multiple selectors.

266 Arrays

CHAPTER 6

REVIEW TERMS AND SYMBOLS

Term	Meaning
addresses:	
int x[20];	given by x (array name)
int i;	given by &i (address of variable)
constant	not available (&233, e.g., is illegal)
int *y;	given by y (pointer name)
array element	&x[i] for array x
array:	row of objects
base address	array name
effective address	array name + selector (*example:* x + i in array x)
homogenous	all elements of same type
structure	
direct access	each element directly accessible
random access	same as direct access
jagged array	varying length of array rows
linear data structure	row of objects
multidimensional	multiple selectors
pointers:	point to memory locations
constants	array names
variables	pointer variable can be changed
content	given by *ptr for a pointer ptr
selection sort	continually select smallest element in subtables of original table, starting with the original table (which is also a subtable of itself) until we obtain a subtable with one entry

EXERCISES

1. What is the difference between &x[i] and x[i] for an array x?
2. Give a declaration to initialize each of the following one-dimensional arrays with the corresponding values:

   a. x of type int with the following entries:

   $$1, 1, 2, 3, 5, 8, 13, 21, 34, 55, 89, 144$$

   b. y of type double with the following entries:

   $$1.6, 1.61, 1.618, 1.6180, 1.61803$$

   c. z of type char with the following entries:

   $$\text{'c', 'a', 'l', 'l', 'm', 'e', 'I',}$$
   $$\text{'s', 'h', 'm', 'a', 'e', 'l', '!'}$$

3. Give sample declarations with initial values for *each* cell for the following two-dimensional arrays:

   a. box[2][10] of type int   **c.** ch[6][20] of type char

   b. letter[3][5] of type char   **d.** value[3][4] of type double

CHAPTER 6   **Exercises   267**

4. Give sample declarations with initial values for *each* cell for the following three-dimensional arrays:
   a. box[2][3][5] of type int
   b. symbol[3][4][6] of type char
   c. digital[4][5][6] of type double
5. Write a program to print out the contents of each cell of each array initialized in Exercise 2.
6. Write a program to print out the contents of each cell of each array in Exercise 3.
7. Write a program to print out the contents of each cell of each array in Exercise 4.
8. What is the difference between the base of an array and the effective address of an array element?
9. Write a choice() function that uses a selector value passed to it along with the base address for an array and prints out the content of an array, all selected by the user. Write a program that uses the choice() function to do the following things:
   a. Builds an array of 25 random numbers in the range from zero to 99.
   b. Allows the user to choose an array cell to inspect.
   c. Calls the choice() function with the array address and the selector value for a chosen cell.
   d. Displays the content of the selected cell.
10. Add to the program in Exercise 9 an except() function that does the following:
   a. Uses a selector value passed to it to check if the value is in an acceptable range (i.e., 0 to 49).
   b. Prints an error message, if the *selected* value is unacceptable.
   c. Allows the user to try another value.
   Run your program with
   d. Array with 50 random numbers and selector values of 65, -75, 52, 43.
11. Write a **C** program that prints out the following table:

base	cell	cell address	cell
address	address	- base addr.	content

   in terms of the arrays in Exercise 2.
12. For an array x, explain what the following expression indicates:

   $$\&x[i] - \&x[0]$$

13. Which of the following array declarations within a function will produce error(s) (explain why)?

   a. int cell[2] = {5};
   b. int cell[2] = {1, 5};
   c. int cell[2] = {1, 5, 9};
   d. char ch[2][3] = {
       "today"
       "mm. . ."
       };

   e. static int a[2][3] = {
       {0, 1, 0}
       };
   f. static char x[5] = {"mmmmm"};
   g. static double y[2][3] = {
       {3.0, 3.1, 3.14},
       {2.0, 2.7, 2.71}
       };

14. *Caesar cipher method:* Write a function encrypt() to encrypt a message by replacing each character (spaces, punctuation marks, and letters) by a character three positions forward in the ASCII character table. For example, we can have the following plaintext and encryption:

268 Arrays

CHAPTER 6

> plaintext: SECURE ALL MESSAGES
> ciphertext: VHFXUH#DOO#PHVVDJHV

Notice a problem with this method. That is, it is possible to run past the end of the character table. This problem can be handled by circling back to the beginning of the character table, starting with '!', to avoid error. Write a program that uses the encrypt() function. Your program should print the plaintext and ciphertext for each run. Run your program for

a. C is terse. !

b. Why is it most hackers confuse Halloween and Christmas? Because 31(Oct) = 25(Dec). (Jon L. Bentley (1984, p. 291)). !

15. Write a function decrypt() that decrypts messages using the Caesar system given in Exercise 14. Add this function to the program in Exercise 14. Then give the user the following options:

a. Encrypt a message.

b. Decrypt a cipher text supplied by the user.

Run your program for the cipher texts produced by Exercise 14a and b.

16. Carry out the refinement of the program in Figure 6.9 described in Section 6.4.1. Give a sample run.

17. Carry out the refinement of the build_table() function given in Section 6.4.1 using the suggestion given in Section 6.4.2. Give a sample run.

18. Carry out the refinement of the get_freq() function in Figure 6.11 described in Section 6.4.4. Give a sample run.

19. Make it possible for the user to quantify the stars in the spikes printed by the program in Figure 6.11. Also carry the other two refinements of Figure 6.11 described in Section 6.4.5. Give sample runs illustrating the various cases.

20. Define a select() function and carry out the refinement of the program in Figure 6.20 described in Section 6.8.1. Give a sample run.

21. Modify the program in Figure 6.20 so that the numbers of comparisons and moves made to complete the selection sort are computed. Print a table with the following headings:

tablesize	compares used	moves made

Also modify the program in Figure 6.20 so that it uses the seed from the previous sort as the basis for a new sort. Then generate 20 different random-number tables and record the number of compares and moves made for each sort in the preceding table.

22. Write a program to measure the randomness of the random-number generator introduced in Lab 3 Project of Chapter 5. Display the number of occurrences of each sample in a distribution of numbers generated by this generator. Use the range 1 to 10 for sample sizes.

23. Enhance the program in Exercise 22 so that it produces the following table:

sample	count using sqr() method	count using remainder method

Produce random-number tables using the rnd() generator in Figure 6.6 and the remainder generator from Knuth in Lab 3 Project of Chapter 5. Give several runs to compare the two generators.

CHAPTER 6   Lab projects   269

24. Refine the program in Figure 6.20 so that the user can choose to display an ordered list in descending or ascending order. Run your program using seed = 1.61803 to construct a table of 50 random numbers.

25. Write a findmax() function to find the largest number in a list of numbers. Write a program that uses findmax to carry out a selection sort of a list of numbers. Allow the user to display the sorted numbers in ascending or descending order. Run your program with
    a. Seed = 2.71828 for a list of 50 random numbers.
    b. Seed = 3.141592654 for a list of 50 random numbers.

26. *Exception handling:* Refine the build_table() function in Figure 6.4 as follows:
    a. Print a message telling the maximum number of entries possible.
    b. Put in a check to check when the user has only five entries left to enter before reaching the end of the array. (Print a warning message.) Give a sample run.

LAB PROJECTS

1. Write a program to compute powers of numbers using repeated addition. Let the user select the base and exponent to be used. Run your program for
   a. 2^{100} **b.** 3^{50} **c.** 16^{50} **d.** 5^{50}

2. Enhance the program in Lab Project 1 so that the user can make the following choices:
   a. Produce a table of powers *and* specify the starting and end powers to be computed as well as the amount to increment the exponent.
   b. Produce a single power.
   Run your program for
   c. Table of powers of 3 from 3^0 to 3^{50} with the exponent incremented by 2.
   d. Table of powers of 3 from 3^{25} to 3^{50} with the exponent incremented by 5.
   e. Table of powers of 2 from 2^0 to 2^{100} with the exponent incremented by 5.

3. Write a select_word() function that can be used to sort an array of words and is the counterpart of the select() function in Figure 6.20. Also define a findword() function that is the counterpart of the findmin() function in Figure 6.20. Use findword() to identify the word that belongs alphabetically at the beginning of a list of words. Write the counterpart of the program in Figure 6.20 to sort a list of words, putting them in alphabetic order. Run your program for
   a. Combined list of review words beginning with the letter *c* from Chapters 4 and 5.
   b. Names of American league west baseball teams.

4. Write the following functions:
   a. Product() to compute the product *kA*, where *k* is a constant and *A* is a rectangular array. For example, what follows is the product *2A:*

   $$2A = 2x \begin{pmatrix} 6 & 9 \\ 4 & 2 \end{pmatrix} = \begin{pmatrix} 12 & 18 \\ 8 & 4 \end{pmatrix}$$

   b. Transpose() to compute the transpose of a matrix (rectangular array) A^T, where A^T represents the array *A* after the rows and columns of array *A* have been interchanged. For example, if *A* is given by

270   Arrays   CHAPTER 6

$$\begin{pmatrix} 6 & 9 \\ 4 & 2 \end{pmatrix}$$

then

$$A^T = \begin{pmatrix} 6 & 4 \\ 9 & 2 \end{pmatrix}$$

Write a program that uses the product() and transpose() functions to compute the products and transpose of the following arrays:

c.$\begin{pmatrix} 2 & 1 & 3 \\ 5 & 7 & 11 \\ 5 & 2 & 1 \end{pmatrix}$

d.$\begin{pmatrix} 10 & 65 & 9 \\ 68 & 72 & 1 \\ 3 & 5 & 55 \end{pmatrix}$

5. *Matrix transpose cipher:* Write a function encrypt() to encrypt a message using the following technique:

   a. Put the ASCII codes for a message into a two-dimensional array (matrix).
   b. Use the transpose() function from Lab Project 4 to find the transpose of the ASCII code matrix from part a.
   c. Produce an encryption of the original message written with the ASCII codes taken from the columns of the transpose of the original matrix from part a.

   For example, we can have the following plaintext and encryption:

plaintext:			matrix:	
usefunctions	u	s	117	99
	e	f	115	116
	u	n	101	105
	c	t	102	111
	l	o	117	110
	n	s	110	115

   transpose:

   $$\begin{pmatrix} 117 & 115 & 101 & 102 & 117 & 110 \\ 99 & 116 & 105 & 111 & 110 & 115 \end{pmatrix}$$

   cipher text:
   117 99 115 116 101 105 102 111 117 110 110 115

   d. Write a program to test the use of the new encrypt() function in terms of the messages in Exercise 14a and b.

CHAPTER 6   **Lab projects   271**

6. Write a decrypt() function to take the transpose of an array of codes from Lab Project 5. Then use the rows of the transpose matrix to produce a plaintext. This time convert the codes to ASCII characters.

7. Knuth (1981) introduced a procedure for extended precision multiplication. A pseudo-code rendition of Knuth's procedure is given in Figure 6.25. Write an extend() function in **C** to implement Knuth's procedure. Write a program that uses extend() to compute the following products:
   a. 130767436800 x 16
   b. 130767436800 x 130767436800
   c. 9999999999 x 9999999999999
   d. 123456789 x 987654321

8. Revise the program written for Lab Project 1 so that Knuth's method in Figure 6.25 is used to compute powers of numbers. Run your revised program for parts a through d of Lab Project 1.

```
PROCEDURE KNUTH:

BEGIN

1.   Insert FACTOR NO. 1 (with M digits) into ARRAY U with
     dimension M

2.   Insert FACTOR NO. 2 (with N digits) into ARRAY V with dimension
     N

3.   Initialize the product array W so that W(M+1) through W(M+N)
     are zero

4.   Set up a counter J (for FACTOR NO. 1) equal to N

5.   Repeat the following steps UNTIL J <= 0:
     5.1   IF V(J) <> 0 Then execute the following steps:
           5.1.1 Initialize counter I (for FACTOR NO. 2) equal to M
           5.1.2 Initialize carry K equal to zero
           5.1.3 REPEAT the following steps UNTIL I <= 0:
                 5.1.3.1 T:=V(I)*V(J)+W(I+J)+K
                 5.1.3.2 W(I+J):=TMOD BASE
                 5.1.3.3 K: = TDIV BASE
                 5.1.3.4 K: = I - 1
           5.1.4 W(J): = K
           ELSE
                 W(J): = 0
     5.2   J: = J - 1

6.   Write out W(1) through W(M+N) as the answer

7.   End Procedure Knuth
```

Figure 6.25   Knuth's Extended Precision Product Procedure

272 Arrays   CHAPTER 6

SELECTED SOLUTIONS

Exercise 6

```
extern char letter[3][5] = { {´a´,´b´,´c´,´d´,´e´},
                             {´A´,´B´,´C´,´D´,´E´},
                             {´1´,´@´,´#´,´$´,´%´} };
extern double value[3][4] = { {1.2, 1.3, 1.4, 1.5},
                              {2.6, 2.7, 2.8, 2.9},
                              {3.0, 3.1, 3.2, 1.76} };

main()
        {
static int box[2][10] = { {1, 2, 3, 4, 5, 6, 7, 8, 9, 10},
                          {10, 9, 8, 7, 6, 5, 4, 3, 2, 1} };
static char ch[6][20] = {´a´};
int i,j;

        printf("box[][]: ");
        for (i = 0;i < 2;++i)
          for (j = 0;j < 10;++j)
            printf("%d, ", box[i][j]);
        printf("\n\nletter[][]: ");
        for (i = 0;i < 3;++i)
          for (j = 0;j < 5;++j)
            printf("%c", letter[i][j]);
        printf("\n\nch[][]: ");
        for ( i = 0;i < 6;++i)
          for (j = 0;j < 20;++j)
            printf("%c", ch[i][j]);
        printf("\n\nvalue[][]: ");
        for (i = 0;i < 3;++i)
          for (j = 0;j < 4;++j)
            printf("%.2f,", value[i][j]);
        }
```

RUN CE66

box[][]: 1, 2, 3, 4, 5, 6, 7, 8, 9, 10, 10, 9, 8, 7, 6, 5, 4, 3, 2, 1,

letter[][]: abcdeABCDE1@#$%

ch[][]: a

value[][]: 1.20,1.30,1.40,1.50,2.60,2.70,2.80,2.90,3.00,3.10,3.20,1.76,

CHAPTER 6   **Selected solutions   273**

Exercise 11

```
#include "lib.h"

tableint(arr,n)
int n, arr[];
        {
        int i, a, b;

        for (i = 0;i <= n;++i)
            {
            a = arr;
            b = &arr[i];
            printf("%d\t%d\t%d\t\t%d\n", a, b, b - a, arr[i]);
            }
        }

tabledouble(arr,n)
int n;
double arr[];
        {
        int i, a, b;

        for (i = 0;i <= n;++i)
            {
            a = arr;
            b = &arr[i];
            printf("%d\t%d\t%d\t\t%.5f\n", a, b, b - a, arr[i]);
            }
        }

tablechar(arr,n)
int n;
char arr[];
        {
        int i, a, b;

        for (i = 0;i <= n;++i)
            {
            a = arr;
            b = &arr[i];
            printf("%d\t%d\t%d\t\t%c\n", a, b, b - a, arr[i]);
            }
        }

main()
        {
static int x[] = {1, 1, 2, 3, 5, 8, 13, 21, 34, 55, 89, 144};
static double y[5] = {1.6, 1.61, 1.618, 1.6180, 1.61803};
static char z[14] =
                {´c´,´a´,´1´,´1´,´m´,´e´,´I´,´s´,´h´,´m´,´a´,´e´,´1´,´!´};

        printf("base     cell       cell address                cell\n");
        printf("address address    - base address            content\n");
```

274 Arrays

CHAPTER 6

Exercise 11 *concluded*

```
printf("----------------------------------------\n");
printf("\n");
tableint(x,11);
tabledouble(y,4);
tablechar(z,14);
}
```

```
RUN CE611

base    cell    cell address    cell
address address  - base address  content
----------------------------------------

6556    6556    0               1
6556    6558    2               1
6556    6560    4               2
6556    6562    6               3
6556    6564    8               5
6556    6566    10              8
6556    6568    12              13
6556    6570    14              21
6556    6572    16              34
6556    6574    18              55
6556    6576    20              89
6556    6578    22              144
6580    6580    0               1.60000
6580    6588    8               1.61000
6580    6596    16              1.61800
6580    6604    24              1.61800
6580    6612    32              1.61803
6620    6620    0               c
6620    6621    1               a
6620    6622    2               l
6620    6623    3               l
6620    6624    4               m
6620    6625    5               e
6620    6626    6               I
6620    6627    7               s
6620    6628    8               h
6620    6629    9               m
6620    6630    10              a
6620    6631    11              e
6620    6632    12              l
6620    6633    13              !
6620    6634    14
```

CHAPTER 6   Selected solutions   275

64   **Exercise 15**

```
#include "lib.h"

encrypt(string)
char string[];
        {
        int i = 0;

        do
          if (string[i] != '\n')  /*keep <cr><lf> in tact*/
            string[i] = string[i] + 3;
        while (string[++i] != '!');
        }

decrypt(string)
char string[];
        {
        int i = 0;

        do
          if (string[i] != '\n')  /*keep <cr><lf> in tact*/
            string[i] = string[i] - 3;
        while (string[++i] != '!');
        }

readstr(string)
char string[];
        {
        int i = 0;

        do
          string[i] = getchar();
        while string[i++] != '!');
        }

main()
        {
        char ans, ch[256];

        printf("\ta) encrypt.\n");
        printf("\tb) decrypt.\n");
        printf("Choice? a/b -:> ");
        ans = getchar();
        getchar();                      /*remove <cr><lf> from input stream*/
        printf("\n\nOriginal text: ");
        readstr(ch);
        if (ans == 'a' || ans == 'A')
          encrypt(ch);
        else
          decrypt(ch);
        printf("\n\nResultant text: %s", ch);
        }
```

276 Arrays   CHAPTER 6

Exercise 15 *concluded*

```
RUN CE615

        a) encrypt.
        b) decrypt.
Choice? a/b -:> a

Original text: C is terse.!

Resultant text: F#lv#whuvhl!


RUN CE615

        a) encrypt.
        b) decrypt.
Choice? a/b -:> b

Original text: F#lv#whuvhl!

Resultant text: C is terse.!


RUN CE615

        a) encrypt.
        b) decrypt.
Choice? a/b -:> a

Original text: Why is it most hackers confuse
Halloween and Christmas?  Because 31 (Oct) =
25 (Dec).  (Jon L. Bentley (1984))!

Resultant text: Zk|#lv#lw#prvw#kdfnhuv#frqixvh
Kdoorzhhq#dqg#FkulvwpdvB##Ehfdxvh#64#+Rfw,#@
58#+Ghf,1##+Mrq#Ol#Ehqwoh|#+4<;7,,!


RUN CE615

        a) encrypt.
        b) decrypt.
Choice? a/b -:> b

Original text: Zk|#lv#lw#prvw#kdfnhuv#frqixvh
Kdoorzhhq#dqg#FkulvwpdvB##Ehfdxvh#64#+Rfw,#@
58#+Ghf,1##+Mrq#Ol#Ehqwoh|#+4<;7,,!

Resultant text: Why is it most hackers confuse
Halloween and Christmas?  Because 31 (Oct) =
25 (Dec).  (Jon L. Bentley (1984))!
```

CHAPTER 6   Selected solutions   277

Exercise 16

```
#include "c66.h"
#include "lib.h"


buildtable(x,n)
int n, x[];
        {
        double newseed;
        int i = 0;

                printf("\n\n Enter seed for random number generator:  ");
                scanf("%f", &newseed);
                init(newseed);
                while (i < n)
                        x[i++] = chop(100 * rnd());
                return(i-1);
        }

fill_cells(x, n)
int x[], n;
        {
        int i = 0, max = n;
        double newseed;
        char ans;

        printf("Enter ´r´ for random nos, ´k´ for kb nos, for the array:   ");
        ans = getchar();
        if (ans == ´r´)
                return(buildtable(x,max));
        else
                {
                printf("\n\n");
                printf("Enter x[i] 1 (to continue), x[i] 0 (to stop) \n\n");
                return(build_array(x, n));
                }
        }
main()
        {
        int box[50];
        int limit;

                printf("\n\n");
                limit = fill_cells(box, 50);
                printf("\n\n %40s \n\n", "Copy of array:");
                drawline();
                printf("\n\n %10s %10d \n\n", "limit =", limit);
                print_array(box, limit);
        }


RUN CE616

Enter ´r´ for random nos, ´k´ for kb nos, for the array:   r


 Enter seed for random number generator:  1.61803
```

Exercise 16   *concluded*

Copy of array:

----

limit =   49

65	40	58	92	50	32
0	92	56	76	25	56
70	80	57	79	53	51
34	17	96	88	23	40
60	1	95	81	69	70
81	65	40	57	83	84
85	99	10	51	36	30
85	1	94	70	82	70
82	74				

RUN CE616

Enter ´r´ for random nos, ´k´ for kb nos, for the array: k

Enter x[i] 1 (to continue), x[i] 0 (to stop)

 ---->12 1

 ---->21 1

 ---->45 1

 ---->40 1

 ---->10 1

 ---->400 1

 ---->7 1

 ---->1 0

Copy of array:

----

limit =   7

12	21	45	40	10	400
7	1				

CHAPTER 6   Selected solutions   279

Exercise 18

```
#include "newlib.h"
#include "c66.h";

init_array(x, n)
int x[200], n;
            {
            int i = 0;

            while (i <= n)
                    x[i++] = 0;
            }

get_freq(x, n,top)
int x[200],n,top;
            {
            int i = 0, no;

            while (i <= n) {
                    no = chop(top * rnd()) + 1;
                    x[no] = x[no] + 1;
                    ++i;
                    };
            }

show_freq(x, n)
int x[200],n;
            {
            int i = 1,newmax,j;

            printf("\n\n%10s %10s %30s", "random", "frequency", "frequency");
            printf("\n\n %10s %10s %30s", "number", "count", "polygon");
            printf("\n\n n.b.: each star represents 10 occurrences of a rnd no.");
            printf("\n\n");
            drawline();
            printf("\n\n");
            while (i <= n) {
                    printf("%10d %10d %5s", i, x[i], "|");
                    newmax = x[i] / 10;
                    for (j = 0; j <= newmax; ++j)
                            printf("%1c", '*');
                    ++i;
                    printf("\n\n");
                    };
             drawline();
             printf("\n\n\n");
            }

main()
            {
            int count[200];
            int limit,bound;
            double newseed;
```

280 Arrays

CHAPTER 6

Exercise 18 *continued*

```
      int max = 200;

            printf("\n\n Enter floating pt seed for rnd nos:  ");
            scanf("%f", &newseed);
            init(newseed);
            do
              {
                printf("\n\n Enter upper bound:  ");
                scanf("%d",&bound);
                if (bound > max)
                    printf("\nchoice too big.\n");
              }
            while (bound > max);
            printf("\n\n Enter limit in rnd range 1 ... limit:  ");
            scanf("%d", &limit);
            init_array(count, bound);
            get_freq(count, limit,bound);
            show_freq(count, bound);
        }
```

```
RUN CE618

 Enter floating pt seed for rnd nos:  3.1415927


 Enter upper bound:  20


 Enter limit in rnd range 1 ... limit:  3000


    random  frequency                   frequency

     number       count                    polygon

 n.b.: each star represents 10 occurrences of a rnd no.

 ----------------------------------------------------------------

         1      159     |****************

         2      155     |****************

         3      167     |*****************

         4      137     |**************

         5      145     |***************

         6      143     |***************
```

CHAPTER 6

Exercise 18 *concluded*

```
        7      136    |**************
        8      129    |*************
        9      153    |****************
       10      143    |***************
       11      162    |*****************
       12      145    |***************
       13      149    |***************
       14      140    |***************
       15      147    |***************
       16      128    |*************
       17      147    |***************
       18      177    |******************
       19      160    |*****************
       20      179    |******************
```

282   Arrays   CHAPTER 6

Exercise 20

```
#include "c66.h"
#include "newlib.h"

static int limit = 0;
static int box[50] = {0};

findmin(x, n)
int x[], n;
        {
        int i = 0, max = n, min;
        int p = 0;

        min = x[i]; i = 1;
        while (i <= max) {
                if (min > x[i]) {
                                min = x[i];
                                p = i;
                                }
                ++i;
                }
        return(p);
        }

fill_cells(x, n)
int x[], n;
        {
        int i = 0, max = n;
        double newseed;
        char ans;

        printf("Enter r for random nos, k for kb nos for array:    ");
        ans = getchar();
        if (ans == ´r´) {
                printf("\n\n Enter seed for random number generator:");
                scanf("%f", &newseed);
                init(newseed);
                while (i < max) {
                                x[i++] = chop(100 * rnd());
                                }
                return(i - 1);
                }
        else
                {
                printf("\n\n");
                printf("Enter x[i] 1 (to continue), x[i] 0 (to stop)\n\n");
                return(build_array(x, n));
                }
        }
select()
        {
        int buff, position;
```

CHAPTER 6   **Selected solutions   283**

Exercise 20   *continued*

```
                          printf("\n\n");
                          limit = fill_cells(box, 50);
                          printf("\n\n %40s \n\n", "Copy of array:");
                          drawline();
                          printf("\n\n %10s %10d \n\n", "limit =", limit + 1);
                          print_array(box, limit);
                          printf("\n\n");
                          drawline();
                          printf("\n\n");
                          printf("\n\n\t\tSorted Array\n\n");
                          drawline();
                          printf("\n\n");

                          do      {
                                      position = findmin(box, limit);
                                      if ( position != limit)
                                       {
                                         buff = box[limit];
                                         box[limit] = box[position];
                                         box[position] = buff;
                                       }
                                      --limit;
                                      }
                          while (limit != 0);

                          print_array(box, 49);
                          drawline();
                  }

main()
        {

              select();

        }


RUN CE620

Enter r for random nos, k for kb nos for array:    r


 Enter seed for random number generator: 2.71828


                          Copy of array:

---------------------------------------------------------------------

    limit =          50

         33          10          56          71          88          19
```

284 Arrays   CHAPTER 6

Exercise 20 *concluded*

15	87	14	82	72	95
81	63	25	56	72	93
58	91	42	74	14	79
46	0	88	22	31	93
65	37	39	52	43	81
66	48	13	75	18	8
40	54	61	14	77	32
3	10				

Sorted Array

95	93	93	91	88	88
87	82	81	81	79	77
75	74	72	72	71	66
65	63	61	58	56	56
54	52	48	46	43	42
40	39	37	33	32	31
25	22	19	18	15	14
14	14	13	10	10	8
3	0				

CHAPTER 6   Selected solutions   285

Exercise 22

```
#include "lib.h"
#include "c66.h";

random()
        {
        static long x = 377;
        int a = 637, b = 3109, c = 9423;

        x = (a * x + b) % c;
        return(x);
        }

init_array(x, n)
int x[], n;
        {
        int i = 0, max = n;

        while (i <= max)
                x[i++] = 0;
        }

get_freq(x, n)
int x[],n;
        {
        int i = 0, max = n, no;

        while (i <= 1000) {
                no = chop(max * (double)random() / 9423) + 1;
                x[no] = x[no] + 1;
                ++i;
                }
        }

show_freq(x, n)
int x[],n;
        {
        int i = 1, max = n, newmax;

        printf("\n\n");
        printf("%10s %10s %30s", "random", "frequency", "frequency");
        printf("\n\n %10s %10s %30s", "number", "count", "polygon");
        printf"\n\n n.b.: each star represents 10 occurrences of a rnd no.");
        printf("\n\n");
        drawline();
        printf("\n\n");
        while (i <= max) {
                printf("%10d %10d %5s", i, x[i], "|");
                newmax = x[i] / 10;
                for (j = 0; j <= newmax; ++j)
                        printf("%1c", '*');
                ++i;
                printf("\n\n");
```

286 Arrays

Exercise 22 *concluded*

```
                }
        }
main()
        {
        int count[11];
        int limit;                          /*rnd range: 1 ... limit*/

                printf("\n\n Enter limit in rnd range 1 ... limit:  ");
                scanf("%d", &limit);
                printf("\n");
                init_array(count, 10);
                get_freq(count, limit);
                show_freq(count, 10);
        }
```

RUN CE622

 Enter limit in rnd range 1 ... limit: 10

    random frequency   frequency

    number   count   polygon

----

        1   109 |**********

        2   96 |*********

        3   104 |**********

        4   77 |********

        5   91 |*********

        6   98 |*********

        7   108 |**********

        8   103 |**********

        9   117 |***********

       10   98 |*********

CHAPTER 6

Selected solutions   287

Exercise 23

```
#include "lib.h"
#include "c66.h";

long prime = 0;          /*seed for random()*/

random()
        {
        int a = 637, b = 3109, c = 9423;

        prime = (a * prime + b) % c;
        return(prime);
        }

init_array(x, n)
int x[], n;
        {
        int i = 0, max = n;

        while (i <= max)
                x[i++] = 0;
        }

get_freq(x, y, n)
int x[],y[],n;
        {
        int i = 0, max = n, no;

        while (++i <= 1000) {
                no = chop(max * (double)random() / 9423) + 1;
                x[no] = x[no] + 1;
                no = chop(max * rnd()) + 1;
                y[no] = y[no] + 1;
                }
        }

show_freq(x, y, n)
int x[],y[],n;
        {
        int i = 0, max = n;

        printf("\n\n");
        printf("%10s %20s %20s", "random", "count using", "count using");
        printf("\n %10s %20s %20s", "number", "sqr() method", "rem. method");
        printf("\n\n");
        drawline();
        printf("\n\n");
        while (i++ < max)
                printf("%10d %20d %20d \n\n", i, x[i], y[i]);
        }
main()
        {
        int count[11], count2[11];
```

288 Arrays

CHAPTER 6

Exercise 23   *continued*

```
        int limit;                          /*rnd range: 1 ... limit*/
        double no;

                printf("\nEnter floating point seed -:> ");
                scanf("%f", &no);
                printf("\n");
                init(no);
                printf("\nEnter prime seed -:> ");
                scanf("%f", &prime);
                printf("\n\n Enter limit in rnd range 1 ... limit:  ");
                scanf("%d", &limit);
                printf("\n");
                init_array(count, 10);
                init_array(count2, 10);
                get_freq(count, count2, limit);
                show_freq(count, count2, 10);
        }
```

RUN CE623

Enter floating point seed -:> 1.61803

Enter prime seed -:> 3

 Enter limit in rnd range 1 ... limit: 10

random number	count using sqr() method	count using rem. method
1	81	121
2	106	91
3	95	93
4	112	83
5	109	103
6	105	83
7	97	100
8	113	103
9	92	110
10	90	113

CHAPTER 6   **Selected solutions 289**

Exercise 23   *concluded*

```
RUN CE623

Enter floating point seed -:> 1.61803

Enter prime seed -:> 5

 Enter limit in rnd range 1 ... limit:  10
```

random number	count using sqr() method	count using rem. method
1	110	121
2	106	91
3	99	93
4	101	83
5	97	103
6	105	83
7	105	100
8	101	103
9	96	110
10	80	113

Lab Project I

```
#include "lib.h"

init(x)
int x[];
        {
        int i;

        for (i = 0;i <= 80;++i)
          x[i] = 0;
        }

copy(x,y)
int x[], y[];
        {
        int i;

        for (i = 0;i <= 80;++i)
          y[i] = x[i];
        }

printresult(x)
int x[];
        {
        int i = 0;

        while (x[i] == 0)
          ++i;                          /*don't print out initial 0's*/
        do
          {
          printf("%d", x[i++]);
          if (i % 3 == 0 && i != 81)
            printf(",");
          }
        while (i <= 80);
        printf("\n");
        }

compute(x,n)
int n, x[];
        {
        int j, i = 80, y[81];

        copy(x,y);
        for (j = 1;j < n;++j)      /*same as multiplying n times*/
          {
          for (i = 80;i >= 0;--i)
            x[i] += y[i];
          }
          carry(x);
        }

carry(x)

 int x[];
        {
        int a;
```

290

Lab Project 1 *concluded*

```
        for (a = 80;a > 0;--a)
          while (x[a] > 9)
            {
            x[a] -= 10;
            x[a-1] += 1;
            }
        }

main()
        {
        int i,no,power,arr[81];

        printf("Enter number, power. (#,#)-:> ");
        scanf("%d,%d", &no, &power);
        printf("\n");
        init(arr);
        arr[80] = no;   /*initialize for 1st power*/
        for (i = 1;i < power;++i)
          compute(arr,no);
        printf("%6d \n%5d %10s", power, no, "equals:  ");
        printresult(arr);
        }
```

RUN CL61

Enter number, power. (#,#)-:> 2,100

    100
      2 equals: 1,267,650,600,228,229,401,496,703,205,376

RUN CL61

Enter number, power. (#,#)-:> 3,50

    50
     3 equals: 717,897,987,691,852,588,770,249

RUN CL61

Enter number, power. (#,#)-:> 16,50

    50
    16 equals: 1,606,938,044,258,990,275,541,962,092,341,162,602,522,202,993,78
2,792,835,301,376

RUN CL61

Enter number, power. (#,#)-:> 5,50

    50
     5 equals: 88,817,841,970,012,523,233,890,533,447,265,625

291

292 Arrays

Lab Project 3

```
#include "lib.h"
#define ARLIM1 50
#define ARLIM2 20

static int limit = 0;

prints(x, n)
char x[ARLIM1][ARLIM2];
int n;
        {
        int i;

        for (i = 0;i <= n;++i)
           {
           printf("%-20s",x[i]);
           if (i % 3 == 2)              /*three per line*/
             printf("\n");
           }
        }
findword(x, n)
char x[ARLIM1][ARLIM2];
int n;
        {
        int i = 0, max = n;
        int p = 0;                      /* a crucial step! */
        char *min;

        min = x[i]; i = 1;
        while (i <= max) {
                if (strcmp(min, x[i]) < 0) {
                        min = x[i];
                        p = i;
                        }
                ++i;
                }
        return(p);
        }

fill_cells(x, n)
char x[ARLIM1][ARLIM2];
int n;
        {
        int i = 0, max = n;

        printf("Enter words with ´!´ as sentinel.\n");
        do
          {
          printf("\nWord-:> ");
          scanf("%s", x[i]);
          ++i;
          }
        while ((*x[i-1] != ´!´) && (i < max));
```

CHAPTER 6

Selected solutions   293

Lab Project 3   *continued*

```
        return(i-2);    /*last postition filled*/
        }
select_word(x, n)
char x[ARLIM1][ARLIM2];
int n;
        {
        char buff[20];
        int position;

        do      {
                position = findword(x, n);
                strcpy(buff, x[n]);          /* Swapping min with */
                strcpy(x[n], x[position]); /*last ele. in box*/
                strcpy(x[position], buff);
                --n;
                }
        while (n != 0);
        }
main()
        {
        char box[ARLIM1][ARLIM2];

                printf("\n\n");
                limit = fill_cells(box, ARLIM1);
                printf("\n\n %40s \n\n", "Copy of array:");
                drawline();
                printf("\n\n %10s %10d \n\n", "limit =", limit);
                prints(box, limit);
                printf("\n\n");
                drawline();
                printf("\n\n");
                printf("\n\n\t\tSorted Array\n\n");
                drawline();
                printf("\n\n");
                select_word(box, limit);
                prints(box, limit);
                printf("\n\n");
                drawline();
        }


RUN CL63

Enter words with ´!´ as sentinel.

Word-:> cast

Word-:> char

Word-:> long
```

294 Arrays   CHAPTER 6

Lab Project 3 *continued*

```
Word-:> mask

Word-:> canonical

Word-:> continue

Word-:> else

Word-:> do

Word-:> iterate

Word-:> switch

Word-:> !


                        Copy of array:

-------------------------------------------------------------------------------

    limit =          9

cast                char                long
mask                canonical           continue
else                do                  iterate
switch

-------------------------------------------------------------------------------



                   Sorted Array

-------------------------------------------------------------------------------

canonical           cast                char
continue            do                  else
iterate             long                mask
switch

-------------------------------------------------------------------------------


RUN CL63

Enter words with ´!´ as sentinel.

Word-:> Twins

Word-:> A´s
```

CHAPTER 6   **Selected solutions 295**

Lab Project 3 *concluded*

```
Word-:> Royals

Word-:> Angels

Word-:> Whitesox

Word-:> !

                        Copy of array:
-----------------------------------------------------------------------------

    limit =         4

Twins              A´s                    Royals
Angels             Whitesox

-----------------------------------------------------------------------------


            Sorted Array
-----------------------------------------------------------------------------

A´s                Angels                 Royals
Twins              Whitesox

-----------------------------------------------------------------------------
```

RELATED READINGS

Bentley, Jon L., , "Programming Pearls," *Communications of the Association for Computing Machinery,* Vol. 27, No. 4 (April 1984), p. 291.

Bosworth, B., *Codes, Ciphers, and Computers.* Rochelle Park, N.J.: Hayden Book Co., Inc., 1982. See Chapters 4 (Caesar Ciphers) and 5 (Matrix Ciphers).

Feuer, A. R., *The C Puzzle Book.* Englewood Cliffs, N.J.: Prentice-Hall, Inc., 1982. See pp. 51–60 (Pointers and Arrays) and pp. 129–140 (Solutions to Problems).

Knuth, D. E., *The Art of Computer Programming,* Vol. 2, Seminumerical Algorithms. Menlo Park, CA: Addison-Wesley Publishing Co., 1981.

Wirth, N., *Algorithms + Data Structures = Programs.* Englewood Cliffs, N.J.: Prentice-Hall, Inc., 1976. See Section 1.6 on arrays.

7

Structures

[A record] aids greatly in displaying logical connections between pieces of data.

*Robert L. Kruse**

AIMS
- Introduce Declarations and Operations with Structures and Pointers to Structures.
- Show How to Access Members of a Structure.
- Show How Pointers Can Be Used to Reference Structures in Functions.
- Give Examples of How Pointers to Structures Can Be Passed to and from Functions.
- Introduce a New Findmin() Function That Returns a Pointer to the Position of a Structure with the Smallest Key.
- Introduce the Use of Keys to Sort an Array of Pointers.
- Introduce a Hash Search for a Structure.
- Show How Structures Can be Nested.
- Suggest Uses of Typedef and Unions.

**Data Structures and Program Design*, Prentice-Hall, Inc., Englewood Cliffs, N.J., 1984.*

297

298 Structures

CHAPTER 7

7.1 INTRODUCTION

A *structure* is a collection of components. The components of a structure can be of various types, not just one type. A structure component is called a *member*. In Pascal, a structure is called a record. The syntax diagram for a structure is given in Figure 7.1.

A structure name is called a *tag*. The term *identifier* in Figure 7.1 refers to a variable, which is a struct. For example, we can declare the following struct for musicians:

```
struct album {
    char disc[20], artist[20];
    int year;
} x, y;
```

This declaration includes two identifiers x and y of type *album*. We can also use the following technique to separate the declaration of a struct from a declaration of variables of type album:

Declaration of struct   **Declaration of variables**

```
Struct album {
    char disc[20], artist[20];
    int year;
};
```

```
struct album x, y;
```

Members of a struct can be accessed using a point (.) in the following way:

identifier . member identifier

For example, we can print the members of the preceding struct for the variable x using the following technique:

```
print("%s %s %d",
        x.disc;
        x.artist;
        x.year);
```

This chapter shows how pointers can also be used to access the members of a struct. In addition, we deal with a key concern in C programs that use structures: the design of functions that can be used to build and use structures. We introduce functions to build structures. We also introduce functions to construct and manage arrays of pointers to structures. We show how to edit an existing structure. We also show how to construct a hash table and to carry out a hash search.

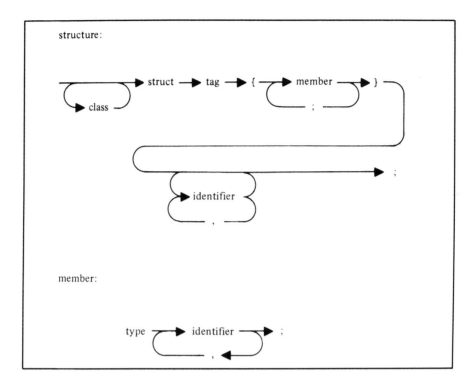

Figure 7.1 Syntax Diagram for a Structure

7.2 POINTERS TO STRUCTURES

We can declare a pointer to a struct. For example, we can use

struct album *ptr_a, *ptr_b, x, y;

This says *a* and *b* can be used as pointers to a struct of type album. A *pointer* to a *structure* identifies the location of a structure in memory, its beginning address. We initialize a pointer to a struct using the following technique:

ptr_a = &x

Now ptr_a has the beginning address of the struct identified by *x*.

To access the member of a struct using a pointer, the following format is used:

pointer_name -> member name

300 Structures   CHAPTER 7

The arrow in this construction consists of a minus sign followed by the greater than symbol (>). For example,

1. ptr_a -> disc *points to a disc name.*
2. ptr_a -> artist *points to an artist's name.*
3. ptr_a -> year *points to an album year.*

If we use

$$ptr\_a \ = \ \&x;$$
$$ptr\_b \ = \ \&y;$$

this gives ptr_a the address of the structure identified by &x and ptr_b the address of the structure identified by &y. The contents of one member can be assigned to a corresponding member of another structure of the same type as follows:

$$ptr\_b \ -> \ disc \ = \ ptr\_a \ -> \ disc$$

This puts a copy of x.disc into y.disc and

$$ptr\_b \ -> \ year \ = \ ptr\_a \ -> \ year$$

puts a copy of x. year into y.year in this second assignment.

Why bother with pointers to structures? They are easier to work with than structures themselves. In addition, most **C** compilers put restrictions on the use of structures that force the use of references (pointers) to structures rather than manipulate structures themselves. For example, it is normally not possible to assign one structure to another. However, it is possible to set up more than one pointer to the same structure. If it is necessary to make a duplicate of a structure in memory, this needs to be done member by member.

The arrow (->) and point (.) notation can be used in several ways. If *x* is a structure of type part, we can use either of the following methods to select (gain access to) the qty member of the structure:

$$x.qty \ \ is \ equivalent \ to \ \ (\&x) \ -> \ qty$$

If ptr is a pointer to a structure of type part, we can use either of the following methods to select the qty member:

$$ptr \ -> \ qty \ \ is \ equivalent \ to \ \ (*ptr).qty$$

Finally, the arrow (->) has the same precedence as parentheses () or square brackets [ ]. These symbols are left associative. If they are used in the same expression together or more than once, they are evaluated from left to right. They have the highest precedence among **C** operators.

CHAPTER 7   **7.4 Functions and pointers to structures**   **301**

7.3 INITIALIZING STRUCTURES

A structure can be initialized if it is in the *extern* and/or *static* storage class. For example, we can initialize a structure *x* of type *album* as follows:

```
static struct album x = {
        "Petrushka",
        "Stravinsky",
        1967
        };
```

This specifies the contents of the members corresponding to the declarations in the declaration of the *album* structure. This says position is important. If the string "Stravinsky" were put before "Petrushka," then

$$x.disc = "Stravinsky"$$

and

$$x.artist = "Petrushka"$$

which is not what we want. Selection of the entries used to initialize a structure must be made with care.

7.4 FUNCTIONS AND POINTERS TO STRUCTURES

In Figure 7.2 we show a build_struct() function. This function uses the following structure:

```
struct part {
        char name[20];
        int qty;
        };
```

It returns a pointer *x* to a newly constructed structure. That is, it returns the beginning address of the new structure. Notice that it is necessary to use

$$\&x \rightarrow qty$$

with the scanf() function if the argument is not a string.

    We can print the content of a structure referenced by build_struct() using the function shown in Figure 7.3. Rather than pass the struct itself, a pointer to the struct is passed to this function in a call by reference. The print_struct() function argument is an alias for an actual pointer to a struct of type part. A complete program to illustrate the use of these two functions is given in Figure 7.4.

302 Structures   CHAPTER 7

```
        struct part *build_struct()

          {

          struct part *x;

          printf("Enter part name:  ");

          scanf("%s", x -> name);

          printf("\n\n Enter part quantity:  ");

          scanf("%d", &x -> qty);


          return(x);              /*returns ptr to struct*/

          }
```

Figure 7.2   Build_struct() Function

```
        print_struct(x)

        struct part *x;          /*pointer to struct*/

          {

          printf("\n %30s %20d",

                  x -> name,

                  x -> qty);

          }
```

Figure 7.3   Print_struct() Function

CHAPTER 7   **7.4 Functions and pointers to structures   303**

```
        #include "newlib.h"

        struct part {
                char name[20];
                int qty;
                };
        /*------------------------------------------------------------*/

        struct part *build_struct()
                {
                struct part *x;

                printf("Enter part name:  "); scanf("%s", x -> name);
                printf("\n\n Enter part qty:   "); scanf("%d", &x -> qty);
                return(x);
                }
        /*------------------------------------------------------------*/

        print_struct(x)
        struct part *x;
                {

                printf("\n\n %30s %20d", x -> name, x -> qty);

                }
        /*------------------------------------------------------------*/

        main()
                {
                struct part *this, *that;

                that = build_struct();
                printf("\n\n"); drawline();
                printf("\n\n %40s \n\n", "Copy of new structure:"); drawline();
                print_struct(that);

                }

RUN C74

Enter part name: wheels


 Enter part qty:   233


---------------------------------------------------------------------------

                Copy of new structure:

---------------------------------------------------------------------------

                        wheels              233
```

Figure 7.4   Program to Build and Print a Structure

304 Structures

CHAPTER 7

7.5 OPERATIONS WITH POINTERS TO STRUCTURES

It may not be apparent that the print_struct() function in Figure 7.2 can be used in two different ways:

1. To receive a pointer address in

print_struct(that);

2. To receive a reference to a struct rather than a pointer in

print_struct(&copy);

where copy is the name of a structure, *not* a pointer to a structure.

That is, &copy is the beginning address of a structure, whereas *that contains the beginning address of a struct but is not the name of a separate struct. We illustrate some of the operations that are possible with pointers to structures in Figure 7.5. Notice how

this = ©

makes the pointer *this* refer to the structure labeled *copy*. The

print_struct(this);
print-struct(&copy);

will print the same thing. We make *this* point to a different structure by using

this = &xerox;

Notice that

xerox -> qty = 21

changes the *qty* member of the xerox structure. We extract the contents of the struct members using

*a = that -> name;
b = that -> qty;

Finally, notice that we copy the members of one structure to another using the following assignments:

that -> name = this -> name;
that -> qty = this -> qty;

CHAPTER 7   **7.5 Operations with pointers to structures 305**

```
#include "newlib.h"

struct part {
        char name[30];
        int qty;
        };
/*---------------------------------------------------------------*/

struct part *build_struct()
        {
        struct part *x;

        printf("Enter part name:   "); scanf("%s", x -> name);
        printf("\n\n Enter part qty:   "); scanf("%d", &x -> qty);
        return(x);
        }
/*---------------------------------------------------------------*/

print_struct(x)
struct part *x;
        {

        printf("\n\n %30s %20d", x -> name, x -> qty);

        }
/*---------------------------------------------------------------*/

main()
        {
        struct part *this, *that, *build_struct();
        static struct part copy = {
                "Tom",
                233
                };
        static struct part xerox = {
                "Tumty! Tumty! Tum-tumtoes!",
                55
                };
        static char *a = "aaaabbbbbcccccddddd";
        int b;

        that = build_struct();
        printf("\n\n copy of entered structure members \n");drawline();
        print_struct(that);
        this = &copy;
        printf("\n\n Result of init. pointer with structure address \n");
        drawline();
        print_struct(this);
        print_struct(&copy);
        this = &xerox;
        printf("\n\n Result of changing pointer: \n"); drawline();
        print_struct(this);
```

Figure 7.5 Operations with Structures

306 Structures   CHAPTER 7

```
          xerox -> qty = 21;
          printf("\n\n Change in member of structure \n");drawline();
          print_struct(&xerox);
          *a = that -> name;
          b = that -> qty;
          printf("\n\n Copy of members of a struct \n");drawline();
          printf("\n\n %30s %20d", *a, b);
          that -> name = this -> name;
          that -> qty = this -> qty;
          printf("\n\n Copying members of one struct to another \n");drawline();
          print_struct(that);

          }


RUN  C75

Enter part name:  wheels


 Enter part qty:    55


 copy of entered structure members
 ----------------------------------------------------------------------------

                          wheels                      55

 Result of init. pointer with structure address
 ----------------------------------------------------------------------------

                            Tom                      233

                            Tom                      233

 Result of changing pointer:
 ----------------------------------------------------------------------------

     Tumty! Tumty! Tum-tumtoes!                       55

 Change in member of structure
 ----------------------------------------------------------------------------

     Tumty! Tumty! Tum-tumtoes!                       21

 Copy of members of a struct
 ----------------------------------------------------------------------------

                          wheels                      55

 Copying members of one struct to another
 ----------------------------------------------------------------------------

     Tumty! Tumty! Tum-tumtoes!                       21
```

Figure 7.5 *concluded*

CHAPTER 7   **7.7 Arrays of pointers to structures** **307**

7.6 ARRAY OF STRUCTURES

It is possible to set up arrays of structures. For example, we can set up an array of structures of type *album* using the following declaration:

struct album card[2000];

This tells **C** to reserve room in memory for 2000 structures of type album. An array of structures can be initialized as follows:

struct album sample[5] = {
    {"Die Fledermaus", "J. Strauss", 1890},
    {"Sleppytime Gal", "R. Whiting", 1938},
    {"Camelot", "F. Loewe", 1940},
    {"Over the Rainbow", "H. Arlen", 1940},
    }"Petrushka", "I. Stravinsky", 1967}
    };

This makes

sample[0] = {"Die Fledermaus", "J. Strauss", 1890};
sample[1] = {"Sleepytime Gal", "R. Whiting", 1938}

and so on.

We can select, for example, the members of the sample[0] struct using

sample[0].disc;
sample[0].artist;
sample[0].year

We can also set up an array of pointers to structures. These are convenient to use in passing information about a structure to a function.

7.7 ARRAYS OF POINTERS TO STRUCTURES

The syntax for a declaration of an array of pointers *to structures* is as follows:

struct tag *name[size];

This says name[i] is a pointer to a structure identified by *tag*. In Figure 7.6 we give a show() function to exhibit the contents of members of a structure referenced by an array pointer. Notice that the show() argument list is constructed in the following way:

1. *x* is an alias for a pointer to a structure of type part.

308 Structures

CHAPTER 7

```
            show(x, n)

            struct part *x[ ];

            int n;

                {

                int i;


                for (i  294    <= n; ++i)

                        printf("\n\n %30s %20d",

                                x[i] -> name,

                                x[i] -> qty);


                }
```

Figure 7.6   Show() Function for an Array of Structures

2. *n* is a value parameter used to carry the number of array pointers that
show() will use.

Declaring an array of pointers does not guarantee that **C** will reserve memory for the structures corresponding to pointers in an array of pointers. To get
around this problem, there is a memory allocation function

$$malloc()$$

that uses an integer argument to allocate bytes of memory to a variable. For
example,

$$x = malloc(20)$$

will allocate 20 bytes to *x*. It is possible to determine the number of bytes needed
for a structure by using the size of operator. For example,

$$size\ of(struct\ album)$$

determines the number of bytes needed for an *album* structure. Then, if x[i] points
to an *album* structure, we can allocate memory to x[i] as follows:

$$x[i] = malloc(size\ of(struct\ album))$$

In Figure 7.7 we show an init() function to initialize each of the structures

CHAPTER 7   **7.8 Refinement: counting bytes used by structures**   **309**

```
init(x, n)

struct part *x[ ];

int n;

    {

    int i;

    for (i = 0; i <= n; ++i)
            x[i] = malloc(sizeof(struct part));


    }
```

Figure 7.7   Init() Function

referenced by an array of pointers. It will be necessary to modify the build_struct()
function in Figure 7.2 to accommodate an array of pointers to structures. The
heading for the new build_struct() function is given next:

$$\text{build\_struct}(x, n)$$
$$\text{struct part } *x;$$
$$\text{int } n;$$

It will be helpful to imitate the build_array() function given in Chapter 6.
That is, we should make n in the build_struct() argument list an upper bound on
the number of pointers that can be used. The user can then enter 1 or more structures without worrying (too much!) about how many structures need to be loaded.
We can make build_struct() return the number of pointers used during its execution. We show this new version of build_struct() in the program in Figure 7.8.

7.8 REFINEMENT: COUNTING BYTES USED BY STRUCTURES

We can enhance the table printed by indicating the number of bytes used for the
structures constructed *during* the execution of the program in Figure 7.8. How?
Take the product of the number of structures loaded times the size of one structure. In addition, the total number of bytes made available by the init() function
can be calculated. Finally, a percentage can be calculated:

$$\text{bytes used } = x\% \text{ of total available}$$

These refinements are left as an exercise.

```
#include "newlib.h"

struct part {
        char name[20];
        int qty;
        };
/*--------------------------------------------------------------------------*/

init(x,n)
struct part *x[];
int n;
        {
        int i;

        for (i = 0; i <= n; ++i)
                x[i] = malloc(sizeof(struct part));

        }
/*--------------------------------------------------------------------------*/

show(x,n)
struct part *x[];
int n;
        {
        int i;

        for (i = 0; i <= n; ++i)
                printf("\n\n %30s %20d", x[i] -> name, x[i] -> qty);

        }
/*--------------------------------------------------------------------------*/

build_struct(x, n)
struct part *x[];
int n;
        {
        int i = 0, yes = 1;

        while ((yes == 1) && (i <= n)) {
                printf("\n\n Enter part name:  ");
                scanf("%s", x[i] -> name);
                printf("\n\n Enter part qty:  ");
                scanf("%d", &x[i] -> qty);
                printf("\n\n Again?--1=Y,0=N:  ");
                scanf("%d", &yes);
                ++i;
                }
        return(i - 1);
        }
/*--------------------------------------------------------------------------*/

main()
        {
        struct part *box[20];
        int limit = 20;

        init(box, limit);
        limit = build_struct(box, limit);
```

Figure 7.8 Program to Build an Array of Structures

```
        printf("\n\n"); drawline();
        printf("\n\n %40s \n\n", "Collection of structures:");
        drawline();
        show(box, limit);
        }
```

RUN C78

 Enter part name: wheels

 Enter part qty: 21

 Again?--1=Y,0=N: 1

 Enter part name: antenna

 Enter part qty: 233

 Again?--1=Y,0=N: 1

 Enter part name: strut

 Enter part qty: 14

 Again?--1=Y,0=N: 1

 Enter part name: mmmmmmmmmmm

 Enter part qty: 89

 Again?--1=Y,0=N: 0

            Collection of structures:
----

                    wheels   21

                   antenna   233

                     strut   14

                mmmmmmmmmmm   89

Figure 7.8 *concluded*

312 Structures

CHAPTER 7

7.9 SWAPPING POINTERS TO STRUCTURES

In Figure 7.9 we show a swap() function to swap pointers to structures. This gives us a way to change pointers to structures, rather than manipulate or change the structures themselves. This also gives us an efficient way to set up a selection sort of structures.

```
swap(x, i, j)

struct part *x[ ];

int i j;                /*pointer indices*/

    {

    struct part *buff;

    buff = x[i];

    x[i] = x[j];

    x[j] = buff;


    }
```

Figure 7.9 Swap() Function

In Figure 7.10 we show a program to swap pointers. The sample run in Figure 7.10 is deceptive. The second list shows the first and last structures in reverse order. However, this does not mean the structures stored in memory have changed positions. In fact, the structures originally entered have *not* been moved. Only the pointers to these structures have been changed.

7.10 REFINEMENT: SELECTION SORT OF STRUCTURES

The swap() function can be used to build a selection sort of a collection of structures. To do this, we need to modify the findmin() function given in Chapter 6. A modified findmin() function can be used to determine the pointer to a structure relative to a sort key. A *sort key* is a structure member name like *qty* in the *part* structure. This key can be used to organize structures. For example, we can organize the part structures as follows:

Name:	Wheels	Antenna	Clips	Buttons
Quantity:	2	11	14	34

CHAPTER 7

7.10 Refinement: Selection sort of structures 313

```
#include "newlib.h"

struct part {
        char name[20];
        int qty;
        };
/*-----------------------------------------------------------------*/

swap(x, i, j)
struct part *x[];
int i, j;
        {
        struct part *buff;

        buff = x[i];
        x[i] = x[j];
        x[j] = buff;

        }
/*-----------------------------------------------------------------*/

init(x,n)
struct part *x[];
int n;
        {
        int i;

        for (i = 0; i <= n; ++i)
                x[i] = malloc(sizeof(struct part));

        }
/*-----------------------------------------------------------------*/

show(x,n)
struct part *x[];
int n;
        {
        int i;

        for (i = 0; i <= n; ++i)
                printf("\n\n %30s %20d", x[i] -> name, x[i] -> qty);

        }
/*-----------------------------------------------------------------*/

build_struct(x, n)
struct part *x[];
int n;
        {
        int i = 0, yes = 1;

        while ((yes == 1) && (i <= n)) {
```

Figure 7.10 Program to Swap Pointers to Structures

314 Structures

CHAPTER 7

```
            printf("\n\n Enter part name:  ");
            scanf("%s", x[i] -> name);
            printf("\n\n Enter part qty:  ");
            scanf("%d", &x[i] -> qty);
            printf("\n\n Again?--1=Y,0=N:  ");
            scanf("%d", &yes);
            ++i;
            }
        return(i - 1);
        }
/*------------------------------------------------------------------------*/

main()
        {
        struct part *box[20];
        int limit = 20;
        struct part *buff;

        init(box, limit);
        limit = build_struct(box, limit);
        printf("\n\n"); drawline();
        printf("\n\n %40s \n\n", "Original collection of structures:");
        drawline();
        show(box, limit);
        printf("\n\n"); drawline();
        printf("\n\n %40s \n\n", "Result of swapping pointers:"); drawline();
        swap(box, 0, limit);
        show(box, limit);
        }


RUN C710

  Enter part name:  wheels


  Enter part qty:  233


  Again?--1=Y,0=N:  1


  Enter part name:  strut


  Enter part qty:  2


  Again?--1=Y,0=N:  1


  Enter part name:  antenna
```

Figure 7.10 *continued*

CHAPTER 7

7.10 Refinement: Selection sort of structures

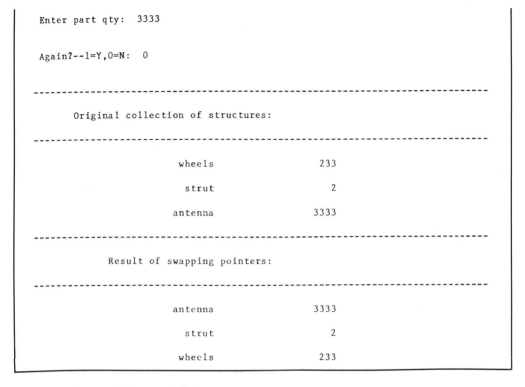

Figure 7.10 *concluded*

That is, the part structures have been ordered in terms of quantities (from smallest to largest). The following loop can then be used to carry out a selection sort of an array of pointers to structures:

```
do {
    position = findmin(box, limit);
    swap(box, position, limit);
    --limit;
}
while (limit != 0);
```

A program to carry out a selection sort of a collection of part structures is given in Figure 7.11. The sort key in the modified findmin() function is *qty*. Notice that

```
x[i] -> qty
```

points to this key.

316 Structures   CHAPTER 7

7.11 REFINEMENT: VARYING THE SORT KEY

The findmin() function is limited to one sort key, *qty*. The formal parameter list
should be enlarged to include a sort key selector. We can use

        findmin(x, n, key)
        struct part *x[ ];
        int n;   /*member of pointers*/
        int key;   /*sort key*/

Then a switch statement can be used to choose the appropriate while-loop, which
is selected using the sort key value. This refinement is left as an exercise.

7.12 REFINEMENT: INTRODUCING A SELECT() FUNCTION

The do-loop in main() in Figure 7.11 should be put into a select() function. We
can use

        select(x, n, key)
        struct part *x[ ];
        int n, key;

as the function heading for this new function. This refinement is left as an exercise.

7.13 EDITING A STRUCTURE

In Figure 7.12 we show an edit() function that can be used to edit an *album* structure. In effect, this function writes over the old members of a structure. Calling
this function is made tricky by the normal way lists are numbered. For example,
we can construct the following list:

Item	Album	Artist	Year
1.	Chocolate Soldier	O. Straus	1954
2.	Music Man	M. Willson	1940
3.	Die Fledermaus	J. Strauss	1899
4.	Evergreen	B. Streisand	1977
5.	Copacabana	B. Manilow	1978

CHAPTER 7

7.13 Editing a structure 317

```
#include "newlib.h"

struct part {
        char name[20];
        int qty;
        };
/*----------------------------------------------------------------------*/
findmin(x, n)
struct part *x[];
int n;
        {
        int i = 0, max = n, min;
        int location = 0;

        min = x[i] -> qty; i = 1;
        while (i <= max) {
                if (min > x[i] -> qty) {
                        min = x[i] -> qty;
                        location = i;
                        }
                ++i;
                }
        return(location);
        }
/*----------------------------------------------------------------------*/

swap(x, i, j)
struct part *x[];
int i, j;
        {
        struct part *buff;


        buff = x[i];
        x[i] = x[j];
        x[j] = buff;


        }
/*----------------------------------------------------------------------*/

init(x,n)
struct part *x[];
int n;
        {
        int i;

        for (i = 0; i <= n; ++i)
  x[i] = malloc(sizeof(struct part));


        }
/*----------------------------------------------------------------------*/
```

Figure 7.11 Selection Sort of Pointers to Structures

318   Structures   CHAPTER 7

```
show(x,n)
struct part *x[];
int n;
        {
        int i;

        for (i = 0; i <= n; ++i)
                printf("\n\n %30s %20d", x[i] -> name, x[i] -> qty);

        }
/*-------------------------------------------------------------------------*/

build_struct(x, n)
struct part *x[];
int n;
        {
        int i = 0, yes = 1;

        while ((yes == 1) && (i <= n)) {
                printf("\n\n Enter part name:   ");
                scanf("%s", x[i] -> name);
                printf("\n\n Enter part qty:   ");
                scanf("%d", &x[i] -> qty);
                printf("\n\n Again?--1=Y,0=N:   ");
                scanf("%d", &yes);
                ++i;
                }
        return(i - 1);
        }
/*-------------------------------------------------------------------------*/

main()
        {
        struct part *box[20];
        int limit = 20, copy, position;
        struct part *buff;
        init(box, limit);
        limit = build_struct(box, limit);

        copy = limit;
        printf("\n\n"); drawline();
        printf("\n\n %40s \n\n", "Original collection of structures");
        drawline(); printf("\n\n");
        show(box, limit);
        printf("\n\n"); drawline(); printf("\n\n");
        do {

                position = findmin(box, limit);
                swap(box, position, limit);
                --limit;
            }
        while (limit != 0);
```

Figure 7.11   *continued*

CHAPTER 7   7.13 Editing a structure   319

```
            printf("%40s \n\n", "Sorted structures:"); drawline();
            show(box, copy);
            }

  RUN C/11

   Enter part name:  wheels

   Enter part qty:  21


   Again?--1=Y,0=N:  1


   Enter part name:  mmmmmmmmmm


   Enter part qty:  2


   Again?--1=Y,0=N:  1


   Enter part name:  antenna


   Enter part qty:  144


   Again?--1=Y,0=N:  1


   Enter part name:  strut


   Enter part qty:  55


   Again?--1=Y,0=N:  1


   Enter part name:  chip


   Enter part qty:  1001


   Again?--1=Y,0=N:  0


  ----------------------------------------------------------------------
```

Figure 7.11   *continued*

320 Structures CHAPTER 7

```
*        Original collection of structures

-----------------------------------------------------------------------------


                    wheels                        21

                    mmmmmmmmmm                     2

                    antenna                       144

                    strut                          55

                    chip                          1001

-----------------------------------------------------------------------------

              Sorted structures:

-----------------------------------------------------------------------------


                    chip                          1001

                    antenna                       144

                    strut                          55

                    wheels                         21

                    mmmmmmmmmm                      2
```

Figure 7.11 *concluded*

If we use sample[] as an array of pointers to these structures, then

sample[0] = {"Chocolate Soldier", "O. Straus", 1954}

This conflicts with the numbering of the displayed list. We can get around this problem by using

sample[i-1] = edit(sample[i-1])

after the user has selected item i in the preceding list. We show a program to carry out this idea in Figure 7.13.

7.14 REFINEMENT: SELECTING A MEMBER TO EDIT

The edit() function in Figure 7.11 can be improved by selecting the member that should be changed. This can be done with a switch statement inside a while-loop

CHAPTER 7   **7.15 A hash search for a structure   321**

```
struct album *edit(recrd)

struct album *recrd;

    {

    char dummy[5];

    gets(dummy);

    printf("\n\n New album name? \n\n");

    gets(recrd -> disc);

    printf("New album´s artist? \n\n");

    gets(recrd -> artist);

    printf("New album´s year? \n\n);

    scanf("%d", &recrd -> year);

    return(recrd);


    }
```

Figure 7.12   Edit Function

that feeds the switch statement with one or more members to edit. This refinement is left as an exercise.

7.15 A HASH SEARCH FOR A STRUCTURE

The term *hashing* is derived from the fact that a search key is hashed or "chopped off." The idea is to construct a hash table so that the keys are smeared across a hash table. For this reason, a hash table is also called a scatter storage table. A hash search starts by using part of a search key selected by the user. A hash search through a hash table is based solely on a comparison of keys. With a hash search, a structure can usually be found in two or three comparisons. This search is independent of the hash table size. This makes a hash search very efficient. Its running time will be proportional to 1.

322 Structures

CHAPTER 7

```c
#include "newlib.h"

struct album
        {
        char disc[30], artist[20];
        int year;
        };


/*--------------------------------------------------------------------------*/

init(x, n)
struct album *x[ ];
int n;
        {
        int i;

        for (i = 0; i <= n; ++i)
                x[i] = malloc(sizeof(struct album));

        }
/*--------------------------------------------------------------------------*/

build(hits,limit)
struct album *hits[];
int limit;
        {
        int i;
        char dummy[5];

        init(hits, limit);
        printf("Creating a list of top ten records...\n\n");
        --limit;
        for (i=limit; i>=0; i--) {
                printf("enter record name--> ");
                gets(hits[i]->disc);
                printf("\n\nenter artist------> ");
                gets(hits[i]->artist);
                printf("\n\nenter year made----> ");
                scanf("%d", &hits[i]->year);
                printf("\n");
                gets(dummy);
                }
        }
/*--------------------------------------------------------------------------*/


show(hits,limit)
struct album *hits[ ];
int limit;
        {
        int i;
```

Figure 7.13 Program to Edit a Structure

CHAPTER 7   7.15 A hash search for a structure   323

```
            printf("\n\n\t\tTOP 5 ALBUMS OF THE 1960s\n");
            printf("\t\t~~~ ~ ~~~~~~ ~~ ~~~ ~~~~~\n\n");
            printf("  %-30s%-20s%-10s\n\n", "Album", "Artist", "Year");
            for (i=0; i<limit; i++)
            printf("%d. %-30s%-20s%-10d\n", i+1, hits[i]->disc, hits[i]->artist,
                                           hits[i]->year);
            printf("\n\n");
            }
/*-------------------------------------------------------------------*/


struct album *edit(recrd)
struct album *recrd;
        {
        char dummy[5];

        gets(dummy);
        printf("\n\nNew album name?\n\n");
        gets(recrd->disc);
        printf("New album´s artist?\n\n");
        gets(recrd->artist);
        printf("New album´s year?\n\n");
        scanf("%d", &recrd->year);
        return(recrd);
        }
/*-------------------------------------------------------------------*/

main()
        {
        struct album *hold[5];
        int new;

        build(hold, 5);
        show(hold,5);
        printf("Which record should be changed (enter number) ?  ");
        scanf("%d", &new);
        hold[new-1] = edit(hold[new-1]);
        printf("\n\n\tNew List:\n\n");
        show(hold, 5);
        }


RUN C713

Creating a list of top ten records...

enter record name--> mmmmmmmmmmmmmm


enter artist------> x

enter year made----> 1962

enter record name--> Petrushka
```

Figure 7.13   *continued*

324 Structures   CHAPTER 7

```
enter artist------> Stravinsky


enter year made----> 1960

enter record name--> Die Fledermaus


enter artist------> J. Strauss


enter year made----> 1899

enter record name--> Music Man


enter artist------> M. Willson


enter year made----> 1940

enter record name--> Chocolate Soldier


enter artist------> O. Straus


enter year made----> 1954



              TOP 5 ALBUMS OF THE 1960s
              ~~~ ~ ~~~~~~ ~~ ~~~ ~~~~~


        Album                    Artist          Year

   1. Chocolate Soldier       O. Straus         1954
   2. Music Man               M. Willson        1940
   3. Die Fledermaus          J. Strauss        1899
   4. Petrushka               Stravinsky        1960
   5. mmmmmmmmmmmmmm           x                 1962


Which record .should be changed (enter number) ?   5

   New album name?

   I wanna hold your hand!
   New album´s artist?

   Beatles
   New album´s year?

   1960
```

Figure 7.13   *continued*

CHAPTER 7   **7.15 A hash search for a structure** **325**

```
    New List:


          TOP 5 ALBUMS OF THE 1960s
          ~~~ ~ ~~~~~~ ~~ ~~~ ~~~~~

      Album                    Artist          Year

   1. Chocolate Soldier        O. Straus       1954
   2. Music Man                M. Willson      1940
   3. Die Fledermaus           J. Strauss      1899
   4. Petrushka                Stravinsky      1960
   5. I wanna hold your hand!  Beatles         1960
```

Figure 7.13 *concluded*

The use of a hash table has two problems:

1. Determining a hash table address using a hash key.
2. Determining what to do if a collision occurs; that is, if we hash to a hash table cell that is filled, we must have some means of resolving the collision.

In this section we will use what is known as the *open addressing* technique to resolve hash table collisions:

```
* * * * * * * * * * * * * * * * * * * *
*                                     *
*  Open addressing technique: continue looking  *
*  in hash table until a vacancy is found.      *
*                                     *
* * * * * * * * * * * * * * * * * * * *
```

To carry out a hash search using open addressing, two functions are needed:

1. A hash function to calculate the initial hash table address.
2. A rehash function to calculate an alternative hash table address, if collision occurs.

The construction of hash and rehash functions is an art that requires imagination and insight concerning the members of a structure. If we use a part number, for example, which is a string of characters, we can add up the ASCII codes for the characters and divide by the hash table size to determine a hash table address.

326 Structures

CHAPTER 7

```
hash(s)

char s[10]

    {

    int m

    for (m = 0, *s != `\0`; )

            m += *s++;


    return(m % TABLESIZE);


    }
```

Figure 7.14   Hash() Function

We show a hash() function to carry out this idea in Figure 7.14. The hash() function may return a hash table address for a nonempty table cell. Collision occurs in this case. Then we compute an alternative hash table address using the rehash() function in Figure 7.15.

A generalized version of the rehash function used in Figure 7.15 is as follows:

```
rehash(x, c)
int x, c;
    {
    return((x + c) % TABLESIZE);
    }
```

The x value is taken from a hash function and used in this function if a collision occurs. The choice of the c value and TABLESIZE is crucial. If c and TABLESIZE have common factors, then table positions will be missed. For example, we can use the following two forms of the return statement for the preceding rehash function:

(a) poor rehash: (b) good rehash:
    return((x + 2) % 10);   return((x + 2) % 11);

A check on these two return statements will show that version (a) misses table positions, whereas version (b) tracks through the entire table. What happens? Start

CHAPTER 7   **7.15 A hash search for a structure   327**

```
rehash(address)

int address;

    {

    return ((address + 1) % TABLESIZE);

    }
```

Figure 7.15   Rehash() Function

with x from the hash function in Figure 7.14. Use this as the initial value of x in the rehash function. Then the value returned by the rehash function becomes the *new* value of x in the next call to the rehash function. For example, if we hash to location 7, which is filled, use

rehash(7, 2) to produce 9 in version (a)

Then, if collision results, use

rehash(9, 2) to produce 1 in version (a)

and so on. It is left as an exercise to verify that version (a) misses some table positions, whereas version (b) can be used to scan an entire table with 11 entries.

We can start, for example, with the following structure concerning owners of various cars:

```
struct node {
    char no[10];        /*id number*/
    char name[15];      /*client name*/
    char car[10], city[10], state[10], zip[10];
};
```

We can use the start_table() function in Figure 7.16 to build a hash table. The start_table() function relies on the use of the strcmp() function from the standard C library. If the compared strings are the same, strcmp() returns a one; otherwise, it returns a zero. The init() function used is essentially the same used earlier. This function guarantees storage is available for the structures to be used. The start_table() also relies on the presence of nulls in the empty cells (the cells not yet used).

The implementation of hash(), rehash(), and start_table() is shown in a program in Figure 7.17.

328 Structures

CHAPTER 7

```
start_table(x, n)
struct node x[];
int n;
        {
        char id_no[10];

        int i = 0, count = 0, yes = 1;

        while ((yes == 1) && (i < n)) {

                printf("\n\n"); drawline();

                printf("\nEnter id number:  ");scanf("%s", id_no);

                printf("\n");

                count = 0;

                i = hash(id_no);

                printf("\ninitial address = %5d", i);

                while ((x[i].no[0] != ´\0´) && (count < SIZE)) {

                        i = rehash(i);

                        ++count;

                        }

                if (count < SIZE) {

                        strcpy(x[i].no, id_no);

                        printf("\n\nName: ");scanf("%s", x[i].name);

                        printf("\n\n car:  ");scanf("%s", x[i].car);

                        printf("\n\n city: ");scanf("%s", x[i].city);

                        printf("\n\n state: ");scanf("%s", x[i].state);

                        printf("\n\n zip code: ");scanf("%s", x[i].zip);

                        }
                else
                        printf("\tSorry, no room for your entry.");

                printf("\n\n Again?--1=Y, 0=N:   ");scanf("%d", &yes);

                printf("\n");

                }
        }
```

Figure 7.16 Hash_table() Function

CHAPTER 7   **7.15 A hash search for a structure   329**

```
#include "newlib.h"

#define SIZE 11

struct node {
        char no[10];
        char name[15];
        char car[10], city[10], state[10], zip[10];
        };
/*------------------------------------------------------------------*/

hash(s)
char s[10];
        {
        int m = 0;

        while (*s != '\0')
          m += *s++;
        return(m % SIZE);
        }
/*------------------------------------------------------------------*/

rehash(address)
int address;
        {

        return((address + 1) % SIZE);

        }
/*------------------------------------------------------------------*/

start_table(x, n)
struct node x[];
int n;
        {
        char id_no[10];
        int i = 0, count = 0, yes = 1;

        while ((yes == 1) && (i < n)) {
                printf("\n\n"); drawline();
                printf("\nEnter id number:  ");scanf("%s", id_no);
                printf("\n");
                count = 0;
                i = hash(id_no);
                printf("\ninitial address = %5d", i);
                while ((x[i].no[0] != '\0') && (count < SIZE)) {
                        i = rehash(i);
                        ++count;
                        }
                if (count < SIZE) {
                        strcpy(x[i].no, id_no);
                        printf("\n\nName: ");scanf("%s", x[i].name);
```

Figure 7.17   Program with a Hash Search

330 **Structures**

CHAPTER 7

```
                                printf("\n\n car:  ");scanf("%s", x[i].car);
                                printf("\n\n city: ");scanf("%s", x[i].city);
                                printf("\n\n state: ");scanf("%s", x[i].state);
                                printf("\n\n zip code: ");scanf("%s", x[i].zip);
                                }
                        else
                                printf("\tSorry, no room for your entry.");

                        printf("\n\n Again?--1=Y, 0=N:  ");scanf("%d", &yes);
                        printf("\n");
                        }


        }
/*----------------------------------------------------------------------*/

printheading()
        {
        printf("\n\n %5s %15s %10s %10s %10s %10s %10s \n\n",
                "cell",
                "name",
                "id. no.",
                "car",
                "city",
                "state",
                "zip code");
        drawline(); printf("\n\n");
        }
/*----------------------------------------------------------------------*/


print_hashtable(x, n)
struct node x[];
int n;
        {
        int i;

        printheading();
        for (i = 0; i < SIZE; ++i)
          if (strcmp(x[i].no, "\0") == 1)
                printf("\n\n %5d", i);
          else
                printf("\n\n %5d %15s %10s %10s %10s %10s %10s",
                        i,
                        x[i].name,
                        x[i].no,
                        x[i].car,
                        x[i].city,
                        x[i].state,
                        x[i].zip);
        printf("\n"); drawline(); printf("\n");
        }
/*----------------------------------------------------------------------*/
```

Figure 7.17 *continued*

CHAPTER 7

7.15 A hash search for a structure   331

```
hashsearch(x, n, key)
struct node x[];
int n;
char key[10];
        {
        int count = 0, spot;

        spot = hash(key);
        while ((strcmp(x[spot].no, key) != 0) && (count < SIZE)) {
                spot = rehash(spot);
                ++count;
                }
        if (count < SIZE) {
                printheading();
                printf("\n\n %20s %10s %10s %10s %10s %10s \n\n",
                        x[spot].name,
                        x[spot].no,
                        x[spot].car,
                        x[spot].state,
                        x[spot].city,
                        x[spot].zip);
                drawline();
                }
        else
                printf("Entry not found!");

        }
/*-----------------------------------------------------------------------*/

main()
        {
        struct node t[SIZE];
        char number[10];
        int limit = SIZE, yes = 1;

        start_table(t, limit);
        print_hashtable(t, limit);

        while (yes) {
                printf("\n\n Enter id number of item you wish to retrieve: ");
                scanf("%s", number);
                hashsearch(t, limit, number);
                printf("\n\n Again?--1=Y, 0=N: "); scanf("%d", &yes);
                }

        }
```

Figure 7.17   *continued*

332 Structures   CHAPTER 7

```
RUN  C717

--------------------------------------------------------------------------------
Enter id number:  cg16

initial address =     8

Name: j

  car:  vw

  city: avon

  state: mn

  zip code: 56310

  Again?--1=Y, 0=N:  1


--------------------------------------------------------------------------------
Enter id number:  ty96

initial address =     7

Name: k

  car:  ford

  city: collegeville

  state: mn

  zip code: 56321

  Again?--1=Y, 0=N:  1
```

Figure 7.17 *continued*

CHAPTER 7   7.15 A hash search for a structure   333

```
-------------------------------------------------------------------------------
Enter id number:  vy33

initial address =     0

Name: tom

 car:  dusenberg

 city: N.Y.

 state: N.Y.

 zip code: 20017

 Again?--1=Y, 0=N:  0


  cell            name    id. no.      car       city      state   zip code
-------------------------------------------------------------------------------


   0              tom     vy33   dusenberg       N.Y.      N.Y.      20017

   1

   2

   3

   4

   5

   6

   7              k       ty96     ford collegevilmn       mn        56321

   8              j       cg16      vw       avon          mn        56310

   9

  10
```

Figure 7.17 *continued*

334 Structures

CHAPTER 7

```
------------------------------------------------------------------

 Enter id number of item you wish to retrieve:  ty95
Entry not found!

 Again?--1=Y, 0=N: 1


 Enter id number of item you wish to retrieve:  ty96


  cell            name    id. no.       car      city      state    zip code

------------------------------------------------------------------



                    k      ty96      ford        mn collegevilmn      56321

------------------------------------------------------------------

 Again?--1=Y, 0=N: 0
```

Figure 7.17 *concluded*

7.16 REFINEMENT; KEEPING TRACK OF THE CELL USED

When a hash search is made using the program in Figure 7.17, no indication of the cell containing the desired record is given. The first column in the printed table is left blank.

In addition, when the hash table is printed out completely, the position of the empty cells is printed and nothing else. The word *empty* should also be printed in the leading (name) column to explain the blank line to the reader.

These refinements are left as an exercise.

7.17 REFINEMENT: KEEPING TRACK OF THE COMPARISONS USED

No effort is made in the program in Figure 7.17 to keep track of the number of comparisons used in a hash search. If more than one hash search is made, the average number of comparisons made should also be computed. A note of the form

note: x comparisons made during this hash search.

should be printed for each entry found *and* for hash search failures. In addition,

CHAPTER 7

the following note should be printed after the user finishes searching for table entries:

note: average no. of comparisons made =

These refinements are left as an exercise.

7.18 REFINEMENT: DELETIONS AND INSERTIONS

A new delete() and a new insert() function should be added to the program in Figure 7.17 so that the user can have the option of deleting unwanted table entries or inserting new ones. This suggests the need for a menu-driven program. The main() function should be used to print a menu of the following form:

1. Build new table.
2. Inspect table.
3. Make hash search.
4. Insert a new table entry.
5. Delete an old table entry.

Item 4 is also new. This will allow the user to add a new record to an existing table. The user should also be allowed to inspect a hash table. These refinements are left as an exercise.

7.19 REFINEMENT: EDITING A HASH TABLE ENTRY

A new item should be added to the menu developed in the previous section.

6. Edit a table entry.

This means an edit() function should be introduced to allow the user to change one or more of the components of an entry. This implies the need for a secondary menu that allows the user to select the component to be changed. This refinement is left as an exercise.

7.20 NESTED STRUCTURES

Structures can be nested. For example, we can make the album structure a component of the part structure introduced earlier. We can do this as follows:

```
struct part {
    char name[20];
```

336 Structures   CHAPTER 7

> struct album x;
> int qty;
> };

Then

> struct part item;

declares that item is one of these structures. To access a member of the album component of this structure, we can use

> item.x.member

For example, each of the members of *x* is accessed in the following way:

> item.x.disc
> item.x.artist
> item.x.year

If ptr is a pointer to one of these item structures, we can use

> ptr -> x -> member

to access one of the members. For example,

> ptr -> x -> year

accesses the year.

We can use the preprocessor define command to simplify the declaration of a nested structure. For example, we can use

> #define MUSIC struct album

to use as a substitute for struct album. Then the preceding declaration will have the following form:

> struct part {
> char name[20];
> MUSIC x;
> int qty;
> };

7.21 CREATING NEW TYPE NAMES WITH TYPEDEF

A *typedef* can be used in C to create names of new types. For example, we can have the following declaration:

CHAPTER 7   **7.21 Creating new type names with typedef   337**

```
typedef struct {
        char name[20];
        MUSIC x;
        int qty;
        } inventory;
```

Then we can use

```
inventory x, y, z;
```

to declare that *x, y,* and *z* are of type *inventory*. This gives us another way to simplify the use of nested structures and an alternative to the use of the *define* command shown in the previous section. That is, we can use the following typedef declaration to make album itself a data type:

```
typedef struct {
        char disc[20], artist[20];
        int year;
        } album;
```

Then we can declare the part structure as follows:

```
struct part {
        char name[20];
        album x;
        int qty;
        };
```

We can also "nest" typedefs. How? We can use typedef to declare the preceding structure itself a data type as follows:

```
typedef struct {
        char name[20];
        album x;
        int qty;
        } inventory;
```

The *typedef* facility can also be used with nonstructural types. For example, we use the following declarations:

```
typedef char name[20];
typedef int qty;
typedef int box[20];        /*array of integers*/
```

Then

338 Structures   CHAPTER 7

```
name a, b, c,;         /*says a, b, c are names*/
qty x, y;              /*says x, y are quantities*/
box now, then          /*says now, then are arrays
                         of type box*/
```

7.22 UNIONS

Unions are used in place of structures to conserve storage. A union advises a **C** compiler to store the members of a union using overlays. When one member of a union is accessed, the other members of a union will usually be held in secondary storage until they are needed. When a member is retrieved from secondary storage, it is written over an area of storage allocated for a member of the same union previously used. This process is called *overlaying*. It is wise to use unions instead of structures, when a union will be bulky or when memory is being used up by structures.

A union has the same format as a structure. The word *union* is used in place of the word *struct*. For example, we can use the following declaration:

```
union album {
        char disc[20], artist[20];
        int year;
        } x, y;
```

This says *x* and *y* are unions. Then we can use the following nested structure:

```
typedef struct {
        char name[20];
        union album x;
        int qty;
        } inventory;
```

This says that inventory is a structure when it contains a union.

7.23 SUMMARY

A *structure* is a collection of components of one or more types. A *tag* is the name of a structure. A *member* is a component of a structure. Each member of a structure will have its own identifier *and* its own type. All members of a structure can be of the same type. It is also possible for the members of a structure to be a mixture of types.

The tag of a structure is used to pull the members of a structure together. A tag of a structure is used to identify the logical relation between the members. A

CHAPTER 7   **7.23 Summary   339**

tag is also used to identify the beginning address of a structure in memory. For example, if x is the tag of a structure, then &x is the beginning memory address of this structure. Finally, the tag of a structure is used to access its members. This is done using the point (.) notation.

For example, if x is an *album* structure defined in this chapter, then

                                x.artist

gives access to the artist member of this structure. We can use

                            struct album *ptr;

to declare *ptr* as a pointer to an album structure. This declaration does not, as a rule, allocate storage for the corresponding structure. It lets *ptr* be used to hold the beginning address in memory where the corresponding structure will be kept. To access a member of a structure with a pointer, the arrow notation (->) is used. This is a minus sign (-) followed by a greater-than symbol (>). For example, we can access the artist component of the album structure using the following technique:

                             ptr -> artist

Pointers offer an efficient way to work with structures. Why? Rather than move structures about in memory, pointers to structures can be manipulated. We demonstrated how this is done in the swap() function in Figure 7.9, for example.

An array of pointers to structures can be set up using a struct declaration and a star (*) prefix. For example, to have an array of pointers to structures of type album, we can use the following declaration:

                          struct album *window[3000];

This says

                       window[0], . . . , window[2999]

is an array of 3000 pointers to album structures.

340 Structures CHAPTER 7

REVIEW TERMS AND SYMBOLS

Term	*Meaning*
arrays of pointers	collection of pointers to structures
arrays of structures	collection of structures
hash	address calculation
hash search	compute location of a structure
hash table collision	hash to an occupied table cell
initialized structures	structures in extern and/or static storage class
malloc()	a standard C function to allocate memory
member	component of a structure
open addressing technique	continue looking in a hash table until a vacancy is found
overlaying components	components are made to share the same area of memory
pointer to a structure	address of a structure
rehash	compute alternative hash address
scatter storage technique	smear keys to structures throughout a hash table
sort key	member of a structure used to organize structures
strcmp(x, y)	returns a 1 if the strings x and y are equal; otherwise, it returns a zero
structure symbols:	collection of logically related members
->	ptr -> member selects a member of a structure when *ptr* is a pointer to a structure
	tag . member selects a member of a structure when *tag* is the name of a structure
&	&tag identifies the memory location of a structure when *tag* is the name of a structure
typedef	facility provided by C to define new types (a naming facility)
union	components (members) of a union are overlayed in memory to save storage

EXERCISES

1. If x is a tag for a structure and ptr is a pointer to the same structure, what is the difference between x and ptr?
2. If a structure is initialized, what storage classes can be used for the initialized structure?
3. What method can be used to determine the number of bytes needed for a structure? Illustrate your answer by showing how to determine the number of bytes for the *album* structure declared in Section 7.1.
4. Write a program to determine the sizes of the following structures:
   a. struct lc {

CHAPTER 7   **Exercises   341**

```
char author[30], title[50], lc_no[20], isbn[20];
int weight;
};
```

   b. struct album x;   /*defined in Section 7.1*/
   c. struct part x;   /*defined in Section 7.4*/
   d. struct node x;   /*defined in Figure 17.17*/

5. Write the structures in Exercise 4 as unions and write a program to determine if the size (in bytes) of the unions is the same in the corresponding structures.

6. Using

$$\text{struct album *ptr, x;}$$

which of the following methods of accessing the artist member of this structure is legal?

   a. ptr -> artist   **b.** (*ptr) . artist
   c. (&x) -> artist   **d.** (*ptr) -> artist
   e. x -> artist   **f.** ptr . artist

7. Write a short program to verify your assertions in Exercise 6 using only the correct methods of accessing a member of a structure.

8. What is wrong with following assignment?

$$\text{*ptr } = \text{ x}$$

where x is an album structure and ptr is a pointer to this structure.

9. Carry out the refinement of the program in Figure 7.8 described in Section 7.8. Give a sample run.

10. Write a program to carry out a selection sort of the node structures given in Figure 7.17. Build an array of 15 pointers to these nodes. Then use *name* as the sort key. *Hint:* If x and y are strings, then

strcmp (x, y) = $\begin{cases} \text{integer} > 0, \text{ if } x \text{ is lexicographically} \\ \qquad\qquad\qquad \text{greater than } y \\ \text{zero, if } x = y \\ \text{integer} < 0, \text{ if } x \text{ is lexicographically} \\ \qquad\qquad\qquad \text{less than } y \end{cases}$

Give a sample run.

11. Refine the findmin() function used in Exercise 10 so that the user can select the sort key to use. Your program should do the following things:
   a. Allow the user to choose one of the members of the node structure as a sort key.
   b. Call findmin() with an indication of the sort. *Hint:* The easiest way to do this is to use an integer value, which permits selection of the correct findmin() search with a switch statement.

12. Carry out the refinement of findmin() used in Figure 7.12 and described in Section 7.11.

13. Carry out the refinement of the program in Figure 7.11 described in Section 7.12 [i.e., introduce a select() function].

14. Carry out the refinement of the program in Figure 7.13 described in Section 7.14 [i.e., modify the edit() function used in this program so that the user can select the member to edit].

342 Structures

CHAPTER 7

15. Start with an initial hash value of 7. Then rehash. Use the two rehash functions *a* and *b* given in Section 7.15. In each case, rehash repeatedly until the initial rehash value is obtained a second time. Indicate which table entries are missed (if any) by each function.

16. Carry out the refinement of the program in Figure 7.17 described in Section 7.16 (i.e., print out the cell containing a structure that has been found in a hash search). Give a sample run.

17. Carry out the refinement of the program in Figure 7.17 described in Section 7.17. Your refined program should tabulate the number of comparisons used by a hash search and the average number of comparisons used when more than one search is made. Give a sample run.

18. Carry out the refinement of the program in Figure 7.17 described in Section 7.18. Introduce a delete() and an insert() function to handle deletions and insertions *after* a table has been built. You should also print the menu described in Section 7.18. Give a sample run.

19. Carry out the refinement of the program in Figure 7.17 described in Section 7.19. This time introduce a new edit() function to handle changes in table entries. Your edit() function should allow the user to select a particular member to edit. You should also expand menu-driven in main(). That is, allow the selection of a menu item by the user to determine what the processor does next. Give a sample run.

20. Write a program that builds an array of pointers to nested structures described in Section 7.20. *Caution:* You should use the modified versions of build_struct() and print_struct() given in Figure 7.4, rather than lump things together in main(). Give a sample run.

21. Refine the program in Exercise 20 using the typedef facility suggested in Section 7.21. Also introduce a select_member() function to select a member to be printed. Allow the user to choose the members to print. Give a sample run.

LAB PROJECTS

1. One method of hashing is called *folding*. The folding method chops up a hash key into segments and adds the segments to get a hash value. For example, if the hash key is a social security number (taken as a string) like

555-12-9198

then we can use

$$\text{sum} = \text{'5'} + \text{'5'} + \text{'9'} + \text{'8'}$$

in

sum % tablesize

to obtain a hash value. Write a fold_hash() function that uses the folding method on social security numbers. In our example, the first two and the last two digits of the social security number string are folded. Use this method in your function.

CHAPTER 7   **Selected solutions**   **343**

2. Write a program that uses fold_hash() and rehash_fold() to build a hash table with the following structures:

> struct person {
>   char name[20], ss_no[11], position[20];
>   int yrs_experienvce, age;
>   };

Then your program should do the following things:

a. Print the following menu:

    1. Build table
    2. Show table
    3. Insert new entry
    4. Delete old entry
    5. Edit entry
    6. Search for a record that is printed
    7. Sort entries

Give a sample run.

3. Refine Lab Project 2 so that the user can select a section of the hash table to print in sorted order in terms of a *user-selected* sort key.

SELECTED SOLUTIONS

Exercise 5

```
#include "c66.h"
#include "newlib.h"


union lc {
        char author[30],title[50],lc_no[20],isbn[20];
        int weight;
    };

union album {
        char disc[20],artist[20];
        int year;
    };

union part {
        char name[20];
        int qty;
    };

union node {
        char no[10];
        char name[15];
        char car[10],city[10],state[10],zip[10];
    };
```

344 Structures   CHAPTER 7

Exercise 5 *concluded*

```
main()
   {

      drawline();
      printf("\n\nThe size of union lc is: %6d\n\n",sizeof(union lc));

      drawline();
      printf("\n\nThe size of union album is: %6d\n\n",sizeof(union album));

      drawline();
      printf("\n\nThe size of union part is: %6d\n\n",sizeof(union part));

      drawline();
      printf("\n\nThe size of union node is: %6d\n\n",sizeof(union node));

      drawline();
      printf("\n\n\n");

      }


RUN CE75

----------------------------------------------------------------------------

The size of union lc is:      50

----------------------------------------------------------------------------

The size of union album is:      20

----------------------------------------------------------------------------

The size of union part is:      20

----------------------------------------------------------------------------

The size of union node is:      15

----------------------------------------------------------------------------
```

CHAPTER 7 Selected solutions **345**

Exercise 11

```c
#include "newlib.h"

struct node {
        char name[15];
        char car[10],city[10],state[10],zip[10];
        };


findmin(x, n,choice)
struct node *x[];
int n,choice;
        {
        static struct node  *min;
        int i = 0, max = n,  result;
        int location = 0;

        switch (choice) {

        case 1: {
            min  = x[i] ; i = 1;
            while (i <= max) {
                    result = strcmp(min -> name,x[i] -> name);
                    if (result > 0) {
                            min = x[i];
                            location = i;
                            }
                    ++i;
                    }
                    }
        break;

        case 2: {
            min = x[i]; i = 1;
            while (i <= max) {
                    result = strcmp(min -> car,x[i] -> car);
                    if (result > 0) {
                            min = x[i];
                            location = i;
                            }
                    ++i;
                    }
                    }
        break;

        case 3: {
            min = x[i]; i = 1;
            while (i <= max) {
                    result = strcmp(min -> city,x[i] -> city);
                    if (result > 0) {
                            min = x[i];
                            location = i;
                            }
```

346 Structures   CHAPTER 7

Exercise 11   *continued*

```
                                ++i;
                                }
                            }
                    break;

                    case 4: {
                        min = x[i]; i = 1;
                        while (i <= max) {
                            result = strcmp(min -> state,x[i] -> state);
                            if (result > 0) {
                                    min = x[i];
                                    location = i;
                                    }
                            ++i;
                            }
                        }
                    break;

                    case 5: {
                        min = x[i]; i = 1;
                        while (i <= max) {
                            result = strcmp(min -> zip,x[i] -> zip);
                            if (result > 0) {
                                    min = x[i];
                                    location = i;
                                    }
                            ++i;
                            }
                        }
                    break;

                    }        /* switch */

                    return(location);
                    }


        swap(x, i, j)
        struct node *x[];
        int i, j;
                {
                struct node *buff;


                buff = x[i];
                x[i] = x[j];
                x[j] = buff;


                }

        init(x,n)
        struct node *x[];
```

CHAPTER 7   **Selected solutions 347**

Exercise 11 *continued*

```
int n;
        {
        int i;

        for (i = 0; i <= n; ++i)
 x[i] = malloc(sizeof(struct node));

        }

show(x,n)
struct node *x[];
int n;
        {
        int i;

        for (i = 0; i <= n; ++i)
                printf("\n\n %15s %10s %10s %10s %10s",
                                x[i] -> name,
                                x[i] -> car,
                                x[i] -> city,
                                x[i] -> state,
                                x[i] -> zip);

        }
build_struct(x, n)
struct node *x[];
int n;
        {
        int i = 0, yes = 1;

        while ((yes == 1) && (i <= n)) {
                printf("\n\n Enter name:  ");
                scanf("%s", x[i] -> name);
                printf("\n\n Enter car:  ");
                scanf("%s", x[i] -> car);
                printf("\n\n city:  ");
                scanf("%s",x[i] -> city);
                printf("\n\n state:  ");
                scanf("%s",x[i] -> state);
                printf("\n\n zip code:  ");
                scanf("%s",x[i] -> zip);

                printf("\n\n Again?--1=Y,0=N:  ");
                scanf("%d", &yes);
                ++i;
                }
        return(i - 1);
        }

main()
        {
        int style,choice;
```

348 Structures   CHAPTER 7

Exercise II   *continued*

```
struct node *box[20];
int limit = 20, copy, position;
struct node *buff;

init(box, limit);
limit = build_struct(box, limit);

copy = limit;
printf("\n\n"); drawline();
printf("\n\n %40s \n\n", "Original collection of structures");
drawline(); printf("\n\n");
show(box, limit);
do {
limit = copy;
printf("\n\n"); drawline();
printf("\n\n menu: \n ");
printf("<1> sort by name.\n <2> sort by car.\n");
printf(" <3> sort by city.\n <4> sort by state\n");
printf(" <5> sort by zip.\n Enter choice:  ");
scanf("%d",&style);
do {

        position = findmin(box, limit,style);
        swap(box, position, limit);
        --limit;
    }
while (limit != 0);
printf("\n\n\n%40s \n\n", "Sorted structures:"); drawline();
show(box, copy);
printf("\n\n");
drawline();
printf("\n\n");
printf("Sort again? <1>=yes, <0>=no:  ");
scanf("%d",&choice);
}
while ( choice == 1);

}
```

```
RUN  CE711

 Enter name:  albert


 Enter car:  ford


 city:  avon


 state:  mn
```

CHAPTER 7   **Selected solutions 349**

Exercise 11 *continued*

```
    zip code:  55310

    Again?--1=Y,0=N:  1

    Enter name:  mike

    Enter car:  dusenberg

    city:  n.y.

    state:  n.y.

    zip code:  20017

    Again?--1=Y,0=N:  1

    Enter name:  betty

    Enter car:  vw

    city:  mahtomedi

    state:  mn

    zip code:  55115

    Again?--1=Y,0=N:  0

-------------------------------------------------------------------

        Original collection of structures

-------------------------------------------------------------------


        albert      ford      avon      mn      55310
```

350 Structures

CHAPTER 7

Exercise II *continued*

```
         mike    dusenberg        n.y.       n.y.      20017

         betty          vw  mahtomedi        mn        55115

----------------------------------------------------------------

menu:
<1> sort by name.
<2> sort by car.
<3> sort by city.
<4> sort by state
<5> sort by zip.
Enter choice:  1



                    Sorted  structures:

----------------------------------------------------------------

         mike    dusenberg        n.y.       n.y.      20017

         betty          vw  mahtomedi        mn        55115

         albert         ford      avon       mn        55310

----------------------------------------------------------------

Sort again? <1>=yes, <0>=no:  1



----------------------------------------------------------------

menu:
<1> sort by name.
<2> sort by car.
<3> sort by city.
<4> sort by state
<5> sort by zip.
Enter choice:  2



                    Sorted  structures:

----------------------------------------------------------------

         betty          vw  mahtomedi        mn        55115

         albert         ford      avon       mn        55310

         mike    dusenberg        n.y.       n.y.      20017
```

CHAPTER 7

Exercise 11   *continued*

```
--------------------------------------------------------------------

Sort again?  <1>=yes, <0>=no:  1


--------------------------------------------------------------------

menu:
<1> sort by name.
<2> sort by car.
<3> sort by city.
<4> sort by state
<5> sort by zip.
Enter choice:  3


                      Sorted structures:

--------------------------------------------------------------------

        mike   dusenberg      n.y.        n.y.      20017

         betty        vw  mahtomedi        mn       55115

         albert      ford      avon        mn       55310

--------------------------------------------------------------------

Sort again?  <1>=yes, <0>=no:  1


--------------------------------------------------------------------

menu:
<1> sort by name.
<2> sort by car.
<3> sort by city.
<4> sort by state
<5> sort by zip.
Enter choice:  4


                      Sorted structures:

--------------------------------------------------------------------

        mike   dusenberg      n.y.        n.y.      20017

         albert      ford      avon        mn       55310
```

352 Structures   CHAPTER 7

Exercise 11   *concluded*

```
            betty       vw  mahtomedi       mn      55115

---------------------------------------------------------------------

Sort again? <1>=yes, <0>=no:  1


---------------------------------------------------------------------

menu:
<1> sort by name.
<2> sort by car.
<3> sort by city.
<4> sort by state
<5> sort by zip.
Enter choice:  5


                    Sorted structures:

---------------------------------------------------------------------

            albert      ford       avon       mn      55310

            betty       vw  mahtomedi       mn      55115

            mike   dusenberg       n.y.      n.y.    20017

---------------------------------------------------------------------

Sort again? <1>=yes, <0>=no:  0
```

CHAPTER 7   Selected solutions   353

Exercise 14

```c
#include "newlib.h"

struct album
        {
        char disc[30], artist[20];
        int year;
        };
/*-------------------------------------------------------------------------*/

init(x, n)
struct album *x[ ];
int n;
        {
        int i;

        for (i = 0; i <= n; ++i)
                x[i] = malloc(sizeof(struct album));

        }
/*-------------------------------------------------------------------------*/

build(hits,limit)
struct album *hits[];
int limit;
        {
        int i;
        char dummy[5];

        init(hits, limit);
        printf("Creating a list of top ten records...\n\n");
        --limit;
        for (i=limit; i>=0; i--) {
                printf("enter record name--> ");
                gets(hits[i]->disc);
                printf("\n\nenter artist------> ");
                gets(hits[i]->artist);
                printf("\n\nenter year made----> ");
                scanf("%d", &hits[i]->year);
                printf("\n");
                gets(dummy);
                }
        }
/*-------------------------------------------------------------------------*/

show(hits,limit)
struct album *hits[ ];
int limit;
        {
        int i;

        printf("\n\n\t\tTOP 5 ALBUMS OF THE 1960s\n");
```

354 Structures   CHAPTER 7

Exercise 14 *continued*

```
        printf("\t\t~~~ ~ ~~~~~~ ~~ ~~~ ~~~~~\n\n");
        printf("  %-30s%-20s%-10s\n\n", "Album", "Artist", "Year");
        for (i=0; i<limit; i++)
        printf("%d. %-30s%-20s%-10d\n", i+1, hits[i]->disc, hits[i]->artist,
                                    hits[i]->year);
        printf("\n\n");
        }
/*------------------------------------------------------------------------*/

struct album *edit(recrd)
struct album *recrd;
        {
        int choice;
        char dummy[5];

        printf("\n\nmenu\n");
        printf("<1> change artist.\n<2> change year\n");
        printf("<3> change record name.\n<4> change entire record.");
        printf("\nEnter choice:  ");
        scanf("%d",&choice);

        gets(dummy);
        printf("\n\n");

        switch (choice) {

        case 1: {
                printf("New album´s artist?\n\n");
                gets(recrd->artist);
        }
        break;

        case 2: {
                printf("New album´s year?\n\n");
                scanf("%d", &recrd->year);
        }
        break;

        case 3: {
                printf("\n\nNew album name?\n\n");
                gets(recrd->disc);
        }
        break;

        case 4: {
                printf("\n\nNew album name?\n\n");
                gets(recrd->disc);
                printf("New album´s artist?\n\n");
                gets(recrd->artist);
                printf("New album´s year?\n\n");
                scanf("%d", &recrd->year);
        }
```

CHAPTER 7

Exercise 14 *continued*

```
        break;
        }  /* switch */
                return(recrd);

        }


/*-----------------------------------------------------------------------------*/

main()
        {
        struct album *hold[5];
        int new,ans;

        build(hold, 5);
        show(hold,5);
        do {
                printf("Which record should be changed (enter number) ?  ");
                scanf("%d", &new);
                hold[new-1] = edit(hold[new-1]);
                printf("\n\n\tNew List:\n\n");
                show(hold, 5);
                drawline();
                printf("\n\nAnother change? <1>= yes,<0>= no:");
                scanf("%d",&ans);
                printf("\n\n");
                drawline();
                printf("\n\n");
                }
        while (ans == 1);
        }


RUN CE714

Creating a list of top ten records...

enter record name--> x


enter artist------> x


enter year made----> 0

enter record name--> Petrushka


enter artist------> Stravinsky


enter year made----> 1960
```

356 Structures   CHAPTER 7

Exercise 14 *continued*

```
enter record name--> Die Fledermaus


enter artist------> J. Strauss


enter year made----> 1999

enter record name--> Music Man


enter artist------> M.Sillson


enter year made----> 1940

enter record name--> Choclate Soldier


enter artist------> O. Straus


enter year made----> 1954



                    TOP 5 ALBUMS OF THE 1960s
                    ~~~ ~ ~~~~~~ ~~ ~~~ ~~~~~


        Album                   Artist          Year

   1. Choclate Soldier       O. Straus          1954
   2. Music Man              M.Sillson          1940
   3. Die Fledermaus         J. Strauss         1999
   4. Petrushka              Stravinsky         1960
   5. x                      x                  0


Which record should be changed (enter number) ?   5


menu
<1> change artist.
<2> change year
<3> change record name.
<4> change entire record.
Enter choice:  4




New album name?
```

CHAPTER 7   **Selected solutions   357**

Exercise 14   *continued*

```
I Wanna Hold Your Hand!
New album's artist?

Beatles
New album's year?

1960


        New List:


            TOP 5 ALBUMS OF THE 1960s
            ~~~ ~ ~~~~~~ ~~ ~~~ ~~~~~


        Album                   Artist          Year

1. Choclate Soldier            O. Straus        1954
2. Music Man                   M.Sillson        1940
3. Die Fledermaus              J. Strauss       1999
4. Petrushka                   Stravinsky       1960
5. I Wanna Hold Your Hand!     Beatles          1960


------------------------------------------------------------------


Another change? <1>= yes,<0>= no:1



------------------------------------------------------------------

Which record should be changed (enter number) ?   2


menu
<1> change artist.
<2> change year
<3> change record name.
<4> change entire record.
Enter choice:   1


New album's artist?

M. Willson


        New List:
```

358 Structures   CHAPTER 7

Exercise 14   *continued*

```
                    TOP 5 ALBUMS OF THE 1960s
                    ~~~ ~ ~~~~~~ ~~ ~~~ ~~~~~


        Album                    Artist              Year

     1. Choclate Soldier         O. Straus           1954
     2. Music Man                M. Willson          1940
     3. Die Fledermaus           J. Strauss          1999
     4. Petrushka                Stravinsky          1960
     5. I Wanna Hold Your Hand!  Beatles             1960


     --------------------------------------------------------------

     Another change? <1>= yes,<0>= no:1


     --------------------------------------------------------------

     Which record should be changed (enter number) ?   1


     menu
     <1> change artist.
     <2> change year
     <3> change record name.
     <4> change entire record.
     Enter choice:   3




     New album name?

     Chocolate Soldier


         New List:


                    TOP 5 ALBUMS OF THE 1960s
                    ~~~ ~ ~~~~~~ ~~ ~~~ ~~~~~


        Album                    Artist              Year

     1. Chocolate Soldier        O. Straus           1954
     2. Music Man                M. Willson          1940
     3. Die Fledermaus           J. Strauss          1999
     4. Petrushka                Stravinsky          1960
     5. I Wanna Hold Your Hand!  Beatles             1960
```

CHAPTER 7   **Selected solutions   359**

Exercise 14   *concluded*

```
------------------------------------------------------------------

Another change? <1>= yes,<0>= no:1


------------------------------------------------------------------

Which record should be changed (enter number) ?   3


menu
<1> change artist.
<2> change year
<3> change record name.
<4> change entire record.
Enter choice:   2


New album´s year?

1899


         New List:


              TOP 5 ALBUMS OF THE 1960s
              ~~~ ~ ~~~~~~ ~~ ~~~ ~~~~~


      Album                    Artist           Year

   1. Chocolate Soldier        O. Straus        1954
   2. Music Man                M. Willson       1940
   3. Die Fledermaus           J. Strauss       1899
   4. Petrushka                Stravinsky       1960
   5. I Wanna Hold Your Hand!  Beatles          1960


------------------------------------------------------------------

Another change? <1>= yes,<0>= no:0


------------------------------------------------------------------
```

360 **Structures** CHAPTER 7

Exercise 16

```c
#include "newlib.h"

#define SIZE 11

struct node {
        char no[10];
        char name[15];
        char car[10], city[10], state[10], zip[10];
        };
/*------------------------------------------------------------------------*/

hash(s)
char s[10];
        {
        int m = 0;

        while (*s != '\0')
          m += *s++;
        return(m % SIZE);
        }
/*------------------------------------------------------------------------*/

rehash(address)
int address;
        {

        return((address + 1) % SIZE);

        }
/*------------------------------------------------------------------------*/

start_table(x, n)
struct node x[];
int n;
        {
        char id_no[10];
        int i = 0, count, yes = 1;

        while ((yes == 1) && (i < n)) {
                printf("\n\n"); drawline();
                printf("\nEnter id number:  ");scanf("%s", id_no);
                printf("\n");
                count = 0;
                i = hash(id_no);
                printf("\ninitial address = %5d", i);
                while ((x[i].no[0] != '\0') && (count < SIZE)) {
                        i = rehash(i);
                        ++count;
                        }
                if (count < SIZE) {
                        strcpy(x[i].no, id_no);
                        printf("\n\nName: ");scanf("%s", x[i].name);
```

CHAPTER 7   Selected solutions   361

Exercise 16   *continued*

```
                        printf("\n\n car:   ");scanf("%s", x[i].car);
                        printf("\n\n city:  ");scanf("%s", x[i].city);
                        printf("\n\n state: ");scanf("%s", x[i].state);
                        printf("\n\n zip code: ");scanf("%s", x[i].zip);
                        }
                else
                        printf("\tSorry, no room for your entry.");

                printf("\n\n Again?--1=Y, 0=N:  ");scanf("%d", &yes);
                printf("\n");
                }


        }
/*------------------------------------------------------------------*/

printheading()
        {
        printf("\n\n %5s %15s %10s %10s %10s %10s %10s \n\n",
                "cell",
                "name",
                "id. no.",
                "car",
                "city",
                "state",
                "zip code");
        drawline(); printf("\n\n");
        }
/*------------------------------------------------------------------*/

print_hashtable(x, n)
struct node x[];
int n;
        {
        int i;

        printheading();
        for (i = 0; i < SIZE; ++i)
          if (strcmp(x[i].no, "\0") == 0)
                printf("\n\n %5d %15s", i,"empty");
          else
                printf("\n\n %5d %15s %10s %10s %10s %10s %10s",
                        i,
                        x[i].name,
                        x[i].no,
                        x[i].car,
                        x[i].city,
                        x[i].state,
                        x[i].zip);
        printf("\n"); drawline(); printf("\n");
        }
/*------------------------------------------------------------------*/
```

362 Structures   CHAPTER 7

Exercise 16 *continued*

```
hashsearch(x, n, key)
struct node x[];
int n;
char key[10];
        {
        int count = 0, spot;

        spot = hash(key);
        while ((strcmp(x[spot].no, key) != 0) && (count < SIZE)) {
                spot = rehash(spot);
                ++count;
                }
        if (count < SIZE) {
                printheading();
                printf("\n\n %5d %15s %10s %10s %10s %10s %10s \n\n",
                        spot,
                        x[spot].name,
                        x[spot].no,
                        x[spot].car,
                        x[spot].state,
                        x[spot].city,
                        x[spot].zip);
                drawline();
                }
        else
                printf("\n\nEntry not found!");

        }
/*---------------------------------------------------------------------*/

main()
        {
        struct node t[SIZE];
        char number[10];
        int limit = SIZE, yes = 1;

        start_table(t, limit);
        print_hashtable(t, limit);

        while (yes) {
                printf("\n\n Enter id number of item you wish to retrieve: ");
                scanf("%s", number);
                hashsearch(t, limit, number);
                printf("\n\n Again?--1=Y, 0=N: "); scanf("%d", &yes);
                }

        }
```

CHAPTER 7   **Selected solutions   363**

Exercise 16   *continued*

```
RUN CE716

----------------------------------------------------------------------
Enter id number:  cg16

initial address =       8
Name: john

  car:  vw

  city: avon

  state: mn

  zip code: 56310

  Again?--1=Y, 0=N:  1


----------------------------------------------------------------------
Enter id number:  ty96

initial address =       7
Name: ken

  car:  ford

  city: collegevill

  state: mn

  zip code: 56321

  Again?--1=Y, 0=N:  1
```

364 Structures

CHAPTER 7

Exercise 16   *continued*

```
-----------------------------------------------------------------
Enter id number:  vy33

initial address =     0

Name: tom

 car:  dusenberg

 city: ny

 state: ny

 zip code: 20017

 Again?--1=Y, 0=N:  0
```

cell	name	id. no.	car	city	state	zip code

```
-----------------------------------------------------------------
```

cell	name	id. no.	car	city	state	zip code
0	tom	vy33	dusenberg	ny	ny	20017
1	empty					
2	empty					
3	empty					
4	empty					
5	empty					
6	empty					
7	ken	ty96	ford	collegevil	mn	56321
8	john	cgl6	vw	avon	mn	56310
9	empty					
10	empty					

CHAPTER 7

Selected solutions 365

Exercise 16 *concluded*

```
---------------------------------------------------------------------


   Enter id number of item you wish to retrieve: ty97

Entry not found!

 Again?--1=Y, 0=N: 1


 Enter id number of item you wish to retrieve: ty96

    cell            name   id. no.        car      city       state   zip code
---------------------------------------------------------------------


      7             ken     ty96         ford          mn collegevilmn    56321
---------------------------------------------------------------------

 Again?--1=Y, 0=N: 0
```

366 Structures CHAPTER 7

Exercise 18

```c
#include "newlib.h"

#define SIZE 11

struct node {
        char no[10];
        char name[15];
        char car[10], city[10], state[10], zip[10];
        };
/*-------------------------------------------------------------------------*/
hash(s)
char s[10];
        {
        int m = 0;

        while (*s != '\0')
          m += *s++;
        return(m % SIZE);
        }
/*-------------------------------------------------------------------------*/
rehash(address)
int address;
        {

        return((address + 1) % SIZE);


        }
/*-------------------------------------------------------------------------*/
table_entry(x,n)
 struct node x[];
 int n;
        {
        char id_no[10];
        int  count,j;

                printf("\n\n"); drawline();
                printf("\nEnter id number:  ");scanf("%s", id_no);
                printf("\n");
                count = 0;
                j = hash(id_no);
                printf("\ninitial address = %5d", j);
                while ((x[j].no[0] != '\0') && (count < SIZE)) {
                        j = rehash(j);
                        ++count;
                        }
                if (count < SIZE) {
                        strcpy(x[j].no, id_no);
                        printf("\n\nName: ");scanf("%s", x[j].name);
                        printf("\n\n car:  ");scanf("%s", x[j].car);
```

CHAPTER 7   **Selected solutions   367**

Exercise 18   *continued*

```
                        printf("\n\n city: ");scanf("%s", x[j].city);
                        printf("\n\n state: ");scanf("%s", x[j].state);
                        printf("\n\n zip code: ");scanf("%s", x[j].zip);
                        }
                else
                        printf("\tSorry, no room for your entry.");
        }
/*---------------------------------------------------------------------*/

start_table(xx, nn)
struct node xx[];
int nn;
        {
        int k = 0,yes = 1;

        while ((yes == 1) && (k < nn)) {
                table_entry(xx,nn);
                ++k;
                printf("\n\n Again?--1=Y, 0=N:  ");scanf("%d", &yes);
                printf("\n");
                }


        }
/*---------------------------------------------------------------------*/

printheading()
        {
        printf("\n\n %5s %15s %10s %10s %10s %10s %10s \n\n",
                "cell",
                "name",
                "id. no.",
                "car",
                "city",
                "state",
                "zip code");
        drawline(); printf("\n\n");
        }
/*---------------------------------------------------------------------*/

print_hashtable(x, n)
struct node x[];
int n;
        {
        int i;

        printheading();
        for (i = 0; i < SIZE; ++i)
          if (strcmp(x[i].no, "\0") == 0)
                printf("\n\n %5d %15s", i,"empty");
          else
                printf("\n\n %5d %15s %10s %10s %10s %10s %10s",
                        i,
```

368   Structures   CHAPTER 7

Exercise 18   *continued*

```
                                    x[i].name,
                                    x[i].no,
                                    x[i].car,
                                    x[i].city,
                                    x[i].state,
                                    x[i].zip);
                printf("\n"); drawline(); printf("\n");
                }
/*-------------------------------------------------------------------------*/

hashsearch(x, n, key)
struct node x[];
int n;
char key[10];
        {
        int count = 0, spot;

        spot = hash(key);
        while ((strcmp(x[spot].no, key) != 0) && (count < SIZE)) {
                spot = rehash(spot);
                ++count;
                }
        if (count < SIZE) {
                printheading();
                printf("\n\n %5d %15s %10s %10s %10s %10s %10s \n\n",
                        spot,
                        x[spot].name,
                        x[spot].no,
                        x[spot].car,
                        x[spot].state,
                        x[spot].city,
                        x[spot].zip);
                drawline();
                }
        else
                printf("\n\nEntry not found!");

        }
/*-------------------------------------------------------------------------*/

delete(x,n,key)
 struct node x[];
 int n;
 char key[10];
        {
        int count = 0, spot;

        spot = hash(key);
        while ((strcmp(x[spot].no,key) != 0) && (count < SIZE)) {
                spot = rehash(spot);
                ++count;
                }
```

CHAPTER 7   **Selected solutions   369**

Exercise 18   *continued*

```
            if (count < SIZE)
                    x[spot].no[0] = '\0';
            else
                    printf("\n\nEntry not found!\n");


        }
/*-------------------------------------------------------------------------*/

main()
        {
        struct node t[SIZE];
        char number[10];
        int limit = SIZE, entries,choice;
    do {
        printf("\n\tmenu\n");
        printf("<1> Build a new table.\n<2> Inspect the table.\n");
        printf("<3> Make hash search.\n<4> Insert a new table entry.\n");
        printf("<5> Delete an old table entry.\n<6> End.");
        printf("\nEnter choice:  ");
        scanf("%d",&choice);
        switch (choice) {

         case 1:
                    entries = start_table(t, limit);
                    break;

         case 2:
                    print_hashtable(t, limit);
                    break;

         case 3: {
                    printf("\n\n Enter id number of item you wish to retrieve: ");
                    scanf("%s", number);
                    hashsearch(t, limit, number);
                    }
                    break;

         case 4:
                    if (entries < SIZE) {
                      table_entries(t,limit);
                      ++entries;
                      }
                    break;

         case 5: {
                    printf("\n\n Enter id number of item you wish to delete :   ");
                    scanf("%s",number);
                    delete(t,limit,number);
                    }
                    break;
```

370 Structures   CHAPTER 7

Exercise 18   *continued*

```
      case 6:

              printf("\n");
              break;
      }   /* switch */
      }   /* do */
      while ( choice < 6);

      }


RUN CE718

        menu
<1> Build a new table.
<2> Inspect the table.
<3> Make hash search.
<4> Insert a new table entry.
<5> Delete an old table entry.
<6> End.
Enter choice:  1


----------------------------------------------------------------
Enter id number:  cg16


initial address =      8

Name: john


 car:  vw


 city: avon


 state: mn


 zip code: 56310


 Again?--1=Y, 0=N:  1



----------------------------------------------------------------
Enter id number:  ty96


initial address =      7
```

CHAPTER 7   **Selected solutions   371**

Exercise 18   *continued*

```
Name: keith

  car:  ford

  city: college

  state: mn

  zip code: 56321

  Again?--1=Y, 0=N:  1


-------------------------------------------------------------------
Enter id number:  vy33

initial address =     0

Name: tom

  car:  dusenberg

  city: ny

  state: ny

  zip code: 20017

  Again?--1=Y, 0=N:  0


        menu
<1> Build a new table.
<2> Inspect the table.
<3> Make hash search.
<4> Insert a new table entry.
<5> Delete an old table entry.
<6> End.
Enter choice:  2
```

372 Structures

CHAPTER 7

Exercise 18 *continued*

cell	name	id. no.	car	city	state	zip code
0	tom	vy33	dusenberg	ny	ny	20017
1	empty					
2	empty					
3	empty					
4	empty					
5	empty					
6	empty					
7	keith	ty96	ford	college	mn	56321
8	john	cg16	vw	avon	mn	56310
9	empty					
10	empty					

```
        menu
<1> Build a new table.
<2> Inspect the table.
<3> Make hash search.
<4> Insert a new table entry.
<5> Delete an old table entry.
<6> End.
Enter choice:  3


  Enter id number of item you wish to retrieve: cg16
```

cell	name	id. no.	car	city	state	zip code
8	john	cg16	vw	mn	avon	56310

```
        menu
```

CHAPTER 7   **Selected solutions   373**

Exercise 18   *continued*

```
<1> Build a new table.
<2> Inspect the table.
<3> Make hash search.
<4> Insert a new table entry.
<5> Delete an old table entry.
<6> End.
Enter choice:  4


---------------------------------------------------------------------
Enter id number:  br20


initial address =      2

Name: george


 car:  vw


 city: willernie


 state: mn


 zip code: 55115

        menu
<1> Build a new table.
<2> Inspect the table.
<3> Make hash search.
<4> Insert a new table entry.
<5> Delete an old table entry.
<6> End.
Enter choice:  2
```

cell	name	id. no.	car	city	state	zip code
0	tom	vy33	dusenberg	ny	ny	20017
1	empty					
2	george	br20	vw	willernie	mn	55115
3	empty					

374 Structures   CHAPTER 7

Exercise 18 *continued*

4	empty					
5	empty					
6	empty					
7	keith	ty96	ford	college	mn	56321
8	john	cg16	vw	avon	mn	56310
9	empty					
10	empty					

```
     menu
<1> Build a new table.
<2> Inspect the table.
<3> Make hash search.
<4> Insert a new table entry.
<5> Delete an old table entry.
<6> End.
Enter choice:  5


 Enter id number of item you wish to delete :  br20

     menu
<1> Build a new table.
<2> Inspect the table.
<3> Make hash search.
<4> Insert a new table entry.
<5> Delete an old table entry.
<6> End.
Enter choice:  2
```

cell	name	id. no.	car	city	state	zip code

0	tom	vy33	dusenberg	ny	ny	20017
1	empty					
2	empty					
3	empty					
4	empty					

CHAPTER 7 **Selected solutions** **375**

Exercise 18 *concluded*

```
     5                empty

     6                empty

     7                keith      ty96      ford      college        mn      56321

     8                 john      cg16        vw         avon        mn      56310

     9                empty

    10                empty
-------------------------------------------------------------------

          menu
<1> Build a new table.
<2> Inspect the table.
<3> Make hash search.
<4> Insert a new table entry.
<5> Delete an old table entry.
<6> End.
Enter choice:  6
```

376 Structures

Lab Project 2

```
#include "newlib.h"

#define SIZE 11

struct person {
        char name[20],ss_no[12];
        char position[20];
        int yrs_experience,age;
        };
/*------------------------------------------------------------------------*/

fold_hash(s)
char s[12];
        {
        int m = 0;

        m = (int)s[0] + (int)s[1] + (int)s[9] + (int)s[10];

        return(m % SIZE);
        }
/*------------------------------------------------------------------------*/

rehash_fold(address)
int address;
        {

        return((address + 1) % SIZE);

        }
/*------------------------------------------------------------------------*/

table_entry(x,n)
 struct person x[];
 int n;
        {
        char id_no[12];
        int  count,j;

                printf("\n\n"); drawline();
                printf("\nEnter social security number:  ");scanf("%s",id_no);
                printf("\n");
                count = 0;
                j = fold_hash(id_no);
                printf("\ninitial address = %5d", j);
                while ((x[j].ss_no[0] != '\0') && (count < SIZE)) {
                        j = rehash_fold(j);
                        ++count;
                        }
                if (count < SIZE) {
                        strcpy(x[j].ss_no, id_no);
                        printf("\n\nName: ");scanf("%s", x[j].name);
                        printf("\n\n position:  ");scanf("%s", x[j].position);
```

CHAPTER 7   **Selected solutions   377**

Lab Project 2   *continued*

```
                        printf("\n\n years experience: ");
                        scanf("%d",&x[j].yrs_experience);
                        printf("\n\n age: ");scanf("%d", &x[j].age);
                        }
              else
                        printf("\tSorry, no room for your entry.");
        }
/*-------------------------------------------------------------------------*/

start_table(xx, nn)
struct person xx[];
int nn;
        {
        int j,k = 0,yes = 1;

        for (j = 0; j < nn; ++j)
                xx[j].ss_no[0] = '\0';

        while ((yes == 1) && (k < nn)) {
                table_entry(xx,nn);
                ++k;
                printf("\n\n Again?--1=Y, 0=N:  ");scanf("%d", &yes);
                printf("\n");
                }

        return(k);
        }
/*-------------------------------------------------------------------------*/

printheading()
        {
        printf("\n\n  %5s %20s %12s %20s %5s %5s \n\n",
                "no.",
                "name",
                "ss. no.",
                "position",
                "yrs.",
                "age");
        drawline(); printf("\n\n");
        }
/*-------------------------------------------------------------------------*/

print_hashtable(x, n)
struct person x[];
int n;
        {
        int i;

        printheading();
        for (i = 0; i < SIZE; ++i)
          if (strcmp(x[i].ss_no, "\0") == 0)
                printf("\n\n %5d %20s", i,"empty");
```

378 Structures

CHAPTER 7

124 **Lab Project 2** *continued*

```
            else
                    printf("\n\n %5d %20s %12s %20s %5d %5d",
                            i,
                            x[i].name,
                            x[i].ss_no,
                            x[i].position,
                            x[i].yrs_experience,
                            x[i].age);
            printf("\n"); drawline(); printf("\n");
            }
/*------------------------------------------------------------------------*/

hashsearch(x, n, key)
struct person x[];
int n;
char key[12];
        {
        int count = 0, spot;

        spot = fold_hash(key);
        while ((strcmp(x[spot].ss_no, key) != 0) && (count < SIZE)) {
                spot = rehash_fold(spot);
                ++count;
                }
        if (count < SIZE) {
                printheading();
                printf("\n\n %5d %25s %15s %25s %9d %9d \n\n",
                        spot,
                        x[spot].name,
                        x[spot].ss_no,
                        x[spot].position,
                        x[spot].yrs_experience,
                        x[spot].age);
                drawline();
                }
        else
                printf("\n\nEntry not found!");

        }
/*-------------------------------------------------------------------------*/

edit(x,n,key)
 struct person x[];
 int n;
 char key[12];
        {
        int count = 0, spot,chosen;

        spot = fold_hash(key);
        while ((strcmp(x[spot].ss_no,key) != 0) && (count < SIZE)) {
                spot = rehash_fold(spot);
                ++count;
```

CHAPTER 7   Selected solutions   379

125   **Lab Project 2**   *continued*

```
            }
     do {
        if (count < SIZE) {
             printf("menu\n");
             printf("<1> Change the name.\n");
             printf("<2> Change the position.\n<3> Change the yrs of exp.\n");
             printf("<4> Change the age.\n <5> End edit.\n");
             printf("Enter choice:   ");
             scanf("%d",&chosen);

             switch (chosen)  {

             case 1: {
                printf("\n\nEnter new name: ");
                scanf("%s",x[spot].name);
                printf("\n\n");
                }
                break;

             case 2: {
                printf("\n\nEnter new position:   ");
                scanf("%s",x[spot].position);
                printf("\n\n");
                }
                break;

             case 3:  {
                printf("\n\nEnter new yrs. of experience:   ");
                scanf("%d",&x[spot].yrs_experience);
                printf("\n\n");
                }
                break;

             case 4:  {
                printf("\n\nEnter new age:   ");
                scanf("%d",&x[spot].age);
                printf("\n\n");
                }
                break;

             case 5:
                     printf("\n\n");
                     break;

             }   /* switch */

        }
        else
                printf("\n\nEntry not found!\n");
     }  /* do */
```

380 Structures   CHAPTER 7

Lab Project 2 *continued*

```
            while ( chosen < 5);

            }
/*--------------------------------------------------------------------------*/

delete(x,n,key)
 struct person x[];
 int n;
 char key[12];
            {
            int count = 0, spot;

            spot = fold_hash(key);
            while ((strcmp(x[spot].ss_no,key) != 0) && (count < SIZE)) {
                        spot = rehash_fold(spot);
                        ++count;
                        }

            if (count < SIZE)
                        x[spot].ss_no[0] = '\0';
            else
                        printf("\n\nEntry not found!\n");

            }
/*--------------------------------------------------------------------------*/

findmin(box,n)
struct person *box[];
int n;
            {
            struct person *min;
            int i = 0, max = n;
            int location = 0;

            min = box[i];
            i = 1;
            while (i <= max) {
               if(strcmp(min -> ss_no,box[i] -> ss_no) > 0) {
                        min = box[i];
                        location = i;
                        }
               ++i;
               }

            return(location);

            }
/*--------------------------------------------------------------------------*/

sort_entry(y,n)
struct person *y[];
```

CHAPTER 7   Selected solutions   381

Lab Project 2   *continued*

```
int n;
        {
        int max = n, j;

        printheading();

        for (j = 0;j < max; ++j)
           printf("\n\n %5d %20s %12s %20s %5d %5d",
                        j,
                        y[j] -> name,
                        y[j] -> ss_no,
                        y[j] -> position,
                        y[j] -> yrs_experience,
                        y[j] -> age );

        printf("\n");
        drawline();
        printf("\n\n");

        }
/*--------------------------------------------------------------------*/

swap(box,i,j)
struct person *box[];
int i,j;
        {
        struct person *buff;

        buff = box[i];
        box[i] = box[j];
        box[j] = buff;

        }

/*--------------------------------------------------------------------*/

selection(xx,bound)
struct person *xx[];
int bound;
        {
        int position,max = bound;

        do {
            position = findmin(xx,max);
            if ( position < max)
                swap(xx,position,max);
            --max;
            }
        while ( max != 0);

        sort_entry(xx,bound);
        }
```

382 Structures   CHAPTER 7

Lab Project 2 *continued*

```
/*-------------------------------------------------------------------*/

init(x,n)
struct person *x[];
int n;
        {
        int max = n,j;

        for ( j = 0; j <=n; ++j)
             x[j] = malloc( sizeof( struct person));

        }

/*-------------------------------------------------------------------*/

main()
        {
        struct person t[SIZE];
        struct person *tab[SIZE];
        char number[12];
        int limit = SIZE, entries,choice;
    do {
        printf("\n\tmenu\n");
        printf("<1> Build a new table.\n<2> Inspect the table.\n");
        printf("<3> Make hash search.\n<4> Insert a new table entry.\n");
        printf("<5> Delete an old table entry.\n<6> Edit a table entry.\n");
        printf("<7> Sort table by soc. sec. no.\n<8> End.\nEnter choice:  ");
        scanf("%d",&choice);
        switch (choice) {

         case 1:
                 entries = start_table(t, limit);
                 break;

         case 2:
                 print_hashtable(t, limit);
                 break;

         case 3: {
                   printf("\n\nEnter soc. sec. no. of item you wish to retrieve: ");
                   scanf("%s", number);
                   hashsearch(t, limit, number);
                 }
                 break;

         case 4:
                 if (entries < SIZE) {
                    table_entries(t,limit);
                    ++entries;
                    }
                 break;
```

CHAPTER 7   **Selected solutions   383**

Lab Project 2   *continued*

```
case 5: {
            printf("\n\n Enter soc. sec. number of item you wish to delete :  ");
            scanf("%s",number);
            delete(t,limit,number);
            }
            break;


case 6: {
            printf("\n\n Enter soc. sec. number of item you wish to edit :  ");
            scanf("%s",number);
            edit(t,limit,number);
            }
            break;

case 7:  {
            int k,i = 0;

            init(tab,entries);

            printf("\n");
            drawline();
            printf("\n");

             for ( k = 0; i  < entries; ++k)  {
              if (strcmp(t[k].ss_no, "\0")  != 0)  {
                tab[i] = &t[k];
                ++i;
                }
             }

            selection(tab,entries);
            }
            break;

case 8:
            printf("\n");
            break;
}    /* switch */
}  /* do */
while ( choice < 8);

}
```

RUN CL72

        menu
<1> Build a new table.
<2> Inspect the table.
<3> Make hash search.
<4> Insert a new table entry.

384 Structures

CHAPTER 7

Lab Project 2 *continued*

```
<5> Delete an old table entry.
<6> Edit a table entry.
<7> Sort table by soc. sec. no.
<8> End.
Enter choice:  1


-------------------------------------------------------------------------------
Enter social security number:  847-93-8888


initial address =      0

Name: fred


  position:  farmer


  years experience: 5


  age: 29


  Again?--1=Y, 0=N:  1



-------------------------------------------------------------------------------
Enter social security number:  384-83-8451


initial address =      0

Name: george


  position:  gardener


  years experience: 3


  age: 33


  Again?--1=Y, 0=N:  1



-------------------------------------------------------------------------------
```

CHAPTER 7   **Selected solutions   385**

Lab Project 2   *continued*

```
Enter social security number:  012-40-9192

initial address =      6

Name: philip

 position:  painter

 years experience: 1

 age: 19

 Again?--1=Y, 0=N:  1


-------------------------------------------------------------------------
Enter social security number:  557-35-9784

initial address =      5

Name: dan

 position:  dentist

 years experience: 5

 age: 35

 Again?--1=Y, 0=N:  0


        menu
<1> Build a new table.
<2> Inspect the table.
<3> Make hash search.
<4> Insert a new table entry.
<5> Delete an old table entry.
<6> Edit a table entry.
<7> Sort table by soc. sec. no.
<8> End.
Enter choice:  2
```

386 **Structures**

CHAPTER 7

Lab Project 2 *continued*

no.	name	ss. no.	position	yrs.	age
0	fred	847-93-8888	farmer	5	29
1	george	384-83-8451	gardener	3	33
2	empty				
3	empty				
4	empty				
5	dan	557-35-9784	dentist	5	35
6	philip	012-40-9192	painter	1	19
7	empty				
8	empty				
9	empty				
10	empty				

```
      menu
<1> Build a new table.
<2> Inspect the table.
<3> Make hash search.
<4> Insert a new table entry.
<5> Delete an old table entry.
<6> Edit a table entry.
<7> Sort table by soc. sec. no.
<8> End.
Enter choice:  7
```

no.	name	ss. no.	position	yrs.	age
0	fred	847-93-8888	farmer	5	29
1	dan	557-35-9784	dentist	5	35
2	george	384-83-8451	gardener	3	33
3	philip	012-40-9192	painter	1	19

CHAPTER 7   **Selected solutions   387**

Lab Project 2   *concluded*

```
        menu
<1> Build a new table.
<2> Inspect the table.
<3> Make hash search.
<4> Insert a new table entry.
<5> Delete an old table entry.
<6> Edit a table entry.
<7> Sort table by soc. sec. no.
<8> End.
Enter choice:  2
```

no.	name	ss. no.	position	yrs.	age
0	fred	847-93-8888	farmer	5	29
1	george	384-83-8451	gardener	3	33
2	empty				
3	empty				
4	empty				
5	dan	557-35-9784	dentist	5	35
6	philip	012-40-9192	painter	1	19
7	empty				
8	empty				
9	empty				
10	empty				

```
        menu
<1> Build a new table.
<2> Inspect the table.
<3> Make hash search.
<4> Insert a new table entry.
<5> Delete an old table entry.
<6> Edit a table entry.
<7> Sort table by soc. sec. no.
<8> End.
Enter choice:  8
```

388 Structures CHAPTER 7

RELATED READINGS

Feuer, A. R., *The C Puzzle Book*. Englewood Cliffs, N.J.: Prentice-Hall, Inc., 1982, pp. 61–69 on structures.

Kernighan, B. W., and **D. M. Ritchie,** *The C Programming Language*. Englewood Cliffs, N.J.: Prentice-Hall, Inc., 1978, Chapter 6 on structures.

8

Linked Lists

Lists are a particularly flexible structure because they can grow and shrink on demand, and elements can be accessed, inserted, or deleted at any position within a list.

A. V. Aho, J. E. Hopcroft, and J. D. Ullman*

AIMS

- Introduce Linked Lists, Both Singly Linked and Multilinked Lists.
- Use Recursive Functions to Build Lists.
- Suggest a Recursive Definition for a List
- Introduce Insert() and Delete() Functions for Singly Linked Lists.
- Show How a Search Key Can be Used to Produce an Insertion Sort with a Linked List.
- Introduce a New() Function to Handle Dynamic Allocation of List Nodes.
- Construct Insert() and Delete() Functions for Binary Trees.
- Show How an In-order Traversal of a Binary Tree Can be Used to Produce a Tree Sort.

**Data Structures and Algorithms*, Addison-Wesley Publishing Co., Reading, Mass., 1983, p. 37.

390   Linked lists   CHAPTER 8

8.1 INTRODUCTION

A structure that contains a component that is a pointer to itself is called a *self-referential structure*. For example, the following person structure contains a link pointer to a person structure:

```
struct person {
    char  name[30];
    int  PO_box;
    struct  person  *link;
};
```

A *singly linked list* is a collection of self-referential structures of the same type, each containing a pointer to the next structure in the list or to nothing. A pointer that points to nothing in a linked list is called a *nil pointer*. The structures of a linked list are also called *nodes*. A node used merely to point to the beginning of a linked list is called a *list head* or *head node*. A head node is used to simplify the problem of inserting and deleting nodes in a linked list. The head node is never deleted from the list. We illustrate the use of a head node with the person structure in Figure 8.1.

A linked list is a *dynamic data structure* because its nodes are created and destroyed during the execution of a program. We can append a node to the next node in Figure 8.1 using the following technique:

1. Append node to list by making next -> link point to a new person structure, using

$$next \rightarrow link \ = \ malloc \ (sizeof \ (struct \ person));$$

2. Assign contents to the components of the new node in the following way:

$$next \rightarrow link \rightarrow name \ = \ ''Goldberry'';$$
$$next \rightarrow link \rightarrow PO\_box \ = \ 29$$

In Figure 8.2, we show the results of these two steps.

8.2 RECURSION

A linked list can be given a recursive definition in the following way:

1. The head node is a structure.
2. The successor of a node is a node that is a structure.

steps:

1. allocate storage to two nodes

    struct person *head, *next;

    head = next = malloc (sizeof (struct person))

result:

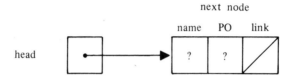

2. fill next node:

    person -> name = "Tom";
    PO   -> PO_box = 193 ;

result:

Note:

    link

    means link points to nil
    (i.e. it points to nothing)

Figure 8.1 Beginning a Linked List

step 1: make next -> link point to the new node:

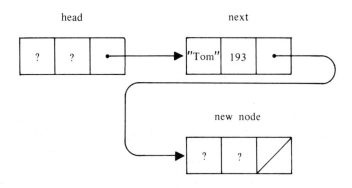

step 2: Initialize members of new node:

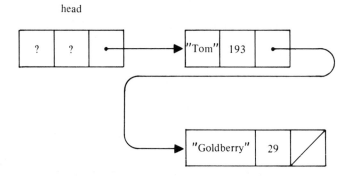

Figure 8.2 Appending a Node to a Linked List

That is, each node in the list is explainable in terms of its successor, except the last node that points to *nil*. A linked list can be explained in terms of its sublists. This idea can be used to advantage to create a function to append nodes to a singly linked list. How?

In C, it is possible for a function to include a statement that calls the function itself. This is called a *recursive function*. For example, we can use the following function to compute three different sums:

CHAPTER 8   8.2 Recursion   393

function add(x, y, z)
int x, y, z;
{
if z < 100
    add(x + 5, y + 5, x + y);
printf("%20d %20d %20d", x, y, z);
}

This function will continue calling itself while $z < 100$. Each recursive call entails the use of a stack by the processor. It uses a stack to save the return address, which is the address of the *next* statement following the recursive call. If this function calls itself 10 times, it will pop the return address to the statement following the recursive call 10 times. This means it will execute the statement following the recursive call as many times as the function calls itself. Once the last return address has been popped, the processor executes the statement following the recursive call once more and then returns control to the calling function.

We illustrate the use of the add() function in a program in Figure 8.3.

```
#include "newlib.h"

add(x, y, z)
int x, y, z;
        {
        if (z < 100)
                add(x + 5, y + 5, x + y);
        printf("%20d %20d %20d \n\n", x, y, z);
        }

main()
        {
        int a, b, sum;

        while (1) {
                printf("\n\nEnter 3 integers:   ");
                scanf("%d %d %d", &a, &b, &sum);
                printf("\n\n %40s \n", "results of recursion:");
                drawline(); printf("\n\n");

                add(a, b, sum);

                printf("\n\n"); drawline();
                }

        }
```

Figure 8.3   Recursive Function

394 Linked lists   CHAPTER 8

```
RUN C83


Enter 3 integers:  0 0 0


                    results of recursion:
-----------------------------------------------------------------------
              55                  55              100

              50                  50               90

              45                  45               80

              40                  40               70

              35                  35               60

              30                  30               50

              25                  25               40

              20                  20               30

              15                  15               20

              10                  10               10

               5                   5                0

               0                   0                0


-----------------------------------------------------------------------
Enter 3 integers:  ^C
```

629   **Figure 8.3**   *concluded*

8.3 APPENDING NODES TO A LINKED LIST

We can use a recursive function to append nodes to a linked list. An append()
function that can be used to do this is given in Figure 8.4. This function does three
things:

1. Receives a pointer to the node pointed to by the head node; this is the
initial value of *point*.

CHAPTER 8   **8.3 Appending nodes to a linked list 395**

2. Searches through the linked list for the node with a nil pointer; in effect, the following sequence of calls to append() takes place:

> append (point -> link), if
> > point -> link is not *nil;*
>
> append (point -> link -> link), if
> > point -> link -> link is not *nil;*
>
> .
>
> .
>
> .
>
> until a link pointer is found that points to nil.

Then the recursion stops.

3. Dynamically (during execution of the program) allocate storage for a new node with the new() function shown in Figure 8.5.

```
struct person *append(point)

struct person *point;

    {

    if (point -> link == ´\0´) {

        printf("\n\n Enter name:  \n");

        scanf("%s", point -> name);

        printf("\n Enter PO Box:  \n");

        scanf("%d", &point -> PO_box);

        new(point -> link);

        }

    else

        append(point -> link);

    return(point);

    }
```

Figure 8.4 Recursive Append() Function

396 Linked lists   CHAPTER 8

```
                        new(x)

                        struct person *x;

                            {

                            x = ALLOCATE;

                            }
```

Figure 8.5 New() Function

Initially, a list is empty and is begun with the following assignment:

$$head = next = ALLOCATE$$

where we define ALLOCATE as follows:

$$\#define\ ALLOCATE\ malloc(sizeof(struct\ person))$$

Notice that the assignment symbol (=) is right associative (it is evaluated from right to left if more than one assignment symbol occurs in the same statement). In the preceding multiple assignment statement, memory is allocated *first* to the structure pointed to by *next;* then head is assigned the address of the *next* structure. In effect, *head* is used to hold a copy of the address in memory of the first node of the linked list.

In Figure 8.6, we show a program that uses append() to build a singly linked list.

8.4 INSERTING A NODE INTO A LINKED LIST: INSERTION SORT

The program in Figure 8.5 builds an unordered linked list. That is, a singly linked list is built by this program without concern about the nonpointer members of a new node relative to the members of earlier nodes. Each new node is merely appended to the old list.

Figure 8.7 shows how a new node can be inserted into a linked list using name as an insertion key. The trick is to make

$$arrow \rightarrow link$$

point to

$$next \rightarrow link$$

CHAPTER 8   **8.4 Inserting a node into a linked list: insertion sort**   **397**

```
#include "newlib.h"

#define yes          1
#define ALLOCATE malloc(sizeof(struct person))

struct person
            {
            char name[30];
            int PO_box;
            struct person *link;
            };
/*---------------------------------------------------------------------*/
struct person *new(x)
struct person *x;
        {

        x = ALLOCATE;
        return(x);

        }

/*------------------append structure to list---------------------------*/

struct person *append(point)
struct person *point;
        {
        if (point -> link == ´\0´)
                {
                    printf("\n\n %20s", "Enter name:   ");
                    scanf("%s", point -> name);
                    printf("\n %20s", "Enter PO box:   ");
                    scanf("%d", &point -> PO_box);
                    point -> link = new(point -> link);
                }
        else
                append(point -> link);
        return(point);
        }
/*-------------------end append----------------------------------------*/

main()
        {
        struct person list[10], *next, *head;
        int repeat=yes;

        head = next = ALLOCATE;
        while (repeat == yes)
                {
                next = append(next);
                printf("\n another? (y=1/n=0) \n\n");
                  scanf("%d", &repeat);
                }
                /* listing the linked structures */
        printf("\n\n"); drawline(); printf("\n\n %40s \n\n", "linked list");
```

Figure 8.6   Program to Build a Singly Linked List

```
        drawline(); printf("\n\n");
        next = head;
        while (next->link != ´\0´)
                {
                    printf("%30s %20d \n", next -> name, next -> PO_box);
                next = next->link;

                }
        }
```

RUN C86

        Enter name: Goldberry

    Enter PO box: 192

 another? (y=1/n=0)

1

        Enter name: Tom

    Enter PO box: 193

 another? (y=1/n=0)

1

        Enter name: Tracy

    Enter PO box: 028

 another? (y=1/n=0)

1

        Enter name: x

    Enter PO box: 028

 another? (y=1/n=0)

0

----

                                 linked list

                    Goldberry   192
                          Tom   193
                        Tracy   28
                            x   28

Figure 8.6 *concluded*

steps to insert a new node

1. create new node:

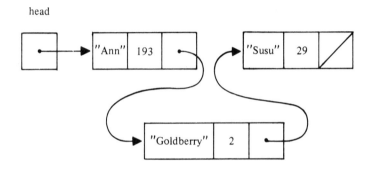

Figure 8.7 Steps to Insert a New Node

during a traversal of a list. Each time there is a failure to find a place to make an insertion, an extra pointer (call it *back*) is used to make a copy of the address of the new node. Then the new node is given the address of the *next* pointer to a list node. We use the following assignments to do this:

```
back = arrow;      /*save address of arrow*/
arrow = arrow -> link;
```

An insert() function to handle list insertions using this technique is shown in Figure 8.8. In effect, this function gives us the basis for an insertion sort.

8.5 DELETING A NODE FROM A LINKED LIST

A node can be deleted from a linked list using the technique shown in Figure 8.9. To delete a node, the following steps are used:

400 Linked lists

CHAPTER 8

```
struct person *insert(point, entry)
struct person *point;
struct person *entry;
        {
        struct person *arrow, *back, *first;
        int nl;

        first = arrowl = arrow = point;    /*copy addr. of point*/
        nl = strcmp(entry -> name, arrow -> name);
        while ((nl >= 0) && (arrow != point)) {
                back = arrow;
                arrow = arrow -> link;
                nl = strcmp(entry -> name, arrow -> name);
                }
        entry -> link = arrow;
        if (arrow == point)
                first = point = entry;
        else
                back -> link = entry;

        return(first);  /*returns pointer to beginning of list*/
        }
```

Figure 8.8   Insert() Function for Singly Linked Lists

1. Use an arrow pointer in

$$\text{next} = \text{arrow};$$
$$\text{arrow} = \text{arrow} \to \text{link};$$

to traverse a list, letting arrow begin by pointing to the list head.

2. Continue traversing a list until a match is found between

$$\text{arrow} \to \text{key}$$

and a target with the key type.

3. Then use

$$\text{next} \to \text{link} = \text{arrow} \to \text{link}$$
$$\text{free (arrow)}$$

The free() function is a standard C function that frees up memory used by a structure. A delete() function to carry out these ideas is given in Figure 8.10. The delete() function will print a message, if the target is not found. This function returns a pointer to the beginning of the revised list (the *first* pointer is used to do this).

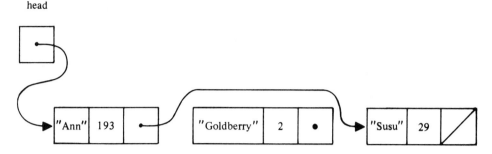

Figure 8.9 Deletion of a Node

```
struct person *delete(arrow, target)
struct person *arrow;                       /*initialized with list head addr*/
char target[MAX];                           /*search key*/
        {
        struct person *next, *first;

        first = arrow;
        while (! cmpstr(arrow -> name, target) && arrow -> link != NULL) {
                next = arrow;
                arrow = arrow -> link;
                }                           /*stop traversal at this point*/
        if (cmpstr(arrow -> name, target)) {
                if (cmpstr(first -> name, target))
                        first = arrow -> link;
                else
                        next -> link = arrow -> link;
                free(arrow);                /*standard C fn to free up
storage*/
                }
        else
                printf("\n %s not found in list \n\n", target);

        return(first);                      /*return ptr to beginning of list*/
        }
```

Figure 8.10 Delete() Function for Singly Linked Lists

8.6 LIST PROCESSING

The functions introduced so far in this chapter allow us to do the following things:

1. Build an unordered list with the append() function.
2. Build an ordered list with the insert() function.
3. Delete a node from either an unordered or ordered list.

402 Linked lists

CHAPTER 8

This is the beginning of list processing. A program to do these three things is given in Figure 8.11.

8.7 REFINEMENT: A COMPLETE LIST PROCESSING PROGRAM

A complete list processing program should be able to do the following things:

1. Inspect a node in a list (this is found using one or more search keys like name and PO_box).
2. Edit the members of a node.
3. Insert a new node.
4. Delete a node.
5. Combine two or more linked lists into one list.
6. Split a list into two or more lists.
7. Make a copy of a list.
8. Print the contents of a list.
9. Determine the number of nodes in a list.
10. Sort the list.
11. Search (traverse) a list to find a particular node.

The program in Figure 8.11 takes care of items 3, 4, 8, 10, and 11 in the preceding list. It remains to add new functions to the program of Figure 8.11 to build a complete list processing program.

8.7.1 Refinement: Inspect a List Node

The insert() and delete() functions in Figure 8.11 both show how to search through (traverse) a linked list using one search key. In both cases, a person's name is used as the search key. An inspect() function can be defined using the following technique:

1. Call inspect() with a search key (let the user choose the search key to use).
2. Traverse the list using

```
while(((entry -> key) != target) && (arrow != NULL)) {
    back = arrow;
    arrow = arrow -> link;
}
```

If the desired node is found, then print its contents. This refinement is left as an exercise.

CHAPTER 8   **8.7 Refinement: a complete list processing program**   403

```c
#include "newlib.h"

#define yes           1
#define NL              printf("\n")
#define MAX          20
#define MAX1         30
#define MAX2         15
#define ALLOCATE  malloc(sizeof( struct person ))
char z[]="zzzzzz";

struct person
            {
            char name[MAX];
            char addr[MAX1];
            char phone[MAX2];
            struct person *link;
            };
/*--------------------------------------------------------------------*/
struct person *new(x)
struct person *x;
        {

        x = ALLOCATE;
        return(x);

        }

/*--------- procedure to append structure to the list---------------*/

struct person *append(point)
struct person *point;
        {
        char dummy[MAX];
        if (point->link == NULL) {
                gets(dummy);
                printf("enter name:\n\n");
                gets(point->name); NL;
                printf("enter address:\n\n");
                gets(point->addr);NL;
                printf("enter phone:\n\n");
                gets(point->phone);NL;
                point -> link = new(point -> link);
                }
        else
                append(point -> link);
        return(point);    /* returns pointer to new structure */
        }
/*--------- procedure to insert into the list----------------------*/

struct person *insert(point, entry)
struct person *point;
struct person *entry;
```

Figure 8.11   List Processing Program

404 **Linked lists**   CHAPTER 8

```
        {
        struct person *arrow,*back,*first;
        int nl;

        first = arrowl = arrow = point;
        nl=strcmp(entry->name,arrow->name);
        while (nl >= 0  && arrow != NULL) {
                back = arrow;
                arrow = arrow->link;
                nl=strcmp(entry->name,arrow->name);
                }
        entry->link = arrow;
        if (arrow == point)
                first  = point = entry;
        else
                back -> link = entry;
        return (first);  /* returns pointer to beginning of the list */
        }
/*--------- procedure to delete a node from list--------------------------*/
struct person *delete(arrow,target)
struct person *arrow;
char target[MAX];
        {
        struct person *next, *first;

        first = arrow;
        while (! cmpstr(arrow->name , target  ) &&  arrow->link != NULL) {
                next = arrow;
                arrow = arrow->link;
                }
        if (cmpstr(arrow->name , target)) {
                if (cmpstr(first->name , target))
                        first = arrow->link;
                else
                        next->link = arrow->link;
                free(arrow);
                }
        else
                printf("\n\n %s %20s \n\n", target, "not found in list");
        return (first);  /* returns pointer to beginning of the list */
        }
/*--------- procedure to list the linked structure----------------------*/

printlist(point)
struct person *point;
        {

        while (point->link != NULL) {
                printf("%-20s\t%-30s\t%-15s\n",
point->name,point->addr,point->phone);
                point = point->link;
```

Figure 8.11 *continued*

CHAPTER 8

8.7 Refinement: a complete list processing program   405

```
        }
      }
/*-----------------------------------------------------------------------*/

header()
      {
      drawline(); printf("\n\n");
      printf("\t\tLocal Hobbitville Telephone Directory\n");
      drawline(); printf("\n\n");
      printf("Name\t\t\tAddress\t\t\tPhone\n");
      printf("----\t\t\t-------\t\t\t-----\n");
      }
/*-----------------------------------------------------------------------*/

main()
      {
      struct person *head, *next, *newhead, *newnext, *newnode;
      int    option, choice=1, flag=0, flag2=0;
      char out[MAX],dummy[MAX];

      while (choice == yes) {
            printf("\nmenu:\n");
            printf("-->1. build unordered list\n");
            printf("-->2. delete entry from list\n");
            printf("-->3. build ordered list (insertion sort)\n\n");
              drawline(); printf("\n\n");
            printf("\n %s", "Your choice:  ");
            scanf("%d\n", &option);
            switch(option)
                    {
                    case 1:
                            option = yes;
                          head = next = new(next);
                      while (option == yes) {
                          next = append(next);
                          printf("another? (y=1/n=0)\n\n");
                          scanf("%d\n", &option);
                              }
                    next = head;
                    header();
                    printlist(next);
                          NL; drawline(); NL;
                    break;
                      case 2:
                    printf("\n\n Deletion from:\n");
                    printf("1. Append List\n");
                    printf("2. Inserted List\n\n");
                    scanf("%d\n", &option);
                            if (option == 2) {
                    next = newnext->link;   head = newhead->link;
                                    }
                    next = head;
```

Figure 8.11   *continued*

406 Linked lists

CHAPTER 8

```
                    option=yes;
                    while (option == yes) {
                            printf("\n\n");
                            gets(dummy);
                     printf("enter name you wish to delete:\n\n");
                            gets(out);
                            head = delete(head, out);
                            printf("\n\n Another deletion?--1=Y, 0=N: ");
                            scanf("%d", &option);
                            }
                            printf("\n\n");
                            header();
                            printlist(head);
                            printf("\n\n"); drawline(); printf("\n\n");
                            break;
                    case 3:
                            option = yes;
                    newhead =  newnext = new(newnext);
                    newnext = newhead;
                    newnode= new(newnode);
                    strcpy(&newnode->name,z);
                    newhead=insert(newnext,newnode);
                    while (option == yes) {
                            newnext = newhead;
                            newnode = new(newnode);
                            gets(dummy);
                            printf("\n\n %s \n\n", "Enter name:");
                            gets(newnode -> name);
                            printf("\n %s \n\n", "Enter Address:");
                            gets(newnode -> addr);
                            printf("\n %s \n\n", "Enter phone no.:");
                            gets(newnode -> phone);
                            newhead = insert(newnext, newnode);
                            printf("\n\n %s \n\n", "Again (1=Y, 0=n): ");
                            scanf("%d\n", &option);
                            }
                            header(); NL;
                            printlist(newhead -> link);
                            printf("\n\n"); drawline(); printf("\n\n");
                            break;
                }                 /* endswitch */
        printf("\n\n"); drawline(); printf("\n\n");
        printf("Do you want to go to the menu? (y=1/n=0)\n\n");
        scanf("%d\n", &choice);
        }          /* end while */
}
```

Figure 8.11 *continued*

CHAPTER 8　　　　　**8.7 Refinement: a complete list processing program　407**

```
RUN  C811

menu:
-->1. build unordered list
-->2. delete entry from list
-->3. build ordered list (insertion sort)

-----------------------------------------------------------------------------

 Your choice:   3

 Enter name:

tom

 Enter Address:

down under

 Enter phone no.:

none


 Again (1=Y, 0=n):

1

 Enter name:

susu

 Enter Address:

nearby

 Enter phone no.:

na


 Again (1=Y, 0=n):

1

 Enter name:

sam
```

Figure 8.11　*continued*

408   **Linked lists**   CHAPTER 8

```
 Enter Address:

down under

 Enter phone no.:

ext. 82


 Again (1=Y, 0=n):

0
-------------------------------------------------------------------------------
               Local Hobbitville Telephone Directory
-------------------------------------------------------------------------------

Name                    Address                 Phone
----                    -------                 -----

sam                     down under                          ext. 82
susu                    nearby                              na
tom                     down under                          none


-------------------------------------------------------------------------------



-------------------------------------------------------------------------------

Do you want to go to the menu? (y=1/n=0)

1

menu:
-->1. build unordered list
-->2. delete entry from list
-->3. build ordered list (insertion sort)

-------------------------------------------------------------------------------


 Your choice:  2


 Deletion from:
1. Append List
2. Inserted List

2
```

Figure 8.11   *continued*

CHAPTER 8   **8.7 Refinement: a complete list processing program   409**

```
enter name you wish to delete:

sandy


 sandy     not found in list



 Another deletion?--1=Y, 0=N: 1

enter name you wish to delete:

sam

 Another deletion?--1=Y, 0=N: 1

enter name you wish to delete:

tom

 Another deletion?--1=Y, 0=N: 0

--------------------------------------------------------------------------

                 Local Hobbitville Telephone Directory
--------------------------------------------------------------------------

Name                    Address                 Phone
----                    -------                 -----
susu                    nearby                  na


--------------------------------------------------------------------------



--------------------------------------------------------------------------

Do you want to go to the menu? (y=1/n=0)

 0
```

Figure 8.11   *concluded*

8.7.2 Refinement: Using More Than One Search Key

The inspect() function in Section 8.7.1 and delete() function in Figure 8.11 do not take into account the presence of more than one node where the name members are identical (two persons with the same name). These functions should be refined to allow the user to pass more than one search key. This refinement is left as an exercise.

8.7.3 Refinement: Joining Two Lists

This refinement of the program in Figure 8.11 will require the following significant changes:

1. Allow the user to create a list; then, using a second list head, create a second list (*example:* the user may want to collect separately the telephone directory information for two separate organizations or cities).
2. Introduce a join() function that receives pointers to the two list heads. Use the join() function to traverse the first list until a nil pointer is found; then make this pointer point to the second list head.

The operations of the join() function are depicted graphically in Figure 8.12.

step 1:   get pointers to <u>head1</u> and <u>head2</u> ..

step 2:   make the tail of the first list with <u>head1</u> point to <u>head2</u> :

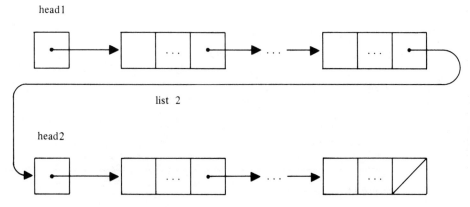

Figure 8.12 Operations of a Join() Function

CHAPTER 8   **8.8 Multilinked lists 411**

8.7.4 Refinement: Using Insert() to Join Two Lists

The join() function in the previous section does not produce an ordered list. Why? No consideration is given to the order of the structures in the second list. This problem can be remedied by modifying the join() function so that either an unordered or ordered list will result when two lists are joined. This can be done by starting at the beginning of the second list and calling insert() with a pointer to a node in the second list. This method will produce an ordered list.

8.7.5 Refinement: Splitting a List into Sublists

One way to split a list into sublists is to set up an array of pointers that can serve as list heads. Then a split() function can be introduced in the program in Figure 8.11 that uses the following arguments:

1. Pointers to two or more list heads.
2. Targets that are used to identify the beginning of each sublist.

For simplicity, suppose the user wants to split a list into two sublists. Then two list heads and one target will be needed in the split() parameter list. The target will be used as a search key to identify the beginning of the second sublist. This assumes the beginning of the first sublist is the first node of the original list. This refinement is left as an exercise.

8.8 MULTILINKED LISTS

A *multilinked list* has nodes with more than one pointer. A *doubly linked list,* for example, is a multilinked list in which each node contains a forward pointer (call it *flink*), which points to the next node, and a backward pointer (call it *blink*), which points to the previous node. If the last flink points to the head node and the blink of the head node points to the last node, then the doubly linked list forms a circular list like that shown in Figure 8.13. A node in a doubly linked list has the following structure:

```
struct node {
    .
    .              data members
    .
    struct node *flink;
    struct node *blink;
};
```

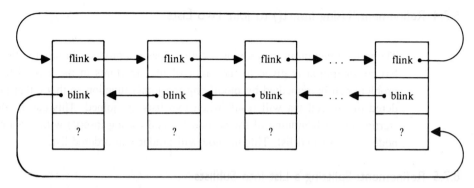

Figure 8.13 Doubly Linked Circular List

8.9 BINARY TREES

Another type of multilinked list is a binary tree that is either empty or is a nonempty list with the following features:

1. There is a beginning node called the *root*.
2. The remaining nodes are organized into two disjoint sets, a left and right subtree, so that all keys in the left subtree are less than and all keys in the right subtree are greater than the key value of the root node.

Each node of the tree will have a *llink* to point left and an *rlink* to point right.

The organization of a sample binary tree is shown in Figure 8.14. Each node in a tree is called a *parent*. In a binary tree, each parent has at most two *children*. A child node is the right or left node pointed to by a parent node. A parent with no children is called a *leaf*. There are four leaves in the tree in Figure 8.14: the nodes with the name members "Bill," "Jan," "Susu," and "Tracy."

To traverse a binary tree means to visit each of the nodes in a tree, starting with the root node. *To traverse left in a binary tree* means visiting each left child starting with the left child of the root and ending with the leftmost child that is a leaf. In a left traversal of a binary tree, the first node visited is the root, which may have no children.

8.10 BUILDING A BINARY TREE

In Figure 8.15 we show an insert() function to build a binary tree. This function uses x as the search key in building a binary tree. The insert() function is recursive. It is called with the search key x and a pointer to the new tree node, which

CHAPTER 8
8.10 Building a binary tree

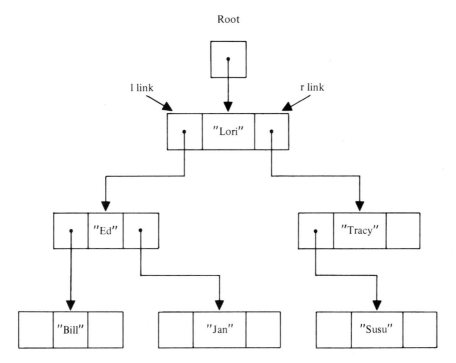

Figure 8.14 Binary Tree

```
struct node *insert(x, branch)
struct node *branch;
int x;
    {
    if (branch == NULL) {
        branch = new(branch);
        branch -> key = x;
        branch -> llink = NULL;
        branch -> rlink = NULL;
        }
    else
        if (x < branch -> key)
            branch -> llink = insert(x, branch -> llink);
        else
            if (x > branch -> key)
                branch -> rlink = insert(x, branch -> rlink);

    return(branch);
    }
```

Figure 8.15 Insert() Function for Binary Trees

414 Linked lists

CHAPTER 8

will be the root the first time this function is called. It uses the following steps:

1. Allocate storage for the new node pointed to by *branch* and initialize the members of the branch node.
2. Traverse left as long as

$$x < branch -> key$$

3. Then traverse right as long as

$$x > branch -> key$$

4. Repeat step 2 and then step 3, if necessary, until a leaf node is reached.

In the preceding algorithm, step 1 gets executed only once, that is, when the insert() function is first called.

8.11 IN-ORDER TREE TRAVERSAL

The steps of an *in-order* tree traversal are given as follows:

1. Traverse left until a leaf node is reached.
2. Visit the current node (do something with its nonpointer members).
3. Traverse right and repeat step 1, if possible.

Using this technique with the sample tree in Figure 8.3, we get the following results from an in-order traversal, where we print the name member each time step 2 is executed:

Bill, Ed, Jan, Lori, Susu, Tracy

In other words, an in-order traversal of an ordered binary tree gives us the basis for a tree sort. A program to carry out a tree sort is given in Figure 8.16.

8.12 REFINEMENT: VISITING A TREE NODE

The insert() function in Figure 8.14 can be turned into a function to visit a node by replacing

$$if (branch == NULL)$$

by

$$if (branch -> key == target)$$

CHAPTER 8   8.12 Refinement: visiting a tree node   415

```c
#include "newlib.h"

#define SENTINEL -999

struct node {
        int key;
        struct node *llink;
        struct node *rlink;
        };
/*-----------------------------------------------------------------------*/

struct node *new(x)
struct node *x;
        {

        x = malloc(sizeof(struct node));
        return(x);

        }
/*-----------------------------------------------------------------------*/

struct node *insert(x, branch)
struct node *branch;
int x;
        {
        if (branch == NULL) {
                branch = new(branch);
                branch -> key = x;
                branch -> llink = NULL;
                branch -> rlink = NULL;
                }
        else
                if (x < branch -> key)
                  branch -> llink = insert(x, branch -> llink);
                else
                  if (x > branch -> key)
                    branch -> rlink = insert(x, branch -> rlink);
        return(branch);
        }
/*-----------------------------------------------------------------------*/

inorder(route)
struct node *route;
        {
        if (route != NULL) {
                inorder(route -> llink);
                printf("%d\t", route -> key);
                inorder(route -> rlink);
                }
        }
/*-----------------------------------------------------------------------*/
main()
```

Figure 8.16   Tree Sort Program

416   **Linked lists**   CHAPTER 8

```
        {
        struct node *z[10];
        int entry=0,choice=1,i=0;

        while (choice == 1)
              {
                printf("Enter list of nos. to be ordered: (-999 to stop) \n");
                printf("\n\n %20s", "Enter an integer: ");
                scanf("%d", &entry);
              while (entry != SENTINEL) {
                        z[i] = insert(entry, z[i]);
                        printf("\n %20s", "Enter an integer: ");
                        scanf("%d", &entry);
                        }
              printf("\n");
              drawline();
              printf("The ordered list:\n\n");
              inorder(z[i]);
              printf("\n");
              drawline();
              printf("Again? (y = 1/n = 0): \n\n");
              scanf("%d", &choice);
              i++;
              }
        }
```

```
RUN C816

Enter list of nos. to be ordered: (-999 to stop)


    Enter an integer: 45
    Enter an integer: 2
    Enter an integer: -1
    Enter an integer: 55
    Enter an integer: -3
    Enter an integer: 99
    Enter an integer: -99
    Enter an integer: 0
    Enter an integer: 3
    Enter an integer: 21
    Enter an integer: -999
--------------------------------------------------------------------------------
The ordered list:

-99     -3      -1      0       2       3       21      45      55      99
--------------------------------------------------------------------------------
Again? (y = 1/n = 0):

0
```

Figure 8.16   *concluded*

CHAPTER 8   **8.14 Analysis of a tree sort   417**

Instead of looking for a leaf node, we will look for a node using *target* as a search key. If a node is found with

branch -> key

corresponding to the target value, then a visit occurs. During a visit to a node, the user can do the following:

1. Print the contents of the node members.
2. Edit the node members.

The use of a visit() function can be added to the program in Figure 8.16 to allow the user to visit a node in a tree. This refinement is left as an exercise.

8.13 DELETING A NODE FROM A BINARY TREE

A function to delete a node from a binary tree is given in Figure 8.17. The delete() function is recursive. It uses the value of z as the target, which it compares with

limb -> key

It traverses a tree looking for a match between the target and limb -> key. If the target is located at a leaf, the leaf is deleted by using

limb = NULL

If the target node has a right child but no left child, this node is deleted by using

limb = limb -> rlink

If the target node has a left child but no right child, the node is deleted from the tree by using

limb = limb -> llink

Finally, we have a case where the target node has a left and a right child. In this case the findmin() function in Figure 8.18 is used to delete the target node.

8.14 ANALYSIS OF A TREE SORT

The height of a binary tree equals the number of branches between the root and the lowest leaf. The maximum number of nodes can be computed with the tree height h using the following formula:

418 **Linked lists** CHAPTER 8

```
struct node *delete(target, limb)
struct node *limb;
int target;
        {
        struct node *buff;

        if (limb != NULL)
          if (target < limb -> key)
                limb -> llink = delete(target, limb -> llink);
          else
                if (target > limb -> key)
                  limb -> rlink = delete(target, limb -> rlink);
          else
                if (limb -> llink == NULL && limb -> rlink == NULL)
                  limb = NULL;
          else
                if (limb -> llink == NULL)
                  limb = limb -> rlink;
          else
                if (limb -> rlink == NULL)
                  limb = limb -> llink;
          else
                {
                buff = findmin(limb -> rlink);
                buff -> llink = limb -> llink;
                limb = limb -> rlink;
                }
        return(limb);
        }
```

Figure 8.17   Delete() Function for Binary Trees

```
struct node *findmin(bough)
struct node *bough;
        {
        if (bough -> llink == NULL)
                return(bough);
        else
                bough -> llink = findmin(bough -> llink);

        }
```

Figure 8.18   Findmin() Function

CHAPTER 8

8.14 Analysis of a tree sort

```
* * * * * * * * * * * * * * * * * * * * * * * * * * *
*                                                   *
*   maximum no. of nodes in a binary tree equals  2^{h+1} - 1  *
*                                                   *
* * * * * * * * * * * * * * * * * * * * * * * * * * *
```

Examples of binary trees with the maximum nodes and corresponding node counts are given in Figure 8.19. Notice that it takes at most $h + 1$ comparisons to make a search from the root to a leaf of a binary tree. For any binary tree with n nodes, we can use the fact that

$$n <= 2^{h+1} - 1$$

Then

$$n + 1 <= 2^{h+1}$$

If we take the binary log (i.e., the log of a number base 2) of both sides of this inequality, we get

$$\lg(n + 1) <= h + 1$$

The notation lg stands for $\log_2$ (a binary log). This inequality gives us a way to talk about the maximum number of comparisons in a binary search using the number of nodes in a sorted binary tree. That is, the maximum number of comparisons in a binary search is approximately $\lg(n + 1)$. In the construction of a binary tree with n nodes, used in a tree sort, a tree search will be carried out n times. This says the running time of a tree sort like that in Figure 8.16 will be proportional to $n * \lg(n + 1)$.

This is an improvement over a selection sort, for example, which has a running time proportional to n^2. For example, with a list with 100 elements, a select-

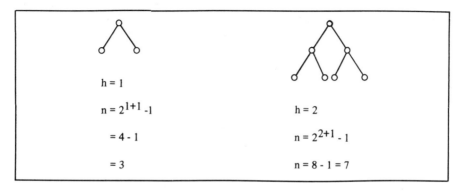

Figure 8.19 Binary Trees with Heights

420 **Linked lists**   CHAPTER 8

ion sort will require 100^2 comparisons (or 10,000 comparisons), whereas the construction of a sorted binary tree for the tree sort will take $100 * \lg(101)$ or 666 comparisons (or about 9000 fewer comparisons).

8.15 SUMMARY

A *linked list* contains nodes with one or more pointers to other nodes in the list. A *list node* is a structure containing at least one pointer to itself. A structure with a pointer to itself is called a *self-referential structure*.

A *singly linked list* is a collection of nodes in which each node contains a pointer to the next node, except the last node, which points to *nil*. A pointer that points to nil points to nothing. A NULL is used in C to provide a nil pointer. A NULL is an ASCII zero; NULL is a standard constant in C.

A *multilinked list* is a collection of nodes in which each node will have pointers to two or more nodes in the list. For example, a binary tree is a multilinked list. A binary tree has a root node that contains pointers to two disjoint subtrees, a left and a right subtree. A binary tree is a recursive structure, since it is defined in terms of its subtrees, and each subtree is defined in terms of its right and left subtrees, and so on.

A *search key* in a list node is a node member used to search through a list. In Figure 8.11, for example, a name is used as a search key to decide where to insert a new node (this is case 3) in a list. The use of the name search key in Figure 8.11 induces a lexicographic ordering of the names in a list. The tree sort in Figure 8.16 uses a numeric search key to produce an ordered list.

A linked list is a dynamic data structure. We introduced a new() function in Figures 8.16 and 8.11 to create new nodes during the execution of a program. When the basis for a linked list is declared in a program, it is not necessary to specify how many nodes will be needed in the list. This is a powerful feature of linked lists. These lists can grow *and* shrink on demand during the execution of a program. This makes a linked list far superior to an array in situations where it is not known how big a list needs to be. That is, a linked list is a good data structure to use when there is uncertainty about the list size. For example, a linked list is an ideal data structure to use in an airline reservation system where the number of reservations changes from moment to moment.

CHAPTER 8   **Review symbols and terms 421**

REVIEW SYMBOLS AND TERMS

Term	*Meaning*
binary tree	root with disjoint left and right subtrees
blink	backward link
child	offspring of a tree node
doubly linked list	each node in the list has a blink and flink
dynamic data structure	constructed during execution of a program (*example:* linked list)
flink	forward link
free()	standard **C** function to free up storage
height of a tree	number of branches between the root and lowest leaf
in-order traversal	traverse left, visit node, traverse right
lg x	$\log_2 x$ (a binary log of x)
linked list	nodes of list contain one or more pointers to other nodes in the list
list head	first node in a linked list
list processing:	
1. build unordered list	append new nodes to list
2. build ordered list	insertions made relative to a key
3. delete	point past node to be deleted
4. inspect	visit node
5. combine	join two or more lists with pointers
6. split	separate list into sublists
7. copy	duplicate nodes of a list
8. print	display nodes of a list
9. sort	use sort key to arrange nodes
10. search through	traverse
llink	left link
multilinked list	list nodes have more than one pointer
$n * \lg(n + 1)$	proportional to running time of a tree sort
nil	nothing (points to nothing)
NULL	ASCII zero
parent node	tree node with zero or more offspring
recursive function	function that calls itself
rlink	right link
self-referential structure	a structure with a pointer to itself
singly linked list	each node in list has a pointer to the next node, except the last node, which points to *nil*
traverse list	search through list nodes
visit node	inspect node

EXERCISES

1. What is the difference between a singly linked and a multilinked list?
2. Suggest how to turn a singly linked list into a circular list.
3. Write a program that constructs a circular list using the following structure:

    struct node {
        char name[20];
        struct node *link;
    };

    Then use the program to do the following things:
    a. Construct a list with the following five names: Goldberry, Tom, Bilboe, Gandalf, Tolkien.
    b. Print five copies of the list by circling through the list five times.
4. Write a recursive function factorial() to compute factorials.
5. Write a program that uses factorial() in Exercise 4 to produce a table of factorials with the following heading:

    Your program should allow the user to choose the initial and final value of n to be used. Run your program for
    a. Initial value of $n = 3$, final value of $n = 6$.
    b. Initial value of $n = 0$, final value of $n = 7$.
6. Write a recursive length() function to count the number of non-whitespace characters in a string. Write a program that uses length() to print a message with the following format:

    <string> has ___ non-whitespace characters.

    Run your program with the following strings:
    a. Structures are called "records" in some languages, most notably Pascal (K & R, p. 119).
    b. Its integration of pointers, arrays and address arithmetic is one of the major strengths of [C] (K & R, p. 96).
7. Carry out the refinement of the program in Figure 8.11 described in Section 8.7.1. Define an inspect() function as part of this refinement.
8. Refine the program in Exercise 7 so that the user can call the inspect() function with a chosen search key. Allow the user to choose one of the three nonpointer members (name, address, phone no.) as the search key to use as the search in the inspect function. Give a sample run.
9. Carry out the refinement of the inspect() function described in Section 8.7.2. That is, allow the user to call inspect() with a choice of one of the pairs of search keys:

    name, address
    name, phone number

    Give a sample run using a list that contains two or more nodes for which the name members are identical.

10. Define a join() function described in Section 8.7.3. Add the join() function to the program in Figure 8.11 and allow the user to do the following things:
    a. Construct two lists.
    b. Use join() to join two lists.
    c. Print a copy of the joined lists.
    d. Inspect a node in the joined lists.
    Use the new program to construct telephone directories for two villages, Hobbitville and Down under.
11. Carry out the refinement of the join() function described in Section 8.7.4 so that joining two lists results in an ordered list.
12. Develop a split() function described in Section 8.7.5 and add this function to the program in Figure 8.11. Allow the user to specify one or more (up to three) search keys to split a list into sublists. The new program should do the following:
    a. Prompt for the search keys to be used to identify the beginning and ending nodes of the sublists.
    b. Use split() to construct the sublists.
    c. Print the sublists.
    Give a sample run.
13. Give the heights of the trees shown in Figure 8.20.

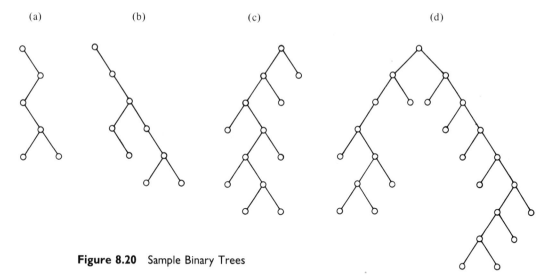

Figure 8.20 Sample Binary Trees

14. Each of the following represents the number of nodes in a sorted binary tree like the tree built in Figure 8.16. Compute the maximum number of comparisons needed to carry out a tree search in one of these trees:
    a. $n = 100$ b. $n = 1000$
    c. $n = 10,000$ d. $n = 100,000$

Note: $\lg x$ equals $\ln x/\ln 2$, where $\ln x = \log_e x$ (the natural log of x on most calculators).

424 Linked lists   CHAPTER 8

15. Modify the program in Figure 8.16 so that it uses random numbers to build a binary
    tree and carry out a tree sort. Allow the user to do the following things:
    a. Choose the seed.
    b. Choose the number of random numbers to be put into the sorted binary tree.
    Then have your program print out the following table:

Tree Size	Total Comparisons Used in Sort	$n * \lg(n+1)$

    Run your program for
    c. Seed = 2.71828, n = 100
    d. Seed = 2.71828, n = 1000
    e. Seed = 2.71828, n = 10,000
    f. Seed = 2.71828, n = 100,000

16. The international telegraphic code (a variation of the code invented by Samuel F. B.
    Morse in 1844) is given in Table 8.1. Write a Morse() function that stores the Morse
    code table (each symbol and its Morse code) in a binary tree. Then write an encode()
    function to code a plaintext in Morse and a decode() function. Take a message enci-
    phered in Morse code and produce the plaintext. Write a program that uses these new
    functions to do the following:
    a. Encrypt the following message:

    Tom went walking on up the Withywindle (Tolkien).

    b. Decrypt the following coded message:

    ```
    _ _  ·  _ _ _  · _ · ·  _ · ·  _  · · ·  · ·  _ _
    · _ _  _ · _ _  · _ · · · ·  · · ·  _  · · · ·
    _  · _ _  · ·  _  · · · ·  _ · _ _  · _ _
    · ·  _ ·  _ · ·  · _ · · ·
    ```

TABLE 8.1   International Telegraphic Code

Symbol	Code	Symbol	Code	Symbol	Code
A	· _	J	· _ _ _	S	· · ·
B	_ · · ·	K	_ · _	T	_
C	_ · _ ·	L	· _ · ·	U	· · _
D	_ · ·	M	_ _	V	· · · _
E	·	N	_ ·	W	· _ _
F	· · _ ·	O	_ _ _	X	_ · · _
G	_ _ ·	P	· _ _ ·	Y	_ · _ _
H	· · · ·	Q	_ _ · _	Z	_ _ · ·
I	· ·	R	· _ ·	&	· · · · ·

---

17. Add to the program in Figure 8.16 the delete() function described in Section 8.11.
    Allow the user to delete a node using *name* as the search key. Give a sample run. Be
    sure to build in a provision for a search failure when the desired node is not found.

CHAPTER 8   **Lab projects   425**

18. Write a visit() function for the program in Figure 8.16 so that the user can specify a search key for a tree node the user wishes to visit. Then allow the user to do the following things:
   a. Print contents of node.
   b. Change a member of the node and print revised node.
   Give a sample run.

LAB PROJECTS

1. Use a linked list to write an airline reservation system using the following structure:

```
struct node {
    char last_name[15], first_name[ ];
    char origin[15], destination[15];
    char flight_no[6], seat_no[ ];
} passenger;
```

Your reservation system should allow a ticket agent to do the following things:
a. Make a reservation (insertion).
b. Cancel a reservation (deletion).
c. Change a reservation (edit).
d. Confirm a reservation (inspection, using first and last name as search keys).
e. Print a copy of reservations arranged alphabetically by last name (sort).
f. Determine how many reservations have been made (count).
Introduce a function to handle each of these procedures. Give a sample run, using the following instructions:
g. Make reservations for the following passengers.

First name	Last name	Origin	Destination	Flight no.	Seat no.
Bilboe	Baggins	Down under	Brandywine RV	NW201	21A
Ailinel	Tar-Alderion	Rohan	Mpls	U507	2B
Aldor	Rohan	Aldburg	SF	U507	2C
None	Morgoth	Middle Earth	Erebor	U507	3A
Corufin	Feanor	Down under	Withywindle	A375	40B

   h. Cancel the reservation for Morgoth; print revised list.
   i. Change seat number for Aldor Rohan to 2A.
   j. Confirm a reservation for Gimli Durin. Print search failure message. Since there is no reservation for this dwarf, make one. Print revised list.
   k. Determine how many reservations have been made up to this point.
2. Write an Olympiad message center program that uses a binary tree to store messages by last name for senders and receivers. Your program should allow the user to do the following things:
   a. Send a message.
   b. Retrieve a message, if there is one.

426   Linked lists   CHAPTER 8

c. Change a message.

d. Print a copy of a message.

e. Print a copy of the full names of all persons (by country) who have messages.
Give a sample run.

SELECTED SOLUTIONS

Exercise 6

```
# include "newlib.h"

#define NOWHITE  (box[i] != ' ') && (box[i] != '\t') && (box[i] != '\n')
/*------------------------------------------------------------------*/
length (box, i, count)
char box[100];
int i, count;
        {
        if (box[i] != '\0')
           if (NOWHITE)
              count = length(box,++i,++count);
           else
              count = length(box, ++i, count);

        return(count);

        }

/*------------------------------------------------------------------*/
main()
        {
        char x[100];
        int tally, index, choice = 0;

        do {
            tally = 0; index = 0;
            printf("\nEnter string of 100 characters.\n");
            printf(" (Pad with spaces if necessary)\n>");
            scanf("%100c",x);

            tally = length(x,index ,tally);

            printf("\n\n");
            drawline();
            printf("\nThe entered string:\n");
            printf("\n\n %100s \n has %5d non-white space characters.",x,tally
);
```

CHAPTER 8

Selected solutions 427

Exercise 6 *concluded*

```
            printf("\n\n");
            drawline();
            printf("\n\nRun Again? <1> = Yes, <0> = No:  ");
            scanf("%d", &choice);
            }
        while (choice == 1);
```

Enter string of 100 characters.
 (Pad with spaces if necessary)
>   Structures are called "records" in some languages,
     most notably Pascal.

The entered string:

       Structures are called "records" in some languages,
     most notably Pascal.

  has   62 non-white space characters.

Run Again? <1> = Yes, <0> = No: 1

Enter string of 100 characters.
 (Pad with spaces if necessary)
        Its integration of pointers, arrays and address arithmetic is
 one of the major strenghts of [c]

The entered string:

       Its integration of pointers, arrays and address arithmetic is
 one of the major strenghts of [c]

  has   80 non-white space characters.

Run Again? <1> = Yes, <0> = No: 0

428   Linked lists   CHAPTER 8

Exercise 7

```c
#include "newlib.h"

#define yes             1
#define NL                      printf("\n")
#define MAX        20
#define MAX1          30
#define MAX2          15
#define ALLOCATE  malloc(sizeof( struct person ))
char z[]="zzzzzz";

struct person
                {
                char name[MAX];
                char addr[MAX1];
                char phone[MAX2];
                struct person *link;
                };
/*------------------------------------------------------------------------*/

struct person *new(x)
struct person *x;
                {

                x = ALLOCATE;
                return(x);

                }

/*--------- procedure to append structure to the list---------------*/

struct person *append(point)
struct person *point;
                {
                char dummy[MAX];
                if (point->link == NULL) {
                        gets(dummy);
                         printf("\n\n");
                        printf("enter name:\n\n");
                        gets(point->name); NL;
                        printf("enter address:\n\n");
                        gets(point->addr);NL;
                        printf("enter phone:\n\n");
                        gets(point->phone);NL;
                        point -> link = new(point -> link);
                            }
                else
                        append(point -> link);

                return(point);          /* returns pointer to new structure */
                }
```

CHAPTER 8   **Selected solutions   429**

Exercise 7   *continued*

```
/*--------- procedure to insert into the list---------------------------*/

struct person *insert(point, entry)
struct person *point;
struct person *entry;

                {
                struct person *arrow,*back,*first;
                int nl;

                first = arrow = point;
                nl=strcmp(entry->name,arrow->name);
                while (nl >= 0  && arrow != NULL) {
                        back = arrow;
                        arrow = arrow->link;
                        nl=strcmp(entry->name,arrow->name);
                        }
                entry->link = arrow;
                if (arrow == point)
                        first  = point = entry;
                else
                        back -> link = entry;
                return (first);     /* returns pointer to beginning of the list
*/
                }
/*--------- procedure to delete a node from list-------------------------*/

struct person *delete(arrow,target)
struct person *arrow;
char target[MAX];
                {
                struct person *next, *first;

                first = arrow;
                while (! cmpstr(arrow->name,target) && arrow->link != NULL)
                     {
                     next = arrow;
                     arrow = arrow->link;
                     }
                if (cmpstr(arrow->name , target)) {
                        if (cmpstr(first->name , target))
                                first = arrow->link;
                        else
                                next->link = arrow->link;
                        free(arrow);
                        }
                else
                        printf("\n\n %s %20s \n\n",target,"not found in
list");

                return (first);     /* returns pointer to beginning of the list
*/
                }
```

430 Linked lists   CHAPTER 8

Exercise 7 *continued*

```
/*--------- procedure to list the linked structure---------------------*/
printlist(point)
struct person *point;
                {
                while (point->link != NULL) {
                  printf("%-20s\t%-30s\t%-15s\n",
                              point->name,point->addr,point->phone);
                  point = point->link;

                  }
                }
/*--------------------------------------------------------------------*/

header()
                {
                drawline(); printf("\n\n");
                printf("\t\tLocal Hobbitville Telephone Directory\n");
                drawline(); printf("\n\n");
                printf("Name\t\t\tAddress\t\t\t\tPhone\n");
                printf("----\t\t\t-------\t\t\t\t-----\n");
                }

/*--------------------------------------------------------------------*/

inspect(entry)
struct person *entry;
        {
        struct person *arrow;
        char dummy[MAX], tag1[MAX];

        gets(dummy);

        arrow = entry -> link;

        printf("\nEnter key name:");
        gets(tag1);
        while ((strcmp(entry -> name,tag1) != 0) && (arrow != NULL)) {
            entry = arrow;
            arrow = arrow -> link;
            }

        printf("\n\n");
        if (strcmp(entry -> name,tag1) == 0) {
            header();
            printf("%-20s\t%-30s\t%-15s\n",entry
->name,entry->addr,entry->phone)
;
            }
        else
            printf("\nEntry not found.\n\n");
```

CHAPTER 8   **Selected solutions   431**

Exercise 7   *continued*

```
        }

/*--------------------------------------------------------------------*/

main()
        {
        struct person *head, *next, *newhead, *newnext, *newnode;
        int    option, choice=1, flag=0, flag2=0;
        char out[MAX],dummy[MAX];

        while (choice == yes) {
                printf("\nmenu:\n");
                printf("-->1. build unordered list\n");
                printf("-->2. delete entry from list\n");
                printf("-->3. build ordered list (insertion sort)\n");
                printf("-->4. inspect an entry from the list\n\n");
                drawline(); printf("\n\n");
                printf("\n %s", "Your choice:   ");
                scanf("%d\n", &option);
                switch(option) {

                    case 1:
                            option = yes;
                            head = next = new(next);
                        while (option == yes) {
                            next = append(next);
                            printf("another? (y=1/n=0)\n\n");
                            scanf("%d\n", &option);
                            }

                    next = head;
                    header();
                    printlist(next);
                            NL; drawline(); NL;
                break;
                    case 2:
                    printf("\n\n Deletion from:\n");
                    printf("1. Append List\n");
                    printf("2. Inserted List\n\n");
                    scanf("%d\n", &option);

                            if (option == 2) {
                        next = newnext->link;
                            head = newhead->link;
                            }
                    next = head;

                    option=yes;
                    while (option == yes) {
                            printf("\n\n");
                            gets(dummy);
                    printf("enter name you wish to delete:\n\n");
```

432 Linked lists

CHAPTER 8

142 **Exercise 7** *continued*

```
                                     gets(out);
                                     head = delete(head, out);
                                     printf("\n\n Another deletion?--1=Y, 0=N:
");
                                     scanf("%d", &option);
                                     }
                                  printf("\n\n");
                                  header();
                                  printlist(head);
                                  printf("\n\n"); drawline(); printf("\n\n");
                        break;

                   case 3:
                                 option = yes;
                       newhead =  newnext = new(newnext);
                       newnext = newhead;
                       newnode= new(newnode);
                       strcpy(&newnode->name,z);
                       newhead=insert(newnext,newnode);
                       while (option == yes) {
                                     newnext = newhead;
                                     newnode = new(newnode);
                                     gets(dummy);
                                     printf("\n\n %s \n\n", "Enter name:");
                                     gets(newnode -> name);
                                     printf("\n %s \n\n", "Enter Address:");
                                     gets(newnode -> addr);
                                     printf("\n %s \n\n", "Enter phone no.:");
                                     gets(newnode -> phone);
                                     newhead = insert(newnext, newnode);
                                     printf("\n\n %s \n\n","Again (1=Y, 0=n):
");
                                     scanf("%d\n", &option);
                                     }
                                  header(); NL;
                                  printlist(newhead -> link);
                                  printf("\n\n"); drawline(); printf("\n\n");
                        break;

                   case 4:
                                  printf("\n\n");
                                  drawline();
                                  printf("\n\tinspection choice\n");
                                  printf("--->0 Entry in unordered list.\n");
                                  printf("--->1 Entry in ordered list.\n");
                                  printf("Enter choice:  ");
                                  scanf("%d",&option);

                                  if (option == 0)
                                     inspect(head);
                                  else
                                     inspect(newhead -> link);
```

CHAPTER 8   Selected solutions   433

143   **Exercise 7**   *continued*

```
                            break;

                    }              /* endswitch */


                    printf("\n\n"); drawline(); printf("\n\n");

                    printf("Do you want to go to the menu? (y=1/n=0)\n\n");
                    scanf("%d\n", &choice);

            }              /* end while */
    }



menu:
-->1. build unordered list
-->2. delete entry from list
-->3. build ordered list (insertion sort)
-->4. inspect an entry from the list

--------------------------------------------------------------------------

 Your choice:  3

 Enter name:

tom

 Enter Address:

nearby

 Enter phone no.:

1471


 Again (1=Y, 0=n):

1


 Enter name:

susu

 Enter Address:
```

434 Linked lists   CHAPTER 8

Exercise 7 *continued*

```
down under
 Enter phone no.:
2582

 Again (1=Y, 0=n):

1

 Enter name:

sam
 Enter Address:

nearby
 Enter phone no.:

3693

 Again (1=Y, 0=n):

0
--------------------------------------------------------------------------
                  Local Hobbitville Telephone Directory
--------------------------------------------------------------------------

Name                    Address                 Phone
----                    -------                 -----

sam                     nearby                          3693
susu                    down under                      2582
tom                     nearby                          1471


--------------------------------------------------------------------------


--------------------------------------------------------------------------

Do you want to go to the menu? (y=1/n=0)

1

menu:
```

CHAPTER 8   Selected solutions   435

Exercise 7 *continued*

```
-->1. build unordered list
-->2. delete entry from list
-->3. build ordered list (insertion sort)
-->4. inspect an entry from the list

--------------------------------------------------------------------------------


Your choice:  4


--------------------------------------------------------------------------------
         inspection choice
--->0 Entry in unordered list.
--->1 Entry in ordered list.
Enter choice:  1

Enter key name:tom


--------------------------------------------------------------------------------
             Local Hobbitville Telephone Directory
--------------------------------------------------------------------------------

Name                    Address                 Phone
----                    -------                 -----
tom                     nearby                              1471


--------------------------------------------------------------------------------

Do you want to go to the menu?  (y=1/n=0)

1

menu:
-->1. build unordered list
-->2. delete entry from list
-->3. build ordered list (insertion sort)
-->4. inspect an entry from the list

--------------------------------------------------------------------------------


Your choice:  4


--------------------------------------------------------------------------------
         inspection choice
--->0 Entry in unordered list.
--->1 Entry in ordered list.
```

436   Linked lists   CHAPTER 8

Exercise 7   *concluded*

```
Enter choice:  1

Enter key name:joe


Entry not found.


-----------------------------------------------------------------------------

Do you want to go to the menu? (y=1/n=0)

0
```

RELATED READINGS

Kernighan, B. W., and **D. M. Ritchie,** *The C Programming Language.* Englewood
   Cliffs, N.J.: Prentice-Hall, Inc., 1978. See Section 6.5 (Self-Referential Structures).
Tolkien, J. R. R., *Unfinished Tales.* Boston: Houghton Mifflin Co., 1980. Good source
   of information about Tolkien's "travelers" used in Lab Project 1.

9

Files

From the point of view of the programmer, storage space and computation time are two distinct resources and I regard it as one of the responsibilities of the programmer—rather than the system—to allocate them....

Edsger W. Dijkstra*

AIMS
- Introduce the Sequential and Direct-access File-handling Functions Available in C.
- Show How External Files Can be Used to Feed a Binary Tree to Produce a Tree Sort of the File Components.
- Show How Files of Numbers, Strings, and Structures Can Be Built.
- Suggest How a File Directory System Can Be Built to Enhance Several Programs.

9.1 INTRODUCTION

A *file* is an organized collection of components. The standard C library includes a variety of functions that make it possible to set up and use external disk files. A sampler of these file-handling functions is given in Table 9.1.

The fprintf() and fscanf() functions in Table 9.1 are the counterparts of the familiar printf() and scanf() functions. The printf() function works with a stream

---

*"Notes on Structured Programming," in O.–J. Dahl, E. W. Dijkstra, and C. A. R. Hoare, *Structured Programming*, Academic Press, Inc., New York, 1972, p. 42.

437

438 Files

CHAPTER 9

TABLE 9.1   Sampler of File-handling Functions in C

Function Format	Description
fscanf(fd, ctrl-s, arg(s))	Like scanf(), except that now, instead of the input stream, the argument(s) get their values from an external file specified by **fd**
fprintf(fd, ctrl-s, arg(s))	Like printf(), except that now, instead of **stdout**(to a screen), the values of the argument(s) are sent to an external file specified by **fd**
read(fd, buff, size)	Read up to size characters from an **fd** file to **buff** in memory
write(fd, buff, size)	Write size characters to **fd** file
lseek(fd, offset, sense)	The (long) offset is used to modify the read/write pointer for the binary file **fd** under control of sense
fopen(fd, mode)	Opens file **fd** and returns pointer to buffer used for the file **fd** with modes ''r'' (read), ''w'' (write), ''a'' (append)
fclose(fd)	Clears file buffer and frees up channel used to communicate with file **fd**
close(fd)	Returns -1, if file **fd** cannot be opened

file called *stdout,* which is used to send a stream of characters to a screen. By contrast, the fprintf() function uses a file descriptor (fd) to identify an external file on a secondary storage like a disk or diskette. The output form fprintf() goes to the fd external file, instead of a screen.

Similarly, the familiar scanf() function uses a stream input file called *stdin,* which is a stream of characters coming from a keyboard. The counterpart of a scanf() is the fscanf() function, which gets its input from an external file specified by the file descriptor fd.

These powerful and useful functions are used with what are known as sequential files. To access a sequential file component, it is necessary to start with the first file component. This is done by moving a file pointer to the beginning of the sequential file. Then the file pointer is moved from component to component until the desired component is found. In this chapter, we show how to build and use sequential files using the fprintf() and scanf() functions.

In addition, the standard C library provides functions that make it possible to set up direct-access files. These files can be accessed nonsequentially by specifying the position of a file component. We also discuss how this function can be used.

CHAPTER 9   **9.2 Building a file of random numbers 439**

9.2 BUILDING A FILE OF RANDOM NUMBERS

A buildfile() function is given in Figure 9.1. The line

FILE *fp, *fopen();

is equivalent to

struct file *fp, *fopen();

In this declaration, FILE is a macro that is replaced by *struct file* by the C preprocessor. The statement

fp = fopen(''rnd.nos'', ''w'');

does the following things:

1. Declares that rnd.nos is the name of the new external file.
2. Opens the rnd.nos file for writing with the ''w'' mode switch.
3. Assigns the beginning address of the new file to *fp*.

```
buildfile()

    {

    int i, n;

    FILE *fp, *fopen();

    fp = fopen("rnd.nos", "w");

    for (i = 1; i <= MAX: ++i)

        {

        fprintf(fp, "\n");        /*needed filler*/

        fprintf(fp, "%12d", rand());

        }

    printf("\n\n");

    fclose(fp);

    }
```

Figure 9.1   Buildfile() Function

440   Files   CHAPTER 9

The statement

$$fprintf(fp, \ ''\%12d'', \ rand())$$

does the following things:

1. Specifies the location of the initial file component of the rnd.nos with the pointer fp.
2. Gives ''%12d'' as the control string to use when writing to the rnd.nos file (this formats the entries made to the file).
3. Calls the standard **C** random-number function, which returns a random number to be loaded into the rnd.nos external file.

The statement

$$fprintf(fp, \ ''\backslash n''); $$

advances the rnd.nos file pointer to the beginning of the next line. Finally, after the rnd.nos file has been built, the following statement is used to free up the channel used to communicate between the processor and secondary memory:

$$fclose(fp);$$

9.3 INSPECTING THE CONTENTS OF AN EXTERNAL FILE

An inspect_file() function is given in Figure 9.2. This function is the counterpart of the buildfile() function. The statement

$$fp \ = \ fopen(''rnd.nos'', \ ''r'');$$

opens the rnd.nos file for reading with the ''r'' node switch. The declaration

$$FILE \ *fp, \ *fopen();$$

is repeated, which will not be necessary if this declaration is put at the beginning of a program that uses fp as a file pointer. We illustrate how this is done in a program in Figure 9.3. The buildfile() function in this program is limited to file components that are integers. We can also construct a function that builds a file of members of structures.

9.4 FILE OF STRUCTURES

In Figure 9.4 we show a construct() function that builds a file of team records. The technique used in the construct() function is similar to that used in the build-

CHAPTER 9   9.4 File of structures   441

```
showfile()

{

int i, num;

FILE *fopen(), *fp;

fp = fopen("rnd.nos", "r");

for (i = 1; i <= MAX; i++)

    {

    if (i % 8 == 1)

            printf("\n");

    fscanf(fp, "%d", &num);

    printf("%d\t", num);

    }

printf("\n\n");

fclose(fp);

}
```

Figure 9.2   Showfile() Function

file() function. The members of each structure are written on separate lines of the
buffer for the team.dat file. We have found that it is better to allocate storage for
each new structure that is copied to a file. We do this inside the for-loop of Figure
9.4 with the following assignment:

p[i] = malloc(sizeof(struct team));

A function to inspect this new file will start by moving the team.dat file
pointer back to the beginning of the file. Then the components of each record are
obtained one by one using a fscanf(). We show a program to carry out this idea
in Figure 9.5.

442 Files   CHAPTER 9

```c
#include "newlib.h"

#define MAX 200
FILE *fp, *fopen();

/*----------------------------------------------------------------------*/

buildfile()
        {
        int i, n;

        fp= fopen("rnd.nos", "w");

        for(i=1;i<=MAX;++i)
                {
                 fprintf(fp, "\n");
                 fprintf(fp,"%12d", rand());
                }
        printf("\n\n");
        fclose(fp);
        }                /* end of buildfile */
/*----------------------------------------------------------------------*/

inspect(fname)
char fname[10];
        {
        int i, num;

        fp = fopen("rnd.nos", "r");
        printf("THE RANDOM NUMBERS CREATED IN RND.NOS ARE:\n\n");
        for (i=1; i<=MAX; i++)
                {
                if (i % 8 == 1)
                        printf("\n");
                fscanf(fp,"%d"   , &num);
                printf("%d\t", num);
                }
        printf("\n\n");
        fclose(fp);
        }                /* end of showfile */
/*----------------------------------------------------------------------*/

main()
        {
         buildfile();
         inspect("rnd.nos");
        }
```

Figure 9.3 Program to Build a File of Random Numbers

CHAPTER 9   **9.4 File of structures 443**

```
RUN C93


THE RANDOM NUMBERS CREATED IN RND.NOS ARE:


0          21468    9988     22117    3498     16927    16045    19741
12122      8410     12261    27052    5659     9758     21087    25875
32368      26233    15212    17661    20496    8191     23065    23471
32096      10781    14596    23212    24244    5661     514      25643
1350       19576    8051     18234    16882    13023    5983     21166
23479      9992     31833    27345    12782    23097    4112     19915
17992      22933    29621    13004    27273    20265    529      12287
3590       18358    12130    4910     26335    2364     2809     6453
29437      17995    16020    12328    3274     14857    10108    12356
4019       30978    25950    14230    18527    691      31466    5229
11436      24532    23597    27265    5998     22889    1711     32480
998        5255     32588    22172    1284     7911     20946    5174
29789      14380    28256    16329    5354     25588    121      26102
9606       4256     7147     14739    7974     24292    23394    9234
6869       22029    19659    28851    7031     4373     18282    32362
14138      12392    1978     9358     23771    7284     11528    13894
12446      25843    29902    20659    15626    18680    20432    24541
29544      13243    11512    1631     14330    14884    5618     21458
30204      25880    31111    30203    30556    21639    16314    20660
31800      1842     933      10395    19995    21309    3856     19580
19191      23416    29654    27007    9186     3437     24312    30225
19345      29737    382      24467    20629    27595    11026    26309
8023       462      29274    22257    26580    3606     1816     983
8985       20668    2564     14939    29822    8345     1637     4081
25250      30356    26993    15556    9258     25004    4970     4970
```

Figure 9.3 *concluded*

444 Files CHAPTER 9

```
construct()

    {

    struct club *p[20];

    int m, i;

    fp = fopen("team.dat", "w");

    for (i = 1; i <= MAX; i++) {

        p[i] = malloc(sizeof(struct team));

        scanf("%s", p[i] -> name);

        printf("\n");

        scanf("%d %d", &p[i] -> win, &p[i] -> loss);

        fprintf(fp, "\n");

        fprintf(fp, "%s", p[i] -> name);

        fprintf(fp, "\n");

        fprintf(fp, "%s", p[i] -> win);

        fprintf(fp, "\n");

        fprintf(fp, "%s", p[i] -> loss);

        fprintf(fp, "\n");

        }

    fclose(fp);

    }
```

Figure 9.4 Construct() Function

CHAPTER 9   9.4 File of structures   445

```
#include "newlib.h"

struct club
            {
            char name[20];
            int win, loss;
            };
struct file *fp, *fopen();

construct()
        {
        struct club *p[20];
        int m,i;

        fp = fopen("score.dat", "w");
        printf("This program prints your info to score.dat\n");
        printf("How many teams?\n\n");
        scanf("%d", &m);

        for (i=1; i<=m; i++) {
                p[i] = malloc (sizeof(struct club));
                printf("\n %20s", "Enter team name: ");
                scanf("%s", p[i]->name);
                printf("\n %20s", "Enter wins: ");
                scanf("%d",&p[i]->win);
                printf("\n %20s", "Enter losses: ");
                scanf("%d", &p[i]->loss);
                printf("\n\n");
                fprintf(fp, "\n");
                fprintf(fp, "%s", p[i]->name);
                fprintf(fp, "\n");
                fprintf(fp, "%d", p[i]->win);
                fprintf(fp, "\n");
                fprintf(fp, "%d", p[i]->loss);
                fprintf(fp, "\n");
                }

        fclose(fp);
        }                       /* end construct */
/*-------------------------------------------------------------------------*/

showfile()
        {
        struct club p2[20];
        int i,num, pct;

        fp = fopen("score.dat", "r");
        printf("\nReading from file SCORE.DAT:\n\n");
        printf("How many teams in file?\n\n");
        scanf("%d", &num);
        printf("--------------------------------------------------\n\n");
        printf("\t***NATIONAL LEAGUE BASEBALL SCORES***\n\n");
```

Figure 9.5   Program to Build a File of Structures

```
        printf("NAME\t\t\tWINS\tLOSSES\tPERCENTAGE\n");
        printf("****\t\t\t****\t******\t**********\n\n");
        for (i=1; i<=num; i++) {
                fscanf(fp, "%s", p2[i].name):
                fscanf(fp,"%d",&p2[i].win);
                fscanf(fp, "%d", &p2[i].loss);
                printf("%-20s\t %d\t  %d\t", p2[i].name, p2[i].win, p2[i].loss);
                pct = (p2[i].win * 100 / (p2[i].win + p2[i].loss));
                printf("  %d%%\n", pct);
                }

        printf("\n");
        fclose(fp);
        }              /* end showfile */
/*--------------------------------------------------------------------------*/

main()
        {
        int choice, option=1;

        while (option == 1)
                {
                printf("\n----------------------------------------------\n\n");
                printf("Menu:\n--->1. See copy of old file\n");
                printf("--->2. Build new file\n--->3. None of these\n\n");
                printf("choose one of the following menu items:  ");
                scanf("%d", &choice);
                printf("\n\n");

                switch(choice)
                        {
                        case 1:             showfile();
                                            break;

                        case 2: construct();
                                            showfile();
                                            break;

                        case 3: option = 0;
                                            break;

                        }              /*  switch */
                }      /*  while */
        }              /*  main */



        RUN C95

        -------------------------------------------------

        Menu:
        --->1. See copy of old file
        --->2. Build new file
        --->3. None of these

        choose one of the following menu items:  2
```

Figure 9.5 *continued*

```
This program prints your info to score.dat
How many teams?

3

      Enter team name: Philadelphia

          Enter wins: 89

       Enter losses: 73



      Enter team name: Montreal

          Enter wins: 86

       Enter losses: 76



      Enter team name: Chicago

          Enter wins: 73

       Enter losses: 89



Reading from file SCORE.DAT:

How many teams in file?

3
----------------------------------------------------
         ***NATIONAL LEAGUE BASEBALL SCORES***

NAME                  WINS      LOSSES    PERCENTAGE
****                  ****      ******    **********

Philadelphia          89        73          54%
Montreal              86        76          53%
Chicago               73        89          45%



----------------------------------------------------

Menu:
--->1. See copy of old file
--->2. Build new file
--->3. None of these

choose one of the following menu items:  3
```

Figure 9.5 *concluded*

448 Files   CHAPTER 9

9.5 REFINEMENT: USING A SENTINEL

The programs in Figures 9.5 and 9.3 both rely on a fixed number of components being added to the file. This fixed number is determined by MAX. In Figure 9.5, it was necessary for the user to indicate the number of structures to be put into the team file. Rather than do this, it would be better to set up a sentinel structure to mark the last structure and the end of the file the user wishes to build. For example, we can use

$$\text{while}((\text{strcmp}(p[i] \rightarrow \text{name}, \text{'*'})) \mathrel{!=} 1) \{$$

and enter a star (*) instead of a name when the last structure has been entered. Then inspection of this file would continue until this sentinel structure is found. This refinement is left as an exercise.

9.6 REFINEMENT: DIRECTORY OF AVAILABLE FILES

We can improve the program in Figure 9.5 by allowing for the possibility of more than one file containing team records. For example, if team records were collected for more than one league or more than one sport, these would probably be put into separate files. Then the menu in Figure 9.5 should be enlarged to give the user a chance to see a list of available files. That is, the user should be able to inspect a directory of file names with a description of each file. In addition, this means that each time the program in Figure 9.5 is used the directory file should be updated, if a new file is built.

To update a sequential file, the append "a" mode switch can be used when the file is opened for writing. Additions to the directory file can be made, for example, by using the following assignment;

$$\text{fp} = \text{fopen}(\text{"dir.dat"}, \text{"a"});$$

to specify that dir.dat will be used in the *append* ("a") mode. With the write ("w") and read ("r") modes, the file pointer is moved to the *beginning* of a file. By contrast, the append ("a") mode specifies that the file pointer is to be moved to the end of the file so that the next file component can be appended to the old file. If the file specified is the fopen statement, then a new file is created.

It is advisable to use

$$\text{fp} = \text{fopen}(\text{"dir.dat"}, \text{"w"});$$

to create a new directory file. Then use the append "a" mode to open an old directory file. These two forms of the fopen() function should be used inside a single dir() function to build a directory file.

CHAPTER 9   **9.8 Refinement: using a sentinel   449**

To inspect a directory file, the following while-loop can be used in a show_dir() function:

```
int c;
while ((c = getc(fp)) != EOF) {
        .
        .
        .

}
```

The getc() function retrieves the next character in the fp-file. It returns an EOF if an end of file is reached.

The construction of the dir() and show_dir() functions are left as exercises.

9.7 USING AN EXTERNAL FILE TO BUILD A BINARY TREE

We can modify the tree sort given in Chapter 8 so that it gets its modes from an external file. For example, we can use the rnd.nos file constructed by the program in Figure 9.3. This can be done using the following statements:

```
fscanf(fp, "%d", &entry);
while (entry != endf)
    {
    z[i] = insert(entry, z[i]);
    fscanf(fp, "%d", &entry);
    }
```

The assumption in this loop is the presence of a value of *endf* that can be used to signal the end of the random numbers in the rnd.nos file. It is possible to keep track of the end number in this file without inserting a flag after the last file entry, if the maximum number of file entries is already known. We show how this is done in Figure 9.6. Since we always know the value of *max* in this program, we can use the showfile() function to assign a value to endf. That is, the last entry in the rnd.nos file is assigned to endf. This makes the while loop in main() possible.

9.8 REFINEMENT: USING A SENTINEL

The program in Figure 9.6 can be simplified by eliminating the use of the last entry of the rnd.nos file as a value for endf. Instead, a special value called a *sentinel* can be inserted into the rnd.nos file after the last random number that is entered. The choice of a good sentinel will depend on the acceptable contents of a file. For example, since none of the random numbers will be negative, using a

450 Files

CHAPTER 9

negative entry as a sentinel value will work in the rnd.nos file. Then, instead of using

$$\text{for } (i = 0; i <= \text{mas}; i++) \{$$

in showfile() in Figure 9.6, use

$$\text{fscanf(fp, "\%d", \&num);}$$
$$\text{while (entry != endf) \{}$$

$$.$$
$$.$$
$$.$$

$$\}$$

The insertion of the sentinel into the rnd.nos file should be handled in the build-file() function. This refinement is left as an exercise.

```c
#include "newlib.h"

struct node {
        int key;
        struct node *llink;
        struct node *rlink;
        };
struct file *fp, *fopen();

/*------------------------------------------------------------------------*/

struct node *new(x)
struct node *x;
        {

        x = malloc(sizeof(struct node));
        return(x);

        }
/*------------------------------------------------------------------------*/

struct node *insert(x, branch)
struct node *branch;
int x;
        {
        if (branch == NULL) {
                branch = new(branch);
                branch -> key = x;
                branch -> llink = NULL;
                branch -> rlink = NULL;
                }
        else
```

Figure 9.6 Tree Sort of a File of Random Numbers

```
                    if (x < branch -> key)
                      branch -> llink = insert(x, branch -> llink);
                    else
                      if (x > branch -> key)
                        branch -> rlink = insert(x, branch -> rlink);
          return(branch);
          }
/*----------------------------------------------------------------------*/

inorder(route)
struct node *route;
        {
        if (route != NULL) {
                inorder(route -> llink);
                printf("%d\t", route -> key);
                inorder(route -> rlink);
                }
        }
/*----------------------------------------------------------------------*/

    int max = 0, endf = 0;

    buildrndf()
          {
          int i;

          printf("\n\nHow many random numbers would you like to sort ?   ");
          scanf("%d", &max); printf("\n\n");

          fp = fopen("rnd.nos", "w");
          for (i = 0; i <= max+1; ++i)
                  {
                  fprintf(fp, "\n");
                  fprintf(fp, "%12d", rand());
                  }

          printf("\n\n");
          fclose(fp);
          }
    /*------------------------------------------------------------------*/

    showfile()
          {
          int i, num;

          fp = fopen("rnd.nos", "r");
          printf("The random numbers created are :\n\n");
          for (i = 0; i <= max; i++)
                  {
                  if (i % 10 == 1)
                          printf("\n");
                  fscanf(fp, "%d", &num);
                  if (i == max)
                          endf = num;
                  else
                  printf("%d\t", num);
                  }
          printf("\n\n");
          fclose(fp);
          }
```

Figure 9.6 *continued*

452 Files CHAPTER 9

```
/*--------------------------------------------------------------------*/

main()
        {
        struct node *z[100];
        int entry = 0, choice = 1, i = 0;
        while (choice == 1)
                {
                buildrndf();
                showfile();
                fp = fopen ("rnd.nos", "r");
                fscanf(fp, "%d", &entry);

            while (entry != endf)
                    {
                    z[i] = insert(entry,z[i]);
                    fscanf(fp,"%d", &entry);
                    }
            printf("\n");
            drawline();
            printf("\n\n");
            printf("The ordered list :\n\n");
            inorder(z[i]);
            printf("\n");
            drawline();
            printf(" How about another list? (y = 1/n = 0)   ");
            scanf("%d\n", &choice);
            fclose(fp);
            i++;
            }
    }
```

```
RUN C96

How many random numbers would you like to sort ?   10




The random numbers created are :

0
21468   9988    22117   3498    16927   16045   19741   12122   8410


------------------------------------------------------------------------

The ordered list :

0      3498    8410    9988    12122   16045   16927   19741   21468   22117
------------------------------------------------------------------------
 How about another list? (y = 1/n = 0)   0
```

Figure 9.6 *concluded*

CHAPTER 9   **9.9 Tree sort of an external file of names**   **453**

```
            buildstr()

            {

            char name[20];


            fp = fopen("string.s", "w");

            strcpy(name, "dummy string");

            while((cmpstr(name, "*")) != 1)  {

                  printf("\n Enter string: (a *, to stop)");

                  scanf("%s", name);

                  printf("\n");

                  fprintf(fp, "\n");

                  fprintf(fp, "%s", name);

                  fprintf(fp, "\n");

                  }


            printf("\n\n");

            fclose(fp);

            }
```

Figure 9.7 Buildstr() Function

9.9 TREE SORT OF AN EXTERNAL FILE OF NAMES

In Figure 9.7 we show a buildstr() function to build a file of names. This function inserts a star (*) as a sentinel into the string.s file after the last name has been entered. Notice, also, that this sentinel is used to control the execution of the following while-loop:

$$\text{while ((cmpstr(name, ''*'')) != 1) \{}$$

.

.

.

}

454 Files

CHAPTER 9

Initially, the *name* variable is assigned a value with the following statement:

strcpy(name, "dummy string");

This initial value of name does not get into the string.s file. It merely serves as a beginning value for the while Boolean expression to check. By using a sentinel, we eliminate the need to know ahead of time how many names the user wishes to enter. The sentinel stored after the last name in the string.s file can also be used to advantage in a function to inspect the contents of the file.

In Figure 9.8 we give a showfile() function that can be used to inspect the string.s file. This function has the following features:

1. A variable *i* that is used to control the number of names printed on each line. This is done with the statement

if (i % 10 = = 1)
    printf("\n");

Printing will begin on a new line when $i = 11, 21, 31$, etc.

2. Inspection of the first file entry with the following statement:

fscanf(fp, "%s", name);

which gives *name* its initial value checked by the while loop. Notice that this initial value is not printed. [It should be! This is the subject of a refinement of the showfile() function.]

3. Comparison of each file entry with the star (*) sentinel with the following statement:

while ((cmpstr(name, "*")) != 1) {

.

.

.

}

The use of a sentinel also simplifies the use of the string.s file in a tree sort. In Figure 9.9 we show a program that uses the buildstr() and showfile() functions to tree sort the names in the string.s file.

9.10 REFINEMENT: CHOOSING FILES TO SORT

The program in Figure 9.9 should be refined so that the user can do the following things:

CHAPTER 9   9.10 Refinement: choosing files to sort   455

```
        showfile()

        {

        int i = 1;

        char name[20];

        fp = fopen("string.s", "r");

        fscanf(fp, "%s", name);

        while ((cmpstr(name, "*")) != 1) {

            if (i % 10 == 1)

                printf("\n");

            ++i;

            fscanf(fp, "%s", name);

            printf("%s\t", name);

            }

        printf("\n\n");

        fclose(fp);

        }
```

Figure 9.8   Another Showfile() Function

1. Get a copy of available name files using the showdir() function developed earlier.
2. Be able to choose either an existing file (an old file) or a new file to sort; this means the buildstr() function will need to be modified to accept the name of the new file to be built. This will allow the same function to build more than one file of names.
3. Each time a new file is built, a dir() function (see the refinement in Section 9.6) should be used to update a dir.dat file.

These changes to the program in Figure 9.9 are left as an exercise.

```
#include "newlib.h"

struct node {
        char key[20];
        struct node *llink;
        struct node *rlink;
        };
struct file *fp, *fopen();

/*-------------------------------------------------------------------------*/

struct node *new(x)
struct node *x;
        {

        x = malloc(sizeof(struct node));
        return(x);

        }
/*-------------------------------------------------------------------------*/

struct node *insert(x, branch)
struct node *branch;
char x[20];
        {
        if (branch == NULL) {
                branch = new(branch);
                strcpy( branch -> key , x);
                branch -> llink = NULL;
                branch -> rlink = NULL;
                }
        else
                if (strcmp(x , branch -> key) < 0 )
                  branch -> llink = insert(x, branch -> llink);
                else
                  if (strcmp(x , branch -> key) > 0)
                    branch -> rlink = insert(x, branch -> rlink);
        return(branch);
        }
/*-------------------------------------------------------------------------*/

inorder(route)
struct node *route;
        {
        if (route != NULL) {
                inorder(route -> llink);
                printf("%s\t", route -> key);
                inorder(route -> rlink);
                }
        }
/*-------------------------------------------------------------------------*/
```

Figure 9.9 Tree Sort of a File of Names

```c
buildstrf()
        {
        char name[20];

        fp = fopen("string.s", "w");
        strcpy(name, "dummy string");
        while ((cmpstr(name, "*")) != 1) {
                printf("\nEnter string: (a *, to stop)");
                scanf("%s", name);
                printf("\n");
                fprintf(fp, "\n");
                fprintf(fp, "%s", name);
                fprintf(fp, "\n");
                }

        printf("\n\n");
        fclose(fp);
        }
/*-------------------------------------------------------------------------*/

showfile()
        {
        int i = 1;
        char name[20];

        fp = fopen("string.s", "r");
        printf("The  original list is :\n\n");
        fscanf(fp, "%s", name);
        while ((cmpstr(name, "*")) != 1) {
                if (i % 10 == 1)
                        printf("\n");
                ++i;
                printf("%s\t", name);
                fscanf(fp, "%s", name);
                }
        printf("\n\n");
        fclose(fp);
        }
/*-------------------------------------------------------------------------*/

main()
        {
        struct node *z[100];
        int choice = 1, i = 0;
        char entry[20];

        while (choice == 1)
                {
                buildstrf();
                showfile();
                fp = fopen ("string.s", "r");
                fscanf(fp, "%s", entry);
                z[i] = NULL;
                while ((cmpstr(entry, "*")) != 1) {
                        z[i] = insert(entry,z[i]);
                        fscant(fp, "%s", entry);
                        }
                printf("\n");
                drawline();
```

Figure 9.9 *continued*

```
                    printf("\n\n");
                    printf("The ordered list :\n\n");
                    inorder(z[i]);
                    printf("\n");
                    drawline();
                    printf(" How about another list? (y = 1/n = 0)   ");
                    scanf("%d\n", &choice);
                    fclose(fp);
                    i++;
                    }
        }


    RUN C99

    Enter string: (a *, to stop)Gandalf


    Enter string: (a *, to stop)Bilboe


    Enter string: (a *, to stop)Amy


    Enter string: (a *, to stop)Goldberry


    Enter string: (a *, to stop)Tom


    Enter string: (a *, to stop)Tim


    Enter string: (a *, to stop)Elf


    Enter string: (a *, to stop)Hobbit


    Enter string: (a *, to stop)*



    The   original list is :



Bilboe  Amy      Goldberry      Tom      Tim      Elf      Hobbit   *

-------------------------------------------------------------------------

The ordered list :

Amy     Bilboe  Elf     Gandalf Goldberry      Hobbit  Tim     Tom
-------------------------------------------------------------------------
 How about another list? (y = 1/n = 0)  0
```

Figure 9.9 *concluded*

CHAPTER 9   **9.12 Direct-access files   459**

9.11 REFINEMENT: EXTERNAL SORT

It is possible for a file size to grow beyond the capacity of internal memory. It may
not be possible, for example, to bring all the names from string.s into memory all
at once. To avoid this problem, a file is divided into sublists to be brought into
memory. Each sublist is sorted. Then the sorted list can be saved in a separate file
and later merged with the next sorted sublist. This is known as an *external sort*.
One technique for carrying out an external of the string.s file is given by the following steps:

1. Use the beginning letter of each name as a means of constructing a sublist
   loaded into a sort tree. We can start with the letter *A* and scan the string.s
   file for all names beginning with *A*. These names are brought into internal memory where they are loaded into a sort tree.
2. Open a copy.str file to hold the sorted sublist. Each new sublist is appended to the copy.str file. After the last sublist has been merged with
   the sublist in the copy.str file, this new file will contain a complete ordered list.
3. Print out the contents of the copy.str file.

This refinement is left as an exercise.

9.12 DIRECT-ACCESS FILES

It is possible to control the position of a file pointer using the lseek() function,
which is part of the standard **C** library. The general form of the lseek() function
is

lseek(fd, (long) offset, place)

where fd stands for file descriptor,
       offset stands for an integer of type long,
       place stands for the position of the pointer.

The *place* variable can be either 1, 0, or -1. This produces the following three
forms of the lseek() function:

1. lseek (fd, (long) offset, 0), which means that the file pointer is moved
   offset bytes from the beginning of the file descriptor (fd).
2. lseek (fd, (long) offset, 1), which means that the file pointer is moved
   offset bytes from the current position in the file.
3. lseek (fd, (long) offset, 2), which means that the file pointer is moved
   offset bytes from the end of the file.

460 Files   CHAPTER 9

The offset can be either zero, negative, or positive to give complete control of the file pointer. To open a file for direct-access inspection, it is necessary to use the open() function. For example, we can use the following statement:

$$fd = open(frame, 2);$$

The number 2 indicates the access mode. There are three choices for access modes for the open() statement:

1. Mode 0 for reading a file.
2. Mode 1 for writing to a file.
3. Mode 2 for both reading from and writing to a file.

The lseek() function also uses the read() and write() functions. The read() function has the form

$$x = read(fd, buffer, n);$$

The buffer variable gets the contents of the bytes read by this function. The variable n specifies the number of bytes to be read. The read() function returns the number of bytes actually read. The variable x gets assigned this value.

The write() function has the following general form:

$$y = write(fd, buffer, x)$$

The buffer variable provides the beginning address of the bytes to be written to the fd-file. The number x specifies the number of contiguous bytes to be written to the fd-file. We used x in the preceding representation to suggest the use of the value returned from the read() function. The read() function returns the number of bytes written successfully. The value of y will be -1 if there is a write failure.

In Figure 9.10 we give a search() function that uses direct access to inspect an old file. This function receives a file name, which is to be inspected using the direct-access method. This is used in

$$fd = open(fname, 2)$$

which specifies that the *fname* file will be used for *both* reading and writing. The characters in the *fname* file are assigned to the buf-string by using

$$n = read(fd, buf, off);$$

Notice that the off(set) value supplied by the user is used to determine how many bytes are to be read. The value of n returned by the read() function is used by the following statement:

$$write(STDOUT, buf, n);$$

CHAPTER 9   **9.13 Refinement: Another use for a file directory 461**

```
            search(fname)

            char fname[10];

                {

                int off, fd, n, i;

                char buf[60];


                fd = open(fname, 2);


                while (1)

                    {

                    scanf("%d", &off);

                    lseek(fd, (long)off, 0);

                    n = read(fd, buf, off);

                    write(STDOUT, buf, n);

                    }


                close(fd);

                }
```

Figure 9.10 Search() Function

This specifies that the characters stored in the buf-string are written to the output stream specified by STDOUT. This sends the written characters in the buf-string to a screen.

A program that illustrates the use of direct-access inspection of an old file is given in Figure 9.11.

9.13 REFINEMENT: ANOTHER USE FOR A FILE DIRECTORY

The program in Figure 9.11 can be enhanced by giving the user access to a directory of available files before the search() function is called. This can be done by including the showdir() function described earlier in Section 9.6. This refinement is left as an exercise.

462 Files   CHAPTER 9

```
#include "newlib.h"

search(fname)
char fname[10];
        {
        int off;
        int fd, n, i;
        char buf[60];

        fd = open(fname, 2);

        while (1)
                {
                printf("\n %40s", "Enter no. of bytes to inspect: ");
                scanf("%d", &off);
                printf("\n\n");
                printf("\n\n %40s", "Bytes inspected in file:");
                printf("\n\n"); drawline(); printf("\n\n");
                lseek(fd, (long)off, 0);
                n = read(fd, buf, off);
                write(STDOUT, buf, n);
                }
        close(fd);
        }


main()
        {
        char target[10];

        printf("\n\n %40s", "Enter filename to inspect: ");
        scanf("%s", target);
        search(target);

        }


RUN C913

                Enter filename to inspect: string.s

        Enter no. of bytes to inspect: 10




                Bytes inspected in file:
----------------------------------------------------------------------------


Gandalf
```

Figure 9.11 Program That Uses Lseek()

CHAPTER 9   9.14 Refinement: specifying the output file   463

```
           Enter no. of bytes to inspect: 20



                   Bytes inspected in file:
-----------------------------------------------------------------------

Bilboe

Amy

Goldber
           Enter no. of bytes to inspect: 30



                   Bytes inspected in file:
-----------------------------------------------------------------------

ry

Tom

Tim

Elf

Hobbit

*
           Enter no. of bytes to inspect: ^C
```

Figure 9.11   *concluded*

9.14 REFINEMENT: SPECIFYING THE OUTPUT FILE

The program in Figure 9.11 is limited to writing to STDOUT or a screen. It would be better to let the user select the output file. If the output file is not STDOUT, then a showfile() function should be added to this program to let the user inspect a newly created file. This refinement is left as an exercise.

464   Files   CHAPTER 9

9.15 SUMMARY

A file is an organized collection of components, which are usually called records. To use an external file in a C program, it is first necessary to have a declaration like the following:

struct file *fp, *fopen();

This declares that fp will be used as a pointer to a file. Each external file is associated with a buffer inside internal memory. The buffer is used to hold a segment of a file on an external storage device. Typically, a file buffer will contain a copy of one or more blocks (usually 512 bytes) of the external file. The file pointer fp is given the beginning address of the file buffer with the following statement:

fp = fopen(filename, mode);

The user supplies the file name (filename) and the mode switch used in this assignment. If the mode switch is a ''w'' or an ''r'', then the file pointer is moved to the beginning of the file. There is also a third mode switch (the ''a'' switch), which moves the pointer to the end of the file so that a new component can be appended to an old file.

The fopen() function is used when a file is handled sequentially. In a sequential file, reading from and writing to the file start with the beginning of the file. If an fscanf() function is used to scan an external file, the scan must start with the first file component. If an fprintf() function is used to write to an external file, the writing must start at the beginning of the sequential file.

It is also possible to access file components directly in C. This is done using the lseek() function. This function makes it possible to position a file pointer before file access begins.

The use of these direct-access and sequential-access file-handling functions makes it possible for the C programmer to manage rather well one of the two key resources mentioned by Dijkstra (1972): storage space.

CHAPTER 9   Exercises   465

REVIEW TERMS AND SYMBOLS

Term	Meaning
external file	file in a secondary storage device like a disk
external sort	partition a file into sublists that are sorted separately and then merged together
file:	organized collection of records
direct-access file	components addressed directly
directory file	file with names and data about other files
sequential file	access always begins with the first file component and moves across the file from one component to the next
STDIN	stream file from a keyboard
STDOUT	stream file to a screen
sentinel	value used in a Boolean expression to control execution or in a file to mark the end of a file segment (*note:* it is possible to use more than one sentinel in the same file)
symbols:	
"a"	used in fopen() to move a file pointer to the end of a file so that the next component can be appended to the file
"w"	used in fopen() to open a file for writing
"r"	used in fopen() to open a file for reading

EXERCISES

1. What is the difference between the STDIN and STDOUT files?
2. Name C functions that always use the following:
   a. STDOUT file   **b.** STDIN file
3. What is implied by the following terms?
   a. External file
   b. Buffer
   c. Sequential access to a file
   d. Direct access to a file
   e. File pointer

4. What is the difference between the following pairs of functions?
   a. scanf() and fscanf()
   b. printf() and fprintf()
   c. fscanf() and read()
   d. fprintf() and write()
   e. fopen() and open()

466 Files CHAPTER 9

5. Write a text() function to store lines of text in an external file named by the user. Allow up to 258 bytes per line of text.

6. Write an inspect_text() function to inspect a text stored in the file used in Exercise 5.

7. Write a program that combines the use of text() and inspect_text() from the preceding two exercises. Allow the user to enter lines of a text. Use a sentinel to signal when the last line has been entered. Give a sample run using

   a. The First five entries in the Review Words and Symbols.

   b. A passage from a book.

8. Write a scanner() function to add to the program in Exercise 7 so that the user can do the following things:

   a. Scan the external file for a misspelled word and correct it.

   b. Determine the number of words in the text.

   c. Print out all occurrences of words with a prefix selected by the user.

   Run your program for

   d. Misspelled word (your choice).

   e. Count of words in the texts built by Exercise 7.

   f. All words beginning with the letter *t*.

9. Carry out the refinement of the program in Figure 9.5 described in Section 9.5.

10. Carry out the refinement of the program in Figure 9.5 described in Section 9.6. This means it will be necessary to define both a dir() and a show_dir() function that can be used in the program in Figure 9.5 and in other programs that follow. Put these new functions into a separate file called dir.h, which can be *included* in this and other source texts. Give a sample run. Use a menu in the new program to allow the user to see the directory of available files.

11. Carry out the refinement of the program in Figure 9.6 described in Section 9.8. Give a sample run.

12. Carry out the refinement of the program in Figure 9.9 described in Section 9.10. In doing this, include the following features in Figure 9.9:

   a. The ability to create more than one name file.

   b. A menu that has the following entries:

      1. See directory.

      2. Build new name file (allow the user to select the name of the new file); also, in this step, be sure to add the *new* file name to the directory file.

      3. See old file of names.

      4. Print tree sort of names.

   Give a sample run as follows:

   c. Create the following files: file called elf.dat with the following entries:

   > Wolf, Yavanna, Zamin, White Lady, Weathertop,
   > Westernesse, Vilya, Uruks, Thurin, Taras,
   > Varda, Nenya, Eowyn

   File called c.dat with the following entries:

   > lint, fscanf, printf, alloc, malloc, sizeof,
   > do, while, if, switch, for, main, else, char,
   > int, strcpy, strlen, pipe, fprintf

   d. Print directory of available files (include string.s used in Figure 9.9 earlier).

   e. Print tree sort of each set of names.

CHAPTER 9   Selected solutions   467

13. Modify the program in Figure 9.9 so that an external sort is used. That is, build a
sorted binary tree from segments of a name file, and put the sorted segments in a separate file. Append each new sorted segment to the last until all the names have been
taken from a name file (see the discussion of how to do this in Section 9.11). Give a
sample run.
14. Is it possible to use the C direct-access functions on a file that has been built previously
using the sequential-access functions? Test your assertion using the program in Figure
9.13.

LAB PROJECTS

1. Using direct-access functions, construct a hash table in an external file using the zip
member of the following structure as the hash key:

struct phone_dir {
    char name[20], address[30], city[15],
        state[2], zip[10], no[10];
}

Define the following functions:
a. construct() to build the hash table in the external file called phone.dir.
b. inspect() to allow the user to find a particular file component using a hash search.
Give a sample run.
2. Define the program in Lab Project 1 so that the user can
a. Construct more than one phone directory.
b. Inspect a directory file containing the names of all files containing phone directories.
Give a sample run using directories for two cities of your own choice.

SELECTED SOLUTIONS

Exercise 9

```
#include "newlib.h"

struct club
                {
                char name[20];
                int win, loss;
                };
struct file *fp, *fopen();

construct()
                {
                struct club *p[20];
                int i=0;

                fp = fopen("score.dat", "w");
```

468 Files   CHAPTER 9

Exercise 9 *continued*

```
            printf("This program prints your info to score.dat\n");
            do {
                    p[i] = malloc (sizeof(struct club));
                    printf("\n %20s", "Enter team name: ");
                    scanf("%s", p[i]->name);
                    printf("\n %20s", "Enter wins: ");
                    scanf("%d",&p[i]->win);
                    printf("\n %20s", "Enter losses: ");
                    scanf("%d", &p[i]->loss);
                    printf("\n\n");
                    fprintf(fp, "\n");
                    fprintf(fp, "%s", p[i]->name);
                    fprintf(fp, "\n");
                    fprintf(fp, "%d", p[i]->win);
                    fprintf(fp, "\n");
                    fprintf(fp, "%d", p[i]->loss);
                    fprintf(fp, "\n");
                    }
            while (p[i++]->name[0] != '*');

            fclose(fp);
            }                       /* end construct */

/*--------------------------------------------------------------------------*/

showfile()
            {
            struct club p2[20];
            int i=0, pct;

            fp = fopen("score.dat", "r");
            printf("\nReading from file SCORE.DAT:\n\n");
            printf("---------------------------------------------------\n\n");
            printf("\t***NATIONAL LEAGUE BASEBALL SCORES***\n\n");
            printf("NAME\t\t\tWINS\tLOSSES\tPERCENTAGE\n");
            printf("****\t\t\t****\t*****\t**********\n\n");
            fscanf(fp, "%s", p2[i].name);
             while (p2[i]->name[0] != '*')
                    {
                    fscanf(fp,"%d",&p2[i].win);
                    fscanf(fp, "%d", &p2[i].loss);
                    printf("%-20s\t %d\t  %d\t", p2[i].name, p2[i].win, p2[i].
loss);
                    pct = (p2[i].win * 100 / (p2[i].win + p2[i].loss));
                    printf("  %d%%\n", pct);
                    ++i;
                     fscanf(fp, "%s", p2[i].name);
                    }

            printf("\n");
            fclose(fp);
            }                       /* end showfile */

/*--------------------------------------------------------------------------*/
```

CHAPTER 9   **Selected solutions   469**

Exercise 9 *continued*

```
main()
              {
              int option=1;

              while (option != 3)
                    {
                    printf("\n-------------------------------------------------\n
\n");
                        printf("Menu:\n--->1. See copy of old file\n");
                        printf("--->2. Build new file\n--->3. None of these\n\n");
                        printf("choose one of the following menu items:  ");
                         scanf("%d", &option);
                        printf("\n\n");
                        switch(option)
                                {
                                case 1: showfile();
                                        break;

                                case 2: construct();
                                        showfile();
                                        break;

                                }                   /*  switch */
                    }         /*  while */
              }         /*  main */



Ready
run e99

-----------------------------------------------

Menu:
--->1. See copy of old file
--->2. Build new file
--->3. None of these

choose one of the following menu items:  2


This program prints your info to score.dat

     Enter team name: Philadelphia

          Enter wins: 89

        Enter losses: 73


      Enter team name: Montreal

          Enter wins: 86

        Enter losses: 76
```

470 **Files** CHAPTER 9

Exercise 9 *concluded*

```
        Enter team name: Chicago

            Enter wins: 73

          Enter losses: 89


        Enter team name: *

            Enter wins: 0

          Enter losses: 0



Reading from file SCORE.DAT:

-------------------------------------------------

        ***NATIONAL LEAGUE BASEBALL SCORES***

NAME                     WINS   LOSSES  PERCENTAGE
****                     ****   ******  **********

Philadelphia             89      73      54%
Montreal                 86      76      53%
Chicago                  73      89      45%


-------------------------------------------------

Menu:
--->1. See copy of old file
--->2. Build new file
--->3. None of these

choose one of the following menu items:  3


Ready
```

RELATED READING

Dahl, O.–J., E. W. Dijkstra, and **C. A. R. Hoare,** *Structured Programming*. New York: Academic Press, Inc., 1972.

Appendixes

A: Character Representations in ASCII and EBCDIC

B: Common Syntax Errors in C programs

C: The C Language

    C.1 Compiling C Programs under UNIX

    C.2 Compiling C Programs under RSTS/E Using Whitesmith C

    C.3 Syntax Rules Using BNF

    C.4 C Syntax

APPENDIX A

Character Representations in ASCII and EBCDIC

Character	*ASCII Code*	*Dec*	*Hex*	*EBCDIC Code*	*Dec*	*Hex*
blank	00100000	32	20	01000000	64	40
.(period)	00101110	46	2E	01001011	75	4B
(	00101000	46	28	01001101	77	4D
+	00101011	43	2B	01001110	78	4E
$	00100100	36	24	01011011	91	5B
*	00101010	42	2A	01011100	92	5C
)	00101001	41	29	01011101	93	5D
-	00101101	45	2D	01100000	96	60
/	00101111	47	2F	01100001	97	61
,(comma)	00101100	44	2C	01101011	107	6B
'(apostrophe)	00100111	39	27	01111101	125	7D
=	00111101	61	3D	01111110	126	7E
A	01000001	65	41	11000001	193	C1
B	01000010	66	42	11000010	194	C2
C	01000011	67	43	11000011	195	C3
.	.	.	.	.	.	.
.	.	.	.	.	.	.
.	.	.	.	.	.	.
I	01001001	73	49	11001001	201	C9
J	01001010	74	4A	11010001	209	D1
K	01001011	75	4B	11010010	210	D2
.	.	.	.	.	.	.
.	.	.	.	.	.	.
.	.	.	.	.	.	.

474 APPENDIX A

Character	ASCII Code	Dec	Hex	EBCDIC Code	Dec	Hex
R	01010010	82	52	11011001	216	D8
S	01010011	83	53	11100010	217	D9
T	01010100	84	54	11100011	226	E2
.	.	.	.	.	.	.
.						
.	.	.	.	.	.	.
Z	01011010	90	5A	11101001	233	E9
a	01100001	97	61	10000001	129	80
b	01100010	98	62	10000010	130	82
c	01100011	99	63	10000011	131	83
.	.	.	.	.	.	.
.						
.	.	.	.	.	.	.
1	01101001	105	69	10001001	137	89
j	01101010	106	6A	10010001	145	91
k	01101011	107	6B	10010010	146	92
.	.	.	.	.	.	.
.						
.	.	.	.	.	.	.
r	01110010	114	72	10011001	153	99
s	01110011	115	73	10100010	162	A2
t	01110100	116	74	10100011	163	A3
.	.	.	.	.	.	.
.						
.	.	.	.	.	.	.
z	01111010	122	7A	10101001	169	A9
0(zero)	00110000	48	30	11110000	240	F0
1	00110000	49	31	11110001	241	F1
2	00110010	50	32	11110010	242	F2
.	.	.	.	.	.	.
.						
.	.	.	.	.	.	.
9	00111001	57	39	11111001	249	FA

APPENDIX B

Common Syntax Errors in C Programs

In what follows, we state some of the common C bugs and how to correct them.

Missing {

   Example:

```
main ( )
        printf("Hello");
        }
```

   Correction:

```
main ( )
        {
        printf("Hello");
        }
```

Missing ;

   Example:

```
main ( )
        {
        printf("Hello")
        }
```

   Correction:

```
main ( )
        {
        printf("Hello");
        }
```

Misplaced braces

   Example:

```
main
        }
        printf("Hello");
        {
```

   Correction:

```
main
        {
        printf("Hello");
        }
```

476 APPENDIX B

Unclosed Comment
    Example: /* My First program *
    Correction: /*My First program */

Using /n instead of \n
    Example: printf("Hello/n");
    Correction   printf("Hello\n");

Using ; after the function heading
    Example: hello ( );

```
                                {
                                printf("Hello");
                                }
```

    Correction: hello ( )

```
                                {
                                printf("Hello");
                                }
```

Using ; after for
    Example: for(i = 1;i<10; + +i);
    Correction: for(i = 1;i<10; + +i)

Using = instead of = =
    Example: if (i=l)

```
                                   printf("\n");
```

    Correction: if (i = = l)

```
                                   printf ("\n");
```

Treating a char as a string
    Example: main ( )

```
                                {
                                char C = 'a';
                                printf("%S",C);
                                }
```

    Correction: main ( )

```
                                {
                                char C = 'a';
                                printf("%C",C);
                                }
```

Common Syntax Errors in C Programs   477

Missing * and & operators

Example:

```
main ( )
{
char leta,*letb,C;
leta = 'a';
letb = leta;
C = letb;
.
.
.
}
```

Correction:

```
main ( )
{
char leta,*letb,C;
leta = 'a';
letb = & leta;
C = * letb;
.
.
.
}
```

Using single quotes instead of double quotes

Example: printf ('\n');

Correction: printf ("\n");

Uninitialized external variable

Example:

```
int i;
main ( )
{
.
.
.
}
```

Correction:

```
int i = o;
main ( )
{
.
.
.
}
```

478 APPENDIX B

Pointer to double is assigned to a pointer to int

Example:
```
main ( )
{
int *r;
double x = 11.3;
r = & x
.
.
.
}
```

Correction:
```
main ( )
{
int * r, x;
x = 11.3;
r = & x;
.
.
.
}
```

Undeclared identifier

Example:
```
main ( )
{
int i;
print f ("%d", i*j);
}
```

Correction:
```
main ( )
{
int i; j = 5;
print f ("%d", i*j);
}
```

Missing ; after function call

Example: main ( )
                            {
                            .
                            .
                            .
                            hello ( )
                            .
                            .
                            .
                            }

Correction: main (   )
                            {
                            .
                            .
                            .
                            hello ( );
                            .
                            .
                            .
                            }

Declaring function argument after the function brace

Example: fact (x)
                            {
                            int x;
                            .
                            .
                            .
                            }

Correction: fact (x)
                            Int x;
                            {
                            .
                            .
                            .
                            }

APPENDIX C

The C Language

C.I COMPILING C PROGRAMS UNDER UNIX

C.I.I Creating the Source Program

Creating the source C program can be done by using the UNIX text editor ed as follows:

1.1 Type ed followed by filename.c
1.2 The editor responds with a question mark, '?'
1.3 Type filename.c after the question mark, and hit <CR>
1.4 Type a (for append)
1.5 Type your C program.
1.6 Type one period to leave the text mode, and hit <CR>.
1.7 Type w (this command puts your program into a file named filename.c and gives the number of characters in the filename.c)
1.8 Type q to quit the editor.

The following are the steps for creating the source program to print a welcome message.

```
ed welcom.c
?welcom.c
a
main()
    {
    printf("Welcome to the 'c' programming/n");
    }
```

The C Language 481

                    w
                    q

C.1.2 Compiling

To compile the program, type the command

cc filename.c

C.1.3 Executing the Program

To run your program, type the command

a.out

C.1.4 Error Detection

Type

lint filename.c <CR>

C.2 COMPILING C PROGRAMS UNDER RSTS/E USING WHITESMITH C

C.2.1 Creating a File to Store the C Program

The first step in running a **C** program is to write it and store it in a file with the extension c. This can be done using a text editor. The **C** compiler accepts a free-format program, which means that the user can use blanks, tabs, new lines, and form feeds to make the program readable.

C.2.2 Compilation

The compilation process proceeds as follows: Type

cc filename <CR>

You will receive two prompts like the following:

!*** processing started on 31-Aug-83 at 02:45 PM ***
Ready
!*** processing ended on 31-Aug-83 at 02:46 PM ***
Ready

The previous two prompts indicate the end of the compilation process.

482 APPENDIX C

C.2.3 Running the C Program

To run the C program, type

run filename <CR>

C.2.4 Detection of Errors and How to Correct Them

The C compiler detects the syntax errors in the program. Such errors as missing semicolons, undefined identifiers, and missing braces can be identified by listing the file that contains the compilation process. This file is known as the LOG file. To print the LOG file, type

filename.LOG <CR>

C.3 SYNTAX RULES USING BNF

BACKUS–NAUR FORM

A C program is built by a sequence of characters that include lowercase letters, uppercase letters, digits, special characters and nonprinting characters such as blanks, new lines, and tabs. The smallest individual unit of a program is known as a token. In C there are six classes of tokens: identifiers, keywords, constants, strings, operators, and other separators. The syntax rules of C can be described by using a rule system based on the Backus–Naur Form (BNF).

The BNF formalism is a scheme that uses symbols to help define a language's syntax. It was first used in 1960 to describe ALGOL 60. The BNF symbols with their definitions are known as BNF productions. These productions do not explain the semantics of the language, but they precisely specify its syntax. Every production is reduced to symbols that are not defined further. Such symbols are known as terminal symbols. Characters, words, and signs are examples of terminal symbols.

The following table gives the production symbols that we will use in describing the C syntax.

Symbol	Meaning		Symbol	Meaning
Italics	Indicates a syntax class		[]opt	Optional items
:=	Is defined to be		{}rep.0+	Repeat the items 0 or more times
!	Means or		{}rep.1+	Repeat the items 1 or more times
[]	One of the enclosed items			

The C Language 483

C.4 C SYNTAX

In this section we introduce the C syntax using the previously mentioned production symbols.

C.4.1 Keywords

keyword : =	!auto	!double	!if	!static
	!break	!else	!int	!struct
	!case	!enum	!long	!switch
	!char	!extern	!register	!typedef
	!continue	!float	!return	!union
	!default	!for	!short	!unsigned
	!do	!goto	!sizeof	!void
				!while

C.4.2 Identifiers

identifier : = {letter!_} rep.1 + {letter!_!digit} rep.0 +
letter : = lowercase_letter ! uppercase_letter
lowercase_letter : = a ! b ! c ! . . . ! z
uppercase_letter : = A ! B ! C ! . . . ! Z
digit : = 0 ! 1 ! 2 ! 3 ! 4 ! 5 ! 6 ! 7 ! 8 ! 9

Examples: idno
idnumber
id_no
no23

C.4.3 Declarations

type : = char ! int ! float ! short ! long ! double !
        unsigned char ! unsigned short !
        unsigned long ! unsigned

declaration : = type identifier {, identifier} rep.0 + ;

Examples: int i;
float speed, time, height;
char a, c;

484 APPENDIX C

C.4.4 Relational Operators

$$\text{relational\_operator} := \; > \; ! \; >= \; ! \; < \; ! \; <= \; ! \; == \; ! \; !=$$

C.4.5 Arithmetic Operators

$$\text{arithmetic\_operator} := \; + \; ! \; - \; ! \; * \; ! \; / \; ! \; \%$$

C.4.6 Logical Operators

$$\text{logical\_operator} := \; \&\& \; | \; !! \; | \; << \; | \; >> \; | \; ! \; \sim \; \& \; | \; \hat{} \; | \; -$$

C.4.7 Relational Operators and Expressions

$$\text{relational \_expression} := \text{expression} < \text{expression}$$
$$\text{!expression} > \text{expression}$$
$$\text{!expression} <= \text{expression}$$
$$\text{!expression} >= \text{expression}$$

Examples: (r + 2.3) < (x + Y)
a > x
d - 5 <= a + b

C.4.8 The Compound Statement

$$\text{compound statement} = \text{'\{' statement \{ ';' statement\} '\}'}$$

Example: {
    int i, product = 1;
    for (i = 1; i < n; ++i)
        product *= m;
    return (product);
}

C.4.9 if_else_statement

$$\text{if \_else\_statement} := \text{if (expression) statement}$$
$$\text{else statement;}$$

Examples: if (a == b) printf("/n%d",b * b)
else printf("/n%d",a * a);

The C Language   485

C.4.10 while_statement

while_statement := while (expression) statement

Examples: while (i + + <= n)
result *= i;
while ((strcmp (x,key) != 0) && (count < size))
spot = rehash (spot);
+ +count;

C.4.11 for_statement

for_statement := for (expression; expression;
expression;) statement

Examples: for (i = 0; i < mX; + +i)
printf("-");
for (i = 0; i < SIZE; + +i)
add + = mat[i];

C.4.12 do_statement

do_statement := do statement while (expression);

Example: do {
add + =k;
scanf("%d",&k);
while (k>0);
}

C.4.13 Increment and Decrement Operators

increment_expression := + +variable ! variable + +
decrement_expression := --variable ! variable --

Examples: + +i   which is equivalent to i = i + 1;
i+ +   which is equivalent to i = i + 1;
--i   which is equivalent to i = i - 1;
i--   which is equivalent to i = i - 1;

486 APPENDIX C

C.4.14 The Switch Statement

switch_statement : = switch (integral_expression)
                              switch_statement_list
switch_statement_list : = {case_label :} rep.0 + statement
                              !{ [local_declaration_list]opt
                              {switch_statement_list}
                              rep.0 +}
case_label : = default ! case integral_constant_
                                                        expression

Example: switch(a) {
             case 'r' :
                     printf(" the r case");
                     break;
             case 's' :
                     printf(" the s case");
                     break;
             default :
                     printf("default");
             }

C.4.15 One-dimensional Array Initialization

one_dimensional_array_initializer : = {initializer {,
                                           initializer} rep.0 +
initializer : = [constant_expression]opt

Examples: static int array[8] = {0,2,5,6,3,7,9,10};
              float ary[] = {3.2,4.9,7.1};

C.4.16 Structure Declarations

structure_declaration : = struct tag declarator_list;
tag : = identifier
declarator_list : = [declarator]opt {,declarator} rep.0 +
structure_type : = struct tag member ! struct tag !
                         struct member
member : = {{type_specifier declaration_list ;}
                                           rep.1 +}

Examples:

```
struct node {
        int one;
        char two;
} item[23];
struct club {
        char name [20];
        int win, loss;
};
struct item {
        char code[5];
        float price;
} items[50];
typedef struct {
        float real;
        float immag;
} complex;
complex z,y,a[30];
struct node {
        int num;
        struct node *left;
        struct node *right;
};
```

Glossary

Accumulator: Register used by a CPU to do arithmetic and hold operands used in calculations by processor.

Actual parameter: An argument in a function call.

Algorithm: A set of precise directions for performing some procedure, a step-by-step method that produces a result in a finite time, which dates back to the publication of the first algebra textbook by Mohamed Ibn Musa Al-Khowarizmi (A.D. 825).

Array: A series of items (numbers or strings) arranged in an orderly pattern; an ordered arrangement of elements in one or more dimensions.

ASCII: American Standard Code for Information Interchange. It is a standardized 7-bit code representing 128 characters by which textual information is recorded on most computers.

Atomic statement: A statement that specifies a single action.

B: B is a system language developed in Bell Laboratories.

BCPL: Basic Combined Programming Language developed in 1969 by Martin Richards at Cambridge University.

Bit: Binary digit; smallest unit of information in a machine.

Block structure: A programming language concept that allows related declarations and statements to be grouped together.

BNF: The Backus–Naur form, named after John W. Backus (USA) and Peter Naur (Denmark), is the best-known example of a metalanguage, i.e., one that syntactically describes a programming language.

Buffer: An area of storage that temporarily holds data that will be delivered to a processor.

Bug: An error in either the logic or the syntax of a computer program.

Byte: A given number of bits to form a storage location.

C: A general-purpose programming language designed by Dennis M. Ritchie (1972) as an alternative to the B language.

Call by value: Use an argument in a function call to pass a value to a function.

Call by reference: Use an argument in a function to pass an address to a function.

Counter: A storage location used to accumulate quantitatively and often used to control program loops.

CPU: The central processing unit of the computer.

Debugging: The process of detecting, locating, and correcting any mistakes in a computer program; the process of testing a program for errors.

EBCDIC: Extended Binary Coded Decimal Interchange Code. It was developed by IBM for use on the IBM System 1360.

Editing: The process of modifying data, a program, or a file; the alteration of program format.

Field: A unit of data within a record.

FIFO: First in, first out, a technique for dealing with a queued list of items. Additions are made at one end (the tail) and deletions are made at the opposite end (the front).

Formal parameter list: Parameter list in a function heading.

489

490 Glossary

Global variable: Variable declared outside a function.

Hash: Address calculation.
Hashing: Operations done to transform one or more fields into a different arrangement.
Hash search: Computing location of a structure.
Hash table collision: Hash to an occupied table cell.

Indirect address: An instruction code and an address that point to a location in memory.

LIFO: Last in, first out, a technique for dealing with a stacked list of items. Additions and deletions are made at the same end (the top).
List processing: The collection of operations that must be performed on list-structured data.
Local alias: Formal parameter that is another name for a memory address identified in call by reference.
Local variable: Variable declared in a function block.

Macro: A single computer instruction that stands for a given sequence of instructions.
Metalanguage: A set of symbols and words used to describe another language.

Open addressing technique: Continue looking in a hash table until a vacancy is found.
Operand: A quantity that is operated on.
Operating system: The software that initiates the interaction of the components of a computer so that they constitute a useful system.

Operator: A term that specifies operation.
Operator associativity: Evaluation of an expression from left to right or right to left.
Overlaying components: Components are made to share the same area of memory.

Polish notation: A notation devised by the Polish logician Jan Lukasiewicz (1951). The notation places operators before or after their operands; the need for parentheses is eliminated, provided each operator has a fixed number of operands.

Register: Small, high-speed storage inside a processor.

Storage class: Specifies how much memory to use and lifetime of storage used during program execution.
Syntax: Arrangement of tokens used by a part of a language (especially a statement).
Syntax diagram: Graphical representation of language syntax.

Tokens: Smallest parts of a computer program.

UNIX: A general-purpose time-sharing system developed at Bell Laboratories by Ken Thompson and Dennis Ritchie.

Value parameter: A formal parameter that receives a value from a function argument.
Variable parameter: A formal parameter that receives an address from a function argument; a local alias for a memory location identified by an argument in a function call.

Index of Programs

Figure	Program Title	Figure	Program Title
2.6	Arithmetic operators 30	8.11	List processing 403
6.15	Array of pointers 245		
6.13	Array of pointers and contents 242	6.11	Measuring randomness 239
6.17	Array of strings 247		
		4.14	Nested and compressed assignments 150
5.12	Build a form letter 188		
7.8	Building an array of structures 310	3.16	Nested blocks 85
3.15	Building a powers table 82	5.7	Nested while-loop 183
7.4	Building structures 303		
		7.5	Operations with structures 305
1.3	C source text 10		
3.10	Call by value and call by reference 73	3.17	Parallel blocks 88
3.4	Calling a function with one parameter 61	2.9	Personal C library 37
		4.5	Pointing to strings 125
6.5	Constructing an array of numbers 229	4.12	Powers of 2 using left-shift operator 145
6.9	Constructing an array of random numbers 235	4.7	Powers of 2 with type long 130
		4.1	Printing ASCII characters and codes 118
8.6	Creating a linked list 397		
		4.3	Printing string constants 123
7.2	Draw a sketch 302		
		8.3	Recursive summary functions 393
7.13	Edit a structure 322		
		6.20	Selection sort 253
6.22	Factorials 259	7.11	Selection sort of pointers to structures 317
6.19	Finding the smallest and second smallest number 251	4.13	Shift operators 147
2.12	Floating-point output sampler 42	2.7	Signed and unsigned maxint values 33
2.5	For-loops 26	5.16	Simulating the roll of a die 194
		4.6	Sizeof operator 129
5.18	Gries's coffee can problem 198	4.4	Streamlined local library 124
		4.11	Stripping the bits off a number 142
6.17	Hash search 247	7.10	Swapping pointers to structures 313

492 Index of Programs

Figure	Program Title	Figure	Program Title
8.16	Tree sort 415	4.8	Use of type short to save storage 134
9.9	Tree sort of an external file 456	2.8	User-defined C library 36
4.9	Types float and double 137	5.2	Using an if-else statement 173
		6.7	Using external functions 233
3.6	Use of global variables 65		
3.7	Use of global variables—type Int and Char 67	2.15	Von Neumann time machine 46
3.13	Use of return statement 78		
3.18	Use of static and auto storage classes 91	5.6	While-loop 181
		5.14	While-loop with rand() 192

Index of Functions

Figure	Function	Figure	Function
8.4	Append () 395	6.10	Get-freq () 237
5.5	Atou () 180	7.14	Hash () 326
6.4	Build-array() 228	7.7	Init () 309
7.2	Build-Struct () 302	8.15	Insert () (binary tree) 413
7.7	BuildStr () 309	8.8	Insert () (linked-list) 400
6.16	Build-text () 247	5.11	Insert-word () 187
5.8	Chop () 185	3.14	K and R power function 81
9.4	Construct () (files) 444	8.5	New () 396
8.10	Delete () (linked lists) 401	7.3	Print-Struct () 302
7.12	Edit () 321	7.15	Rehash () 327
6.6	External function library 231	5.15	Rnd () 193
4.10	Extract () 141	9.10	Search () 461
6.8	Fill-cells () 234	5.17	Select () 196
8.18	Findmin () 418	7.6	Show () 308
6.18	Findmin () (binary tree) 249	6.12	Show-addresses () 241
3.9	Function with a local alias 72	9.8	Show file () 455
3.5	Function with more than one formal parameter 63	7.16	Start-table () 328
		5.13	Strlen () 191
3.3	Function with one formal parameter 61	7.9	Swap () 312

Index of Syntax Diagrams

Figure	Diagram	Figure	Diagram
6.2	Array declaration 225	3.12	Return statement 77
5.10	Do-loop 187	2.13	Scan f ( ) 43
2.4	For statement 25	7.1	Structure 299
3.2	Function 59	5.3	Switch statement 177
2.3	Identifier 22	5.4	While-loop 179
5.1	If statement 173	2.11	%d and %f 41
2.10	Print f ( ) 39		

Index of Terms and Subjects

SYMBOLS

!,   21, 94, 117, 139
!=,   21, 140
%,   21, 28, 29, 81
&,   18, 21, 49, 140, 149, 243, 299, 304, 340
&&,   21, 27, 139
*,   21, 27, 121, 129, 243, 299
+,   21, 29
++,   21, 27, 28, 94
-,   21, 27, 29
--,   21, 29, 31
l,   21, 300, 301, 304, 339, 340, 390
/,   21, 29
<,   21, 175

<<,   21, 140, 144
<=,   21, 117, 119, 179
=,   18, 23, 29
==,   20, 117, 171, 175
>,   9, 18, 175
>=,   18
>>,   21, 140, 146, 179
[ ],   45, 243, 263
\,   21, 38, 39
∧,   21, 140
| |,   21, 139
~,   21, 140
.,   21, 339, 346
{ },   18, 23, 49

TERMS

actual parameter   64, 97
ALGOL   17
array   222, 227, 232, 256, 266
    of pointers   243
    of strings   246
    of structures   307
    two dimensional   263
    multidimensional   258
as   6, 12
ASCII   5, 12, 43
atomic statement   48, 49
auto   21, 46, 93, 98

B   5, 11, 12
BCBL   5, 11, 12
\b   39, 120
binary tree   412, 449
bit   3, 12, 20
BNF   20, 49
Boolean   138, 153
Break   21, 69, 77, 170, 176, 202

C   1, 5, 11, 12
%c   38, 40, 61, 66
C compiler   2

C vocabulary   20
call by reference   70, 97
call by value   70, 79
case   21, 64, 77, 76
cc   6, 12
ccp   6, 7, 12
char   21, 45, 64, 66, 116, 124, 127, 151, 224, 258
comment   22, 49
compound statement   22, 49
continue   21
control structure   169, 201

%d   25, 40
#define   7, 8, 12, 34, 35
\ddd   39, 120
default   21, 64, 172, 177
do   21, 170, 185, 315
double   21, 49, 84, 131, 136, 151, 224, 225
dynamic data structures   390

%e   40
EBCDIC   5, 12
else   21, 172
enum   21
exp( )   33, 49
extern   21, 90, 95, 98, 264
external sort   459

%f   40
fclose( )   438
fd   460
FILE*   349
files   437, 448, 459, 461
   direct access   459
   external   439, 440
   output   463
   random numbers   439
   sequential   437, 465
   structures   440
float   21, 132, 151
fopen( )   438
for   21, 24, 49, 117, 122, 170
formal parameter   60, 97
fp   439

fprintf( )   438
fputs( )   438
fscanf( )   438
functions   57, 97, 301

%g   40
getchar( )   171
gets( )   122
global variables   64, 97
goto   21
Gries Coffee Can Problem   195

hash search   321, 325

#include   7, 8, 12, 23, 39, 35, 50
if   20, 21, 23, 81, 170, 172
insertion sort   396
int   21, 50, 64, 128, 151, 224, 258
invariant assertion   18, 19
iteration control   170, 178, 201

ld   6, 12
library of functions   231
linked lists   384, 394
      appending nodes   394
      deleting nodes   399
      inserting nodes   396
list   12
list processing   401
local alias   72, 74, 97
local variables   64, 87
log( )   33, 50
long   21, 128, 132
lseek   438, 450

machine   2
      codes   3
      organization   3
macro   50
main( )   15, 23
malloc( )   308, 441

Index

memory   3
    address   3, 12
    location   3, 12
multilinked lists   411

\n   120
nested if   175
nested structures   335
nested while   185
noise words   12

%o   46
operating systems   2
operators   115
    prefix   29, 50
    postfix   29, 50

Pascal   17, 58
pdp-11   11
PL/1   58
pointers   75, 121, 124, 240, 243
    constants   240, 265
    to structures   299, 301, 312
    variables   240
preprocessor   12
program development cycle   17, 19

\r   39, 120
random numbers   191, 232, 236
read   438, 460
recursion   390
register   3, 12, 21, 90, 95, 98
return   21, 77, 144, 227

%s   40, 46, 49, 66
scanf( )   18, 23, 41, 43, 46, 50, 66, 122, 127
shift left operator   144, 147
shift right operator   145, 147
short   21, 128, 134, 136
signed integers   32, 50
sizeof   21, 308
sqrt( )   27
static   21, 90, 93, 98, 225, 264
storage class   90
strcpy( )   75, 98, 454
string constant   121, 124
struct   21, 298, 299, 307, 327, 390
structure   297, 301, 309, 312, 321
switch   21, 69, 77, 98, 170, 176

\t   27, 120
types   115
typedef   21, 336

%u   40
union   21, 338
UNIX   2
unsigned integers   21, 32, 128

value parameter   70, 98
variable parameter   70, 98
void   21

while   18, 20, 21, 22, 170, 179, 184, 453
    nested   185
write   348, 460

%x   40